IRAN

Having been ruled, more or less continuously, by a range of monarchical dynasties for three millennia, the end of the monarchy in Iran was relatively sudden, taking place in two short years. Since then, Iran has gone through tumultuous change, yet is still apparently caught in a cycle of transition. Iran has now created a complex but unique and non-transferrable system of government, but the question to be asked is whether the Islamic republic has lived up to its founding expectations, serving the Iranian people and helping them to realize their aspirations.

This book is the first comprehensive analytical study of the forces which have been shaping and changing modern Iran and its relations with the rest of the world. It looks at the roots of the 1979 revolution and the forces unleashed during the modernization process under the Pahlavi monarchy. Applying a range of theoretical approaches to understanding the Islamic republic's neo-authoritarian political system, Anoushiravan Ehteshami reflects on how the country's new elite emerged and how these new political forces have changed Iran, the stresses on its political system, the forces shaping the country's political economy, and the Islamic republic's international relations. As some of Iran's leaders appear to crave permanent revolution as their means of staying in power, this book argues that the struggle for the soul of the Islamic republic has mired the country in a cycle of change: Constant reform and transition. The republic finds itself stuck in transition.

Written in a clear and insightful manner, this book provides an unparalleled analysis of the Islamic Republic of Iran as a major regional actor and gives fresh insights into the political workings of the world's only Shia, and revolutionary, Islamic republic. It will be of great importance to students and scholars of Middle East Politics and International Relations, as well as the policy community whose gaze is never too far from this unique country.

Anoush Ehteshami is Professor of International Relations, and the Nasser al-Mohammad al-Sabah Chair in International Relations and Director of the HH Sheikh Nasser al-Mohammad al-Sabah Programme in International Relations, Regional Politics and Security at Durham University.

The Contemporary Middle East
Edited by Professor Anoushiravan Ehteshami

Institute for Middle Eastern and Islamic Studies, University of Durham

For well over a century now the Middle East and North Africa countries have formed a central plank of the international system. **The Contemporary Middle East Series** provides the first systematic attempt at studying the key actors of this dynamic, complex, and strategically important region. Using an innovative common format – which in each case study provides an easily-digestible analysis of the origins of the state, its contemporary politics, economics and international relations – prominent Middle East experts have been brought together to write definitive studies of the MENA region's key countries.

Books in the series

Tunisia
Stability and Reform in the Modern Maghreb
Christopher Alexander

Libya
Continuity and Change
Ronald Bruce St John

Lebanon
The Politics of a Penetrated Society
Tom Najem

Libya
Continuity and Change 2nd Edition
Ronald Bruce St John

Morocco
Challenges to Tradition and Modernity 2nd Edition
James N. Sater

Tunisia
From stability to revolution in the Maghreb 2nd Edition
Christopher Alexander

The United Arab Emirates
Power, Politics and Policymaking
Kristian Coates Ulrichsen

Iran
Stuck in Transition
Anoushiravan Ehteshami

IRAN

Stuck in Transition

Anoushiravan Ehteshami

LONDON AND NEW YORK

First published 2017
by Routledge
2 Park Square, Milton Park, Abingdon, Oxon OX14 4RN

and by Routledge
711 Third Avenue, New York, NY 10017

Routledge is an imprint of the Taylor & Francis Group, an informa business

© 2017 Anoushiravan Ehteshami

The right of Anoushiravan Ehteshami to be identified as author of this work has been asserted by him in accordance with sections 77 and 78 of the Copyright, Designs and Patents Act 1988.

All rights reserved. No part of this book may be reprinted or reproduced or utilised in any form or by any electronic, mechanical, or other means, now known or hereafter invented, including photocopying and recording, or in any information storage or retrieval system, without permission in writing from the publishers.

Trademark notice: Product or corporate names may be trademarks or registered trademarks, and are used only for identification and explanation without intent to infringe.

British Library Cataloguing in Publication Data
A catalogue record for this book is available from the British Library

Library of Congress Cataloging in Publication Data
Names: Ehteshami, Anoushiravan, author.
Title: Iran: stuck in transition / Anoushiravan Ehteshami.
Other titles: Contemporary Middle East (Routledge (Firm))
Description: Milton Park, Abingdon, Oxon: Routledge, 2017. | Series: The contemporary Middle East | Includes bibliographical references and index.
Identifiers: LCCN 2016036333 | ISBN 9780415710831 (hardback) | ISBN 9780415710855 (pbk.) | ISBN 9781315271569 (ebook)
Subjects: LCSH: Iran—Politics and government—1997– | Iran—Politics and government—1979-1997. | Iran—Economic conditions—1997– | Iran—Foreign relations—1997–
Classification: LCC DS318.9 .E38 2017 | DDC 955.05/4—dc23
LC record available at https://lccn.loc.gov/2016036333

ISBN: 978-0-415-71083-1 (hbk)
ISBN: 978-0-415-71085-5 (pbk)
ISBN: 978-1-315-27156-9 (ebk)

Typeset in Bembo
by codeMantra

To Emma, for a lifetime of love and happiness

CONTENTS

Chronology ix

Introduction 1
Narrating Iran in the twenty-first century 3

1 **Modern state formation** 15
Introduction 15
Historical legacy 17
Emergence of a modern state 18
The last Pahlavi 20
Revolution 23
The birth of the Islamic republic 27

2 **Politics of the Islamic republic** 32
Introduction 32
Constitutional arrangements 34
The first ten years 39
The second republic 43
1997: Tehran spring 49
Neoconservatism rears its head 57
Nezam in crisis: Iran's tenth presidential elections 63
    Velvet revolution or velvet coup? 75
    Post-election crisis and the region 84
Lame duck president? 87
2013: clocks go forward or back? 92
Political power and nuclear politics 96
Authoritarian state, democratic society 104

3 Iran's political economy   115
Context   115
Iran's economic development in the post-Second World War period   117
   Oil drives change   119
   State-society relations under the monarchy   121
   Consolidation of dependent capitalism under the monarchy   125
Iran's economy under the Islamic republic   129
   War and the economy   133
The nineties: challenging taboos   135
Khatami: torn between economics and politics   140
Ahmadinomics takes hold   142
A new golden age?   146
State-society relations under the Islamic republic   150
Sanctions and the economy   154
After the sanctions   158

4 International relations   168
Introduction   168
Historical features of Iran's international relations   171
International relations of a modern state: the Pahlavis   173
International relations of the Islamic republic   178
   The war years   183
   The pragmatists take charge   192
      Improvements in international relations   195
   Détente and the dialogue of civilizations   199
      Iran and 9/11   207
      Nuclear politics takes over   210
   From Khatami to Ahmadinejad   218
   Foreign policy of the neoconservatives   219
      Nuclear crisis deepens   221
      Populist Iran responds to encirclement   226
      The Islamic republic's '1969 moment'   228
      The Arab uprisings   233
   Rouhani aims to open up 'new horizons'   235
      Success of nuclear diplomacy   237
      Geopolitical uncertainties shape policy   241
Conclusion   250

Conclusion   268

Bibliography   277
Index   289

CHRONOLOGY

2400–539 BC	Pre-Iranic Period, Elamite Kingdom.
708 BC	The Median Kingdom is established.
639 BC	The ultimate collapse of Elamite Kingdom.
612 BC	Cyaxares King of Media allies with Babylonians. He invades Nineveh and ends the Assyrian Empire.
558 BC	Cyrus ascends to power and moves the capital of Achaemenid Empire to Susa.
550 BC	Cyrus defeats the Median King Astyages and annexes Media to Achaemenid Empire.
512 BC	Darius succeeds his cousin Cambyses, Cyrus, son.
334 BC	Alexander the Great invades Asia.
330 BC	Alexander the Great brings down the Achaemenid Empire.
323 BC	Alexander the Great dies, and his empire is divided among his Generals.
320 BC	The Seleucid Empire is founded. The name of the Empire is referred to the Roman General Seleucid, who became the ruler of the Eastern provinces of the Roman Empire, what is known today as Lebanon, Syria, Iraq, Iran, and Afghanistan.
247 BC–224 CE	The Parthian Empire rules the area.
224 CE	Ardeshir I establishes the Sassanian Empire.
609 CE	The Rise of Islam in the Arab peninsula.
635 CE	Omar, the Second Caliph of Islam, launches his campaign against the Sassanian Empire.
637 CE	The Muslim Arab armies bring the Sassanian Empire to an end.
819–999 CE	The Samanid Empire emerges, the first Iranian Empire to be established after the Arab conquest.
934 CE	Ali Buya seizes control over Fars and Shiraz and establishes the Buyid dynasty.
945 CE	The Buyids conquer Baghdad.
999 CE	The Ghaznavids conquer the Samanid capital, Bukhara, and bring down the Sassanian Empire.

1038 CE	Toghrul Beg defeats Ghaznavids and establishes the Seljuk Empire.
1055 CE	The Seljuk Empire expands and conquers from the Buyids.
1077–1231 CE	The Khwarezmid dynasty establishes its rule in Persia by Anush Tegin Gharchai.
1294 CE	Kublai Khan dies, and the Mongol Empire falls apart into four Khanate Empires; among them was the Ilkhanate dynasty in Persia.
1256–1353 CE	The grandson of Genghis Khan, Hulagu Khan, rules the Ilkhanate dynasty in Persia.
1335–70 CE	The Chobanids, Jalayirids, Injuids and the Muzaffarids ruled separate parts of the area.
1370 CE	Timur establishes the Timurid dynasty.
1501 CE	Ismail Shah establishes the Safavid rule in the area and changes the faith of the empire from Safaviyya founded by Safi-ad-Din Ardabili to Shiism.
1510 CE	Ismail Shah conquered the city of Herat.
1514 CE	Battle of Chaldiran between the Safavid Empire and the Ottoman Empire takes place after the defeat of Shah Ismail I against Sultan Selim I.
1555 CE	The treaty of Amasya is signed between the Safavid Empire and the Ottoman Empire after Shah Tahmasp of Persia's defeats in the 1532–55 and 1578–90 wars.
1590 CE	The Treaty of Constantinople is signed between the Safavid Empire and the Ottoman Empire after the defeat of the Persians in 1578–90 war.
1603 CE	War erupts again between the Safavid Empire and the Ottoman Empire.
1612 CE	Treaty of Nasuh Oasha was signed by Shah Abbas I of Persia and Sultan Ahmed I of the Ottoman Empire.
1618 CE	The treaty of Serav is signed after a decisive Safavid victory over the Ottomans.
1639 CE	Sultan Murad IV and Shah Safi sign the Treaty of Zuhab and end the 1623–39 war for the Ottomans.
1651–53 CE	Russo-Persian War erupts.
1707 CE	While in prison by the Safavid court in Isfahan, Shah Mir Wais Ghilji convinces the Shah Sultan Hossein to allow him to perform pilgrimage to Mecca (which was under the Ottoman Empire authority) and succeeds to obtain a verdict fatwa to rise against the 'Shiite' Safavids.
1709 CE	Chief leader of the Pashtuns Shah Mir Wais Ghilji began his campaign against the Safavids and succeeded to enter Kandahar.
1722–23 CE	Russo-Persian war erupts and Russia regains influence in the north frontiers of Persia.
1722–29 CE	The Ghilzai Dynasty rules Persia.
1732 CE	Sultan Mahmud and Shah Tahmasp II sign the treaty of Ahmed Pasha between Persia and the Ottoman Empire, which ended the 1730–35 war.

Chronology

1736 CE	Nader Shah Afshari establishes the Afsharid Dynasty in Persia.
1736 CE	Nader Shah Afshar and Sultan Mahmud I sign the treaty of Constantinople and end the 1730–36 war for the Afshars.
1746 CE	Nader Shah and Sultan Mahmud I sign the agreement of Kerden after 1743–46 war.
1776 CE	Karim Shah Zandi conquers Basra.
1778 CE	Karim Shah declares Tehran the second capital.
1779 CE	Karim Shah loses Basra to the Ottomans again.
1790 CE	The Zand Dynasty begins to rule Persia with Shiraz as its capital.
1794 CE	The last king of Zand Dynasty, Loft Ali Khan, is killed in Bam and the Qajar dynasty starts to rule Persia.
1796 CE	Agha Mohammad d Khan Qajar establishes the Qajar Dynasty, conquers Mashhad and ends the Afshar Dynasty.
1796 CE	Agha Mohammad Khan defeats the Russian army in 1796 war.
1823 CE	Fath-Ali Shah Qajar signs the treaty of Erzurum with Sultan Mahmud II.
1828 CE	The Treaty of Turkmenchay is signed between the Persian Empire and the Russian Empire after the 1826–28 war.
1848 CE	Nasser al-Din Shah Qajar comes to power and fails to prevent the British and the Russian influence over Persia.
1856–57 CE	The Anglo-Persian War starts, and Britain blocks Qajar's control of Herat.
February 1857 CE	The Battle of Khushab takes place. This battle was followed by the Battle of Mohammerah near Basra in March, followed by another battle, the battle of Ahvaz on April in the same year.
April 1857 CE	The Treaty of Paris ends the Anglo-Persian War.
1880 CE	The Qataris cracks down Sheikh Abdullah's Kurdish revolt.
1881 CE	Russia seizes control over the northeastern borders of Persia.
1896 CE	Mirza Reza Kermani, a student of Jamal a-Din al-Afghani and revolutionist, assassinates Nasser al-Din Shah. Mozaffar-e-din, Nasser al-Din's son, becomes king.
1905–06 CE	The constitutional revolution against Mohammad Ali Shah Qajar takes place.
October 1906 CE	The first legislative assembly, the Majlis, draws up a constitution for the empire.
December 1906 CE	Mozaffar-e-din Shah signs the constitution.
1907 CE	Britain and Russia sign the Anglo-Russian Agreement and agree to divide Persia into spheres of influence.
June 1908 CE	Mohammad Ali Shah bombs the Majlis building and abolishes the parliamentary government.
July 1909 CE	The constitutional forces succeed in regenerating the constitution, and Mohammad Ali Shah is sent to exile in Russia.
July 1909 CE	The Majlis votes to 'appoint' Ahmad Shah, Mohammad Ali Shah's 11-year-old son, as king.

xii Chronology

July 1910 CE	Russian military forces step up actions in Persia.
December 1911 CE	Russian troops siege the Majlis building and succeed to suspend the constitution.
1914–18 CE	The First World War ravishes Europe and leaves Persia vulnerable.
1979 CE	The Bolshevik revolution succeeds in ending Tsarist Russia and establishes the Soviet Union.
1919 CE	The Anglo-Persian Agreement is signed, and the Majlis refuses to approve it.
1921 CE	Brigade officer Reza Khan leads a coup and establishes a pro-British rule in Tehran. He becomes the Chief of Staff, and Zia ad-Din Tabatabai becomes the prime minister of Persia. Three months later, Reza Khan forces Tabatabai to leave Persia.
1921 CE	Brigade Reza Khan cracks down on the Simko Shikak's Kurdish revolt against the Qajar dynasty.
February 1921 CE	Persian and Soviet Russia sign the Treaty of Friendship.
1923 CE	Ahmad Shah Qajar appoints Reza Khan premier and leaves for Europe.
April 1926 CE	Reza Khan Pahlavi becomes the Shah of Persia.
1926 CE	Simko Shikak second Kurdish revolt against the Pahlavi Dynasty is cracked again.
1932 CE	Reza Shah cancels the Anglo-Persian oil agreement.
1936 CE	Reza Shah changes the name of Persia to Iran.
1939 CE	Reza Shah leans towards Germany in the Second World War.
1941 CE	Hitler attacks USSR and transports war materials to his armed forces in USSR though Iran.
August 1941 CE	USSR and Britain invade Iran and replace Reza Shah with his son, Mohammad Reza Shah.
1948 CE	With Soviet backing, Qazi Mohammad announces the Kurdish Republic of Mahabad in the north. The republic lasted for eleven months, and Qazi Mohammad was captured and sentenced to death.
June 1953 CE	Britain proposes to the US to replace Prime Minister Mossadeq for his collaboration with the Iranian Tudeh (communist) party. Eisenhower administration approves the proposal. In August, the Shah appoints Zahedi as prime minister. Mossadeq refuses to step down, a few days later; the Shah's forces defeat Mossadeq and his followers.
1955 CE	Iran joins the Baghdad Pact.
1963 CE	The Iranian authorities arrest the prominent Shia cleric, Ayatollah Ruhoullah Khomeini, for his opposition to the Shah's reform revolution.
1964 CE	Ayatollah Khomeini is sent to exile.
1968 CE	The Ba'ath party comes to power in Iraq and claims Khuzestan as Arab territory. It starts to support the insurgents in Khuzestan and Baluchistan against the Shah. The Shah on his side began to support the Kurdish rebels in Iraqi Kurdistan against the Ba'ath regime.

1971 CE	The Shah of Iran sponsors a coup against the Ba'ath regime in Iraq and backs Sultan Qaboos against Iraqi-backed rebels.
1975 CE	Iran and Iran sign the Algiers accord demarcating their border.
January 1978 CE	*Ettela'at* newspaper publishes article denouncing Ayatollah Khomeini as non-Iranian and a British agent.
1978–79 CE	Revolution erupts against the Shah's regime.
February 1979 CE	The Shah leaves Iran to exile, and Ayatollah Khomeini returns to the country and establishes the first republic of Iran, and the first revolutionary Islamic republic in the world.
February 1979 CE	Ayatollah Khomeini becomes Iran's Supreme Leader, Faqih.
October 1979 CE	The constitution of the Islamic Republic of Iran is adopted.
November 1979–January 1981 CE	Fifty-two American diplomats and citizens were held as hostages for 444 days in Tehran.
September 1980–August 1988 CE	Iran-Iraq War.
3 July 1988 CE	The United States Navy shoots down Iran Air civilian flight 655 over the Persian Gulf, causing the death of all 290 people on board.
21 July 1988 CE	Ayatollah Khomeini accepts UNSC Resolution 598.
8 August 1988 CE	Iran-Iraq War ends.
February 1989 CE	Ayatollah Khomeini issues his famous verdict, fatwa, to kill Salman Rushdie, the British-Indian writer, for publishing his book the *Satanic Verses*.
3 June 1989 CE	Ayatollah Khomeini dies.
4 June 1989 CE	The Assembly of Experts elects the president of Iran Seyed Ali Khamenei as Iran's new Supreme Leader, and Ali-Akbar Hashemi Rafsanjani is elected as the first executive president of the country.
1993	Rafsanjani wins elections and starts his second term in office.
1995 CE	The United States ceases trade activities with Iran, accusing the country of supporting terrorism and pursuing a WMD programme.
August 1997–2005 CE	The reformist Mohammad Khatami elected with large majority as president of the country.
2001 CE	Iran cooperates with the United States against the Taliban regime in Afghanistan.
January 2002 CE	President of the United States, George W. Bush, describes Iran, along with Iraq and North Korea, as 'axis of evil' countries for their support of international terrorism and pursuing nuclear weapons programmes.
March 2003 CE	The United States invades Iraq and ends Saddam Hossein's regime in Iraq.
September 2003 CE	The International Atomic Energy Agency (IAEA) calls on Iran to suspend all the uranium enrichment activities.
October 2003 CE	Iran accepts IAEA's request to suspend the enrichment activities.
June 2004 CE	IAEA castigates Iran for its lack of cooperation with the agency.

2004–January 2016 CE	Iran-IAEA tensions remain but negotiations also take place.
August 2005 CE	Neoconservative Mahmoud Ahmadinejad elected president of Iran.
August 2009 CE	Ahmadinejad is controversially reelected to the presidency. As a result, his opponent, the reformist Mir-Hossein Mousavi, leads massive protests across the country in dispute of the results of the elections. In the end, the Supreme Leader approves Ahmadinejad's reelection and accuses the protests of a foreign-sponsored conspiracy.
August 2013 CE	Hassan Rouhani is elected president of the country.
April 2015 CE	President Hassan Rouhani agrees to the outlines of a nuclear deal with IAEA.
20 September 2015 CE	UN atomic inspectors visit Iran's military-designated Parchin site.
23 November 2015 CE.	The Russian president, Vladimir Putin, visits Tehran.
January 2016 CE	Iran- P5+1 (the US, UK, France, China, Russia, and Germany) deal is signed, and the international sanctions are lifted.
2 January 2016 CE	Saudi Arabia executes the Shia cleric, Shaikh Nimr al-Nimr. Saudi-Iranian relations hit a new low.
23 January 2016 CE	Iran and China sign a twenty-five-year strategic agreement.
28 January 2016 CE	The Italian prime minister visits Tehran.
5 February 2016 CE	A Japanese economic delegation visits Tehran.
16 February 2016 CE	Ghana President Mahama is the first African leader to visit Tehran after the nuclear deal.
February 2016 CE	Austria's Raiffeisen Bank International (RBI), the first European Bank, announces plan to open a branch in Iran.
27 February 2016 CE	Swiss President Johann Schneider-Ammann visits Tehran.
8 March 2016 CE	Iran embarks on a series of missiles tests.
20 March 2016 CE	Ayatollah Ali Khamenei says that the US is undermining Iran's banks.
25 March 2016 CE	Iran to boost security and trade ties with Pakistan.
11 April 2016 CE	Russian S-300 air defence missiles arrive in Iran as part of a major arms deal.
12 April 2016 CE	President Nursultan Nazarbayev of Kazakhstan visits Tehran.
12–18 April 2016 CE	Italy extends $5 billion credit line and export guarantees to Iran.
2 May 2016 CE	South Korean President Park Geun-hye visits Tehran
16 May 2016 CE	High Representative of the European Union for Foreign Affairs and Security Policy Federica Mogherini visits Tehran, at the head of a large EU delegation, to discuss regional security and trade opportunities.
22–24 May 2016 CE	Indian Prime Minister Narendra Modi visits Tehran to boost political and economic relations.
23 May 2016 CE	The United States kills the Taliban leader Akhtar Mohammad Mansour on his way to Pakistan right after visiting Iran.

INTRODUCTION

This book is about modern Iran after its mass-based 1979 revolution. More precisely, this book is about the political order that followed the fall of the monarchy – the Islamic Republic of Iran and its political, economic and foreign relations complexities. It was conceived when Dr Mahmoud Ahmadinejad, representing a new blend of Iranian neoconservatism, emerged victorious from the second round of voting in Iran's ninth presidential poll in 2005. But the book began to take shape during the second term of Ahmadinejad's presidency, arguably the country's darkest days since the war years in the 1980s. His second-term administration, coming to power on the back of suspected massive electoral fraud in the June 2009 presidential poll and intra-elite in-fighting, started with heavy-handed clamped down on society in an unprecedented way. Much of the efforts of the government and security establishment were put towards trying to stop the revolt against the regime that had followed the election result. His administration closed off all major avenues for free expression, put away large numbers of the country's political reformists, used torture and forced into exile many thousands for standing up for their electoral rights, muffled the media, and in this process thoroughly securitized society.

Externally, Ahmadinejad's policies also cost the Iranian society dearly. His populist rhetoric and aggressive policies caused a rupture in Iran's relations with its main trading partners in Europe, in the process diverted Iran from its traditional markets, and also caused a rift in the normal flow of diplomacy with its hinterland. With regard to the nuclear crisis, particularly, which had become a national foreign policy problem during the presidency of Hojjatoleslam Mohammad Khatami, Ahmadinejad's hostile negotiating tactics pushed Iran further into the arms of the UN Security Council and its strict treatment of Iran as a non-compliant state and a violator of its NPT commitments. His administration's hostility and provocative acts became so brazen that from 2010 his policies ended up putting Iran under the toughest multilateral sanctions regime ever. Society was being squeezed internally and externally.

This book started during this dark period, and as the budding Green Movement slowly submerged under intense pressure from the regime, as much as from lack of ambition, it was hard to see how Iran's youthful and networked society would recover from this crisis. Yet it did, and the prose of this book took shape under circumstances from whence it started, during an era of hope and optimism following the election victory in June 2013 of Hojjatoleslam Hassan Rouhani, a popular cleric and regime insider with close links to the reformers as well as the centrist and conservative factions of the elite. Iran's fortunes had apparently changed with the blink of an eye, and once the nuclear negotiations resulted in the lifting of all multilateral sanctions on the country in January 2016, everything now seemed possible. The government's diplomatic machinery went into overdrive and cultivated economic partnerships with the East and the West. This level of change promised a very different Islamic republic to the one nurtured and developed in the preceding years. How was this level of change achieved and what caused the volte-face?

This research project has focused on Iran not only because it is, and is perceived to be, an influential regional, and increasingly pan-Asian, power, and not solely for its strategic and geopolitical assets that have shaped its relations with the outside world, or its own worldview; but for the fact that we have in front of us a country with a strong revolutionary legacy and unique in modern revolutions for being rooted in religious traditions and a novel political system based on a particular theo-political ideology, going through a process of fundamental change. The aim is to better understand the internal and external forces that have influenced this revolutionary regime's formation and identity and the processes of political change that have shaped its economy and international relations since the Islamic revolution of 1979. This book is, at its heart, an attempt at a better understanding of change in a revolutionary regime. Its purpose is to show how social and political forces in a revolutionary environment, which articulates resistance, can accommodate internal pressures for reform and democratization and external pressures to conform to the conditions of the prevailing international order.

While its place in the twentieth century–born world of modern nation-states is certainly different from the old times, one cannot underestimate the role that history has continued to play in the country's self-perception and also in determining its role in the Westphalian system of states.

The introductory chapter will trace the conditions under which a modern state has grown out of the ancient Persian Empire. The geographical, socioeconomic and political contours of modern Iran will be examined and the milestones in the modern history of the country will be highlighted in order to provide a backdrop for the detailed analysis of the country's politics, economics and international relations.

Narrating Iran in the twenty-first century

The essence of this book is to try to engage with the theoretical and methodological problems associated with contextualization of a modern republic, which, unlike so many others in the non-Western world, has the base of an ancient civilization to draw on and a long tradition of governance.[1] This is a new republic in old clothes – the old clothes of Persian Empires and of Islamic traditions. This book addresses the problems of governing through a combination of 'Iranianness' and 'Islamicness' through a series of focused discussions on the politics, political economy and international relations of the Islamic Republic of Iran – the essence of the country. The study is based on the observation that this state has been shaped as much by revolutionary ideology and history as by the 'fixed' forces of geography, geopolitics, and a robust nation-state identity. But to better understand the interplay between these forces, the research will build its narrative around answering three critical questions:

- How does one *consider* Iran? If one were to strip the country of its 'Islamic' republican order, how different would Iran of the twenty-first century be from the Pahlavi state? What has changed, what has remained familiar, and what can be considered as more permanent?
- How does one *view* Iran? Does Iran provide a new model for other would-be revolutionaries of the East? Is the republic a conformist or a revisionist state? Does its ruling political regime really want to change the world and remake it in its own image, bring about a different international order more in keeping with its values? Or, in the last analysis, does it believe in 'live and let live'? Does rhetoric disguise a desire to conform? How can we determine whether it is a status quo power or a subversive one?
- How does one *evaluate* Iran? In a normative sense, can one quantify the performance of the republic? Has the Islamic republic lived up to its founding expectations, has it served the Iranian people and helped realize their aspirations as it so confidently espouses to have done so on the anniversary of the revolution in February of every year?

I have aired these, and adaptations of these questions, at different gatherings over the years and have been fortunate enough to receive immensely helpful comments from a small army of scholars, observers and analysts who have unselfishly shared their own insights and observations with me and have willingly and constructively contributed to my own thinking about this unique and most interesting of modern republics. It transpired very quickly, and not unexpectedly, that no single set of answers could be given to any of these questions, and the area of disagreement was really quite extensive. Why was that? Why was it so hard to reach consensus in narrating Iran? For me, the difficulty lies in our interpretations of the 'state of Iran' today. The issue is how to get beyond the polemics driving debates about Iran for a deeper new study of Iran that can capture the essence of state formation in this ancient land, explain the drivers of change in the country, and understand how and where it aims to locate itself amongst an increasingly interdependent world of weak and powerful states. How does it see itself and what impressions have political and economic transformations of the last two generations made on the republic? Where does one begin narrating Iran of today? Iran is a complex historical, social, political and territorial entity, with multiple identities – in terms of nationalities, tribal communities, localities – and historical narratives, so on what ground should one place one's first step?

First, what is Iran today? Clearly, it is an Islamic republic, but unlike the Islamic monarchy of Saudi Arabia, for example, which uses the Quran as its constitution, Iran has a written constitution and one which Western constitutional experts can instantly recognize. So, the question follows, how republican and how Islamic is the Islamic Republic of Iran? How do its Islamic and republican components interact? Is the IRI a constitutional republic? If so, who holds sovereignty, and where do the revolutionary masses fit in? Like republican regimes the world over, this Islamic republic has in place the three distinct and separate branches of state craft enshrined in its written and (the twice) popularly endorsed constitution. The independence of the executive, legislative and judiciary are enshrined in the constitution and the three branches of governance operate separately but in a related fashion. To inhibit the emergence of a strongman dictatorship, the republic has layers upon layers of institutional checks and balances. Although the fifteen-member Council of Guardians (CG) has the authority to vet all legislation put forward by the elected parliament, if the latter is dissatisfied with the CG's treatment of its proposed laws, then (under the rules of the 1989 amended constitution) it can refer the contested legislation to another state body – the Expediency Council (EC) – for adjudication. The EC can, in the interest of the system (the nezam), in effect overrule the CG.

On top of the republic's governance institutions sits the Supreme Leader – always a cleric – but who is not necessarily senior in theological circles. He is the highest religious and political authority of the republic. The qualities of the Leader, according to the constitution, should include piety and administrative competence: "Better versed in Islamic regulations or in political and social issues". Note that no longer is religious supremacy a requirement for this important office. The Supreme Leader is himself 'elected' by yet another popularly elected body, the Assembly of Experts (AE). The AE role is to elect and also monitor the performance of the Leader. Underpinning the institutions of the state, which the constitution also stresses, is the role of the (Shia) clerical establishment, with Article 4 stating that "all civil, criminal, financial, economic, administrative, cultural, military, political, and all other statutes and regulations (must) be in keeping with Islamic measures;... the Islamic legal scholars of the Guardian Council will keep watch over this". And on the importance of the role of the Leader, Article 5 states that "during the absence of the hidden Twelfth Imam government and leadership of the community in the Islamic Republic of Iran belong to the rightful God fearing... legal scholar (Faqih) who is recognized and acknowledged as the Islamic leader by the majority of the population". The responsibilities of the Supreme Leader are only vaguely stated in the constitution, thus any 'violation' by the Supreme Leader would likely be dismissed almost immediately. Furthermore, the constitution empowers the Leader, tenured for life, above all others, which has resulted in Ayatollah Ali Khamenei creating a government within a government – a vast centralized bureau (Beit Rahbari) of some 5,000 employees and teams of experts and advisers reporting directly to him. The Leader is served by a "vast network of commissars stationed in strategic posts throughout government bureaucracies, dedicated to enforcing his authority".[2] Added to this are his formal roles as the Commander-in-Chief of the armed forces, overseeing the appointment and performance of every local Imam of Friday Prayer leader in the country, and the head of the state-run radio and television, which places him both at the heart and above the state.

Clearly, Iran has created a complex but unique and non-transferrable system of government that can work only in this country, yet the constitution claims that the Islamic republic would aspire to 'export' the country's morally and politically superior system of government to the rest of the (Muslim) world. With the insertion of the Faqih as the overriding authority of the Islamic republic, and with placing him at the heart of the country's body-politic, Iran has arguably merely created the model of 'Islam in one country'. The tension between Tehran's self-promoted role as the beacon of revolutionary political Islam in the world and the rest of the Muslim world's image of Iran was laid bare following the Arab uprisings in which the masses and the new activists not only did not turn to Tehran for support but actively sought to distance themselves from the Iranian model. Purportedly based on the universal values and teachings of Islam, its revolutionary model, ironically, also made it totally non-transferable – even to other Shia-majority Muslim countries.

Underlining the uniquely local relevance of this republic, in 1989 Ayatollah Khomeini himself made it clear, and indeed mandated, that the affairs of the state always take precedence over religious (Islamic) imperatives: Building a functioning republic has always been more important than creating God's rule on earth. So is this then more of republic than an Islamic one? Secondly, what it is its regime type? Is it democratic, authoritarian, semi-authoritarian, proto-democratic, pseudo-democratic, hybrid? How do we decide? The reality is that the Islamic republic has held dozens of popular, and meaningful, elections since its birth in 1979. And in this regard, it is unique amongst the Muslim countries of the Middle East and North Africa. It held its eleventh successful presidential elections in June 2013, at the same time as local elections, with a 72 per cent voter turnout. The parliament whose term ended in spring 2015 constituted the country's ninth and was elected through peaceful exercise of voter preferences in 2012. People routinely take part in election cycles; elections always go ahead on time, are lively affairs, and even enjoy televised debates. Campaigning is regulated more to ensure fairness and equal say than control the voice of the candidates or the people.

Yet candidates for all contested positions are customarily vetted by the country's central authorities to ensure their 'suitability' for high office in the Islamic republic. For most positions, candidates must be Muslim, provide evidence of probity and contribution to the life of the regime – the ubiquitous nezam (system of governance). But meeting these essential criteria is insufficient for approval. So for example, in the 2013 presidential race, only 8 candidates (all grey men!) out of 680 registered hopefuls were allowed to actually run for this office. The other hundreds were summarily 'disqualified', including the twice former president of the republic, Ayatollah Rafsanjani. He was actually barred from standing for an office that he had already occupied for two successive terms and in fact also competed for in 2005. Despite his national standing and experience as a senior figure in the republic, his candidacy was deemed as too political! What does this episode tell us about the Islamic republic? With factionalism so rife in this polity, do we confuse unregulated in-fighting for plurality and political competition? Elected office holders do make an impact and can determine the direction of travel, but they are all constrained by the pervasive 'red lines' in the regime, and an obvious lack of transparency and accountability.

Furthermore, 'pluracracies' thrive on a free media, uncensored and open. But in the Islamic republic, and despite constitutional assurances regarding a free press, the media is tightly controlled. With self-censorship a necessary professional skill, the scope for debate is both narrowed and scripted. So it needs to be asked, how does debate take place when, since 2000, 150 pro-reform newspapers have been shut down for 'transgression' and when 'Reporters Without Borders' has ranked Iran as the 174th worst offender of press freedom in the world in 2013 out of 179 countries? Censorship alongside a strict penal code, severe punishment of any dissent or free thinking, and routine violation of human rights makes its controlled electoral politics an even less convincing model for freedom-seeking citizens of other Muslim countries. Clearly then, a free polity must be more than a composite of elections, and if in Iran elections are the mainstay of its 'democratic' system – a concept that the founding fathers of the republic were loath to use as to them an Islamic state is by definition superior to all forms of government – one would struggle to find other means of setting this republic apart. So, we can agree that Iran's polity is different, but the question is, is it for this any better, or superior, than others around the world?

How does the Islamic republic project itself, and how does it project power? Is it done in terms of 'soft power' means – religion, ideology, power of history, projection of influence through example – or through conventional measures of power (military might, economic success, technological achievements, geopolitical and resources reserves)? Moreover, what does it stand for? Clearly, the post-Pahlavi regime has pressed the country in a very different direction compared with its predecessor. Bakhash makes the case that "the Islamic revolution and the ideas and ideology to which it gave birth have significantly reshaped Iranian foreign policy". This is very true, and, as he has noted, the revolution helped Iran end its most durable alliances with the West, particularly the United States; severing its strategic partnership with the Western-constructed regional organs; and confronting regional countries which up to the revolution had been its allies.

So relations with Israel and Egypt were cut, and those with the *ancien regime*'s Arab allies (Saudi Arabia, Jordan, and Morocco) were curtailed. Some radical Arab parties, like Syria and the PLO, emerged as new friends, but other radical states, like Iraq, were shunned. Tehran's new foreign policy may have had an ideological underpinning to it but as its policies towards the region's two Ba'athist powers of Iraq and Syria in the 1980s show, it was also dictated by geopolitical imperatives. In this, one can argue that a considerable degree of pragmatism must have crept into its role conception. Furthermore, despite the Islamic republic's strategic mission to de-legitimize the Westphalian international order, in favour of a distant Islamic unity, it has remained an active member of all the intergovernmental organizations that the Pahlavi regime signed Iran into. Indeed, the long (2002–16) diplomatic struggle over its nuclear programme was in part about Iran's efforts to prove to the world that it had remained loyal to the principles of the Non-Proliferation Treaty (NPT; of which Iran is a founding member) and that its policies for acquiring nuclear technology and know-how were wholly consistent with the NPT regime's conditions. Tehran has unfailingly participated in the machinery of the Westphalian system, which its ideological bend opposes as a matter of principle. In this regard, the constitution states with great clarity that the Islamic Republic of Iran will "pave the way for the formation of a unified Ummah [single Muslim entity] in the world".

But for a more structured discussion, one can usefully divide the principles of the Islamic republic's foreign policy into five key components, of which three are particularly significant and relevant to the discussion of this monograph.

- The *first* is that, like the Pahlavis before it, the country's Islamic leadership regards Iran as a regional power with regional and even international aspirations. Tehran regards itself as a legitimate regional actor by virtue of revolutionary zeal: Its mass revolution and popularity of its stance in support of the vulnerable and the deprived is regarded as giving it a voice and a say in affairs affecting the Muslim world. Its Islamic foundations, it claims, coupled with its superior political system, provide it with the moral legitimacy to intervene in the region 'in defence of Muslims' and in support of their perceived causes and values.
- *Second,* given the conditions of its birth – an eight-year long devastating war (1980–88), fought in near-complete isolation – Tehran's international relations have been shaped, above all, by security concerns. The Iranian elite has a dim view of the West and has tended to see the West's pursuit of its interests in the Middle East as part of a devious plot to undermine this self-declared Islamist beacon. For its 'resistance', the regime finds itself in a zero-sum game of chicken that the West plays with it on the regional canvas and even through penetration of its home front – its sacred space. Iran sees dangers and conspiracies behind every Western action, even when Western

action has aided its security – as in the removal of the Taliban and the Ba'ath regime in Afghanistan and Iraq, respectively. Tehran saw ulterior motives for each of these acts: The fact that US/Western troops were ensconced on Iran's borders subsequent to 9/11 might have fed the sense of siege in Tehran and the fear that the West was adding to its forces stationed in Bahrain and other Gulf Arab monarchies as part of a broader encirclement strategy for an inevitable confrontation with the Islamic republic.

- *Third,* the Islamic republic has tried to stamp its own authority on relations with the outside world through a 'counter-hegemonic' foreign policy – that of 'neither East nor West'. Since its birth, it has intermittently sought to build closer relationships with non-aligned or non-US-oriented great or regional powers. 'Looking East' has been one fruitful strategy that emerged as early as the mid-1980s. Another, emerging in the early twenty-first century, was closer links with the populist South American states. It is worth noting, however, that the Shah had also cultivated links with Asian powers and had developed good links with both India and China in the 1970s as well as partnerships with many of the pro-Western Asian countries (such as Taiwan, South Korea, the Philippines, and Singapore), as part of the strategy of diversifying its alliance network.

More generally, Iran's international relations have developed in long cycles since 1980, defined by the force of the key moments in its history and the influence of its popularly elected presidents. Since 1989 and the creation of the executive presidency, the latter's role has become even more significant, though on most strategic issues the Leader has tended to moderate the executive's policies and the real or imaginary 'red lines' that his considerable bureau has drawn. But in the long term, how different has been the IRI's agenda with respect to its immediate neighbourhood compared with that outlined by the Shah in 1974? The monarch said: "We have declared before that we would not want to see any foreign presence in the gulf, England, the United States, or China – our policy hasn't changed". Ayatollah Khamenei repeats the same mantra in all his foreign policy forays.

What is the balance between morality and interest in the IRI's foreign relations? In Syria, Bahrain, Iraq, Palestine, Afghanistan, Yemen, for example, or indeed in terms of relations with the 'Great Satan' itself (the United States), what factors drive its policies? Is it morality, ideology, or pure and simple interest? In the last analysis, is the IRI a 'rational actor', and are Iran's leaders, in the words of President Obama "strategic, and not impulsive. They have a worldview, and they see their interests, and they respond to costs and benefits".

Or does the Iranian political elite represent "a messianic apocalyptic cult", with a death wish, as argued by the Israeli PM and many others in the United States and also in the region itself? Will its aspirational challenge to the Westphalian order (based on the existence of independent nation-states) constantly push it towards policy choices that will create the conditions for the birth of an, albeit ill-defined, Islamic world order? Does this then make the IRI an anti-system state? Are voices like Netanyahu's right after all?

Fourth, how would one describe the Iranian economy? What is it modelled on? What role does the market play in it, and what is the relationship between private capital and the state?

Iran is a medium-sized economy with the potential to become a leading Asian powerhouse. With a well-educated workforce and a population of 75 million people, a GDP of $540 billion ($998 billion in PPP terms), large landmass and plentiful mineral resources, readily available power sources (and one of Asia's largest generators of electricity with 233 billion kilowatt hours of electricity), Iran should be one of Asia's most promising economies.

In terms of GDP and population, Iran is the second-largest country in the MENA region and as such carries significant weight in west Asia. It has mastered advanced technologies (like nuclear technologies) – almost single-handedly – and for these reasons, Iran's potential has resulted in Goldman Sachs listing it as a member of the Next-11 ('N-11') group of emerging economies to follow in the footsteps of the BRICS. Remarkably, despite the pressures of war and sanctions, the Islamic regime has not lost sight of its welfare agenda, which has been part of its revolutionary psyche. As such, it has been keen to develop the country's conditions of living as a priority – all levels of education, housing provision, spread of energy and electricity, access to clean water, transport infrastructure, and healthcare have shown significant improvements. It is remarkable how much progress Iran has made in these fields and under such difficult conditions – capital flight and flight of the professional classes, war, low oil prices, and sanctions would have been major impediments to the revolutionaries' plans for economic development.

Data gathered from national sources, IMF, UNICEF, and the World Bank shows that at the end of the 2010s, some 4.4 million people were enrolled in tertiary education, with nearly 190,000 individuals training to become physicians, and a further 1.6 million were enrolled in engineering and hard sciences programmes; and, with a nearly equal gender balance, 13.2 million children were enjoying formal schooling, with some 60,000 schools serving the country's rural areas. Ninety per cent of the rural communities now have access to clean piped water, and the government's active agricultural support programme has been facilitating the production of basic foods, such as wheat and rice, in the country. Over 35 per cent of government expenditure has tended to go on education, social services and health, with health taking 2 per cent of GDP, and education, 5 per cent. The country has ninety-two institutions of higher learning and a further fifty-six research institutes. A national social security and pension system in place covers over 75 per cent of the population, and also a social welfare net supports the low-income social groups. On average, around 20 per cent of the budget has gone on social welfare since the mid-1990s. Life expectancy is 73, immunization coverage is 99 per cent, and total adult literacy rate stands at an impressive 85 per cent. Tehran has a thriving stock market, and as will be discussed the usual imperatives drive the republic's economic policies.

But, the Islamic republic also faces unique economic challenges: Hydrocarbons, which have been the basis of Iran's economy for a hundred years, have continued to dominate the economy. Manufacturing remains weak, and deep structural problems with the economy remain unresolved. The share of the state sector (including the all-powerful *bonyads*) remains predominant in the economy, acting as the prop for the regime. When compared with other countries, the IRI does not shine: In terms of corruption index, it is ranked 144/177 countries; in terms of competitiveness, it is ranked 66/141; in terms of press freedom, it is 175/179; and in terms of judicial independence, it is ranked 66/142. In terms of globalization (measured by the KOF Globalization Index), the country is ranked 162/181. The Economist Intelligence Unit has placed Iran 150th in the world in terms of quality of life.

Is the economic system just, then, when 45 per cent of the country's GDP is consumed by 25 per cent of its population, and the bottom 20 per cent receive only 6.4 per cent of the GDP? Iran's Gini index – a statistical measure in which 0 equals absolute equality and 100 equals absolute inequality – has climbed from 38.3 in January 2005, which was already high, to an estimated high of 44.5 today. According to one analysis, 40 per cent of Iranians now live below the international poverty line, almost double the proportion of just eight years ago. As the noted economist Salehi-Isfahani states, "Iran's inequality is caused by inequality at the two extreme ends of the distribution, the very poor and the very rich. Iran's poor are worse off than the poor in Egypt and Malaysia, while its rich are represented in the top decile of the world's income distribution".

More immediately, the currency's collapse has made hard times harder: The dollar went from 870 tomans in 2005 to 3,200 tomans in 2013, which means that a 1-million-toman monthly salary's value dropped from $1,114 in 2005 to just $313 in 2013. Add to this the effects of inflation, and the erosion of real incomes is even greater. The Iranian population's purchasing power dropped by 72 per cent between 2005 and 2013. In this process, the middle classes have been crushed. With unemployment hovering at around 28 per cent, social misery is mounting, with young people under the age of 25 accounting for around 70 per cent of the recorded unemployed. Hyperinflation has remained a real danger for society as prices sometimes have risen by over 40 to 50 per cent on average. By way of a comparison, neighbouring oil states worry about annual inflation rates of only 2.5 per cent, or at worst 3.5 per cent. Iran's GDP contracted by just over 5 per cent in 2012 and 2013, just as Iran had begun enjoying historically unprecedented levels of oil income. Beyond oil, the state has very few other options for generating revenue as 60 per cent of the population do not pay (direct) taxes. And more worrying still, the shadow economy may have grown to 20 per cent of the GDP because of the sanctions, disguising income-generating activities.

But is this telling the whole story? To show the complexity of the picture, I again turn to Salehi-Isfahani, who makes the point that "it may surprise most people that the poorest person in the US has about the same income as the Iranian located at the 20% percentile. So, if the poorest person in the US visited Iran, he or she would have reason to envy the living standard of 80% of Iranians". Of course, most people in Iran have access to clean water, electricity, paved roads, education and such like. So, the question begs itself: By what set of measures do we judge Iran's socioeconomic performance? For Iran's leaders, Islamic economics is the ideal-type, as exemplified in the country's strides towards establishing an interest-free Islamic banking system. But is that it? What else is unique in the economic system of the world's first revolutionary Islamic state?

Fifth, where do the Iranian people fit into the discussion? What do they want, what do they stand for, and how do they exercise their rights and challenge restrictions? What do men and women think? In the first instance, the glass ceiling manifests itself as a glass wall in Iran. It not only keeps women from the highest posts but also keeps women separate from much of the wider world of men and therefore apart from the affairs of the republic. Yet women are massively involved in education and training and make up more than 50 per cent of the country's university population. In fact, thanks to religion legitimizing the education and also social integration of women, they are now a credible and important part of the country's labour force: Women are training to become teachers, lecturers, nurses, physicians, engineers, administrators, managers, filmmakers, lawyers and everything in between. Female students outnumber male students in Iranian universities 2:1. Yet they cannot become judges or run for the presidency on religious grounds, their witness is less credible, and their inheritance entitlement is 50 per cent of their male siblings'.

Then we have social issues to consider. For example, how does one account for Iran's rising divorce rate? Iran's divorce rate of 2.5 per 1,000 of the population is higher than the often derided 'decadent countries' of the West. About 150,000 divorces a year are taking place, meaning that 1 in 6.5 marriages were ending in divorce in 2011, now up to 1 in every 5.2 marriages. It could be argued that with 20 per cent of women in the workplace or actively seeking employment, they are less dependent on men for survival and therefore more able to choose their own destiny. But, according to the head of the research centre at the Ministry of Youth and Sports, Mohammad Tagi Hasanzadeh, the major reasons for the high divorce rate are moral corruption, mental disorder, unemployment, and alimony payments: "A recent study on young couples in Iran suggests that unhealthy relationships and moral degeneration are the leading causes of divorces among the young Iranian couples". Should such problems even exist in an Islamic state in which the family unit is enshrined in its constitution?

Other social problems visible elsewhere are also prevalent. A key crisis is having some four million registered addicts in the country, a total of 2.2 per cent of the population and the highest addiction rate in the world according to the United Nations. How did Iran find itself here?

On a different note, Iran may be seen as an isolated country and did suffer under the most restrictive international sanctions ever conceived, but Iranians are not living in isolation – this is not North Korea. Despite state restrictions, Iran boasts of one of the greatest number of Internet users in the Middle East, and the state endures a substantial blogging community. Thus, in terms of Internet usage, Iran's rate jumped from 250,000 in 2000 to 36.5 million in 2011, just before sanctions bit into the country's ITC provision. In 2009, there were more than 700,000 weblogs written in Persian, compared with about 50 in [Arabic] neighbouring Iraq. Iranians are active, and with over 150,000 of the most highly educated or skilled leaving the country each year, they are also very well aware of the rapid pace of change around them and the great opportunities beyond the republic's borders.

Sixth, and finally, in looking beyond the immediate future, do we know where Iran wants to be by the end of this century? Does it have long-term ambitions? Does it have a strategy for getting there? How will it know when it has arrived? To me, the Islamic republic has not created what might be called a 'legacy state form'. So, taking each of my realms of analysis in turn, it is possible to say that:

- *Economically,* the republic has not established a unique and just economic system, as anticipated by its founding fathers and enshrined in the country's constitution. The economy's performance has been lacklustre for some two decades and there is no 'Islamic alternative' to capitalism or command economic system on display. Furthermore, its corporatist, 'state-capitalist' model is yet to negotiate for itself a place in the global capitalist system beyond exporter of hydrocarbons.
- The *political system* is certainly unique but is it sufficiently pluralist to be internationally credible? The key point is that while Iranian voters do have a say in the election of their representatives and while they vote in very large numbers for both parliamentary and presidential elections, the candidates for high office seem to be pre-selected by entirely unelected organs of the state. Citizens can vote only for what is offered to them. How is this political system superior to any other? Furthermore, when smaller religious groups, seen as minorities by virtue of being non-Muslim, are allocated limited numbers of seats according to their demography, how can one talk of equality and true universal suffrage?
- The IRI's *foreign policy* displays a greater proximity to what might be interpreted as revolutionary. But revolutionism cannot automatically be reduced to adventurism, irredentism, or dogmatism. Revolutionary, if evaluated on its own terms in the Iranian context, can be seen as no more than counter-hegemonism. But in reality, a fuller explanation of the foundations of Iran's international relations does exist, and Islamist Iranian international relations theorists, such as Firooz-Abadi, have argued that in the eyes of the Iranian leadership "an Islamic world system is desirable, utilizing worldwide Islamic values, common human interests, ethical principles and justice. This path will lead to the creation of an Islamic world society which would be devoid of power relations, domination, suppression and violence, and would proclaim the freedom and equality all human beings as citizens of an Islamic

world government". The 'Islamic world society' notion is suspiciously similar to the 'international society' concepts, but the big difference is that with Iran as the custodian of the Islamic universalist ideology, its policies and behaviour can act as the vehicle and can determine the process towards this ideal type.

More fundamentally, where does the territorially defined and geopolitically based 'national interest', an increasingly favourable currency in the Islamic republic, sit in the greater struggle to rid the world of nation-states? How compromised is the Islamic republic to a post-modern international system when it appears strongly wedded to the prevailing 'balance of borders' and territoriality of international politics when it daily commits blood and treasure in defence of neighbouring friendly regimes struggling to take back national territories lost to non-state violent actors?

So, in conclusion, can we say that the Islamic republic has a vision of a utopia? After all, its constitution boldly states that the IRI "intends to establish an ideal and model society on the basis of Islamic norms". In essence, I would say that it may have a vision for such a utopia but has limited means of realizing it. Essentially, the IRI's model is so case-specific that little from it can be extrapolated – transferred. Moreover, what has been built in the IRI is so unique that 'Iranian exceptionalism' makes its Islamist system redundant as a model. Methodologically, if the Islamic republic is a unique creation, then surely it cannot ever be reproduced, and by extension its claim of creating a new pathway for humanity is redundant. If Iran is unique, how then can its practices form a model, a transferable blueprint for the ideal society?

A regime that purports to have a universal answer only reaffirms its own difference. And there is the rub; the story of the Iranian revolution and the history of the Islamic republic is so contested that no single narrative can account for Iran in the twenty-first century. Iran's ideologues, particularly amongst the clerical establishment, consistently claim that the Islamic republic is better and superior in governance and society to other countries. One such figure, Ayatollah Imami Kashani, for example, used to say that "the school of capitalism is detestable and its filthy face is covered in scandals, crimes, corruption, AIDS. Marxism and Communism too is bankrupt. So the only school that can run the world is the school of Islam". The question which begs itself is 'but which Islam?'. Clearly, there is no single 'school of Islam', whether in the social or the political realm. Islamic doctrines are contested across the sects of Islam and also within each sect. Political Islam, moreover, is an un-uniform set of ideas and deeply divided ideologically and in terms of praxis. Political Islam does not represent a common set of practices and cannot be assumed as a model. Yet, in Iran, the assumptions about Islam and state being as one are presented as a unitary whole. But clearly these assumptions – about both Islam and state – are being critically challenged in Iran itself, and the regime is in need of answers if it is to keep the coherence of its message.

Looking at Iran through its own workings and looking at it from the outside – outside of its own terms of reference and political system and in terms of its international relations – will help explain the processes through which the country is governed and state-society relations managed. To better and further understand how the revolution has shaped Iran and how Iranian society and the world has been interacting with this revolutionary state, this book focuses on three core areas of political structures and processes, political economy, and international relations. With a modern historical perspective, this book takes stock of the forces that have changed and shaped Iran.

This book is structured in such a way as to speak to the style of the Contemporary Middle East Series and faithful to the need to develop a fuller understanding of one of the world's last remaining revolutionary states and addressing the core issues that make the Islamic Republic of Iran such an interesting case study and one for further investigation.

Notes

1 Nicola Pedde, 'Challenges for the New Persia', *Aspenia International*, no. 71–72, 2016, pp. 81–92.
2 Karim Sadjadpour, *Reading Khamenei: The World View of Iran's Most Powerful Leader* (Washington, DC: Carnegie Endowment for International Peace, 2008), p. 2.

1
MODERN STATE FORMATION

Introduction

This chapter will focus on the rise of the modern state in Iran, reflecting on the Qajar legacy but focusing in particular on the key structural developments taking place during the reign of the two Pahlavi monarchs. The analysis will flow into a survey of the institutional structures of the modern state and the changes that the 1979 Islamic Revolution brought about. It will aim to explain how the revolution affected the Iranian 'state form' and how historically significant these changes have proved to be. The institutional makeup and constitutional underpinnings of the Islamic republic will also be discussed.

As noted, Iran's experience with republicanism is recent, having been ruled by a range of monarchical dynasties over three millennia. But the end of the monarchy was a relatively sudden act and, for the nature of the revolutionary upheavals, therefore stands out as one of the most significant political developments of our time in terms of an apparently powerful leader of a fast-emerging regional power being challenged, exiled and finally deposed in just two short years between summer of 1977 and winter of 1979.

The development of a constitutional political regime in 1905, on the back of the constitutional movement, which quickly overwhelmed the corroding Qajar dynasty and finally gave birth to a new political order in the 1920s, can be seen as the point of departure for the making of modern Iran. Iran, as an 'empire-country' is a heterogeneous state and in its modern form is an amalgam of nationalities and ethnicities, crisscrossed by tribal communities of different sizes and significance today. Iran's socio-national makeup has over the decades played a significant part in determining the central government's regional policies, resource allocation, and even the country's foreign policy. Three times since the early twentieth century, for example, 'national uprisings' in the Azeri and Kurdish regions of the country have directly challenged the authority of Tehran and forced the mobilization of its military forces to put down such rebellions. So, the nationalities question, rooted in the country's demographic makeup, provides a useful entry point for taking account of the emergence of the modern Iranian state.

Iran's geography forms one of its key characteristics. Geography has had a strong hand in the rise of its civilization and has continued to play its part in determining Iran's history. Rooted in and based on the foundations of a vast multinational empire, Iran's geopolitical presence, its ethnicity, its languages and outlook on life and the surrounding areas have all been shaped by geography. Empire and geography have ensured that Iran be a heterogeneous country and home to many ethnicities.

Iran is not a demographically homogeneous country and is, indeed, by any international comparison one of the most ethnically diverse countries of the world. Being a multi-ethnic and multinational state brings its own unique pressures on the central authorities. National policies tend to underline the centre's keenness to control the provinces as tightly as possible, particularly as the majority of the country's minorities occupy the territorial edges of Iran. Thus, Kurdish, Lur and Azeri regions stretch from the foothills of the Zagros Mountains to the Aras River in the north (bordering Iraq, Turkey, Armenia and Azerbaijan); the Arabs live in the oil-rich province of Khuzestan in the southwest (bordering Iraq and Kuwait); the Baluch region is in the southeast and shares its lineage with the Baluchis of Pakistan; Turkmens live in the northeast and close to the border with Turkmenistan. Geography has dictated that all eight countries with which it has a land border have a linguistic/cultural presence in Iran.

A variety of Indo-European, Semitic and Turkic languages are spoken in Iran, and these are enriched by variations amongst the country's several nomadic tribal communities who in the past have been a source of insecurity for the central government but today travel across the country in smaller numbers in accordance with weather conditions and their established 'ghouch' (travel) customs. Foreign-supported uprisings in demand of autonomy in the Azeri and Kurdish regions since the early twentieth century have made a considerable impression on the Persian masters of the state, adding to the central authorities' nervousness of politicized minorities and the socialization of ethnic (national or tribal) communities – Kurds, Azeris, Bakhtiaris – into activists. In these senses, Iran's ethnic makeup has had a very considerable impact on its modern state structures and has played an important part in the emergence of strong and pervasive central administrative machinery at the heart of the state.

In addition to its varied ethnic communities, Iran also benefits from being a multi-religious and multi-confessional state. Shia Islam accounts for 89 per cent of the country's population, Sunni Islam for a further 10 per cent, and the remainder are Christians, Jews, Zoroastrians, and the unrecognized community of Bahais.[1] As Table 1.1 shows, 'ethnic minorities' as a single category make up nearly 50 per cent of Iran's population, so as a force, ethnic groups have a considerable presence, if not influence, in the country.

TABLE 1.1 Ethnic makeup of Iran

Ethnic group	% of total population	Ethnic group	% of total population
Persian	51	Arab	3
Azeri	24	Lur	2
Mazandarani & Gilaki	8	Baluch	2
Kurd	7	Turkmen	2
		Other	1

Source: CIA World Factbook.

Historical legacy

Persia, as the country was known until the early twentieth century, has been a major power since its emergence as a transcontinental empire in the sixth century BC. Nine centuries before the arrival of Islam on their shores, the Persians of Achaemenid dynasty had created a multinational world empire with a formidable military force and cultural and economic links to match. At its height, the empire stretched from Egypt to the Indus and from the Aral Sea to the Aegean. Following Alexander the Great's destruction of the Achaemenid Empire, the Sassanians under Ardeshir I emerged in the third century to restore Persian greatness with conquest and with security and economic prosperity. This dynasty established a new regional order whose boundaries were constantly tested by the Romans and later Byzantine. The Sassanians also had to defend the empire against Muslim Arab armies coming from the south and west and eventually incorporate Islam into the empire's life in the seventh century. This fundamental change in the empire's belief system did not come at the expense of its well-established customs and cultural mores and Persian identity, which not only remained intact but actually contributed to the development of Islamic empires for centuries to come.

Despite expensive wars, the onslaught of the Mongols and spectacular defeats, the Persian civilization not only survived but also thrived. The Persians played a significant role in the fostering of the ancient Silk Road stretching across the vast Eurasian landmass and later played their part in enriching Islam's empires. Persia, for all its bloody encounters with European powers, including the Ottomans and Imperial Russia, remained a major power until the eighteenth century. In this sense, Iran of today is the product of a deep-rooted transnational empire, with a sophisticated character. Its history and sense of self-worth is embedded in the characters of the world, the Eurasian world, which its civilization helped shape. As a result, it is, as a nation-state, steeped in many layers of identity and histories. The idea of Persia/Iran then is an old one, and the powerful contextual narrative, which has come from its sons – through such literal giants as Ferdowsi, Hafez, Saadi, Roumi – has stamped in the nation's collective memory a strong sense of self-worth and also awareness of the place of age/history at the centre of its self-identity. Pedde argues that Iran is

> The only real nation in the wide area extending from the Eastern Mediterranean to the Indian Ocean that has over 3,000 years of history and identity.... Persia and then Iran have experienced periods of both splendor and decline, economic and military might and crises and defeat, without ever losing an awareness of national identity and a sense of mission. This has brought about an extraordinary fusion of cultural values and political capabilities that has over the centuries made it possible to forge a state administration, an ever-evolving body of legislation and an ability to manage its own role and interaction with the outside world that are virtually unique in the [Middle East] region.[2]

But, history has also given it baggage, which is both positive and negative. The negative baggage follows the Qajar monarchs' inability to secure the empire and its territories and to find a path for Persia to modernize European style. Indeed, Iran's early modern period began with the rise of the Qajar dynasty in 1794. The Qajar shahs faced four distinct sets of pressures as they set about consolidating the Persian Empire. Their first challenge was to secure the empire's territorial integrity, which was being openly contested by European powers. Qajar kings spent much of their reign either trying to stave off encroachments by Russia, the Ottomans, Great Britain, and France or cutting deals with them for the sake of their crown. The second challenge was ensuring internal cohesion. With central authority being as weak as it was in this period, tribal and ethnic rebellions constantly threatened the monarchy's grip on the state. Third, the empire suffered from a stale and corrupt political system. Finally, the Qajars had difficulty developing the Persian economy to keep up with the rapid advances taking place in Europe. Under the Qajars, Iran was in stagnation, experiencing steady decline. External vulnerability and internal disorder provided the backdrop for modernizers, nationalists and progressive clerics to rally in support of constitutionalism in the early twentieth century.

Emergence of a modern state

Iranians, like their Russian counterparts, rebelled against arbitrary rule in 1905 and, in the course of Iran's unique constitutional revolution, managed to create a semblance of a modern and democratic state. But the 1905–21 period in Iran was anything but peaceful and stable and during which central authority weakened considerably. Iran's domestic problems were compounded by the Great War and the eventual demise of two of Iran's neighbours, the czarist order in Russia to the north and the Ottoman Empire to the west and south of the country.[3] But Iran's ties with Germany also exposed it to European geopolitical intrigue in which Berlin threatened to intervene in India (Britain's greatest colony) from Iranian territory.

The price of a constitutional order and the promise of rule of law appeared to be anarchy and social mayhem. And in this context, the Cossack Brigade colonel, Reza Khan, appeared on the scene as the saviour of the nation, following a coup attempt in 1921 against the crown. Patriot and intensely nationalist, Reza Khan's first mission was to restore order to the country, for which the military budget under his control as the commander-in-chief was tripled, outstripping expenditure on other departments "by a margin of four to one".[4] The country was bankrupt at this juncture, and there was little money to be found in the national treasury to finance the newly emerging national army under Reza Khan's command, so Reza Khan appropriated funds from other government departments and collected income accruing from such foreign oil companies as the Standard Oil Company of America active in the country.[5] After Ahmad Shah Qajar, under considerable pressure from the military, had left the country in 1923, Reza Khan had become the country's de facto leader. The Qajar dynasty was voted out by the Majlis on 31 October 1925, and Reza Khan was best positioned to bury this dynasty. But interestingly the constitutionally created Majlis, the source of national authority at the time, reconstituted itself as a constituent assembly, in order to vote for Reza Khan to become king of a new dynasty on 12 December 1925.[6] With this act the Pahlavi dynasty was born, but one of the deputies that objected to Reza Khan transforming himself from prime minister to king was none other than Mohammad Mossadeq – the nationalist aristocrat who became prime minister in the 1950s and also the chief opponent of Reza Shah's successor.

Reza Shah, the founder of the relatively short-lived Pahlavi dynasty (1925–79), is credited with establishing the modern state of Iran. Basing his own strategy on the secular modernist practices of the republic of Turkey under Kamal Ataturk next door, Reza Shah used his sixteen years on the throne to revolutionize the country's administration, class structure, infrastructure, and economic development strategy. Pushing through sweeping changes, which removed the old order and Iran's traditional-style politics for a Western-style governance system, he swiftly marginalized the hard fought for independent parliament, introduced a modern bureaucracy, enhanced educational opportunities and pushed women into public space while curtailing the power of the clerical establishment on society. He was a man with a mission whose reign, often brutal and heavy-handed, dragged Iran into the twentieth century. His rule accelerated the country's modernization, industrialization, urbanization, secularization and bureaucratization. He pushed modernization at a fast pace and did not suffer fools gladly, but his impatience for national development left in its wake many casualties, which included accumulation of land and other assets by the court for patronage, centralization of power relations, repression and suspension of many freedoms, a controlled press, the banning of minority languages, and bureaucratization of politics. Forcing European-style of dress and the broader secularization of the country, as embodied in forced unveiling of women, also left a bad taste in what was still a highly traditional and God-fearing society. His disempowerment of the clerics, beginning before he was 'elected' king, accelerated in the 1930s by the end of which the mullahs had lost much of their cultural, political and economic privileges to the secular state organs, and even Sharia (Islamic legal codes) were being abolished in favour of new civil and criminal codes.

Externally, Reza Shah operated with a deep awareness of Iran's geopolitical vulnerabilities and thus adopted a cautious foreign policy that aimed to reduce Britain's and Russia's hold on the country through building relations with other European countries, notably France, Germany and Italy. This strategy was largely successful in the 1930s and brought in much needed know-how from Germany and Italy in particular. The 1930s had witnessed Germany emerge as Reza Shah's key economic partner: Germany was busily building Iran's roads and highways, railroads, communications networks, power stations, factories and other major buildings and was also supplying it with machinery, tools and all manner of industrial goods. Not surprisingly, on the eve of the Second World War, 26 per cent of Iran's exports had been destined for Germany, compared with 8 per cent to Britain, and Germany accounted for 49 per cent of the country's imports, with just 9 per cent coming from Britain.[7]

Reza Shah's drive for modernization of the country was swiftly derailed once war broke out in Europe and Germany and the Soviet Union became enemies. On one side were Britain and the USSR, which urged Tehran to evict the thousands of German experts and technical advisers out of the country, and on the other side was Germany, which advised the Iranian government that the expulsion of its nationals from Iran would result in the end of diplomatic relations between the two friendly countries. The Iranian government's declaration of neutrality pleased neither side, and with German forces thrusting deep into Soviet territory by the end of August 1941, Iran was under the occupation of the Allies. A chorus of criticism had followed the Iranian government's position, with direct threats from Moscow to deal with Reza Shah once and for all. Following intense BBC broadcasts in Persian in September in which Reza Shah was painted as a Fascist sympathiser and a dictator and the one person responsible for the insecurity crisis facing the country, the ground had been prepared for the Anglo-Soviet military intrusion into Iran. Faced with this situation, Reza Shah abdicated on 16 September and found exile in South Africa soon after.

This episode provided another reminder of European interference in Iran's internal affairs and the geopolitical vulnerability of the country against superior forces. In Europe's battles, Iran's location, natural resources (oil in particular), and infrastructure had become prizes, which Britain and the Soviet Union quickly moved in to preserve for the Allies' cause. Iran, to the dismay of its people, was once again a pawn in the power plays of the great powers. Reza Shah's departure was followed by increases in personal insecurity, tribal and national minority unrest, breakdown of social order, unemployment, and food scarcity.

The last Pahlavi

Mohammad Reza Shah succeeded his father at the height of a national security crisis that had been triggered by the occupation of the country. His rule following the Second World War did not start well because he had to put much of his energies in the 1940s into the restoration of Iran's sovereignty and the removal of Soviet influence in the north and west of the country. The struggle against the Soviets and their local allies took shape in the brewing Cold War, which catapulted the young monarch to the frontline of the geopolitical tussle between East and West. Accompanying the West's Cold War consciousness was America's rapidly growing interest in Iran as a strategic Cold War front-line state and its monarch as an ally.[8] Iran's relations with the United States from the 1940s onwards came to shape the Shah's rule and also the political economy of this oil-rich state, which after the 1953 successful coup to restore the Shah to the Pahlavi throne considerably deepened. This clandestine 'investment' in the 'Peacock throne' against the nationalist popular government of Mohammad Mossadeq seemed to have paid off handsomely shortly after, following Iraq's bloody anti-monarchy revolution in 1958, which descended that country into a bloody chaos and cleared the way for Soviet intervention.

The revolution radicalized the Iraqi state and effectively made Iran the linchpin of the anti-Soviet Baghdad Pact and the defender of America's growing energy and security-related interests in the Persian Gulf. A small measure of this growing relationship is to be found in the developmental and technical aid that poured into Iran from the United States: Technical aid, for example, expanded from just $1.3 million in 1951 to $73 million in 1956, and between 1953 and 1960 a total of $567 million and $450 million were given in economic and military assistance, respectively.[9] Until oil income grew sufficiently, from the second half of the 1960s, in order to support the economy the regime had to rely on US and World Bank assistance for development. As a result, until the advent of the oil era, change had, of necessity, been tempered by externalities and was therefore gradual, incremental and proportionate. This changed dramatically as oil began to feature as a new and independent source of income, which in turn gave the Shah the confidence to be bolder and more daring in his policy choices. The Shah had already shown his preference to rule rather than reign over his country when, subsequent to the attempt on his life in February 1949, he hastily engineered the gathering of a new constituent assembly in March to pass three important laws: That the Senate (upper chamber), half of whose 60 members were crown appointees, be convened; that the Shah be given the power to dissolve both chambers; and that the two chambers establish the basis for their transactions.[10]

But the struggle with Prime Minister Mossadeq in the first three years of the 1950s shaped the Shah's reign. Mossadeq himself was not immune from excesses,[11] of course, but the political uncertainties during his premiership, which were compounded by mounting pressures from the outside (chiefly from Britain and the Soviet Union) and from within (chiefly through agitation by the Soviet-sponsored Tudeh (communist) party and a number of ultra-nationalist and religious groups), ensured that the Shah would secure for his throne the strong hand of the security forces and the military establishment as one of the main pillars of his order. The suppression of the Tudeh party following the return of the monarch on 22 August 1953 from his brief 'foreign travels', the creation of a largely obedient parliament rebuilt around the notion of a two-party system in 1955 (with a loyal opposition in the Mardoum party), a renegotiated oil extraction agreement with foreign companies, and demonstrated support by the United States and Britain for his crown, had by the second half of the 1950s consolidated in the Shah's realm both national political and economic power. The monarch's dissolution of the Majlis and the Senate in May 1961 preceded the introduction of his regime's own revolutionary policies – what became known as the 'White Revolution' – whose six-point plan was introduced via a national referendum in January 1963.[12] The Shah was now portrayed as a reformer with a grand vision for social and economic development of his country, a visionary no less who had stood against the Soviet-style 'Red revolutions' and the 'black reaction' (religious opposition) and in favour of peaceful and consensual change. This was to become welcomed as the 'Shah and people' revolution. It also brought the most vocal backlash against the Shah from the religious community in the figure of Ayatollah Ruhollah Khomeini.

The Shah's 'White Revolution' of the 1960s, focusing on education, health, agricultural reform and female emancipation, was precisely the mobilizing tool that the regime used to catalyse socioeconomic change on a grand scale. This was the Pahlavi's efforts to create a rural base for the regime, but at the same time by redistributing their land with substantial monetary compensation, the monarchy also enabled the landed aristocracy to trade their land for industry and commerce – to become bourgeois. But these and general secularization measures of the regime would generate a backlash – which appeared inevitable in the context of Iran's turbulent political clashes since the Second World War. As Avery astutely noted in 1965,

> It seems inevitable, when we take all these factors into consideration, that the religious classes would feel compelled to make a stand; above all the traditional balance between secular and religious authority, so heavily buffeted by Reza Shah's reforms, was now, under his son, undergoing a disturbance so radical that its future restoration might be placed beyond the bounds of possibility.

The problem, as Avery identified, was an existential one for the clerics as "modernism in the form of a new technical and materialistic control that would supersede for ever the old dispersal of controls under the ultimate guardianship of the nation's recognised spiritual authorities", had been unleashed.[13] In less than twenty years, the mullahs would have their revenge on the Pahlavi dynasty.

By the end of the 1960s Iranian society had become more urbanized and differentiated, and forces of capitalism were now directly shaping social relations. A growing middle class had emerged, which was richer and more mobile and educated than ever before. Young Iranians were travelling abroad for study in the thousands, and the middle classes had discovered the joy of overseas holidays, which had become popular thanks to the reasonable ticket prices charged by the national carrier (Iran Air), the strength of the rial (Iranian currency), and the luxury of visa-free travel to so many parts of the world. These groups were quick to adopt new habits from the West and thus widen the gap between the still majority traditional classes and the modern middle classes. Economic modernity, however, did not bring with it political benefits and in fact had the reverse effect, with the Shah deciding in the mid 1970s to turn the country into a single-party state. The single governing party of Rastakhiz was intended to "become the ultimate tool of ideological dissemination and political control".[14] The party was to secure absolute and unconditional support for the Pahlavi state, and its cadres would be the troopers for achieving this. Only traitors and communists would resist this new dawn, the Shah claimed, and their place was either in jail or in exile.[15] Changing the traditional Persian lunar calendar in 1976 into an invented 'imperial' one, which overnight changed the prefix of Iranian years from 13 to 25, alienated society as a whole and provided more evidence for the increasingly nervous middle classes and the religious and secular opposition that the Shah's megalomania had entered a new phase and with it the depth of the dictatorship.

Despite the Shah's announcements that his people were variously not yet experienced enough for democracy or not interested in it because it was an imported Western practice in any case, the trappings of modern living did not extinguish the thirst for political democracy, which had been in evidence at least since the 1940s. And the tensions between mosque and state had not gone away either. As the country entered the 1970s with a resolute and confident monarch at the helm, the pace of change became even more rapid and uncontrollable. Inflation and lower oil prices had a dampening effect on the overheating economy, which led to substantial cutbacks. Stagnation costed jobs, wages and bankruptcies. Ironically, the change of prime minister – replacing the loyal Abbas Hoveyda with the technocrat Jamshid Amuzegar – in 1977 ensured that austerity measures would be carried out with precision and efficiency, which in the political realm added to the Shah's as yet unarticulated unpopularity. The wave that started in 1977 became a tsunami in less than two years, but while the monarchy was swept away with the revolutionary wave and while the 'ruling class' decamped *en masse* in search of safer postures abroad, we should not overlook the fact that the governance structures that the Pahlavis had established remained. The modern state had been formed by the Pahlavis, and the massive social changes that decades of change had wrought could not be undone.

Revolution

There are only a few occasions of mass mobilization that scholars collectively classify as revolutionary. Many differences remain over the causes of a revolution and identification of the political order that follows it, but over the nature of such an uprising little is in dispute.[16] And when it comes to identifying revolutions, Iran's is one that is regarded as one such event.[17] A mix of economic mismanagement (against rising expectations), repression (administered bluntly), the stifling of independent voices, and apparent erosion of support from the Shah's Western allies (making him appear unprotected in the eyes of disgruntled social forces) arguably ignited protests, which were triggered by an apparent public slight against the exiled Ayatollah Khomeini and his clerical allies in a newspaper article published in Iran's most popular daily (*Etala'at*) in January 1978.

Protest had begun in summer 1977 as prices rose, shortages appeared and intellectuals were allowed, within the rubric of the new Rastakhiz order, to speculate publicly about to how to fix Iran's problems and celebrate its achievements. Like intellectual voices everywhere, the attention of this elite slowly but surely began to shift to the country's more immediate problems and the excesses of the government. International concerns about Iran's human rights provided the echo for wider criticisms. As one of President Jimmy Carter's foreign policy concerns, it was natural that many of America's allies in the developing world would become subject to closer scrutiny, and Iran was no exception. Indeed, the country's appalling human rights record actually made it a natural target of criticism. External commentary emboldened internal opinion on this and also wider social and political issues. But the revolution had deeper roots, and the role of domestic actors and factors in 1977 stands out. An avalanche of activism seemed to have changed the balance of power between the regime and society, and foremost amongst social agitators one can name, from many, the group of lawyers who wrote to the Shah complaining about political interference in the judiciary, the novelists and poets who used the Goethe Institute's premises for critical readings and commentaries, the leaders of the country's liberal voices (the National Front) who in an open letter to the Shah not only criticized the regime's economic policies and its excesses but also demanded an end to dictatorship and compliance with the constitution (which enshrined rule of law and limited the powers of the monarchy), the writers association public letter demanding an end to censorship and repression.[18]

As the Shah and the government were one and the same, criticism of the government morphed into criticism of the political order and soon into attacks on the person of the Shah himself – as the symbol and pinnacle of the Pahlavi regime. Isolated protests in towns and cities gave way to mass demonstrations in the capital and elsewhere, which by the autumn of 1978 were in the hundreds of thousands. The slogan was 'death to the Shah', and demonstrations were accompanied by mass strikes across the public sector, leading to closures and further shortages, while limiting the state's ability to restore order and recreate a semblance of normality. The killing of (thousands of) demonstrators hardened the resolve of the masses and regime violence in turn invited more militancy from the crowd and their willingness to accept hardship as the necessary price for freedom.

The ill-advised newspaper attack on Khomeini, a credible revolutionary personality since the 1960s, had two effects. First, it radicalized many elements of the normally apolitical Shia clerical establishment and encouraged them to join mass protests. Second, and in the absence of any organized political opposition to the Shah – beyond a handful of guerrilla organizations the majority of whose leaders were either in jail, in exile, or dead, and a defunct communist party (Tudeh) – Ayatollah Khomeini and with him the country's vast mosque network became the leaders of the revolutionary wave. In this, Khomeini was supported by the national liberal elite whose members later formed the republic's provisional government. Khomeini's uncompromising stance and his charisma stood in sharp contrast to the hitherto invincible figure of the monarch who now appeared confused, wounded, indecisive and feeble.[19] Lack of direction, indeed action, by the regime had of course emboldened the critics of the regime.[20] But, arguably the monarch's unmistakable indecisiveness, compounded by his apparent willingness to sacrifice his most loyal of allies (like longstanding prime minister and then minister of court, Hoveyda), diminished the resolve of the royalists to stand and fight for the monarchy. They could not be more Shah than the monarch himself, and in the absence of clear and decisive leadership from the top of the pyramid, the rest took flight or remained static until the whole structure gave way to the dynamic pressure from below and from across the country's body politic. The Shah stating that 'I have received the echo of your revolution', while imposing martial law and changing government personnel, showed that he had ran out of options.

Ayatollah Khomeini emerged as the undisputed leader of the movement, and the role that he occupied, coupled with the power and symbolism of Shia Islam, not forgetting the mosque's national network and financial power, gave the colour of religion to this revolutionary movement. The Shia religious establishment, of course, had been a part of the political system since the 1500s and had played a historic role in the constitutional order in the early twentieth century and again in the 1950s and 1960s, so when Khomeini mobilized them in the putsch against the Shah, they did enjoy credibility as well as legitimacy as an independent and trustworthy political voice. Crucially, Khomeini was uniquely placed to use Islam to bring together two distinct social groups in the revolutionary cause. The new urban middle classes saw in Khomeini's challenge to the Shah a religious shield to "defend their political, social, and ideal interests", and the marginalized classes, the most visible victims of the land reforms of the white revolution and now shantytown dwellers, "embraced messianic Shi'ism as a transnational, charismatic solution to mass alienation".[21] Furthermore, the regime's repressive policies had compelled virtually all urban communities, contends Brumberg, "to seek refuge in mass arenas such as religious seminaries, universities, mosques, and ultimately the *streets themselves*".[22] These arenas acted as hubs for mobilization as well and were either already dominated by the religious establishment or were solidly penetrated by forces loyal to the Khomeini-orchestrated revolutionary wave. But this did not mean that other political forces were not independently active. Indeed, the leftists, divided into a number of armed groups, were heavily involved in mass protests against the Shah's security forces, were able to use force against the vestiges of the regime's loyal troops, narrated the revolutionaries' anti-imperialist position, and also played a significant role in articulating a republican order and pushing the clerical establishment towards negotiating such an order with the broad-based revolutionary coalition.

Regime collapse occurred because, in the eyes of his allies and his opponents, the Shah no longer willed to rule and keep the political order in place and also because Khomeini appeared organized, mobilized and eager to bring about change. In January 1978, when the Shah left his country for the last time, all was lost. A year later, the 53-year-old Pahlavi dynasty ended the long line of monarchical order in this ancient land and ushered in a new and untested republican regime. But the nature of the revolutionary outcome was still far from clear in 1978 as this was 'change on the go': "A process or development in which various groupings in Iranian society battled for power and which, on account of its great depth and extent, forced large segments of Iranian public to take part in the development. The revolution developed into a process by which a charismatic leader – Khomeini – established his hegemony", but still not a clear path to his desired outcome of a unique (Shia) theocratic regime.[23] Khomeini's allies and followers, however, stated that the 'Imam' had not only a blueprint for Islamic government, a philosophy for it, a strategy for realizing it, but also a keen sense of occasion and ability to lead the people towards the ideal of '*Houkoomat-e Eslami*' (Islamic Government). Thus, concludes the preface to a learned discussion of Ayatollah Khomeini's thoughts on government: Imam Khomeini,

> by ruling historical events, and having a thorough knowledge of history of Islam and likewise, modern history of Iran and the world, has undertaken to find the causes of weakness and decadence of Muslims. On the other hand, his mastery in other fields such as religion, philosophy, theosophy, ethics and politics made it possible for him to look at every social matter from different perspectives, and find complete and correct answers. In fact, his personality characteristics, deep studies and keen judgement of social and political issues of Iran and the world created a new impression of religion in the mind of the people of the world.[24]

Yet it was Hashemi Rafsanjani, one of Ayatollah Khomeini's closest disciples, who chided parliamentary criticism of the government's tax reforms that 80 per cent of what the regime was doing had had no precedent in Islamic history.

The revolution had created the opportunity, unexpectedly, to give substance to Ayatollah Khomeini's idea of 'Islamic government' and the revolutionary coalition set about drawing up the governance structure of the new republic even before the Shah's last prime minister, Shapour Bakhtiar, was forced out of office in 1979. The assembly that was set up after the fall of the monarchy was charged with working through the final draft of the constitution as prepared by Khomeini's allies and thus presented to the public for their consideration. Schirazi notes that at this point the idea of a constitutional assembly had been rejected and Khomeini's allies moved swiftly to establish and fill a proposed 'assembly of experts'.[25] The clerics dominated the assembly of seventy-two, and with almost all fifty-five of them declaring allegiance to Ayatollah Khomeini it was inevitable that the Velayat-e Faqih (Jurist Consult) would find a place at the heart of the constitution and thus dominate the state structures of the new republic. With this process, Iran's clerics had embarked on a new political experiment and, in their deliberations, had created a unique constitutional order that blended religious designations with secular, Western, republican values and institutions.

The birth of the Islamic republic

Iran is home to the quintessential 'Islamic revolution' – mobilization of many millions under clerical leadership, with gun-toting turbaned mullahs accompanying the masses on the streets of Iran's cities chanting 'Allah o' Akbar'. This was a largely peaceful revolution that did culminate in brief street battles to take down the vestiges of the Pahlavi regime and once the Imperial order had ended, in February 1979, a process of 'republicanization' and Islamization of the state began. The new order was born on 1st of April 1979 and the establishment of the Islamic Republic of Iran. The rapid collapse of the *ancien regime* kept the state machinery intact and enabled the revolutionary forces to take control of state organs without much trauma. But, at the same time, with no organized political machine to manage the transition to a new system, with little statecraft experience, and no blueprint for the operationalization of the successor regime, the rainbow coalition of revolutionary forces spent as much time fighting each other as developing the foundations of the new republic. But foundations were laid and a new political system, based on the revolutionary leader's own interpretation of Islamic government, was established in April 1979. A new constitutional order emerged, in its early years dominated by the clerical establishment. Thus, as a theocratic republic Iran's republican institutions are laced with doctrinal bodies and religious-based organs.

In terms of structure, the Faqih sits at the heart of the political system (nezam) and enjoys wide-ranging powers. Formally his bureau has control of the armed forces, the media, the judiciary, and many other bodies besides. The Faqih is also lodged in the centre of the mechanisms for the regulation of political activity: He appoints half of the twelve-member Council of Guardians (CG), which is the election 'gatekeeper' of the nezam (ultimately determining which individuals can stand for elected office), with the other half being appointed by the judiciary chiefs.[26] The CG, it should be noted, has six Shia clerics as members and six legal experts who also have specialism in Islamic or constitutional law. The Faqih also determines every five years the makeup of the thirty-nine-member Expediency Discernment Council, which was formalized in the revised constitution to resolve legislative disputes between the Majlis and the Guardians, but also to support the Leader in the dispensation of his duties. Through this web and a vast informal network, the Leader has his finger in all the 'orchestrating' organs of the state and from this vantage point can monitor, manipulate and intervene directly (if need be) in the political process and in the country's direction of travel. In recent years, the Leader's 'red lines' have become markers for policy do's and don'ts, going so far as shaping foreign and state policy.

The four-year term presidential office (as head of the executive) is perhaps the most important and powerful elected office of the republic and he (the Islamic dimension of the constitution has been interpreted by the clerical establishment to limit this office to the male population only) is responsible for representing the country internationally, for negotiating treaties and for the implementation of the constitution. He is responsible for all ministerial appointments, a whole host of other state organizations, research and monitoring institutes and affiliates. The other two important elected organs of the state are the four-year term parliament (Majlis) and the eight-year term Assembly of Experts (which elects the Faqih and has the task of monitoring the leader's performance). Amongst its many functions the legislature (the Majlis) not only introduces laws and confirms government-proposed legislation but also reviews and ratifies international treaties, in addition to vetting and confirming/vetoing ministerial nominees. The only other nationally elected body is that of local councils, which have played a far less important role in the governance of Iran compared with the above organs. In addition, the republicans have also shown an interest in direct democracy when required and since 1979 have used referenda on three separate occasions for validation of elite recommendations. The establishment of the Islamic republic, the constitution of the Islamic republic and the 1989 amendments to it were all carried forward via plebiscites.

The key state organ that regularly brings the parallel institutions together and mediates the republic's strategic-level policies is the supreme national security council. This body, which was formalized into an organ of the state in 1989, is largely run by the executive but populated by all those who share power and decision-making. It plays a critical role in encouraging collective decision-making and also unbiased examination of issues of concern to the country. 'Interest' takes form in this forum and strategies for defence of articulated interests emerge in the round of meetings in this council.

So the Islamic republic is characterized by a mixture of secular governance system and unorthodox revolutionary political structures. Furthermore, this regime is child of a modern, urban-based revolution. It is product of a unique revolution in which revolutionary forces used religion, as a form of resistance, and an unorthodox interpretation of religious doctrines, as the model of the post-revolution regime.[27] The new regime, as a consequence, has a very complex DNA and has been infused with the ideals of populist Third Worldism, elements of Shia political doctrines, secular and religious legal structures, and the principles and institutions of republicanism.[28] The Islamic republic, however, appears to suffer from seemingly irreconcilable tensions and the governing system (nezam) seems to be suspended between profoundly different, competing, forces: Ideology and pragmatism; revolutionism and conformism; globalism and isolationism; pluralism and authoritarianism; exceptionalism and universalism.

Moreover, factionalism, in the absence of robust party structures, became ingrained, masquerading as pluralism in the system.[29]

The IRI is a hybrid republic, with all the institutions of a 'typical' republic but only few of the intellectual (liberal) components of a republican regime. There is no enshrined 'people's power' here, and even the individuals who citizens have the right to vote for are previously vetted and in a sense 'preselected'. As one explores the system of governance, it becomes clear that the republican order is based on religious authority and one which only can be interpreted by the clerical establishment. But the people still have a major political role in the republic, a point which the founder of the republic constantly underlined. To Ayatollah Khomeini, the Islamic order should satisfy both the spiritual and material needs of human beings and Islam, the real *political* religion, is based on political activism to meet human beings' material needs in a just and informed way. Khomeini stated:

> Islamic government is a divine phenomenon that with its implementation, children's happiness is best guaranteed in this world... it has the power to eliminate oppressors and plunderers, corruption, aggression and to guide people to the desired perfection. It... intervenes and supervises individual and social, material and spiritual, cultural and political, military and economic spheres and does not leave any point however minute concerning training of human being and society as well as national and spiritual aspects unattended.[30]

The leader of the revolution also was clear on the political process. He said, prior to the revolution, that "we want to form an Islamic republic which is a government based upon the public vote. The final form of government, with regard to the current state of affairs will be defined by the people themselves", and stated again in November 1979 that "it must unerringly respect the public vote everywhere.... The press is free to publish all truths and events; all parties and gatherings by the people are free unless they threaten the interests of the people".[31] Thus, secular institutions of the state were accepted as the building blocks of the new order and so, given Iran's history of democratic struggles, a written constitution recognizing a pluralist political system based on competitive elections for such organs as parliament, presidency and local councils was established. At the same time, revolutionary organs also emerged and evolved alongside existing state institutions and were enshrined in the constitution. Thus, the Guard, revolutionary courts, special clerics court, Islamic banking, Sharia courts, bonyads (foundations, religious and charitable organizations) form the most visible parts of the parallel governance structures. This 'dual institutionalization' serves as one of the main stabilizing pillars of the Islamic republic.[32]

Fred Halliday has cautioned that revolutions "are moments of transition which, once passed, may not need replication. Instead, they lay down an agenda for political and social change that through reform, struggles and democracy may take decades, or centuries, to be achieved".[33] Through this protracted process, the post-revolution regime changes and evolves. The Islamic Republic of Iran has been no exception, and since its founding in 1979 not only has it had to adjust its constitutional order, through a referendum in 1989, to the realities of governance, but it has also been the arena for repeated efforts to change the political balance in favour of the elected institutions of the republic.

The Islamic republic is not too far from Halliday's prediction, and we have seen that after thirty years the regime that followed the revolution is yet to consolidate into a fully stable, albeit unique, sustainable political entity. This is understandable given the fact that it has remained dominated by the first generation revolutionaries who followed Khomeini to power. Although senior in age, and not by any means an allied bloc, this group of clergy-dominated men still retain the levers of power and yet struggle with each other to chart a clear and acceptable path for the future of this political system. They are yet to give way to the emerging generation of post-revolution revolutionaries who perhaps lack the desire to imagine a different nezam, and – as will be shown – by virtue of having a truly instrumentalist approach to power and governance are actually not equipped to instil (meaningful) change from within. The regime's power structures, arguably, keep the whole order – the nezam – in suspended equilibrium.[34]

Notes

1 The followers of the Bahai faith, it should be noted, are persecuted in the Islamic republic, denied all basic rights of worship and assembly, and are also often denied access to basic state services and civic institutions.
2 Nicola Pedde, 'Challenges for the New Persia', *Aspenia International*, no. 71–72, 2016, p. 82.
3 Sir Percy Sykes, *History of Persia* (London: Macmillan, 1921).
4 'Iranian Nationalism and the Great Powers', *MERIP Reports 37*, May 1975, p. 11.
5 Stephanie Cronin, *The Army and the Creation of the Pahlavi State in Iran, 1910–1926* (London: Tauris Academic Studies, 1997).
6 Peter Avery, *Modern Iran* (London: Ernest Benn, 1965).
7 George Kirk, *Survey of International Affairs 1939–1946: The Middle East in the War* (Oxford: Oxford University Press, 1947).
8 Louise Fawcett, *Iran and the Cold War: The Azerbaijan Crisis of 1946* (Cambridge: Cambridge University Press, 1992).
9 James Bill, *The Eagle and the Lion: The Tragedy of American-Iranian Relations* (New Haven, CT: Yale University Press, 1988).
10 Avery, op. cit.
11 Demanding in February 1953 that the Majlis give him unlimited powers or he would dissolve the national assembly and acquire the said powers via a referendum was one example of this.
12 The six had become twelve principles even before the oil boom and to emphasize the rapid pace of change had gone to seventeen on the eve of the revolution.
13 Avery, op. cit, p. 506.
14 Ali M. Ansari, *Modern Iran Since 1921: The Pahlavis and After* (London: Longman, 2003), p. 185.
15 Abbas Milani, *The Shah* (New York, NY: Palgrave Macmillan, 2011).

16 Theda Skocpol, *State and Social Revolutions* (Cambridge: Cambridge University Press, 1979).
17 Theda Skocpol, *Social Revolutions in the Modern World* (Cambridge: Cambridge University Press, 1994).
18 Ibid.
19 We now know of course that the Shah was suffering from cancer at the time and had been considerably weakened by the disease and his intensive treatment.
20 Nikki R. Keddie, *Modern Iran: Roots and Results of Revolution* (New Haven, CT: Yale University Press, 2006).
21 Daniel Brumberg, *Reinventing Khomeini: The Struggle for Reform in Iran* (Chicago, IL: University of Chicago Press, 2001), p. 89.
22 Ibid, p. 92. Emphasis in original.
23 Peter Seeberg, 'The Iranian Revolution, 1977–79: Interaction and Transformation', *British Journal of Middle Eastern Studies*, vol. 41, no. 4, p. 497.
24 Mohsen Dehgani (ed.) *Religion and Politics from Imam Khomeini's Viewpoint: A Collection of Articles* (Tehran: The Institute for Compilation and Publications of Imam Khomeini's Works, 2007), p. 25.
25 Asghar Schirazi, *The Constitution of Iran: Politics and the State in the Islamic Republic* (London: I. B. Tauris, 1997).
26 The parliament has to approve the judiciary's six nominees for the Council of Guardians.
27 Peter Seeberg, 'The Iranian Revolution, 1977–79: Interaction and Transformation', *British Journal of Middle Eastern Studies*, vol. 41, no. 4, pp. 483–97.
28 Ervand Abrahamian, *Khomeinism: Essays on the Islamic Republic* (Berkeley, CA: University of California Press, 1993).
29 Tawfiq Alsaif, *Islamic Democracy and its Limits: The Iranian Experience Since 1979* (London: Saqi, 2007).
30 Majid Karimi and Manssor Limba (eds.) *Sahifeh-ye Imam* (Tehran: The Institute for Compilation and Publication of Imam Khomeini's Works, vol. 21, 2008), p. 402.
31 Saeed Madeh Khaksar (translator), *Sahifeh-ye Imam* (Tehran: The Institute for Compilation and Publication of Imam Khomeini's Works, vol. 4, 2008), p. 266. Interesting that Khomeini talks here of the 'interests of the people', whereas later it would be the interests of the nezam, which were said to be paramount.
32 Mehran Kamrava and Houchang Hassan-Yari, 'Suspended Equilibrium in Iran's Political System', *The Muslim World*, vol. 94, October 2004, pp. 495–524.
33 Fred Halliday, *Revolution and World Politics: The Rise of the Sixth Great Power* (London: Macmillan, 1999), p. 335.
34 Mehran Kamrava and Houchang Hassan-Yari, op. cit.

2
POLITICS OF THE ISLAMIC REPUBLIC

Introduction

Iran had been in a steady state when revolution struck. During the 1970s the opposition to the Shah had either been cowed, exiled or imprisoned. Secular opposition was silent, armed groups were on the run, and the clerical opposition had been jailed or co-opted or was residing in the Shia centres of learning in Iraq and Lebanon. While every evidence in the 1970s showed that the economy was overheating, corruption was threatening social relations, income disparity and alienation were rising, and the regime's heavy-handed approach to problem-solving was generating real discontent, the regime felt confident enough to end the country's two-party system and usher in a new political order through the establishment of a mass membership one-party system – the Rastakhiz (Resurgence) party – devoted to the promotion of the Shah's ambitious socioeconomic plans for the country. In this exercise, the monarchy was essentially attempting to de-politicize politics and turn political discourse and activity into a one-way relationship between ruler and the masses, and political activism into a functional arm of the state.

In the course of Rastakhiz's establishment, at the same time, citizens, intellectual groups and professional associations were encouraged to air their views on the path ahead, and as they did in the hundreds so this period also provided an unprecedented window on the vitality and dynamism of Iranian middle classes and their aspirations. It also, however, highlighted their deep sense of frustration with the status quo. This was not the regime's glasnost moment because the Shah, rather like Khomeini who followed, held Western political systems in contempt, seeing Western democratic systems as offering little more than a sham democracy. Iranians, in his view, were not yet ready for Western-style democracy in any event. Only the monarch knew how to guide the country through the transition to a brighter future and, as father of the nation, he would, of necessity, have to hold tight to the levers of power as he manoeuvred Iran through the process of change. In this task, he would need the services of a united country, orchestrated through a strong one-party order, to help chart the way to the gates of the great civilization. Iran, according to the Shah, would create a political order superior to the deficient Soviet and Western capitalist systems.

Ironically, the establishment of the Rastakhiz party was a step towards the institutionalization of the monarchy and the vehicle for leading the transformational change. Yet it was such unilateral acts, born out of the regime's misplaced self-confidence, that contributed to the destabilization of the Pahlavi order in its entirety. The revolution, lit by small fires at first, became widespread and irreversible, to paraphrase Skocpol,[1] in the autumn of 1978, and as it did so, it soon washed away the imperial order in Iran. Abrahamian succinctly captures the conditions that led to the perfect storm: "The oil boom of the 1970s undermined the economic well-being of the middle class. With the income from petro-dollars, the government embarked on a program of rapid industrialization and further military expansion", and this strategy unleashed the forces that eventually brought down the monarchy. For this strategy:

> Exhausted the urban labor supply and inadvertently drove up industrial wages. This, in turn, attracted agricultural laborers into the cities, drained the rural labor force, and consequently slowed down agricultural production.... The agricultural crisis, together with labor shortages and increasing government expenditures, drove up food prices.... The middle class was also hit with escalating costs for housing and manufactured goods, exacerbated by the influx of over 50,000 Western technicians and military experts.... A middle class family could be paying as much as 50 percent of its annual income for housing.[2]

With the economy at a standstill, national income dropping and external and internal support fast fading, the Shah's departure in January 1979 was the act that expunged the old order. By then much of the ruling class had begun evacuating: "The exodus has been a little undignified. Sometimes it seemed that those who had profited most successfully from the bonanza that the Shah had unleashed were the first to go – with members of the Pahlavi dynasty leading the rush to the exits".[3] The revolution had from that point on, notes Shawcross, become unstoppable, and no force from the Pahlavi order was able or willing to prevent its collapse.[4]

The wholesale departure of the ruling class caused massive economic upset, but it also created the socio-political conditions for the creation of a new order. The Islamic republic's birth was far from certain in the period before the fall of the monarchy and the months following the revolution's victory in February 1979, so much was to be gained through active intervention. Despite the self-assuredness of the victorious religious parties, in the revolutionary chaos it was frankly impossible to see which forces would emerge triumphant to shape the character of the successor political order or the social forces that would lead it. Before February and the plebiscite that led to the establishment of the Islamic republic, the revolution still had many surrogate fathers. What had been clearer, however, was the fact that, unlike its predecessors in the twentieth century, the Iranian revolution was almost entirely urban and led by a loose coalition of middle class actors covering the entire spectrum – from the traditional petit-bourgeois forces to the modern, and the communist left to the liberal secular, and of course armed groups.

Following the unsuccessful revolution of 1905 in which liberal, tribal and religious forces joined arms to create a constitutional monarchy, in 1979 the clerical-led coalition, itself divided into a spectrum of social groups and ethnicities, successfully implemented the maximalist goal of destroying the monarchy in favour of a religious-based republic. The revolution showed itself to be truly authentic, rooted in the country's cultural and religious mores, and was accomplished largely peacefully with a guerrilla phase only at the final stage of the revolutionary process. A focus on the down-trodden echoed the other major revolutions' slogans, but here these were tinged with the narrative of Islam and thus quickly acquired the values of Islam as well as its tools of resistance. In a Muslim society like Iran's, such values as justice, equality, and freedom represented a coded set of aspirations which Iran's ideologue of political Islam, Ali Shariati, had identified as the struggle for a class-less Islamic society. This ideological approach was distinct from Marxism and actually opposed to many tenets of Marxism. To be more accurate, Shariati rejected the political parties and the systems which had been created in the name of Marxism in the Soviet Union and elsewhere.[5]

The legacy of the revolution and state that this legacy has spawned shapes the country's new political discourse, and its political norms are objectively different.

Constitutional arrangements

To understand the Islamic republic, one would need to understand the constitutional settlement that gave form to the Islamist regime – the nezam (or system of governance) as it is known. The constitution, in essence an ideas hodgepodge, can be seen as the best effort to combine features of Western political systems with what Ayatollah Khomeini had put forward in a series of lectures while in exile in Iraq in the second half of the 1960s as a utopian model of an Islamic state. The lectures, which were compiled in 1970 into a volume called *Islamic Government*, were to provide a necessary critique of what Khomeini had viewed as the failures of regimes and constitutional arrangements based on what he saw as no more than the "opinion of the majority". But his critique also enjoyed strong theological reasoning. Thus, in uncompromisingly theological-legal terms, he deliberately set apart his ideal type state from what had gone before:

> Islamic government is neither tyrannical nor absolute, but constitutional....
> It is constitutional in the sense that the rulers are subject to a certain set

of conditions in governing and administering the country, conditions that are set forth in the Noble Qur'an and the Sunna of the Most Noble Messenger.... Islamic government may therefore be defined as the rule of divine law over men.

Going further, and in a tautological fashion, he argued that as the body of "Islamic laws that exist in the Qur'an and the Sunna has been accepted by the Muslims and recognized by them as worthy of obedience", it follows then that "this consent and acceptance facilitates the task of government and makes it truly belong to the people".[6] Furthermore, as "Islamic government is a government of law, those acquainted with the law, or more precisely, with religion – i.e., the *fuqaha* – must supervise its functioning. It is they who supervise all executive and administrative affairs of the country, together with all planning".[7] So if you are a Muslim, you will necessarily believe in the Quran and the Sunna and, given this, whomever that is qualified to implement Islamic law – who by definition must be a cleric – will not only be your legitimate ruler but will also be just! In this manner, Khomeini not only justified the foundations of the Islamic state, which by definition will be just, but at the same time secured the place of the Jurist Consult at the heart of such a state. This would, for all intents and purposes, be an absolutist state in all but name.

But in the cold light of day, when the reality of establishing an Islamic state hit the theologian idealists of the revolution, a series of practical compromises had to be made in order to make the ideal type a functioning state. Compromises, being made during a revolution in full swing, in turn bred serious constitutional inconsistencies. Schirazi, for example, notes that "the Constitution of the Islamic Republic of Iran is full of contradictions".[8] They appear in the principles of the new state, in the complexity of its governance structures, and in the designs for the new economic model of the Islamic republic. The practical policy levels and theoretical tensions between constitutionalism and authoritarianism are palpable in the governance structures developed in the constitution of the republic, which have in turn blighted efforts since 1989 to reform the system.

The contradictions can usefully be divided into two principle groups. The first is identified as the contradiction between the 'Islamic legalist' component of the constitution and its non-religious secular elements: The Godly and the earthly components of it, if you will. In this regard, the tension between where sovereignty lay in the Islamic republic exemplified the problem and brought to centre stage the consequences of placing sovereignty with God and therefore his representatives (Shia clerics for Muslims) on earth. In the course of this narrative, the process of Islamization of the state was institutionalized, but the real secular elements of a constitutional system remained in place.[9] These 'earthly' instruments of government provided the means and protest tools for the reformers, later in the life of the Islamic republic, to challenge the pre-eminence of the Vali-e Faqih in the nezam.

The second constitutional contradiction noted by Schirazi is that between the constitution's democratic (universal suffrage, elected office, etc.) components and its overtly anti-democratic elements. Nima similarly argues that "each of the main principles of the constitution contains its own antithesis; it asserts democratic rights and liberties in general terms while denying them with the qualification 'according to Islamic standards'.... What makes this constitution uniquely retrogressive are those principles which deal directly with the power structure".[10] Such elements as the power of the Leader (who controls the state media, the armed forces, and the judiciary); role and influence of the Council of Guardians (CG) in vetting legislation, appointment of individuals to some of the highest offices of the land, vetting of candidates for electorally contested positions by such authorities as the CG; and, sovereignty – while based on popular will – belonging to the deity and not to the people (or their elected representatives), are the most prevalent undemocratic features of the IRI's constitution. In Omid's words,

> [T]he constitution failed to solve the basic contradiction that is inherent in the concept of an Islamic government. If God is the sole source of all laws; and if the law of God must be unquestionably obeyed, then how can an Islamic government accommodate any notion of democracy, least of all that of a representative legislature? All that a Parliament can do is to plan institutions and delineate administrative paths.[11]

The supremacy of the office of the 'Leader of the Revolution' as Faqih and his influence in virtually all matters of state is the most telling aspect of the republic's authoritarianism because his control of the armed forces and national broadcasting, and the oversight by the twelve-man Guardian Council of the elected chamber's legislative deliberations, gives the Leader unprecedented powers. In a sentence, the real tension in the Islamic republic is between authority and legitimacy.[12] While Khomeini was alive, the tension was moderated by the fact that the Leader ('Imam Khomeini') himself was the legitimate authority of the whole nezam, whose pronouncements helped to provide short-term solutions to the often daily dilemmas that state functionaries faced, and help to codify, and even legitimize, state policy. But after the Imam's death, the tension between legitimacy and authority became much harder to disguise and interestingly, in order to ensure the survival of the nezam in its current form, the elite ensured that authority (power) would provide the source of legitimacy and not the other way around.

Not surprisingly, prior to the success and in the immediate aftermath of the revolution, much of the debates tended to focus on the relationship between the concepts of democracy, political Islam, and republic. In 1979 these debates were heated and were taking place at home, in the workplace and of course in the chamber assembled to draw up the republic's constitution. The clerical lieutenants of the regime, the radical Islamists close to Ayatollah Khomeini, stayed loyal to the principles he had outlined much earlier in the writings and speeches before the revolution. Taking their cue from the Leader, they summarily dismissed putting the word 'democracy' alongside Islam.

So it was then that the written guarantor of pluralism in the country, the idea of a 'democratic Islamic republic' as proposed by Premier Mehdi Bazargan, was reduced to that of an Islamic republic. And when the final constitution was put to the vote in December 1979, it already had enshrined at its heart the concept of the Velayat-e Faqih and with it the dominance of the state by the clerical establishment. Iran was not to be just a republic of Muslims but a republic of Mullahs and a regime form whose institutions would become dominated by the Shia clergy associated with Ayatollah Khomeini. However, the new nezam was not a constitutional dictatorship by any means. It is true that the Leader carries absolute weight and sets all the so-called 'red lines' of the regime; it is the case that the Leader's bureau (Bayt-e Rahbari) has become 'Kremlinesk' in its behaviour and associations, having its fingers in every pie of power, controlling the armed forces as well as the country's state media, and even appointing the head of the judiciary; it is also true that the powerful Council of Guardians (a semi-elected organ of the nezam) acts as a gatekeeper of power and has veto power over all legislation; and finally it is the case that without thorough vetting no one is able to stand for any elected office in the country. The nezam is, at best, a controlled electoral system whose critics claim in which votes do not lead to any meaningful change and cannot challenge the prevailing order. Iran's current Leader and former president provided evidence for this view in saying that the Faqih "deems certain issues to be in the best interest of society and acts on it and this is God's command and this command is obligatory for everyone to obey.... In reality, the legislative and executive bodies owe their legitimacy to their reliance on and authority of the Supreme Islamic Leader. The latter is like a soul within the body of the system".[13] This is unambiguous and clearly places the Faqih above state institutions and also the people: The legitimacy of the state is derived from the Faqih.

But, on the other hand, the constitution itself was drawn up by an elected body (Assembly of Experts). And in the constitution one sees clear lines of accountability as well as division between the various branches of state (the executive, the legislative, and the judiciary); the executive and legislative branches of the state are subject to voter scrutiny (with set terms for both); the head of the executive branch (president) is directly elected at regular intervals of four years and cannot serve more than two consecutive terms; the country enjoys universal suffrage and the regime positively encourages voter participation in Majlis, local council and regional elections; there is diversity (if not plurality) of opinion at all levels; and finally, even the Vali-e Faqih himself is constitutionally held accountable by another elected body.

The contradictions embedded in the Islamic republic's constitutional arrangements carry within them the seeds of the nezam's structural weaknesses, which (as we will see) have tested its legitimacy, in different ways, in the post-Iran-Iraq War period. At the heart of its governance, the issues of who wields power, who has authority, and where responsibility lies, have been omnipresent. In Mozaffari's assessment, in the referendum on the formation of the new Islamic republic (in March 1979), the Iranian people traded their absolutist Shah for an exclusivist regime.[14] It of course was not meant to be like this. From the outset, in the early days of the revolutionary period, one can see that much of the debate surrounding the country's new constitution was a quintessential struggle between democratization and (clergy-dominated) centralization – between republicanism and a unique (Shia-based) version of Islamic government. In short, a straight fight between the proponents of democracy (themselves confused in camps advocating establishing a 'people's democracy', those leaning towards a more secular European-style social democratic model, and others who genuinely believed in an Islamic democracy) who saw legitimacy in a theocracy. In the end, the clerical elite's interpretation of the Velayat-e Faqih placed Islamism at the heart of the state and not republicanism: It placed clericism at the heart of the state.

The absence of clarity in the new regime's mission, persistent ideological ambiguities about the nature of the new republic, the lack of durable political structures to manage elite and intra-elite competition in what was an unsteady national political environment, and the absence of virtually any rules for the new political game encouraged organizational interaction to take place behind closed doors, often at the sub-elite level. The emergence of groups, 'fronts', and 'associations' substituted for political party organization and in the absence of party discipline (a single collective voice) facilitated tactical bloc building and a heavy dose of opportunistic behaviour.[15] Ironically, this multiplicity has given the nezam a degree of durability because the political system is arguably "built on many independent, rival, parallel columns of power that hold the system together... the diversified and vast engagement of various groups brings internal collaboration that resists the intrusion of political outsiders".[16]

The result has been the fragmentation of the revolutionary coalition into factions of the sort instantly recognizable by Sartori: factions of interest (providing tangible rewards) and factions of principle (advancing ideas and ideals).[17] In the Islamic republic's case, grand coalitions did not coalesce in political parties and therefore the factions of interest and principle converged and diverged for maximizing short-term gains. Indeed, the grand factions themselves have been subject to consolidation and sub-fracturing, leading to political organization at the sub-factional level. This in turn has tended to create a mesh of alliances cutting across the 'interest' and 'principle' dimensions. Factions became platforms and informal institutions of power maximization rather than for building support in pursuit of thought-out political programmes. A further feature of the post-revolution political system, then, is factionalism.[18]

Where political party institutions have been weak and vulnerable to arbitrary closure, social and family networks have acted as platforms for political mobilization. Intense ideological differences over the character of this unique Islamic republic have also played an important part in distinguishing political currents in the Islamic republic. Trends have emerged from these currents, which have institutionalized factional rivalries in the regime. Factional structures, competing factional platforms, made elite interaction with the wider public more problematic and voter engagement with the political process more complex. In the absence of nodes, such as political parties, voters (and activists themselves) began building coalitions around a whole host of factors: Personalities, ideological proximity, revolutionary slogans, socioeconomic improvements, neighbourhood and community, kinship, ethnicity and such like. Factional structures became so entrenched that when political parties were finally allowed to enter the political arena in the 1990s, they too tended to behave like factions and in fact reflected the prevailing factional fault lines.

The "forms and functions of the rule-making structures in the Islamic republic were framed with the intention that none would exceed its power to the extent that Khomeini's [Faqih's] authority could be questioned".[19] 'Rule-making' structures, however, were subject to factional manipulation from early on. But in the absence of a blueprint, a model, for Khomeini's Islamic republic, disputes were commonplace and soon after the elimination of the National Front and the other so-called 'liberal-leaning' individuals from power, the clerical establishment began to split along interpretive, ideological, personal, clan, material interests, and even personal preferences lines. Ayatollah Khomeini's "simple emphasis on the Islamicity of the regime did not provide sufficient guidelines to determine the specific policies of the state… its sociocultural policies, the nature of its economic system, and its foreign policy orientation".[20]

While the loose networks and the absence of a strong 'party line' regarding the new republic's orientation may have allowed for more creativity and discussion, nevertheless disagreements over the fundamentals of the new republic "led to the differentiation of factions and the upsurge of factional politics". Factionalism became endemic and institutionalized, plaguing it for all time. As a senior figure such as Rouhani was to observe, well before he had even considered entering the presidential race in 2013, with political parties playing little role in organizing the elite, even the country's supreme national security council had become affected by factionalism, where ministerial representatives (such as foreign affairs, intelligence and defence) would tend to present their case based on their factional affiliations.[21] In reality the republic has come to represent a fragmentation of authority – a 'fragmented autocracy', in the words of Keshavarzian.[22]

The first ten years

Iran's politics in the immediate post-revolution period was dominated by the imperatives of war, the country's first inter-state war for more than a century. The military campaign against Iraq soon became a symbol of the revolutionary struggle against 'global arrogance', but it at once served as a tool in inter-factional battles for control of the instruments of power and access to the largely abandoned industries, businesses, financial institutions and massive assets of the state as well (which will be discussed in more detail in chapter 3).

The theocrats, supported by Ayatollah Khomeini and increasingly in control of the instruments of power, made their move in June 1981 with the impeachment by the clergy-dominated parliament (Majlis) of the country's first elected president, Abolhassan Bani-Sadr. His departure was accompanied by the routing of all other opposition groups over the next two years, starting with the Mojahedin-e Khalq Organization (MKO), who had spent the previous fifteen years waging an urban guerrilla campaign against the Pahlavi regime. The relentless and systematic suppression of Islamic moderates, leftists and Kurdish groups had, by 1984 (and the end of term of the republic's first Majlis), removed from the country's landscape all those revolutionaries whose loyalty to the Islamic republic, as constituted by the allies of Ayatollah Khomeini, was uncertain. As one assessment has it, in less than four years after the revolution, and at the height of the war with Iraq, the "Islamic state and clerical government were secured. In a violent return swing of the pendulum, religious despotism had ousted both secularism and democracy".[23] By this point, even the organization of the first prime minister of the Islamic republic, Prime Minister Bazargan's influential Liberation Front (Movement), had been thoroughly marginalized, delegitimized, and its footprint in the new nezam almost entirely wiped out. The National Front had to contend with being 'tolerated' by the republic's clergy-dominated elite.

At this time a new political elite supporting Ayatollah Khomeini's Islamist regime consolidated its position. A handful of individuals dominated the upper echelons of the nezam – Montazeri, Hashemi Rafsanjani, Khamenei, Mousavi, Karroubi – and, despite their own deep personal and ideological differences, formed the circle of power in the first few critical years of the new republic. While the influence of two individuals in this group – Khamenei and Rafsanjani – has endured and indeed become institutionalized, Montazeri, Mousavi, and Karroubi emerged later in the life of the republic to pose the most serious challenges to its legitimacy since its inception. As will be discussed later, their role in the 2009 presidential elections and their very public demands at that time for political pluralism created seemingly unbridgeable fissures in the regime and also mobilized many millions of Iranians to march in a campaign of civil disobedience against the policies and practices of the regime. Ayatollah Montazeri, Khomeini's erstwhile successor and a strong critic of the regime's authoritarianism since 1988, provided moral and religious cover for the protests and himself paid a high price for his role: Having his gatherings disrupted, his residence raided and himself placed under house arrest until his death in December 2009.

The three parliaments of this decade, effectively the 1980–88 period, were highly ideological and under the masterful control of the speaker, then-Hojjatoleslam Rafsanjani, provided the main vehicle for elite formation and for the shaping of the regime's political identity. The Majlis, as a consequence, also became the national stage for the new regime's political battles and ideological confrontations. With factionalism taking root quickly and becoming rife in the nezam, factional battles soon became evident across the political landscape. Over time, and as individuals became more confident in their place in the nezam, factions morphed into undisciplined and fluid coalitions and, despite displaying strong ideological tones, often appeared opportunistic. These were increasingly akin to loose coalitions, despite clerics making up much of their membership. Indeed, even before the demise of the pro-Khomeini and radical Islamic Republic Party (IRP) in May 1987 at the behest of Khamenei and Rafsanjani, two competing clerical factions had emerged. One, Society of the Combatant Clergy (Jame'ay-e Rouhaniyat-e Mubarez), which predated the revolution, had become the bastion of conservatism in the regime. It came to represent the traditional right and encompass many of the regime's future leaders – Khamenei (president and later Supreme Leader), Rafsanjani (Majlis speaker and later president), Nateq-Nouri (Majlis speaker and presidential candidate), and Rouhani (secretary of the supreme national security council, president). Many of these individuals would break rank in later years and in the end several would come to stand against each other in the republic's fractious politics.

The other main faction, the Association of Militant Clerics (Majma-e Rouhaniyoun-e Mubarez), was more leftist in outlook and included such figures as Mohammad Khatami (cabinet minister and later president), Mousavi-Khoeinia (prosecutor-general), Ali Akbar Mohtashemi (interior minister), and Mehdi Karroubi (head of the well-endowed Martyrs' foundation, Majlis speaker, and presidential candidate). The individuals associated with the provisional government of Mehdi Bazargan had by the end of the first parliament been ousted from all institutions of power and presented virtually no threat to the religious-ideological groups emerging to dominate the key institutions of the new state. Despite constant friction in the ranks, the war in fact helped the Islamic republic's lieutenants, all loyal to Khomeini, to eradicate all opposition to the regime (the middle-class alliance of the secular National Front and Liberation Movement, such armed leftist groups as Peykar, Mojahedin-e Khalq, Fadayeen, the pro-Soviet Tudeh party which had formally supported the new regime) were ruthlessly and systematically eradicated shortly after the escape from Iran in July 1981 of the republic's first popularly elected president, Abolhassan Bani-Sadr. The non-cleric economist, Bani-Sadr, a confidant of Ayatollah Khomeini and his companion in the revolution, was impeached by the Majlis and left the country before he could be prosecuted for misconduct. From 1979 to 1981 his standing had been high, but he had failed to build a powerbase for himself and seemed to have actively alienated his natural allies in the National Front and also the cleric-based IRP. But because he dared to stand outside of factional politics, his public standing was high, and despite standing as an independent candidate in the presidential race he was by far the most popular candidate. In fact, interior ministry data shows that he was elected in the country's first presidential elections with an overwhelming majority, receiving 10.7 million (76.5 per cent) of the 14 million votes cast (73 per cent voter turnout), compared with 2 million votes cast for the second-place candidate (Admiral Ahmad Madani of the National Front).

The religious-ideological elite's favoured candidate, Hassan Habibi of the establishment Islamic Republican Party, received fewer than 675,000 votes in these important elections.

So the new elite, assured of its legitimacy and 'popularity' as measured by voter turnout for parliamentary elections, formed the critical mass of professional politicians of the Islamic republic. Also closely linked with the new elite was the increasingly important revolutionary guard corps whose members were busily defending the new republic from an Iraqi-led coalition of Arab, Western and even Warsaw Pact states. War, ideology and revolutionary fervour provided the context for the emergence of a largely anti-liberal community of policy-shapers and decision-makers in a country bereft of pluralism for over a generation.

The eighties then was a period of consolidation and, despite internal turmoil, repeated assassination of scores of the primary leaders of the revolution, and an all-consuming war, a community of often inter-locking leadership emerged to shape and take control of the political system and the sources of economic power, too. Yet each parliament came to serve a number of often competing interests and legislative priorities.

The end of the war provided the catalyst for political change. Political factions became more vociferous as the national political space stabilized, raising their activities. But at the same time, state policy also began to change, partly in response to the public sentiment that ending war-imposed restrictions must lead to 'letting the air in by opening the windows'. To this end, the interior ministry's announcement that from the end of December 1988 its special commission would be able to receive applications for the establishment of political parties was a clear signal that the political system was preparing to adjust to a new and less restricted public space. Despite the many restrictions being announced in the laws governing the conduct political parties,[24] this news was significant in underscoring the efforts to open the public space following the restrictions of the previous eight years. Soon after, with major structural changes introduced into the political system of the republic, the triple power pillars of the nezam – the Faqih system, the rentier system, and the largely religious-based well-endowed foundations and religious organizations – consolidated their place in the nezam, strengthening the country's emerging clientelist relationships.[25]

TABLE 2.1 Majlis elections in the 1980s (in millions and percentages)

	No. of eligible voters	Votes cast	Voter turnout
First Majlis (1980–84)	20,758,391	10,875,969	52.14%
Second Majlis (1984–88)	24,143,498	15,607,306	64.64%
Third Majlis (1988–92)	27,986,736	16,714,281	59.72%

Source: Ministry of Interior.

The second republic

The end of the war and the death of Ayatollah Khomeini soon after created the conditions for a rearrangement of power relations in the nezam and, in the absence of a premier and the departure of Mousavi from the political scene, energized regime loyalists to consolidate power around a new – Leader-President – axis to be spearheaded by Ayatollah Khamenei and Rafsanjani respectively.[26] Rafsanjani, already the most trusted ally of Khomeini, emerged in 1989 as arguably the most popular and influential political figure of the regime and the hand that steadied the ship during its transitional period. He had, in June 1989, been elected (with 230 votes in favour and just one against) by the 240 deputies present as the speaker of the Majlis for the eighth time in a row, and barely a month later he received 15,537,394 votes cast (96.1 per cent in favour) to become the republic's first executive and, at that point, the country's most popular president.[27] Rafsanjani had the mandate from the people, and the backing of the legislature, for introducing reforms, for change.

The post-Khomeini period was arguably the start of the Thermidor and a new political arrangement. Indeed, the two presidencies following Ayatollah Khomeini's death were in different ways a departure from the statist, ideological order of the 1980s. So, while the 1989–97 period provided the conditions for economic restructuring, reforms and renewal, as will be shown, the 1997–2005 period saw rapid progress towards the introduction of political and social reforms. In both cases leaders were pushed by the electorate's demands for change, and in fact both sets of reforms were spearheaded by popular presidents – Rafsanjani secured 96 per cent of votes cast in 1989 and Khatami received 20 million votes out of 30 million votes cast in 1997.[28] In both cases the electorate was asking for much more than had been offered (or available) by the state. But, as will be shown, in both cases the electorate also quickly found the structural limits of change in the Islamic republic and the boundaries of tolerance in a political system beholden to ideological conservatism and the office of an all-powerful Faqih.

But, back in 1989, in order to secure the regime in the wake of the founder's death, a strategy of consolidation was followed that necessitated the strengthening of the office of the Leader into that of Velayat-e Faqih-e Motalaq (Absolute Guardianship). To this Khomeini himself had alluded prior to his death so all that was needed was a willing stand-in. To ensure stability a more compliant parliament aligned with the Leader's orientation and the pro-market policies of the new president was needed, which was achieved in 1992.

The final plank of the strategy of consolidation was the extinguishing of internal dissent, through the eradication (through execution of thousands) of many of the remaining opponents of the regime – individuals who had been languishing in the country's jails for years or rearrested in 1988 and executed.[29] Taking place a year before the death of Ayatollah Khomeini, the impression was created that all internal dissent against the nezam had consequently been extinguished and the path had been cleared for the Islamic republic to begin its post-war development without fear of opposition emerging in the course of restrictions being lifted on political activity.

As already noted, the precedent for the absolute guardianship had been set by Ayatollah Khomeini himself who had taken the first steps towards the consolidation of the Faqih's place in the nezam. Most importantly, Khomeini encapsulated the essence of absolute guardianship, as the Leader of the Revolution, a Shia Source of Emulation, and founder of the Islamic republic. Uniquely, he embodied the new nezam. But more emphatically, Khomeini himself pointedly advocated absolutism in the nezam. Indeed, in a celebrated declaration in response to an ongoing dispute between the then–prime minister (Mousavi) and the then-president (Khamenei) about the state's imperatives and priorities – in a nutshell about state power versus the principles of religion – Khomeini left no room for ambiguity. His intervention settled the issue but left senior clerics (including his then-successor Ayatollah Montazeri) cold. The very public wrangle between the two highest offices of the republic was becoming unsettling and increasingly acting as a catalyst for intra-factional quarrels – a rallying point for competing opinions amongst the factions. Thus far, partly thanks to the conditions of war and the massive presence of the state in the economy, the need to strike a balance between Islam and state had been sidestepped, or at least had been shelved after Khomeini's earlier interventions in 1982 and 1983 to reassure the traditional bourgeoisie of their favoured position in the face of massive nationalizations of private holdings, major industries, banking, insurance, finance, mining, agribusinesses and others undertaken by the Mousavi government.[30]

Now, with the pressures for improving the people's socioeconomic conditions rising, Khomeini was unequivocal about governance: The imperatives of state took precedence over all other matters, he declared. Khomeini stated as clearly as he could that in his view the government of God had primacy over all others, in fact it had the authority to revoke Sharia law and break promises it had made to the people if state required it, and that all such matters as "prayer, fasting and hajj", were "secondary injunctions" subservient to the will of the government of God. This statement electrified religious circles, leading one, Ali Khamenei – who was soon to become the future Faqih himself – to interpret Khomeini's words as meaning that "the commandments of the ruling jurist are primary commandments and are like the commandments of God".[31] They must be obeyed. As Leader since Khomeini's death in 1989, Ayatollah Khamenei has behaved consistently in accordance with this belief. The death in succession of three traditionalist Grand Ayatollahs (Khoei in 1992, Golpaygani in 1993 and Araki in 1995) removed potential religious hierarchy opposition to Khamenei's efforts to consolidate authority, if not power in the hands of the Leader.

However, the same conditions, namely the end of the war and the death of the founding father of the revolution, which had already allowed for the consolidation of power in the hands of Ayatollah Khomeini's closest allies, also facilitated the reigniting of very public debates in intellectual circles about the future direction of the Islamic republic. The challenge to the sacred cows of the nezam came from the insiders of the regime who now felt confident to break cover and argue for a new (different) 'political contract'.[32] Using Abdolkarim Soroush's argument that religion (sacred and immutable tenets of Islam) must be separated from religious knowledge (which evolves and changes according to human interpretation) in order to enable Muslim society to find solutions to its problems as their premise, the 'new religious thinking' camp came to argue that "the human understanding of Islam is flexible, that Islam's tenets can be interpreted to encourage both pluralism and democracy, and to allow change according to time, place and experience".[33] In the words of Mir-Hosseini and Tapper the question was not "who should rule, but how they should rule, and what mechanisms there should be to curb the excesses of power".[34]

This line of reasoning was flying in the face of the established dogma and the positioning of Khamenei as the all-authoritative Leader, but it had gained traction amongst religious intellectuals and also with several key individuals in positions of authority.[35] One such person was the minister of Islamic guidance in President Rafsanjani's first cabinet, Hojjatoleslam Mohammad Khatami, who in the cabinet's 1989 Majlis vote of confidence was the most popular ministerial nominee (receiving 246 favourable votes from 260 votes cast).[36] By the fourth Majlis, Khatami was a politically battered figure accused of allowing new ideas to penetrate society through issuing licenses for new films, literature, music, concerts, and encouraging the arts more generally.

An apparently more compliant but conservative-dominated parliament emerged in 1992 (the fourth Majlis). The fourth Majlis was in many ways a threshold parliament that saw the sidestepping of some political giants – Mohtashemi, Karroubi, Khoinia, Nabavi, Mousavi-Tabrizi, Ghafari, Khalkhali – and the arrival of many hitherto unknown personalities. Indeed, as many as 181 of the 270 deputies were entering parliament for the first time. This parliamentary transformation towards the end of Rafsanjani's first term in office saw the almost total electoral annihilation of the 160 strong centre-left parliamentary bloc in favour of the market-friendly pro-bazaar conservative-right faction aligned to Ayatollah Khamenei. This right-leaning parliament, now openly supported by the Leader, also started life by criticizing Rafsanjani – this time for what was regarded as the negative cultural aspects of his administration's economic policies. Having engineered the demise of the radical left in one Majlis, he now faced a strong coalition of centre-right forces rising in defence of the spirit of the revolution and demanding government action against the West's purported 'cultural invasion' of Muslim Iran spearheaded by the United States.[37]

Rafsanjani's 'opening up to the world' economic strategy soon became hostage of the right's obsession with cultural permissiveness and so for every step forward in introducing economic reforms he had to take two steps back in keeping the lid on social demands – irritating the same urban-based voters who had formed the backbone of support for him.[38] So voices critical of Rafsanjani's policies on the economy, foreign policy, and social reforms (such as birth control and easing of social restrictions) were not silenced, and immediately after his re-election as president in June 1993 critics from both left and traditional right attacked his policies for allowing a 'cultural invasion' to take place: "We have tried charm and all other peaceful methods to stop the invasion.... It is too late, this is a disease now spreading rapidly. We need shock therapy. The impossibility of peacefully stopping the cultural invasion means a violent clam-down on those who have deviated from the teachings of the Imam [Khomeini]".[39] The message was clear: As far as the traditionalists and leftists were concerned, ill-conceived government-sponsored changes ultimately led to the nezam using its heavy hand; if the government conformed to the teachings of the founding fathers of the revolution, then no harm could come to state or society. At this point the word 'reform' was not a common currency and appeared incompatible with a political system based on the timeless and divine teaching of Islam. At this point, furthermore, the main camps still shared the obsession of a cultural invasion by the West and used this as an effective political weapon against the centrist pragmatist group coalescing around the president.

The eradication of dissenting voices, followed by the MKO's ill-advised frontal military assault on their own country's armed forces in 1988, removed indefinitely from the political scene the challenge of the small but motivated revolutionary armed groups. As their 7,000-strong so-called National Liberation Army of Iran was bombed to dust on Iranian territory by the Islamic republic's armed forces, so were also put to death between July 1988 and January 1989 thousands of political prisoners in Iranian jails. According to Amnesty International, at least 2,000 political prisoners were executed on the orders of Ayatollah Khomeini.[40] These executions removed the remaining reminders of radical alternatives to the established nezam, but they also caused the unbridgeable fissure between Ayatollah Khomeini and his appointed successor, Ayatollah Montazeri, who repeatedly questioned the efficacy, legality and morality of these executions. The removal of Montazeri as Faqih-in-waiting cleared the way for other clerical forces gathered around Ayatollah Khomeini as his closest aides to seek a successor who could defend the nezam. Religious status, Khomeini had already made a secondary consideration, thus clearing the path for the rise of an even Hojjatoleslam to the office of Faqih. The bloodletting also ensured that all the regime's ranks remained loyal to the cause of the nezam and did not question the agreed cessation of hostilities with the eight-year-long enemy of Iraq.

Thus, in the midst of calls for renewal, reconstruction and reform, the revisions made to the constitution in 1989 actually enhanced the power of the non-elected institutions of the nezam at the expense of the country's elected institutions – ironically, the very sources of the regime's legitimacy and popular appeal. Putting the Faqih at the centre of the new constitution changed the country's power relations sufficiently to give the new Leader unrivalled authority and influence in managing the country's domestic and international affairs – which he exercised to the full in his future disputes with such allies as Rafsanjani.

In tandem, the rise of Ayatollah Khamenei as Leader brought to the fore the traditional rightist (conservative) factions of the republic who had been marginalized by the centre-left coalition (which included religious reformers, nationalists, and leftists). The latter forces' inclinations were exemplified in the premiership of Mir Hossein Mousavi whose role as the head of the executive branch often brought him into direct confrontation with the then-president Khamenei. Khamenei's elevation to the mantle of the Leader of the Islamic revolution brought to a swift end the domination of the left forces of the key instruments of power so prevalent in the 1980s. Ironically, the right faction's control of the Majlis after the parliamentary elections of 1992 did not facilitate a smooth transition to a liberalized economy, and this conservative and economically laissez-faire Majlis also questioned the government's reform strategy and as economic problems mounted from 1993 onwards – weak currency, rising prices of basic goods, house price inflation, rising national debt to cover the cost of rising imports – so the Majlis paved the way for the introduction of restrictive legislation and measures, which included support for the regime's new campaign to counter what was presented as the West's cultural onslaught on the Islamic republic. The new norm led to "growing restrictions on press and intellectual freedom, and periodic crackdowns against women who violated the Islamic dress code".[41]

The tension between economic reforms and social freedoms had, from this point, become a national problem to manage. And, in fear of growing civil society activism during Rafsanjani's second term, the conservative-dominated Majlis contributed greatly to a tightening of political and cultural spaces in the country. Following their ousting of Rafsanjani's popular minister of culture and Islamic guidance, none other than Hojjatoleslam Khatami, in 1992, on the grounds of the minister being too soft on efforts to curb the Western cultural invasion of the country following the liberalization of the economy, censorship of the by-now thriving magazines and newspapers, control of publishing, radio and television, scrutiny of theatre and cinema, incrementally increased. These restrictions went hand in hand with intimidation of intellectuals, vigilante beatings of public figures, and the arrest of writers, journalists and newspaper editors on such charges as violating the country's cultural norms, conspiring with foreign powers, drug use, and personal corrupt practices, which ultimately resulted in the silencing of debate and the closure of several leading publications.[42]

During Rafsanjani's second term, the domestic landscape had shifted in favour of the socially conservative forces who saw in Rafsanjani's policies a dilution of the revolutionary (Islamic) values of the country, a threat to the cohesion of the nezam itself, and as such a direct challenge to the national security of the republic. They thus mobilized en masse following the repression of independent and critical voices, to take control of the fifth Majlis, the elections for which took place in March-April 1996.

Iran's parliamentary elections for the fifth Majlis were arguably one of the most important of such elections to date, with the elite hesitantly looking for the republic's place in a world in which the United States had managed to consolidate its regional presence following its devastating military campaign to liberate

TABLE 2.2 Majlis elections in the Era of Reconstruction

	No. of eligible voters	Votes cast	Voter turnout
Fourth Majlis (1992–96)	32,465,558	18,767,042	57.71%
Fifth Majlis (1996–2000)	34,716,000	24,682,386	71.10%

Source: Ministry of Interior.

Kuwait from the clutches of Iraqi forces, in which the collapse of the Soviet Union had created a unipolar order with the US as the only superpower intent on globalizing the former Soviet spaces and Asia. Tehran was faced with the reality of an American 'New World Order' seeking to impose a new peaceful order on the MENA region.[43] These unsettling external developments fed directly into the regime's domestic economic and public policy debates which were informed, first, by the need to protect the country's unique political order, and second, by helping it to develop and recover from a decade of turmoil.

The domestic situation and rapidly changing international conditions sharpened the political battle lines between the conservative faction which, with support from the president himself, had gained control of the Majlis in 1992 and a new grouping of centrist forces coalescing around the president under the banner of the Executives of Construction. The Executives were by no means the largest electoral faction, but in the absence of Karroubi and Mousavi-Khoeinia-led Association of Militant Clerics (who had withheld from participating in the 1996 Majlis elections in protest for the maltreatment of their candidates), the Executives represented the strongest opposition to the conservative-controlled Society of the Combatant Clergy headed by the sitting Majlis speaker and close confidant of the Leader, Ayatollah Ali Akbar Nateq-Nouri. Using the tactics of mass disqualifications (of 8,365 candidates 1,420 were prohibited from standing), the Society managed to reduce the scale of the challenge from the Executives faction, and by working with Coalition of the Imam's Line and by attacking the Executives for their questionable revolutionary credentials, they managed to secure a significant victory in these elections. The Society won 110 of the 270-seat Majlis and the Executives won 80 seats, with the balance of 80 seats being held by such smaller factions as the Society for the Defence of Islamic Values, which in any case tended to support the Society. Their control of the Majlis meant that the last year of Rafsanjani's presidency was lost to domestic wrangling about economic and foreign policy and also the imposition of tighter controls on social relations. The fifth Majlis of course would be in place for much of the term of the next president, who appeared late on the scene in 1997 but happened to be a highly popular social and political reformer.

Nevertheless, the presence of the Executives in the fifth Majlis also showed the consolidation of a pragmatist-reformist grouping emerging at the heart of power in the republic. Energized by the deep debates taking place at the elite level and openly communicated in the national media, and despite the many disqualifications and abstentions, the voters came out in force in 1996 to ensure that the Majlis could represent the diversity of political opinion. "It was in this tetchy atmosphere of political point-scoring, disunity and disillusionment", notes Axworthy, "that Iran slipped into the run-up to the 1997 presidential elections" – the surprising outcome of which would not only tip the electoral balance of power in favour of a new reformist grouping but also threaten to chart a new path for the country's foreign policy (see chapter 4).[44]

In many ways, the results of the 1996 Majlis elections belied the presence of deep socio-political currents clamouring for change, and which manifested themselves fully just a year after the Majlis elections and in the campaign to elect the successor to President Rafsanjani. During Rafsanjani's presidency, social conditions had begun to change and as Iran proved much more receptive to engagement with the outside world so outsiders also increased their engagement with Iran and so interacted more fully with Iran's intellectuals and young population. The more average Iranians saw of the outside world, the more they wanted the chance to share in their apparent freedoms. Cultural openness, manifested in an increasingly thriving art, music, literature (including access to translated Western classics and also from Russia and East Asia), and cinema scene, pushed the boundaries of imagined possibilities further. So, as the vote for the president drew closer, the more agitated and mobilized urban masses became in support of those arguing for deep-seated change. The makings of a vibrant civil society were increasingly in evidence, but as the nineties wore on so, too, were the contours of an alliance of traditional and conservative forces closely aligned with the Leader.[45] This powerful group now stood against change – against what they increasingly saw as Western cultural and economic penetration of an Islamic republic still covered in the blood of martyrs who had died in its protection and one as pure as there had ever been. Reform equalled betrayal, surrender to the evil empire.

1997: Tehran spring

The elections for Iran's second executive president proved more controversial than the first, for in these elections we saw for the first time the articulation of two competing visions for the Islamic republic and two strong currents championing each camp. On one side was the 'establishment' conservative figure of Nateq-Nouri, Majlis speaker and former interior minister, close ally of the Leader, and a core elite member since the revolution. The election appeared his to lose. His main rival was the former Islamic culture and guidance minister forced out of Rafsanjani's cabinet by a combative Majlis who accused him of liberalism. Khatami was the reluctant presidential candidate who entered the race rather late and finally did so because former premier Mousavi, badly bruised by the constitutional and political changes following Ayatollah Khomeini's death in 1989, had flatly refused to re-enter the political ring.

Khatami's campaign gained momentum rapidly when pro-Rafsanjani and pro-left forces combined forces in support of his candidacy. Hojjatoleslam Khatami was elected president in June 1997 at the head of an energetic reform movement (the so-called Dovoum-e Khordad Movement marking Khatami's election day victory in the Persian calendar) bent on at least questioning many of the general principles of governance in post-revolution Iran, if not changing them in favour of 'civil society', greater presence of women in public life, transparency in decisions, and the rule of law (no one or centre of power should be above the law was the message of Khatami).

Nearly 20 years after the revolution and fully aware of the rapid pace of socioeconomic change taking place at home, and the scale of geopolitical changes at the global level, these voices again resurrected the idea of creating an Islamic democracy, a 'theo-democracy', of the sort talked about back, albeit briefly, in 1979. Against the backdrop of such a rigid (anti-Shia) group as the Taleban forcing its way to power in neighbouring Afghanistan, Iranian society's interest in bringing to power a progressive and democracy-leaning president enhanced Khatami's message of democratization as much as his appeal as an establishment 'anti-establishment' figure preaching the message of hope against the regime's preferred candidate's (Hojjatoleslam Nateq-Nouri, Majlis speaker and widely regarded as the Leader's chosen candidate) message of conformity with the dictates of the clerical establishment.

For the pro-Khatami faction, reform and moderation were the essence of survival for the Islamic republic, and these were precisely the counter positions being peddled by those aligning themselves with the Leader and Nateq-Nouri. The new Taliban regime would become a foreign policy headache for Khatami to be sure, but in the heat of the election campaign, Nateq-Nouri's speeches helped Khatami's team to paint the establishment candidate as unimaginative, arrogant, and rather backward-looking. Nateq-Nouri, for all his experience and wisdom, appeared out of touch, even unfashionable. Khatami had captured the imagination and had galvanized the voters. The spectacularly high voter turnout (88 per cent) was a direct result of Khatami's popularity with voters. And while

TABLE 2.3 Presidential elections, 1997

Candidate	No. of votes	Percentage
Mohammad Khatami	20,078,187	69.60
Ali A. Nateq-Nouri	7,242,859	25.00
Reza Zavarei	771,460	2.70
Mohammad Reyshahri	742,598	2.60
Voter turnout	29,067,100	88.00

Source: Ministry of Interior.

this high turnout provided evidence of the legitimacy of the regime, the perennial concern of the political elite, the fact that a 'counter-establishment' figure had so comprehensively defeated the establishment candidate, immediately created more headaches for the Leader-backed conservative and traditionalist camps. Nevertheless, the president had secured a clear mandate for the introduction of political and social reforms.

With a spirit of hope the president and his political allies, active in an increasingly vibrant civil society, set about producing wide-ranging briefs for reform – for staging a "democratic insurgency", according to Tazmini.[46] Through a well-greased think tank close to the presidency (Center for Strategic Research), which was run by an energetic and respected academic (Dr Mohammad Reza Tajik), President Khatami tested the administration's new policy frameworks and disseminated these widely through the country's lively and expansive media. Public debate of this scale and intensity had never taken place in Iran and in these discussions many taboos of the Islamic republic were publicly discussed and in the process new discourses were born. Also, the scale of change being envisaged was unprecedented: In Khatami's Dovoum-e Khordad movement seemed to be laying the ground for a new social contract, a new revolution, and this reality galvanized the right into action. For them, the reform movement was a Western Trojan Horse, an American Fifth Column, at the heart of the revolutionary state. Thus, from 1998 with every step forward, Khatami's administration was forced to take two steps back. The counterattack was undisguised and vicious, enacted in several different ways. One way was intimidation of public figures through media and also physical assaults on them. The killing of several prominent intellectuals, one cycle of which became known as the 'chain murders', was the most graphic manifestation of this strategy.[47]

The second track was suppression of the largely pro-Khatami student movement, which by the late 1990s had grown into a body of over 1.5 million young men and women. In much smaller numbers, the student body had fought and won the war against the Pahlavi monarch, so the masters of the republic were acutely aware of the mobilizing energy of this community that now was vocal and apparently organized – with their own news agency, media outlets and even unions. So the right's focus on this social group was not surprising and was being trailed throughout spring 1999. But the manner of their attack, which commenced with a coordinated assault on a university dorm in Tehran in July 1999 and the killing of several students and arrest of hundreds of others, was unexpected.[48] The well-coordinated attack brought condemnation from the Leader and the president, but the damage had been done and students had been silenced – for a while.

These protests provided the context for a much bigger demarche against the president. So, following the protests, a group of senior Guard officers submitted a threatening letter to the president warning him of their unwillingness to stand by and see the fruits of the revolution squandered: "watching the wilting flower of the revolution".[49] This was no ideal threat and provided the first documented evidence of the Guard's preparedness to intervene in the country's political process, from which the armed forces are constitutionally barred. It was increasingly clear that the Leader and his associates in charge of the key organs of the state had become nervous of the reform movement and viewed it as a clear and present danger to the Islamic republic. From their perspective, Khatami and his allies were directly responsible for fermenting turmoil and attempting to restructure the relationship between the elite and the governed by diminishing the authority of state institutions. This perception of the reform movement was entrenched, and many of the reformist figures continued to be viewed with suspicion amongst the conservative elite. The prosecution and conviction to a five-year jail sentence of a prominent cleric (Abdullah Nouri) and interior minister in the administrations of Rafsanjani and Khatami in 1999 on charges of undermining the core beliefs and values of the Islamic republic was indicative of this line of thinking.

Indeed, following the election crisis of 2009 and the birth of the Green Movement as a new mass-based force to challenge the establishment, the extent of the suspicions against Khatami's reform camp surfaced, showing also the regime's monitoring of the president and his allies. Following the June 2009 election fiasco and the mass street protests, dozens of reformists were arrested and many were charged with anti-state behaviour, the evidence for which had apparently been gathered in the late 1990s and early 2000s. So in August 2009, over 100 figures associated with Khatami's movement were put on trial for spreading discord, disturbing the peace and conspiring to overthrow the legitimate government of the country. A key charge was conspiring to spread secularism in the Islamic republic, as a way of weakening its religious foundations, which the prosecutor directly associated with the visit of Jürgen Habermas to Iran in 2002. The non-partisan, Los Angeles–based *Tehran Bureau* magazine reported that in the trial "the prosecutor outlined the steps that had supposedly been taken by the reformists to move the country toward a secular government, including the fact that the Khatami administration had allowed the formation of the NGOs on a vast scale. Khatami was supposedly quoted as saying in a meeting of the Supreme Council for Cultural Revolution that, 'there is no way of avoiding secularism'".[50] The principal vehicle for this conspiracy, the prosecutor argued, was the Center for Strategic Studies, accused of, according to *Tehran Bureau*, developing the theoretical framework for secularism during the Khatami administration: "the prosecutor claimed that in an analysis prepared by Mohammad Reza Tajik of the Center and presented to Mr. Khatami, it was stated that, 'In the near future no one can resist secularism, and we must also accept this fate of humanity'. According to the prosecutor, inviting Jürgen Habermas to visit Iran in 2002 was done with this purpose in mind. The prosecutor said that when Habermas traveled to Iran, there was a confidential meeting at the home of Mohsen Kadivar … and attended by Saeed Hajjarian and Mohammad Mojtahed Shabestari". Hajjarian, the ideologue of the reform movement, had survived an assassination attempt in March 2000 but was disabled; Shabestari, a prominent cleric and devotee of the founding father of the Islamic republic, had acquired a following for advocating support for democracy from a religious perspective and the separation of government and religion. The cleric, Mohsen Kadivar, is persona non grata in the Islamic republic. He was convicted by the special clerical court in 1999 for his criticism of the Velayat-e Faqih concept and the country's governance system and moved overseas in 2007 where he has since resided.

The third was an assault on the vibrant press and flourishing media that had grown rapidly since Rafsanjani's second term. The relatively unshackled press pushed the boundaries of debate, conducted sensational exposes, and questioned policies and decisions. But it went further and used its privileged position to poke fun at public figures. Targeting prominent individuals had become normal, and former president Rafsanjani had become one such figure. He was berated for seeking election to the Majlis after having served as president, but his failure to secure a seat in the eighth Majlis made him the subject of ridicule. Essentially, old battles were being fought again in the media and so here we had one of the key proponents of reform and a pillar of the establishment being attacked for some of his policies as president and for blocking the left from access to levers of power. "After May 2000", notes Axworthy, "he was not only aligned against the reformists; he was embittered against them too".[51] The ground was ready, in other words, for the right's attack on the 'free' press. The main assault had begun in March and April 2000, following the assassination attempt on Hajjarian, which led to the forced closure of sixteen pro-reform newspapers, including Hajjarian's own popular daily, *Sobh-e Emrouz*. The Leader's statement in April that "the press is spreading anxiety, discord and pessimism" had provided the pretext for the judicial closures,[52] which continued into 2001 with the closure of a further twenty-three newspapers and magazines.[53] In the pre-social media age and online blogosphere, gagging the press was the most effective way of limiting the intellectual influence and mobilizing power of the reform camp. Limiting newspaper and magazine outlets limited freedom of speech and quickly brought to a near halt the public debates about the country's political system and the enhancement of political freedoms and social liberties. To the Leader, in whose view the nezam was as good as an Islamic state could get, such discussions were anathema and close to treason.

The fourth, and arguably most effective, track for containment of the reform movement was the exercise of the institutional power of the Leader-linked elite – those in control of the judiciary, the special clerics court, in the fifth Majlis, the intelligence and IRGC communities, and of course the Council of Guardians. These great institutional levers were used from 1998 to intimidate, mute, jail, and eradicate the mildest form of dissent or opposition to the nezam.[54] The Leader himself had positioned the domestic political struggle in the wider context of Iran's struggles against the United States and could not have stated his position more clearly in declaring: "America sees the Iranian reform movement as a move against the Islamic system. That is their understanding of the Iranian reform movement. America does not really recognize [understand] a group of our brothers and sisters who are known as reformists".[55]

Khatami's legal and political fightback – in terms of challenges to the behaviour of the Guardians Council, decisions of the judiciary, and the setting up of commissions to draft policies for the enhancement of the rule of law and implementation in full of the articles of the constitution (freedom of assembly, of the press, association and assembly, as key issues), and the enhancement of the president's role as the upholder of the constitution, in tandem with powerful pubic speeches in favour of reforms – proved to harden the elite-level opposition to his policies. Presidential speeches on the theme of change were frequent,[56] a most notable of which was delivered on 28 August 2002 – a year into his second term in office and before his presidency would be consumed by the nuclear crisis.[57] Khatami visited all the main themes of his campaigns during this speech and in the process promised to bring two defining pieces of legislation to the Majlis: To enhance the constitutional power of the president – in effect curtailing that of the Leader's – and to end the Guardian Council's right of vetting candidates for elected office. This direct challenge had perhaps come too late in the day to have the desired effect. In fact, the system chose to bypass Khatami's challenge altogether and by rejecting his two important reform bills in May and April 2003 effectively ended any hope of deliberative change being introduced into the principles and institutions of the nezam.

Despite Khatami's second landslide victory in June 2001 then the reform camp had run out of steam and seemingly lacked the will, as well as the appropriate tools, to challenge the continuing dominance of the Leader's institutional allies. As Arjomand observes, the reform camp "either made the tactical mistake of thinking they could appropriate the rhetoric of the Islamic revolution, or much more likely, did not have the courage to dissociate themselves from it because they were afraid of being called traitors. Either way, these good children of Khomeini's revolution lost the power struggle for reform".[58] Those within the system clamouring for change would get another chance in 2009, however, but ended up facing the exact same dilemmas – to detach from the nezam in anticipation of a post-Islamist order or to remain loyal to the principles of the Islamic revolution and fight for change from within the system. As we will see, the new champions of reform tried mass mobilization as the means for generating momentum for their cause and thus trying to put down a different pathway for change in the country. Evidence will show that the reform leadership's inability to imagine, let alone present, itself as an alternative to the ruling Faqih system inevitably robbed the movement of another golden opportunity to democratize this unique political system.

But in the year 2000, Khatami and his allies were riding high and were at that point poised to take control of the Majlis, the essential legislative vehicle to push through Khatami's reform agenda. The reformists, now organized in the Islamic Iran Participation Front (IIPF), capitalized on Khatami's presidential popularity and, through effective use of a professional publicity machine, ran the country's most modern election campaign in 2000, which removed the monopoly of the conservatives from the parliament.[59] The success of reformists in the sixth Majlis,

TABLE 2.4 Majlis elections in the Reform Era

	No. of eligible voters	Votes cast	Voter turnout
Sixth Majlis (2000–04)	38,726,431	26,082,157	67.35%
Seventh Majlis (2004–08)	46,351,032	23,734,677	51.21%

Source: Ministry of Interior.
Note: Majlis expanded its membership from 270 to 290 seats as of 2000.

buttressed by a strong voter turnout (of nearly 70 per cent), was Iran's second political earthquake in less than three years. The reform coalition's victory was emphatic, securing 216 seats out of the 290, with the conservative-leaning Society securing only 74 seats. The IIPF had emerged as the strongest parliamentary coalition in the Majlis since the early days of the revolution and in the highly ideological first and second 'unity Majlises' of that time. Indeed, by the virtue of their success in these elections, the conservatives became even more wary of the reformists and acted to block any 'contrary' legislation from the parliamentarians passing into law. In several instances, the Council of Guardians rejected bills, agreed to have measures considered by the Expediency Council, or simply sat on them. On one important occasion, the Leader himself intervened: He wrote directly to the Majlis members in August 2000, for example, instructing them not to amend the restrictive press law enacted in the seventh Majlis. The law stood and the reformist Majlis was mortally wounded.[60]

The emphatic Majlis victory however did strengthen the platform for Hojjatoleslam Khatami's re-election bid for the presidency in 2001. Despite growing inter-factional and intra-factional tensions, Khatami did manage to excite voters and won the presidential vote by a substantial margin against a relatively weak list of candidates. With a renewed mandate, he began to pursue two profound changes through the reform-friendly sixth Majlis: To give the executive the legal authority to block political trials, and the even more significant legislation to strip the Guardian Council's power of vetting candidates for national elections.

Khatami's second presidential term was highly political and clearly intent on limiting the extensive powers of the conservative-controlled key institutions of the state. Inevitably, the state responded with a vengeance. It took action to prize the Majlis away from Khatami's allies. By 2004 the tide had turned sufficiently against the increasingly squabbling and detached political forces around Khatami that the IIPF's flank was wide open to attack from the right. So, in the light of the reformists' control of the executive and legislative branches of government, the first wave of attack from the conservatives came through dispossession – dispossession of individuals from office. They thus used the trusted route of disqualification of candidates for the seventh Majlis in 2004 – 3,600 candidates were removed from a long list of 8,200. As if this was not bad enough, the body blow came by disqualifying as many as 80 sitting MPs, almost all of whom were Khatami allies. The reform camp was decimated and their half-hearted boycott and their inability to mount a strong campaign cleared the way for the return of the conservatives to the seventh Majlis. The conservatives' election campaign, largely unchallenged, enabled them to take as many as two-thirds of the Majlis seats. Their engineered exclusion, argue Gheissari and Sanandaji, basically politically impaired the pro-reformist camp which may also have cost them the presidency in 2005.[61]

The political atmosphere was further charged by the president's pointed differences with the Leader and with the country's powerful security apparatus. But the right was back in the saddle and in order to turn the tide against the reformists it could now comfortably focus on recovering the presidency as well from the reformists. Not for the first time in Iran, Majlis elections provided the political context – the platform – for the presidential elections. The makeup of 2004 Majlis, now dominated by the conservatives, became the perfect backdrop for the 2005 presidential elections, on which the right had now set its sight. The seventh Majlis also moved quickly to reverse many of Khatami's economic decisions and several of those granted the government by the sixth Majlis.

The limits of Khatami's abilities to change the dynamics of power in the Islamic republic had become clear in 2003, manifesting themselves in two distinct ways. The first was substantial student protests in mid-June against lack of progress in creating opportunity (for employment, leisure, travel, and further study) and for not opening up society. The second was a carefully worded letter sent to the Leader by 127 parliamentarians of the sixth Majlis warning him of the dire national consequences of inaction. In this letter, similar in tone to the one that was sent to Khomeini in 1987, the reform-leaning parliamentarians advised the Leader that "the vast majority of the people are disgruntled and hopeless" and "not much time is left. The destiny of our country can either be dictatorship, or the respect for democratic rules".[62]

This letter was followed by an ever more direct challenge to the conservative leadership, this time in the form of an open letter signed by more than 250 political, religious, and civil society figures (including the pro-reform figure of Ayatollah Montazeri and close allies of Khatami, Saeed Hajjarian and Saeed Pourazizi) and published in the popular daily *Yas-e Nou*. They accused these establishment forces of heresy by portraying themselves as God's emissaries on earth: "considering individuals to be in the position of a divinity and absolute power...is open polytheism [in contradiction to] almighty God, and blatant oppression of human dignity". And as if this was not clear enough, the letter went on to say that "people [and their elected lawmakers] have the right to supervise fully their rulers, criticise them, and remove them from power if they are not satisfied".[63] This was an unprecedented and direct challenge to Ayatollah Khamenei's leadership, and so as not to leave any doubts about the consequences of the status quo, the signatories urged the leadership to accept wholesale change before "the whole establishment and the country's independence and territorial integrity are jeopardised". Relations between the republic's political factions had broken down and each side blamed the other for the political crisis now facing the country.

Khatami, having arrived with the promises of greater liberty, rule of law and a better life, was leaving with a legacy of unfulfilled promises of constitutional accountability (limits to the powers of the Leader, clear delineations in the remits of state institutions, rule of law and transparency). He had not managed to make his reforms irreversible, had not managed to rebalance power towards the elected offices of the state, and had failed to keep public space open and vibrant.[64] Fear of his bold policies had not only strengthened the hand of the security organs in the nezam but also limited his ability to push through the necessary economic reforms to enhance employment opportunities and reduce inflation, despite the eye-catching success of establishing a national fund for future generations. The last word on the state of affairs at the twilight of Khatami's term was provided by the outgoing Friday prayer leader of Isfahan, the moderate Ayatollah Jalaledin Taheri, who in July 2002 summarized the nezam's situation in terms of "despair, unemployment, inflation and high prices, the hellish gap between poverty and wealth, the deep and daily growing distance between the classes, the stagnation and decline of national revenues, a sick economy, bureaucratic corruption, desperately weak administrators, the growing flaws in the country's political structure, embezzlement, bribery and addiction".[65]

As 9/11-generated political storms raged in Iran's neighbourhood and as the country struggled to find a defensible position in the nuclear storm that it itself had started, the leadership appeared divided and fractured. The country was in gridlock. These conditions and the Leader's resolve not to have reformists anywhere near the levers of power again arguably prepared the ground for the return of the trusted conservatives and also the rise of populist politics in the republic. The conservative-dominated seventh Majlis was the unbreakable barrier against the reformists.

Populist politicians, associated with the conservative camp and militantly loyal to the founding principles of the revolution, appeared on the scene. They preached a message of defiance against the West and one of loyalty to the nezam and all its organs.

Neoconservatism rears its head

On many levels the ninth presidential election in June 2005 was a watershed moment for the Islamic republic. It certainly changed the character of the presidency but was also a test for the much-weakened reform camp. This election also marked significant changes amongst the ranks of the conservative and traditional camps in the elite. The right, subsequent to its domination of the Majlis, had actually begun fighting itself. And in the absence of strong political opposition, their squabbles about policy options and their criticisms of the Khatami administration had increasingly acquired strong ideological undertones. The well-endowed traditional conservatives who were firmly entrenched in the bonyads, the judiciary and many other governing councils of the regime were viewed by a new generation of conservatives as out of touch, self-serving by nature, and no longer representative of Khomeini's founding principles. The 'young Turks', these neoconservatives rising from within the ranks of the conservatives and inspired by the radical teachings of such clerics as Ayatollah Mesbah Yazdi, emerged as a group of "hard-line populists who sought the support of the poor".[66] They separated themselves from the mainstream which was now more closely aligned with the interests of the merchant classes and the traditional middle classes who also had had a cultural fright during Khatami's tenure.

Ayatollah Nateq-Nouri, who adopted the position of the head of the Coordinating Council of Conservatives after his electoral loss to Khatami in 1997, vociferously pushed for Ali Larijani (later to become Majlis speaker in his own right) to become the conservatives' presidential candidate. In endorsing Larijani from the six candidates, Nateq-Nouri, as a prominent voice in the conservative camp, at the same time publicly opposed Ahmadinejad's candidacy. He spoke some years later about the process of selecting the conservatives' candidate for that particular election and stated on the record that after three intense meetings with Ahmadinejad, during which Ahmadinejad was given the floor for a solid two hours on one occasion in order to argue for his candidacy and explain his political platform to the prominent conservatives, the collective view apparently was that Ahmadinejad was not fit for this purpose.[67] Having thus rejected his candidacy, we know that Ahmadinejad subsequently turned away from the established conservative camp. His new front (Usulgarayan or Principlists) positioned itself alongside the 'deprived'. His populist platform and rhetoric wrapped itself in Khomeini's ideals while also deliberately eroding the legitimacy of the centrist and conservative forces in the republic – the backbone of the nezam. Ahmadinejad, who had been a former regional governor and a mayor of the capital, was now an anti-establishment insider. To Nateq-Nouri and his colleagues, at least Ahmadinejad's presidency would endanger the country's national cohesion. It was for this reason that other conservative candidates (Larijani, Qalibaf) stayed in the race whose combined total vote in the first round of the poll (17th June with 5.8 million votes) exceeded that of Ahmadinejad's. Analysis of the official data suggests that the conservatives had secured 39.2 per cent of the vote on the 17th of June.

More interesting still was the campaign of the reformist and the subsequent results for the reform camp. This side of the electoral equation was even more divided. The reformers, after their tremendous showing during Khatami's period, failed to field a credible single consensus candidate. Instead, three well-known names (Karroubi, Moin, Mehralizadeh) appeared as candidates of the reform camp. Moin's reputation as a reform-minded intellectual had helped convince reformists to support his candidacy, when it had become clear that Mousavi was not likely to stand. So, the IIPF and the higher body of the Coordinating Council of the Reformist Front endorsed his candidacy, amongst other

TABLE 2.5 Presidential elections, 2005 (first and second round)

Candidate	1st round	Percentage	2nd round	Percentage
Mahmoud Ahmadinejad	5,711,696	19.43	17,284,782	61.69
Ali Akbar Rafsanjani	6,211,937	21.13	10,046,701	53.93
Mehdi Karroubi	5,070,114	17.24	—	—
Mohammad B Qalibaf	4,095,827	13.93	—	—
Mostafa Moin	4,083,951	13.89	—	—
Ali Larijani	1,713,810	5.83	—	—
Mohsen Mehralizadeh	1,224,882	4.38	—	—

Source: Ministry of Interior.

reformist and civil society organizations.[68] Moin, however, was a totally discredited candidate amongst the conservatives for his views on reform and for advocating improved relations with the West. Karroubi, standing to the left of Moin, already had the support of the religious organization which he himself had headed for some time, the Association of Militant Clerics, and also that of the small but intellectually influential Democracy Party of Iran. The third candidate on the reformist side ran as an independent candidate after failing to secure the nomination of his party, the IIPF. Unlike previous elections, the reform side appeared to lack a strategy and not surprisingly splintered this formerly powerful bloc's vote into big and small fragments. As a result, the reformist side appeared disunited and also oblivious to the greater needs of society. The three reformist candidates as a group did not excite the electorate, did not speak with one voice and did not address the big issues facing society. As a result, they secured no more than 35.5 per cent of the total vote on the 17th of June, less than the core conservative candidates.

Splits in both conservative and reformist camps left the path clear for other candidates into which stepped the well-known, two-time president Rafsanjani and the little-known Ahmadinejad. Rafsanjani positioned himself as the centrist candidate with experience and sufficiently healthy links with all factions to be able to break the political gridlock in the country and move the country forward constructively to deal with its domestic and myriad of regional issues. The left, however, had not forgiven him still for his role in weakening them in the 1990s, but having secured the backing of many leading figures and a spectrum of national organizations, he found his flank vulnerable when Nateq-Nouri's key body – the Coordinating Council of Conservatives – refused to support his candidacy. Members of this Council in the end veered towards Ahmadinejad, which probably against Nateq-Nouri's better judgement, emerged as a credible conservative candidate. Rafsanjani could count on the centrist forces, but as the two entrenched political factions were organizing against him as the leading candidate, the chances of being seen as a compromise candidate evaporated.

Ahmadinejad, suddenly, was the right's leading candidate in the race, and the more he challenged the establishment and the more he criticized corrupt practices and attacked such figures as Rafsanjani for their 'Mafiaesk' past, the more popular he became. With the undisguised backing of such grassroots bodies as the Basij, large sections of the IRGC, and the hard-right parliamentary party (Abadgaran-e Iran-e Eslami, or 'Builders of Muslim Iran') Ahmadinejad also had a mobilizing force to rally support for him in the further corners of the country. He lacked the high-level institutional and media support for seeking such high office in Iran when he entered the race, but his mannerisms had touched a nerve, and despite his first campaign video offering "little in the way of discernible policies or ambitions: No promises of improvements to living conditions, no vision for governance and certainly nothing in the way of warmth and charisma",[69] he was challenging the elite candidates to try to right him off.

The interior ministry's published figures for the first round showed that Ahmadinejad beat Rafsanjani not only in the country's largest constituency, Tehran (1.6 million votes against 1.3 million), but also in nine other constituencies.[70] In Qom, Isfahan and Yazd, Ahmadinejad beat Rafsanjani by a considerable margin. The first inconclusive presidential race of the Islamic republic shocked the country. First, because, despite a high voter turnout of nearly 63 per cent, the best-known candidate (Rafsanjani) had managed to secure no more than 6.2 million of the votes cast on 17 June; and second, because a virtual unknown had beaten all the other candidates and was snapping at the heels of Rafsanjani.[71]

A second round, of the two leading candidates, had to take place a week later (24 June 2005). The result of the second round spoke for itself and despite allegations of irregularities in the first round, the outcome arguably represented a clear message of disenchantment with elite politics in Iran. Defeated candidate Karroubi's urging on 23 June – "Go and vote. Otherwise they are going to make an Iranian Taliban here"[72] – seemed to have little effect as voter turnout did not spike. In fact, voters, 59.6 per cent of whom turned out to vote again on the 24th, were sending a clear message to both major factions that a dysfunctional political system was against the country's interests and this message, I contend, the Leader took to heart as he shifted his weight to support Ahmadinejad's presidency. Indeed, disenchanted with the reformists and Rafsanjani's centrists, the Leader's options had by this point become rather limited. In the second round, there was no question that the right and all its institutional might was behind Ahmadinejad – the accidental candidate was within reach of the presidency, the one institution not controlled by the conservative allies of the Leader. Rafsanjani's rear-guard action to 'prevent extremism' proved an insufficient motivator, and while 150 members of parliament publicly came out in his support on the eve of the second ballot with the reform camp still in disarray, Rafsanjani's allies were unsure that they could mobilize sufficient support for him on the 24th. Rafsanjani himself was loath to publicly campaign against Ahmadinejad as a worthy adversary, so while Ahmadinejad crisscrossed the country portraying himself as the people's champion, Rafsanjani seemed detached, aloof even. So, the final count was massively in favour of Ahmadinejad. As Table 2.5 shows, Ahmadinejad had somehow accumulated an additional 11.5 million votes since the first round, and Rafsanjani had amassed only an additional 3.8 million votes, which was far fewer than the statistically available total reformist vote of 10.5 million. Despite a small difference in voter participation, Ahmadinejad's surge was hard to explain and the glaring statistical discrepancy renewed allegations of vote rigging, but Rafsanjani made it clear that he would not mount a legal challenge or demand a recount. What was done was done.

Now in the saddle, Ahmadinejad was poised for a third revolution. He was eager to change everything, and his populist economic policies dictated that he increase spending on the poor and the rural communities. With oil prices on an inexplicable high from 2005 onwards (rapidly rising from $30 per barrel before his election to over $60 in less than a year after he took office), he also had the means to play havoc with the country's structurally weak economic system. The strategy of the new president was the "eradication of poverty" and "all-out development of the country", with little published information on the policies his administration would choose.[73] Populist policies were presented in terms of economic justice, but as defined in Islam. Thus, his first budget was set at the high figure of $217 billion, the bulk of which was to be spent on the public sector and state-linked enterprises. Armed with the slogan of economic justice, the president liberally spent the oil windfall on half-baked development projects and what appeared as welcome changes – the raising of the minimum wage by between 23 per cent and 46 per cent, and higher public sector salaries – but which soon backfired as workers were laid off in large numbers in response, inflation spiralled, and the parliament began showing a keen interest in the administration's public policies.[74] But some of the beneficiaries of these economic policies were those in control of the same state enterprises and with access to state funds – those within the elite and those with access to powerful networks of the bonyads and the Sepah. With increasing sanctions putting additional pressure on the national economy, access became the key to success, and rent collection from illicit trade and financial deals provided a very attractive way of revenue generation and capital accumulation. The politically dominant faction of the petti-bourgeoisie now also had the material means for economic advancement. Shortages, of which there were to be plenty in the next few years, would be just another opportunity for rent collection.[75]

Populism, arguably, had been providing the perfect cover for the rise of the republic's conservative petti-bourgeois forces to positions of power since the early 2000s, and now that they were in charge they were on a mission to rebuild the Islamic republic in their own image and that of the founding father of the republic, Khomeini. They were Khomeini's true followers and flagbearers, whose destiny it now was to correct the path, remove those trying to subvert the nezam with talk of reform, stand up to foreign aggressors, and rebuild the country from bottom up. But the constant harking back to the fundamentals of Khomeini's revolution prepared the ground for the arrival of the defenders of the Islamic revolution, the Revolutionary Guard, to the centre stage of politics. In previous elections we had seen the growing interest of former Guard officers in public office, thus standing in elections for local councils, parliament and the presidency. Indeed, in the 2005 presidential race, half of the candidates had close association with the Guard. But the scale of their presence as ministers in Ahmadinejad's first cabinet was unprecedented. As many as ten of the twenty-five appointed ministers had either served in the Sepah or had worked with it professionally. This was not just the march of the petti-bourgeoisie; it was the arrival of the military class.[76]

The makeup of Ahmadinejad's political regime, coupled with his anti-democratic and authoritarian-populist policies, which had led to the dismissal, exile, arrest and prosecution of scores of reformist activists and public figures, helped further fuel securitization of the state. Of course the external environment added its own pressures on the increasingly paranoid elite, and after more than a decade of relative openness within a year of taking office Ahmadinejad was closing down all the routes for protest. In addition, he began to 'cleanse' the bureaucracy, ministries, and public institutions of reformers and their sympathisers. So, permanent secretaries, university presidents, ambassadors, and central bank officials were unceremoniously removed from their posts and Ahmadinejad allies took their place.

Ahmadinejad's promises of change had started but all the signs of change pointed to a republic of fear being erected. By the end of his term in office, he had managed to deepen social divisions and polarize political interactions, pretty much wreck the economy with his ill-considered policies, and strike at the heart of the hierarchy by systematically antagonizing the Leader's bureau. He seemed unstoppable and even consolidated his powerbase by securing or, more accurately, engineering, a sizeable majority in the eighth Majlis. Though thanks to his quarrelsome and bombastic manner, he quickly alienated the conservative group there and found himself under attack by what should have been a supportive parliament. From the Majlis speaker, Ali Larijani, downwards considerable concern began to be expressed about some of the president's cabinet appointees, his incoherent economic policies, and his antagonism of the international community. His comments about Israel were particularly embarrassing, though not totally divorced from the tone and content of the republic's leaders since the revolution, but his administration's conduct of Iran's nuclear negotiations concerned the establishment the most in his foreign policy forays.

Ahmadinejad did not yield, though, and as he introduced more confusing policies, his allies positioned themselves to take control of the Majlis in 2008, in preparation for having a friendly legislature to see out Ahmadinajad's anticipated second term for which he was set to compete in June 2009. Eligible voters for the eighth Majlis probably numbered as high as 47.6 million and victory would have gifted Ahmadinejad an emphatic endorsement. Yet official data suggests that voter turnout was significantly lower than previous elections, not much higher than 50 per cent for the first time in the history of the Islamic republic.

TABLE 2.6 Majlis elections during Neoconservative Rule

	No. of eligible voters	Votes cast	Voter turnout
Eighth Majlis (2008–12)	43,824,254	22,350,254	51.0%
Ninth Majlis (2012–16)	48,288,799	26,472,760	64.2%

Source: Ministry of Interior.

Some 7,597 candidates registered themselves for the elections. The majority of them (independents and reformists mainly) were disqualified by the Council of Guardians.[77] Unpopularity of the president and his parliamentary allies was bringing into question the legitimacy of the nezam as a whole. The Leader had repeatedly stated that the popularity of the Islamic republic was to be found in its high voter participation. Voters intended to send a message to the leadership: Ahmadinejad was not as popular as the regime thought, and, secondly, the voters missed the presence of the reformists.

In 2012 Majlis elections the conservatives did rather well, despite the political crisis of 2009 following that year's presidential poll, with the United Front of Principlists (headed by the Majlis speaker, Ali Larijani) fielding the highest number of eligible candidates amongst the 3,400 cleared to compete (of the 5,405 who applied). Their coalition (of three parties) secured a total of 148 seats, with the factions closest to the Leader taking the lion's share of the seats. With a relatively high voter turnout (of 64 per cent), this outcome was a significant blow to Ahmadinejad's Monotheism and Justice Front and marked the decline of the neoconservative challenge to the conservative-dominated order. This parliamentary electoral calm, however, betrayed the deep political crisis which followed Ahmadinejad's re-election in June 2009.

Nezam in crisis: Iran's tenth presidential elections

Ahmadinejad's bid for re-election had started in the course of the 2008 Majlis elections campaign, which his allies mobilized for, cowing any opposition. And, despite the evident tensions between himself and the Leader, indeed perhaps because of it, the incumbent positioned himself as the most credible candidate for the presidential office. The president also openly positioned himself as the most credible candidate capable of keeping the reformists at bay. As it emerged that the reformists were lining up some big guns to contest this poll, Ahmadinejad's argument that only he could stave off the assault from the left and centre made even more sense: The incumbent needed to be supported to ensure success and also to ensure that the conservatives would not be the first faction to have a one-term president in the history of the republic. Yet, the conservative hierarchy remained ambivalent and, against established tradition, sought to identify other suitable candidates to run. The truth was that even the sitting, conservative-dominated Majlis had issues with the president and had already censured him for several of his policies and his discourteous behaviour towards the elected chamber. As noted earlier, his election in 2005 had resulted in a palpable de-liberalization of public space, leading to repression of all manner of fora for debate about Iran's domestic situation and its strategic choices. De-liberalization not only closed down much of public space, it also gave rise to the securitization and gradual militarization of politics, the consequences of which were to be felt throughout Ahmadinejad's first term. Society was ready for a fightback, and the 2009 elections provided the target and the momentum.

It was to be expected then that senior figures, including former presidents Rafsanjani and Khatami, began openly to criticize Ahmadinejad's economic and also diplomatic strategies. The criticisms piled up against the background of unprecedented personnel changes at the highest level of his administration. In May 2008, he sacked Iranian Interior Minister Mostafa Purmohammadi without warning or explanation. This was the ninth cabinet minister to be dismissed since 2005. Another minister dismissed was the Economy and Finance Minister Davud Danesh-Jafari, who had protested in public about what he called unrealistic government policies. Ahmadinejad also received criticism on 15 May from Central Bank Governor Tahmasb Mazaheri, who said that the president's decision to set bank interest rates at between 10 and 12 per cent – well below inflation – was unworkable. Soon after, he too was gone: Ahmadinejad's third Central Bank Governor.

Not surprising also that Iran's main reformist groups were now openly criticizing the government and accusing President Ahmadinejad of squandering Iran's windfall oil earnings and driving up inflation. The Islamic Iran Participation Front, for example, stated that the government had not saved enough when oil prices were high to maintain spending for when the price dropped. Mohsen Mirdamadi, the party's secretary general, bitterly complained that President Ahmadinejad's "main campaign slogan [in 2005] was to share oil wealth fairly.... But instead, his economic policies have caused major problems for Iranians, particularly for lower-income people.... Since the revolution, Iran's total oil income has been $700 billion. Over 36 percent of it was earned during the tenure of office by Ahmadinejad, but inflation and unemployment rates are the highest now".[78] So, despite the historically high oil prices for much of his presidency, the economy was in much worse shape at the end of his first term than at any time since the early 1990s. So, despite many warnings about rising prices and inflationary pressures being fuelled by a reckless fiscal and monetary policy (leading to high-profile resignations of both economic minister and the governor of the Central Bank), the president pressed ahead with his ill-conceived and poorly executed economic policies. The warnings had been coming in thick and fast from 2006, of course, most pointedly from the Majlis, which had to approve the annual budgetary allocations and planned investments. Indeed, Iranian parliamentarians expressed what were described as 'grave concerns' over the proposed 2008 budget, describing the projected spending plans as unrealistic.[79] Noteworthy also was the fact that for the first time in the republic's history the budget was being drafted by the presidential office itself instead of the much more inclusive and technocratic-led economic planning body which Ahmadinejad had disbanded.[80] It was estimated that the government would spend around $31 billion in a year beginning 21 March 2008 in hard currency (largely earned from crude oil exports). But even before this request was lodged, it had emerged that the government had already spent just over $120 billion of hard currency since taking power in 2005 – in little more than two years.

Iran's government was on a spending spree, spending the oil price windfall faster than it was coming in. High oil prices helped in shielding the depth of the brewing crisis, with the result that as oil prices began to soften from August 2008, the cracks in Iran's economic façade appeared with great rapidity. For a man, who in summer 2008 confidently claimed that oil prices would never fall below $100 a barrel, the year's end prices would have come as a worrying reality check. The crisis gripping the country now was profound, even though Iran had not been a direct victim of the credit crunch and financial crisis brought upon the more open economies. In Iran's case, the bulk of the $200 billion in oil exports since 2005 had already been spent by 2008, and the strategic oil fund had been raided so intensively that there was probably less than $7.0 billion left in this strategic fund.

Ahmadinejad's position had become so vulnerable that even the former top nuclear negotiator under Khatami, Dr Hassan Rouhani (to be elected president in 2013), blasted him for his economic policies, alleging that the government had withdrawn $46 billion from the Khatami-established strategic fund since 2005, which had dramatically reduced the country's capacity to withstand such economic shocks as falling oil prices. As one analyst has put it:

> In fact, Ahmadinejad has run Iran's economy into the ground. On October 11, just a day after Ahmadinejad declared that inflation was easing, the Central Bank reported that annual inflation had reached 30 percent… Labor and Social Affairs Minister Mohammad Jahromi recently estimated the ranks of the jobless at 3 million, 2.4 million of whom are young people…unemployment among young people [defined as below the age of 35]… is 21.8 percent, or twice the national average. At least 14 million Iranians live below the poverty line [at a per capita monthly income of 969,750 rials (about $100)].[81]

The problems did not end there, for according to the International Monetary Fund, Iran was likely to face an unsustainable budget deficit if the price of oil remained under $75 per barrel. Officially, the government has assumed oil prices of $55 a barrel as its minimum expenditure baseline, but its spending had been so great that the foreign currency reserve fund had been emptied. It is calculated that in 2007/8 alone, as much as $17 billion had been withdrawn from the fund. With its annual budgetary commitments based on the minimum $80 per barrel price of oil (and oil income still accounts for 80 per cent of the government's overall revenue source), Iran was going to be facing some stark choices as the price of oil fluctuated between $50 and $80 after September 2008. This was not good news for the incumbent as he prepared for the presidential race.

As a result of the economic crisis, two important constituencies of the nezam – the bazaar and the low-income urbanized working classes – protested strongly against government policies, and the convergence of their angry complaints and strikes formed the backdrop to the elections. It is arguable that a combination of pressing and complex economic and political factors – namely, international sanctions, economic mismanagement at home and subsequent pressures on Iran's beleaguered private sector and bazaar communities, election fraud and suppression of protesters – combined to create a potent opposition force to the government. The forces ranged against the neoconservatives consolidated into a new coalition of political and economic forces who had suffered under Ahmadinejad's populist order. As Mozaffari argued, "we are seeing a convergence of interests between the economic elite, whose interests are represented by Rafsanjani and the bureaucratic/cultural elite, represented by Musavi".[82]

Arguably, these two communities form the nezam's core and their convergence would not only have alarmed the conservative camp but also the Leader who had experienced the effectiveness of a Rafsanjani-Mousavi partnership during his own term as president in the 1980s. The domestic political price of Ahmadinejad's populism had proved to be high as well, as with Larijani's pointed departure from the administration and his resignation from the posts of secretary of the Supreme National Security Council, and as such as Iran's chief nuclear negotiator. Ahmadinejad's tactics and strategic naivety had pushed such powerful individuals and potential allies as Larijani into a different – competing – camp from his administration. Politically, the departure of such influential figures was damaging to the president, particularly as Larijani subsequently emerged as the Majlis speaker and an institutional rival of Ahmadinejad. Larijani joined forces with the mayor of Tehran, Qalibaf, and of course Rafsanjani. Pressure mounted from the direct intervention of Ayatollah Rafsanjani, who took the unusual step of writing to the Leader just days before the poll accusing the president of lying in his pre-election statements about his achievements in first term in office which included clearing up the corruption of 'leading families', asking the Leader to "put out this fire". In his letter, Rafsanjani noted that "millions of people were witness to [Ahmadi-nejad's] lies and distortions of the truth, which were against religion, law, ethics and fairness and were aimed at the achievements of our Islamic system".[83] The warning had been issued, but Ayatollah Khamenei did not respond.

Yet he and his allies were adamant that things had never been so good for Iranians, and that externally Iran's regional and international standing had improved considerably, too, since their reintroduction of 'revolutionary values' into the republic's international relations. Yet the country was facing a number of uncertainties as it prepared for the tenth race for the presidency, foremost amongst which was the 'Obama effect'. The election of President Barack Obama in the United States – the man who Iranian conservatives were convinced would never be elected to the White House – posed a very different challenge to Iran than his predecessor, for he now reached out to Tehran, and did so very publicly. He not only recognized the regime's legitimacy, which had been one of Tehran's gripes against the US, but he also went further and extended the hand of friendship to Tehran. Between his election victory in November 2008 and his Middle East tour of June 2009, he on three occasions publicly invited Iran to clasp his extended open hand. The US strategy of regime change had given way to engagement and dialogue. Demonization of the US with Obama at the helm, therefore, was going to be a much harder act, and would inevitably affect Tehran's public diplomacy in the region.

President Obama's drive for improved relations with the Muslim world, as set out in his 4th of June 2009 speech in Cairo, resonated with Muslims. From the peace process to Iran's position in the region, all of the core issues were brought under the spotlight. In his new approach to regional engagement, Obama was posing a challenge to Tehran on several fronts: By reaching out to and building bridges with Iran's only real regional ally (Syria), by appearing to be more even-handed as it pressed for the resumption of the peace process, by mending America's strategic partnerships in the Arab world, by engaging Russia and the European Union more closely on dealing with Iran's regional policies, by incrementally increasing the pressure on Iran to limit its nuclear programme and then curtail it, and of course by very openly reaching out to the Muslim world. Iran's sensitiveness to these early overtures was evident in Ayatollah Khamenei's response, which came on the occasion of the twentieth anniversary of the death of his predecessor and in which he suggested that the United States remained so deeply hated that words alone could not change America's standing:

> In the past few years, American governments, especially the government of the foolish former president... have occupied two Islamic countries, Iraq and Afghanistan, under the pretext of the fight against terrorism. You witness that in Afghanistan, American warplanes bomb people and kill some 150 not once, but 10 and 100 times. They kill people continually. So, terrorist groups, do what you are doing there.... If the new president of America wants a change of face, America should change this behaviour. Words and talk will not result in change.[84]

This was an example of the inelastic mindset still dominant in Tehran and resistance at the highest levels to presentation of alternative perspectives on Iran's international diplomacy and public engagement. These very alternative approaches formed the basis of criticisms of Ahmadinejad during the election campaign and made it unlikely that the Leader could have warmed to Mousavi and Karroubi as alternatives to the incumbent, who until that point at least had remained loyal to the Leader.

Of course voices elsewhere, notably in Washington and admittedly on the very right of the political spectrum, argued that "whatever the outcome of Iran's presidential election today, negotiations will not soon – if ever – put an end to its nuclear threat". Solution: An Israeli military strike.[85] Bolton, a White House insider, speculated that a military strike "accompanied by effective public diplomacy could well turn Iran's diverse population against an oppressive regime". It is worth noting that the conventional wisdom outside Iran before polling had been that a Mousavi victory would enable the moderate Arab states and the US to build on the success of the pro-US and pro-Saudi 'March 14' front's parliamentary elections victory in Lebanon a week earlier to try to check Iran's rampant rise in the Levant, and also to open a new chapter in dialogue with the country's emerging leadership over regional security issues.[86] This kind of analysis was to be expected given that indeed of the four presidential candidates, three of them left the door wide open for engagement with the West and the moderate Arab states. Mousavi went so far as to promise a new détente with the West if elected president. These were important elections and defining, in a country whose destiny now seemed to matter to many millions outside of Iran. As Robin Wright had written, "Just one day before the June 12 presidential election, the Islamic republic had never been so powerful. Tehran had not only survived three decades of diplomatic isolation and economic sanctions but had emerged a regional superpower, rivalled only by Israel. Its influence shaped conflicts and politics from Afghanistan to Lebanon".[87]

As has been shown, elections in Iran – though complex and rarely unfettered – have come to play a significant role in the state's political narrative, as well as in the shaping of the country's political landscape. But electoral politics has not been unique to Iran and was indeed one of the region's key strategic drivers in the late 2000s. So, in the first half of 2009 alone, for example, electoral politics in Israel, Kuwait, Lebanon, Kurdish Regional Government had already made a significant impact on the region's strategic landscape, affecting both inter- and intra-state relations. So, it was in this context that Iran's 2009 presidential elections loomed large, for of all the mentioned elections Iran's presidential poll in June was always going to draw Iran's role in the region and its relations with the West. A series of very serious domestic and international challenges formed the backdrop to these elections, it has been noted. Ahmadinejad had raised the stakes so high that this contest was inevitably always going to be a referendum on his first term, and its outcome would be seen as shedding light on the path that the Islamic republic was going to chart for itself.

In the election campaign, Ahmadinejad had established his position on the basis of his administration's material and ideological achievements. The strong alternative narrative – highly critical of Ahmadinejad and his policies – formed the basis of the campaign of the most serious presidential contenders, Mousavi and Karroubi. For the first time, a coalition had been formed: Mousavi, the former prime minister and highly respected politician of the 1980s, had joined forces with the reformist Hojjatoleslam Karroubi, former Majlis speaker and establishment figure, to challenge the incumbent's grip on the executive branch of the republic. But the challenge of the one-time maktabi (advocate of social, cultural, economic Islamization) Mousavi in 2009 threatened to undo the entire system. But many still doubted that these elections would result in any major changes. Indeed, the prominent Paris-based lawyer (Mohammad Seifzadeh) declared that the screening process by the Guardians Council prevented the election from being free and fair and as such the "election is a race between government candidates, not people".[88] Events since have focused on this very issue, but for a time in 2009 the dispute between the 'government candidates' did threaten the foundations of the nezam, and it is arguable that the regime has still not recovered from the fallout of these elections.

Ironically, the Council of Guardians' screening process alluded to by Seifzadeh may actually have deepened the electoral rifts in pitting three powerful forces in front of each other. More immediately, the four candidates who eventually emerged from the Council of Guardians' scrutiny of the 471 applicant candidates were themselves fully aware of this wider, and for some rather troubling, context.[89] Each cut his electoral cloth according to his own vantage point. Ahmadinejad expressed pride in how his economic policies had helped the poor and had turned the direction of resources towards them. He even unveiled an 'economic transformation plan' which would in his second term reform the country's tax and subsidies system, give more freedom to the private sector and reduce Iran's reliance on oil revenues.[90] For the incumbent, there was nothing wrong with Iran's international strategy and posture. Iran standing tall had won the republic respect internationally and had disabled the enemies' efforts to curtail its nuclear programme. As he argued shortly before the poll: "Four and a half years ago, those who went to negotiate said to their interlocutors, after they agreed to freeze all [uranium enrichment], 'We want [nuclear energy for the purposes of] science and technology. Give us permission to operate 20 centrifuges.' But the other side answered insolently... But today, with the grace of God, and thanks to Iran's national unity... nearly 7,000 centrifuges are spinning today at Natanz, mocking them".[91]

He had made maximum use of his overseas trips and explained that he had struck a number of new partnerships – granted with faraway regimes – for the country's benefit. But promoting Iran's ties with the Shanghai Cooperation Organization was seen as a great foreign policy success. If nothing else, he argued, his government had raised the country's reputation and had ended the treacherous compromises of his predecessors. Regionally moreover, because of Iran's demonstrated strength such movements as Hamas and Hezbollah and the Shia forces in Iraq had become so successful in taking control of their respective realms. Others shared in his sense of achievement, of course, and it was not uncommon to see him described as an influential president: "Ahmadinejad's foreign policy has been consistently radical at both the regional and global levels; but, if you listen to him, this radicalism has restored Iran's stature in the eyes of the world to a level befitting its actual power and influence". During Ahmadinejad's tenure, it was added, Iran had successfully constructed a major independent uranium enrichment facility, "resisted economic sanctions imposed by the U.N.

Security Council, and finally forced the United States to propose direct talks on Iran's nuclear enrichment program. He recently stressed that Iran will not negotiate with the United States on suspending enrichment, but that it would be willing to discuss fighting terrorism and resolving regional crises together".[92]

The other three candidates did not quite see things this way, or Ahmadinejad's way. All three, for instance, were critical of Ahmadinejad's economic policies and also his international diplomacy. Karroubi was one of the candidates who used strong rhetoric to challenge Ahmadinejad's regional policies by focusing on such issues as his Holocaust denial: "First of all, the Holocaust existed.... Secondly, the Palestinians themselves say, 'What [is the use] of bringing such things up?' Thirdly, it [the Holocaust issue] is not related to us".[93] Mousavi promised a return to détente and argued that Iran would need to gain the trust of the international community over its nuclear programme. But he stopped short of saying Iran should halt its controversial uranium-enrichment activities. Karroubi was apparently content to leave Iran's nuclear policy in the hands of the Leader; and Rezaei emerged as the only candidate to fathom the idea of establishing a multinational uranium enrichment facility in Iran, which would include even the United States.

Of Ahmadinejad's economic policies the other candidates were particularly critical. Candidate Rezaei and former IRGC commander, for example, warned that under Ahmadinejad Iran was headed towards "an abyss", economically. Mousavi pointedly asked where the oil money that Ahmadinejad had promised to bring to people's tables in 2005 had gone. He also attacked Ahmadinejad's wider economic record – over GDP growth, inflation figures, household income, employment opportunities, government deficit, and mismanagement. Mousavi also took issue with Ahmadinejad's honesty and declared during a live debate on national television:

> One of our problems is that we are facing an amazing phenomenon: someone who can stare at the camera, look you in the eyes, and claim, with the utmost self-confidence, that black is white, that two times two is not four, but ten, and state it so emphatically that some of you are swayed! Nothing is worse than when the government lies to the people – and today we are witnessing exactly that. The only reason I have decided to get involved in this campaign is that I fear the consequences of this phenomenon.[94]

What the country needed, in his view, was good governance, social and political freedoms and social justice in terms of jobs, fairness and eradication of corruption.

Ahmadinejad's throwaway comment that the election was not between four candidates but three against one was not without substance, for the other three candidates had much to criticize on both domestic and external fronts.

The election campaign had an atmosphere of renewal, and voters interpreted this as the dawn of a new period of reform. That voters were getting their hopes high was reinforced by the candidates themselves and their spokespersons who urged voters not to boycott the elections: "Not voting is not a protest, it is retreating". Campaign text messages would warn that "if you plan not to vote, just think about the day after, when you find out Ahmadinejad has been re-elected".[95] It was said by such experienced commentators as Mashaollah Shamsolvaezin that "it seems that the younger generation, women, students, and all of those who had boycotted the election [in 2005] have been inspired by the election in the United States which brought Barack Obama to power, and also by the elections that took place in Iran's neighborhood – in Pakistan, Turkey, and Iraq.... They are not willing not to vote, to throw their vote away by abstaining from voting".[96]

All three candidates also intensively deployed new ICTs and took advantage of the unblocking of Facebook in February 2009 to engage with Iran's young and dynamic population. SMS, Facebook, Myspace and Twitter emerged as the tools of electoral trade and also for challenging the state media's overwhelming support for the incumbent. One website, setadema.com, had even gone so far as asking any Iranian with a telephone to call five of their friends and convince them to vote against Ahmadinejad. As it transpired, the same tools came to play an instrumental role in the post-election protests as well, facilitating the protesters' mobilization strategy and for ensuring that their message was heard outside of Iran. The rest of the world was caught up in Iran's post-election drama in an unprecedented manner. The gap between tradition and modernity, thus, was not only evident in the election campaign but became a significant focus of the post-election crisis, in which the electorate (the society at large) openly challenged the traditional values of the Islamic republic and powerfully posited in front of the government and the Leader a modernist and inclusivist alternative to the nezam of the conservative and neoconservative forces.

The stakes in these elections were high and voter participation (see Table 2.7) testified to the significance of Iran's presidential race in 2009. Remarkably high voter participation rate was indicative of the recognition by Iranians of the significance of the outcome for their own and also the country's future.

Energized by the campaigns of Mousavi and Karroubi and apparently convinced that the prospect of real change taking place in the country was assured, voters flocked to the polls in the millions, waiting at polling stations for hours in order to cast their vote. Messages from the reformists, including the two former presidents, urging the masses to turn out and vote was an additional mobilizing factor and an encouragement to the voters that their votes did count this time, that their decision at the ballot box could change the country's path, and form the first step in improving their daily lives. The allies of the two pro-reform candidates were making a persuasive case and the Leader happily endorsed their call for high voter turnout, safe in the knowledge that this would only raise the regime's legitimacy factor and help improve its international standing at a time when all the talk was

TABLE 2.7 Presidential elections, 2009

Candidate	No. of votes	Percentage
Mahmoud Ahmadinejad	24,527,516	62.63
Mir Hossein Mousavi	13,216,411	33.75
Mohsen Rezaei	678,240	1.73
Mehdi Karroubi	333,635	0.85
Voter turnout	39,165,191	85.00

Source: Ministry of Interior.

military action to curtail its nuclear programme. The same view was shared by some analysts as well, equally interpreting the high voter turnout as a sufficient indicator of the health of the republic's political mechanisms:

> The sole winners of the presidential election of 2009 were the Iranian people, whoever they voted for – some 40 million of them, out of an eligible voting population of 48 million, upward of 80 per cent. This election showed the democratic will of Iranians has matured beyond any point of return, no matter how violently the unelected officials of the Islamic Republic wish to reverse it. It is too late. As made evident during the presidential election of 2009, Iranians are perfectly capable of organising themselves around competing views, campaigning for their preferred candidates, peacefully going to polling stations and casting their vote.[97]

While voter turnout may have demonstrated the 'democratic will' of the Iranian people, the outcome was totally unexpected, with Mousavi's declared vote being so low as to defy logic, the incumbent's being so high as to negate all predictions, and even more remarkably Karroubi's support base of over five million from just four years earlier simply vanishing! It just did not seem possible that Mousavi and Karroubi between them would secure no more than 34.5 per cent of over 39 million votes cast, and that Ahmadinejad would secure over 60 per cent of votes cast – higher even than in 2005. With his presidency apparently in deep crisis, how did he manage to persuade over 24 million people to vote for him? These questions would begin percolating from the minute results were announced on the evening of 12 June.

No one, friend or foe, watching Iranian voters going to the polls in the millions on 12th of June had expected the unfolding of a major political drama in this country, and few, if indeed any, were prepared for the political crisis that followed the announcement of the result early evening local time. Fewer still could have anticipated the crisis of legitimacy faced by the nezam following the announcement of the result. For the presidential race itself, two sets of challenges formed the backdrop to the June vote. Some were 'homegrown' and largely domestic in character, and some others were external and therefore regional and international in nature. But the external challenges, as we saw from John Bolton's analysis, also posed significant domestic difficulties for the regime. The establishment was aware of the fact that Tehran had to manage the consequences for national security of Iran's negotiating position, minimize the impact of sanctions, as well as keep the country's nuclear options intact as it considered its response to the proposed 5+1 package of incentives in exchange for Iran's suspension of its uranium enrichment. The 5+1 negotiating package was delivered in July 2008 and the group was impatiently waiting for Tehran's response. The presidential elections were seen as the catalyst for movement, and hopefully progress, on this front.

At the heart, though, the domestic challenges facing Iran had turned these elections into historic ones. Many of the domestic challenges were arguably of the regime's own making as in gross fiscal mismanagement of the country's substantial oil revenues, absence of financial transparency fuelling speculative investment and trading, rising unemployment and inflation. The country's socioeconomic situation was not rosy. Under Ahmadinejad, the structural problems of the economy had only intensified. When the price of oil was at over $140 a barrel, peaking in July 2008, the Iranian president carried with him an air of total control and indestructibility. The 2007 US National Intelligence Estimate had concluded that Iran was no longer pursuing a nuclear weapons programme, which was interpreted as a victory by Ahmadinejad, and the high price of oil was allowing him to enjoy popular support for his high-spending initiatives. In the words of the *Economist* magazine, "America's belligerence [during the Bush years] allowed Iran's president to pose as a heroic underdog while record oil prices enabled him to pay for a binge in public spending".[98] This president was not about to surrender his mantle.

To the key candidates, the conduct of the election was found to be flawed and they registered their unease before the voting had even started. On the eve of the elections, in fact, Mousavi and Karroubi had taken the unprecedented step of writing to the Guardians Council directly, accusing the interior ministry of printing some 2.6 million more ballot papers than originally stated, implying that these could be used for fraudulent purposes, and added that "supervision over one-third of the ballot boxes has been taken away from the police and given to the Revolutionary Guards, which is against the law and prior norms".[99] Despite these concerns, both Mousavi and Karroubi seemed confident that the election was theirs. So when the results were announced, the sense of shock and dismay was palpable – to them this was an electoral coup de tat against the republic. Indeed, one authoritative observer who has studied the election's official statistics stated that "the data give very strong support for a diagnosis that the 2009 election was affected by significant fraud [and] ballot-box stuffing".[100] Other analysis had similarly raised questions about the validity of the poll:

> The Ministry of Interior authorized deployment of 14,000 mobile voting booths, making it very difficult for candidates to send monitors to

observe the balloting at every booth. Some 14.5 million extra ballots, by some reports, were printed and no clear system was delineated to track them. When several polling stations in urban centers ran out of ballots, Mousavi supporters asked where the extra ballots were, but they could not be found… Communications among campaign workers was hindered when SMS messaging was turned off and a web page associated with the Mousavi campaign was shut down.[101]

Further commentary suggested that "the election result was nothing but a coup in its worst form. I never imagined I would see the day when Ayatollah Khamenei would become a tool in the hands of the Revolutionary Guard".[102]

It was not surprising then that Mir Hossein Mousavi directly challenged the published results. But the fact that he went further and called on his supporters to protest the outcome was a new twist in the saga. This time the main two opposition candidates stood their ground and refused to accept the results as genuine. Mousavi, in a remarkable statement, not only questioned the integrity of the nezam's political institutions but went further and accused the ruling circles of dictatorial practices. He said:

> The noble people of Iran! The results announced for the tenth presidential election are stunning. The people who in the long voting lines witnessed composition of the vote know for whom they themselves voted and look with greatest disbelief at the magic done by those in the [Islamic Republic of Iran] Voice and Vision. Now, most of all they want to know how, by whom and which authorities have planned this great game. I, apart from strongly protesting against the process and blatant and many irregularities of the election day, warn that I will not surrender to this dangerous setting. The result of what we have seen from untrustworthy officials will lead to nothing but shaking of the pillars of the sacred regime of the Islamic Republic of Iran and strengthening of the rule of lies and authoritarianism. I consider it my religious and national duty to disclose the secrets behind this dangerous process and will explain its fatal effects on the destiny of the country and fear that continuation of the current state of affairs forces the entire authorities of the regime to defend lies in the face of the people.… I urge the authorities to stop this trend before it is too late and all to return to the line of law and trustworthiness and they should know that exit from justice harms legitimacy.… Those who have betrayed the popular vote don't fear that this house of the pious is set ablaze… [and] all those popular and official headquarters active in the elections and to stress that before reaching a result which our country deserves there is need for their presence and struggle.[103]

This was not just inflammatory; it was incendiary.

Velvet revolution or velvet coup?

Events following 12 June tell us a great deal more about Iran's domestic and security policies than hitherto available. The campaign to nip in the bud a reformist-led 'velvet revolution', as the Leader and his allies saw things, followed mass protests unseen since 1979. With many millions marching on the streets of the capital and other cities in support of Mousavi and Karroubi, asking 'where is my vote?', the conservative camp closed ranks and unleashed the security establishment in an effort to contain the peaceful mass protests. At this critical juncture, the establishment's only task was to survive. Hossein Aryan put it like this: "the regime is aware that it has lost its credibility in the eyes of many Iranians, and now its survival is the only important issue. No one is worried now about a possible attack by the United States or Israel or any other issue: The IRGC and the supreme leader are now completely focused on what they call 'soft subversion' ".[104]

The summer of 2009 was marked by a period of political unrest, which itself led to the birth of the country's first inner circle–nurtured opposition movement: The so-called Green Movement (Mousavi's election colours). But of equal importance was the manner in which the establishment had engineered its own 'velvet coup' to keep Mousavi out and Ahmadinejad in power. The Leader's unconditional support for Ahmadinejad, apparent even before the election, was surely partly rooted in his desire to keep his old foe (and a Rafsanjani ally) out of power, but his calculations were also partly shaped by the international environment and the real concern that a reform-leaning president might give away too much of Iran's nuclear achievements in search of an illusory 'grand bargain' with the United States in the race to reach a political accommodation with the United States. Having apparently been rebuffed by the US already, Khamenei was, at this point in time, not ready for any compromises.

The ensuing crisis also highlighted the role of security apparatus in Iranian politics today. Though some aspects of the security factor in domestic politics certainly sharpened during Ahmadinejad's first term, security has been a critical factor in Iranian politics for years. Indeed, the context in which much of the republic's internal debates have been shaped over the years has been about concerns over regime security and the parallel concern over threats to Iranian territory and even culture from the US or its regional allies. It is worth recalling that during President Khatami's eight years in office, on at least three occasions concerns over security were used to check his policies and initiatives.[105] Several of his ministers were forced out and he had to sit by while over a dozen pro-reform newspapers were closed down in one day on the orders of the Leader.

Who can also forget the threats issued against his administration by the Guard early in Khatami's term in office? So, militarization is not a new phenomenon, but Ahmadinejad, in partnership with the security apparatus and in full view of the Leader, took it to new and, as we have seen after the 12th of June, rather dangerous heights. Critics from within the establishment and the religious communities had raised the alarm about the decline in standards of this unique Islamic state, one that, if the late Leader, Ayatollah Khomeini was to be believed, "does not resemble states where the people are deprived of all security and everyone sits at home trembling for fear of a sudden raid or attack by the agents of the state".[106] Khamenei's republic appeared so much more similar to what the founder of this state had so vehemently rejected. The regime used mass arrests (even leading to the death of detainees), torture, the detention of dozens of the reformist leaders, and the placing under house arrest of Karroubi and Mousavi without charge or a judicial intervention as instruments to intimidate and blunt Iran's 2009 peaceful uprising. The regime's response to the MENA region's first 'digital uprising'[107] – mass mobilization took place through social media, information and rallies were circulated through social media outlets, images were instantly transmitted through social media, protest protocols were established through social media and with it a whole new digital language of engagement, and the alternative and indeed competing space to that controlled by the state which had been created was repression on a massive scale. Nightly rooftop chants of 'death to dictator' and 'death to Khamenei' were also new and also unprecedented, again inviting the security forces to post paramilitary lookouts on street corners to identify and storm buildings from whence chants were emanating.

Iran's post-election crisis was increasingly less about the disputed poll itself and more about the very nature of power in Iran and the exercise of power. Both sides claimed to be fighting for the soul of the revolution and Khomeini's ideals and values. Yet on the street the protestors seemed to reject the state's narrative of the revolution along with Mousavi's claim to be upholding it. To Iran's digital voices and street marchers, the dominated narrative of the 1979 revolution was a betrayal of the aspirations of first uprising against the monarch – a fabrication. This new so-called Green Movement, sweeping across cityscapes and digital spaces, was no longer about the Islamic revolution or the reform of the rigid Islamic republic; it was about the desire to reconstruct the 1979 revolution's ideals without ideological prejudice. In their self-image, their style of activism, and the articulation of their revolutionary slogans, these digital protestors represented new modes of political engagement, but they also showed in their actions the generational shift engulfing Iranian society. These educated and articulate communities of networked youths were gingerly bypassing the aging regime of the Islamic republic. That this kind of change was inevitable was staring us in the face when we looked at the country's national statistics: By the end of the decade preceding the June 2009 protests, students were "an increasingly large segment of the nation, according to figures released by the Education Ministry. Between 1979 and 1999, when the population doubled, the student body rose almost threefold, from 7 million to 19 million. The overall literacy rate jumped from 58 percent to 82 percent, and the number of university graduates grew ninefold, from a base of 430,000".[108] This community, highly networked by 2009, was the very engine of change that the conservatives had sought to contain.

As such, the crisis quickly became about the essence of the nezam created by the clerical establishment. In this, the balance of power in Iran, legitimacy of the ruling regime, its political and revolutionary identity, ideology of the state, the republic's political culture, its foreign relations, and Iran's place in the Muslim world were all contested. The very edifice of the Islamic republic was under scrutiny. As Wright put it:

> The day after the election, the Islamic republic had never appeared so vulnerable. The virtual militarization of the state has failed to contain the uprising, and its tactics have further alienated and polarized society. It has also shifted the focus from the election to Iran's leadership. The uprising has transformed Iran's political landscape. Over the past month, dozens of disparate political factions have coalesced into two rival camps: the New Right and the New Left.... What was a political divide has become a schism. Many Iranian leaders served time together in the shah's jails; today, their visions of the Islamic republic differ so sharply that reconciliation would be almost impossible.... With each flash point, the regime's image is further tainted, its legitimacy undermined.[109]

Of the many problems befalling the regime after the election, the crisis of legitimacy was perhaps the most important, perhaps second only to regime security. Grand Ayatollah Hossein Ali Montazeri early on in the crisis stated that confronting protesters threatened the legitimacy of the Islamic republic because it was no longer representing the people.[110] He stated stridently that "today, censorship and cutting telecommunication lines cannot hide the truth" of repression and violation of the people's rights. Significantly, other clerics followed suit: Ayatollah Jalaledin Taheri (the former Friday prayers leader in the city of Isfahan), went on the record describing the re-election of Ahmadinejad as "illegitimate" and "tyrannical". Voices from Qom reported:

> With the exception of a few clerics who have ties with the government, the majority of clerics have not issued any statements in support and confirmation of the election results. Ayatollah Safi, Ayatollah Makarem Shirazi, Ayatollah Zanjani, and Ayatollah Montazeri and other figures [not only did not confirm the election results], but made explicit or implicit comments and expressed their protests. The degree of their stances and condemnation have been different but what I want to say is that there are no real divisions.... The independent clerics have expressed their [critical] stances toward the election.[111]

The bottom line, as articulated by a cleric, was that "[a number of clerics] in Qom believe that the way the election was conducted was not correct and healthy, therefore they called for an investigation by an independent group. Many believed, because of the evidence, that there was massive manipulation in the June 12 vote".[112] This belief, and the state's violent and uncompromising reaction to the protests, drove prominent and respected figures, like Ali Reza Beheshi (son of Ayatollah Khomeini's closest ally until his assassination in 1981), to side with Mousavi. Other senior clerics such as Ayatollahs Abdolkarim Ardebili and Yousef Sanei (sitting and former members of the Council of Guardians respectively) also spoke against the government side, and in support of the protestors. The Qom-based Association of Researchers and Teachers also spoke out declaring on its widely read website: "Candidates' complaints and strong evidence of vote rigging were ignored.... Peaceful protests by Iranians were violently oppressed.... The outcome is invalid".[113]

The pervasive crisis of legitimacy thus soon led to the surfacing of deep cleavages within the republic's power elite. Mousavi clearly recognized this when he sent an open letter to the senior clergy in Qom and Mashhad trying to enlist their support for his campaign of resistance:

> No one imagined this degree of forgery in popular vote right in front of the bewildered world opinion conducted by a government which claims to rest upon justice of the religious law... some elements armed with sticks... are using false excuses to attack members of my election headquarters and those bewildered members of the public visiting the headquarters. There is little hope that the honorable Judiciary, which was not even capable of preventing the dominating candidate to be granted an extra televised address can do anything to stop this black violence. As a part of my duty to guard the popular vote, which has been harmed so greatly, I write to you and beg you hoping that your advice to the authorities may prove effective.

Karroubi, himself a cleric of course, went further and said quite bluntly that "I don't consider this government legitimate".[114] The now 'opposition leader' Mousavi followed and stated that "the majority of the society to which I belong will not recognise the legitimacy of the (future) government.... We will have a government that will have the worst relationship with the people".

Mousavi reiterated the call for a complete new vote after the Guardians Council election watchdog on June 30th declared the poll results to be final following a recount of 10 per cent of ballot boxes: "Our historic duty is to continue the protests to defend the rights of the people... and prevent the blood spilled by hundreds of thousands of martyrs from leading to a police state. I will not compromise on people's rights and votes, which have been stolen.... If we do not resist today we will have no guarantee that such bitter events will not happen again in the future". He continued in the same vein by declaring that he had decided to create, with a group of politicians, "a legal political body to defend citizens' rights and votes that were crushed on June 12, publish documents about the frauds and irregularities and to start legal action". In the same breath Mousavi called for a guarantee of freedom of assembly, a free press, the lifting of bans on independent newspapers and websites and for the possibility to have "an independent television network".[115]

Mousavi thus moved to create an organized force against the neoconservative-dominated ruling faction. This, in essence, was to be the reason for the ferocious attacks on him for the accusations against him and Karroubi of engineering a velvet counter-revolution against the Islamic republic. This was sedition in the eyes of the conservatives close to the Leader and also the neoconservatives allied to the president.

Factionalism, while nothing new in Iran, had now become a grave structural problem and barrier to the nezam's functionality. The very factional-based political structure which had allowed for the rise of political plurality and open competition in Iranian electoral politics was now the base of its crisis. Open competition for office, alongside regular and uninterrupted elections in the thirty-year history of the republic, had made the country unique in a neighbourhood of authoritarian regimes and dictatorships. The regime had boasted on countless occasions that it was legitimate precisely because its people had bought into the system through active participation in elections.

Not until 1997 and the emergence of a strong reform camp did factionalist politics arise as a political problem and the fact that elections were now the means through which change could be brought about that kept a new generation of voters mobilized in 2009. In this context, Ayatollah Rafsanjani's Friday prayer sermon on 17 July, his first for many weeks, was a significant one. His message was clear: Measures adopted by Ahmadinejad's side were detrimental to the survival of the Islamic republic, his excesses were creating and perpetuating an unnecessary and dangerous crisis, thus pushing factional stability to breaking point. Moreover, the leadership's decisions so far had been flawed and some of the government's actions were excessive and beyond the law. Indeed, things were so bad that, he reminded the audience, he had discussed the crisis with the Expediency Council, which he chaired, in order to find a compromise path forward. Far from the Leader's message of take heed of the full force of the security forces and put up, Rafsanjani instead spoke of the need to mend fences and that the process should begin by the freeing of those kept captive since the start of the disturbances. His intervention was in stark contrast to that of the Leader's. Thus, he weighed in:

> As far as the (presidential) election… is concerned… we made a very good start. A sound competition took shape and good preparations were made. The four candidates who were approved by the Guardian Council competed against each other and demonstrated a good competition. The people became hopeful that the elections were completely free and they truly demonstrated an unprecedented participation. In these circumstances the conditions were set for the creation of a proud moment for the country. We have to present this glory to the people. It is their right. It was the people who demonstrated a good presence. The people broke a record as far as the presence at the ballot boxes was concerned. We all have to thank the people who participated freely in the election at a time when no other country

has seen such a level of participation. That was very valuable. I wish those conditions could have continued until today, and today we would have been experiencing the most proud moments in the world regardless of the election results. However, developments did not take shape as we wished them to, and I will explain them now.... What I understand is that towards the end of the election campaign we were taken over by doubt... people started to have doubts and the seeds of doubt were sown.... Whether it was unfavorable publicity or the Voice and Vision's [official media outlets of the state] inappropriate actions or other things, seeds of doubt were planted in the minds of the people. We consider doubt the worst disaster.

Doubt came down on our nation like the plague. Of course, there are two separate currents. There is a group of people who have no doubts.... But there is also another group, whose numbers are not few and include a great section of our erudite and knowledgeable people, who say: 'We doubt.' We should take measures to remove this doubt. This period, after the results of the elections, is a bitter era. I do not believe anyone from any faction wanted this to happen. We have all lost in this event.... We need unity today, more than ever.... I have never wanted to abuse this platform in favor of a particular faction, and my remarks have always concerned issues beyond factionalism. I am talking in the same manner today. I am not interested in any faction. In my view, we should all think and find a way that will unite us, to take our country forward.... What should we do? I have a few suggestions. Of course, I have discussed these suggestions with a few jurists and members of the Expediency Council.... We have decided [that] our important issue is that the trust that brought so many people to the polls, and is now harmed, will be restored. This should be our holy objective, that this trust is returned.... If we accept the... two points that we move in line with the law and leave the door to debate, negotiations and reasoning open, perhaps in a short while we will be satisfied. Meanwhile, we have to do other things. Under current circumstances, there is no need for us to have people in prisons. Allow them to return to their families.... Sympathy should be shown to the victims of the recent incidents which took place. We should offer condolences to those who are mourning and bring their hearts closer to the establishment. And this is possible.[116]

His message of reconciliation was received as a betrayal of the Leader who had already painted the protests as a conspiracy against Islam and counter-revolutionary. There was no room for forgiveness of the gang leaders. So, in saying what he did, not only was Rafsanjani continuing to openly challenge the authenticity of the election result and the role of the Guardian Council therein, but most significantly of all, he was implicitly raising doubt about the role that the Leader himself had played. Rafsanjani's call for an 'open debate' was in effect an open rejection of the Leader's comments in his Friday sermon that demanded an end to questioning of the outcome of the poll. Furthermore, Rafsanjani's reference to the Expediency Council would have reminded the people that he was not without his own levers and that he would have to play a central role in the resolution of the crisis. Indeed, despite his publicized views, in the weeks that followed, Rafsanjani did try to mediate and break the dangerous deadlock and bring the Green Movement leaders into direct contact with the Council of Guardians, but mistrust and intransigence on both sides prevented this from happening.[117] In the end, by snubbing Ahmadinejad's swearing in ceremony, he too apparently decided to terminate his mediation efforts.

The response to his challenge was swift. The state media, parliamentarians and members of such bodies as the Council of Guardians lashed out at Rafsanjani almost immediately. Ayatollah Yazdi (a member of the Guardian Council and also Rafsanjani's deputy) openly questioned and rejected his comments. But the most significant retort came from Ayatollah Khamenei himself, who warned just three days later, with Ahmadinejad by his side, that "the elite should be watchful, since they have been faced with a big test. Failing the test will cause their collapse. Anybody who drives the society toward insecurity and disorder is a hated person in the view of the Iranian nation, whoever he is".[118] Rafsanjani would not be immune from removal. To Ayatollah Khamenei, the outcome of the election was a 'divine miracle' and deviation from this view would be tantamount to 'failing the test'.

Others confronted the disgruntled candidates. The rather powerful and pro-Leader Association of the Self Sacrifices of the Islamic Revolution wrote to Mousavi on the 14th in these terms:

> We are witnessing bitter and provocative postures from you.... Despite the fact that all supervisory institutions have approved of the first round of the elections, non-recognition of the result is a sign of non-abiding by the rules of democracy and politics and lack of love towards the noble and magnanimous nation which has served the Islamic revolution for the past thirty years and created the national epic of June 12th.... All legal channels are open to attend to protests of the candidates against any phase of the execution of the elections and you accepted the framework before entering the race and your representatives have been present at all the voting stations. What religious, rational and legal reasons are there to – rather than pursuing the legal channels of documented protest – making undocumented accusations against authorities of the country for involvement in fraud, lying and treason… and provoke to revolt?"

Post-election crisis caused a rupture between the state and the communities of electorates who have historically provided the legitimacy for the regime through their massive participation in major elections. As former President Khatami stated: "Many people voted because we called for a high turnout. With this result and the way of confrontation (with post-election protests) you can be sure that even us (reformers) cannot ask people to take part in the next election.... This is not in the interest of the establishment".[119] The sense of injustice energized the people and at the same time gave Mousavi the strength to speak for them – to carve the role of the political saviour and the opposition leader for himself. The domestic conditions were ripe for the emergence of a real 'opposition' and this was born with the slogan "Ya Hossein, Mir Hossein!" – the slogan Mousavi's supporters were shouting in Iran. Symbolically, this slogan makes a powerful reference to the Shia Islam's obsession with injustice and its roots as a resistance movement – resistance to the tyranny of the Caliphs and struggle for justice. The martyred Imam (Hossein) symbolizes Shia Islam's spirit of resistance and the allusion to Mousavi's name in the same breath provided a powerful symbolic link between his struggle for electoral justice and Imam Hossein's struggle for justice. The symbolism and also the power of the symbol are clear: Mousavi had been elevated to that of a saviour, pure at heart and not fearful of a struggle, albeit an unequal one. So, it is true to say that "this is a movement that has swept across all dividing lines in Iranian society – both rich and poor, the merchants and the intellectuals, the young and old" are now involved in a national campaign.[120]

Mousavi, the classic establishment figure, was now the elderly revolutionary again and the reform leader. Nevertheless, his position was said to be, according to Hossein Marash (spokesman for the Kargozaran), that he was "not the leader of the opposition to the system. He is the leader of a majority who think their rights are trampled on by Mr Ahmadi-Nejad and the Guardian Council".[121] In late June, however, Mousavi seemed more willing to occupy the mantle of opposition leader, and by early July he was sounding and acting like an opposition leader, stating in direct response to the government's announcements:

> Who believes that they [protesters] would conspire with foreigners and sell the interests of their own country? Has our country become so mean and degraded that you [Ahmadinejad and the Leader] attribute the huge protest movement of the nation to foreigners? Isn't this an insult to our nation? You are facing something new: an awakened nation, a nation that has been born again and is here to defend its achievements.... Arrests ... won't put an end to this problem. End this game as soon as possible and return to the nation its sons.[122]

Significantly, these were words spoken in full view of the public and during a meeting with families of those arrested in the post-election crackdown. The public meeting with these families followed days after Ayatollah Rafsanjani had asked for the release of the detainees in his Friday sermon.

And far from being cowed and accepting that Mousavi had wronged the nezam, his allies rallied more strongly and in an effort to maintain the challenge against the results, former president Khatami came out in July to suggest that the "only way out of the current situation is to hold a referendum. People should be asked whether they are happy with the current situation.... If the vast majority of people are happy with the current situation, we will accept it as well".[123] This intervention in effect continued to challenge the outcome of the vote and the Leader's endorsement of the election results.

In all of this, the theocratic basis of the regime had come under intense pressure. This is best demonstrated through a meaningful exchange between two pro-reform clerics. So, when Hojjatoleslam Kadivar asked, "Can implementing justice be suspended... under the pretext of preserving the regime's interests? What is the believers' religious duty if some position holders confuse the regime's interests with their own, and insist on enforcing their mistake?", Ayatollah Montazeri (one of Shia Islam's most senior figures and also a founding member of the Islamic republic, it should be remembered) replied:

> Clearly, it is not possible to preserve or strengthen the Islamic regime via oppression – which contravenes [the precepts of] Islam. This is because the need for a regime stems [in the first place from the need] to dispense justice and to protect [the people's] rights – that is, to implement the directives of Islam. So how can injustice, oppression and [other] contraventions of Islam possibly [serve to] strengthen or preserve a just Islamic regime? A regime that uses clubs, oppression, aggression… rigged elections, murder, arrests, and medieval or Stalin-era torture, [a regime that] gags and censors the press, obstructs the media, imprisons intellectuals and elected leaders on false allegations or forced confessions… is despicable and has no religious merit.… The nation knows that the false confessions and televised interviews were obtained from its imprisoned sons with threats and torture, and that their aim is to cover up the oppression and injustice, and to [present a] distorted [image] of the people's peaceful and legal protest.… The state belongs to the people. It is neither my property nor yours.… When the Shah heard the voice of the people's revolution, it was already too late [for him]. It is to be hoped that the people in charge [today] will not let [themselves] reach the same situation, but will become more amenable to the nation's demands, and as soon as possible.[124]

Indeed, Ayatollah Rafsanjani drew attention to the philosophical substance of the regime in his 16 July Friday sermon in reminding his audience that "the term Islamic Republic is not a ceremonial title. It is both a republic and Islamic. [Both]… have to be together. If one is damaged, then we will no longer have a revolution and an Islamic Republic".[125]

The alternative view was articulated by Ayatollah Mohammad Yazdi who stated categorically that "in Islam, the legitimacy of a government is granted by God and its acceptance by the people".[126] These debates were reminiscent of a bygone era when the Islamic republic was still looking for a soul to inject into the new political order emerging from the theo-political writings of Ayatollah Khomeini. Such issues were last articulated in this manner in the late 1980s when Khomeini's own intervention had ostensibly ended the debates about religion and state in the Islamic republic. In criticizing Rafsanjani's sermon, Yazdi chose to revisit those theo-political debates and drew a different picture of the IRI in which the people had to obey the Leader as the faith's champion on earth. These debates, which had plagued the regime thirty years prior, had returned to test the legitimacy and identity of the Islamic republic, question the source of authority in Iran, and open the hotly contested issues raised during Khatami's presidency regarding the balance between the republican dimension of the nezam and the Islamic side of it. The renewed discussion of such questions was akin to throwing incendiary devices into a smouldering fire – they helped fan the intellectual flames and raised even more questions about the legitimacy of the theocratic dimension of the republic and its relevance to governance.

Post-election crisis and the region

As the drama on the streets of Iran's towns and cities unfolded, Secretary of State Hillary Clinton said, at the end of June, that Tehran now suffered from "a huge credibility gap". The idea that the Shii, as thus far exemplified in the Iranian system, had a working model of political jurisprudence now appeared unproven. Indeed, as the authority of Najaf grew following the 2003 war in Iraq, more questions were raised about the authenticity of Iran's system of government. And the more Iranian citizens questioned their own system, the wider the credibility gap became.

The shockwaves of the post-election crisis in the Islamist regime *par excellance* were felt across the region, just as the shockwaves of its 1979 revolution had been felt well beyond its borders. Political Islam had to find new ways of absorbing the blow to the credibility of its widely used slogan 'Islam is the solution'. The 'solution' patently was not to be found in the world's only revolutionary Islamic state, and this reality energized Sunni Islamist groups to present their own ideas of 'Islamic government', while more extreme Sunni groups saw in the political crisis in Iran the bankruptcy of Shia theology, the Shia model. The pro-Wahhabi and pro-al-Qaeda radical Sunni groups jumped on the crisis in Iran to mount new ideological and political attacks on an apparently vulnerable regime. By attacking the Shia-based power of the regime, they could try to discredit the Shia as a viable political community in the Muslim world and also contain their political pressure in the GCC countries. The damage to Iran's credibility as a just and accountable Islamic state model was so great that it could no longer claim the mantle of legitimate revolutionary leadership of the umma, which to Ayatollah Khamenei was a personal and political blow for which he held Mousavi and Karroubi directly responsible. These gentlemen's sedition was against the Islamic republic, which by definition was against Islam.

On the nuclear front, as Iran had remained unwilling to reduce let alone suspend its enrichment activities, it was difficult to see how the parties could avert further tensions. Of course, the elections in Iran could have played a crucial part in giving the new president the mandate to negotiate a way out of the crisis. A post-Ahmadinejad president in 2009 could have used his new mandate to re-open unconditional dialogue with the IAEA and the 5+1 even if the nuclear issue was not an electoral issue, on the basis that he was elected to improve Iran's relations with the outside world and to improve the socioeconomic situation at home. By 13 June, that opportunity was in doubt. Indeed, the strategic climate considerably worsened. We see here an example of the seriousness of the situation:

> In short, the stolen election and its tumultuous aftermath have dramatically highlighted the strategic and tactical flaws in Obama's game plan. With regime change off the table for the coming critical period in Iran's nuclear program, Israel's decision on using force is both easier and more urgent. Since there is no likelihood that diplomacy will start or finish in time, or even progress far enough to make any real difference, there is no point waiting for negotiations to play out. In fact, given the near certainty of Obama changing his definition of 'success,' negotiations represent an even more dangerous trap for Israel. Those who oppose Iran acquiring nuclear weapons are left in the near term with only the option of targeted military force against its weapons facilities. Significantly, the uprising in Iran also makes it more likely that an effective public diplomacy campaign could be waged in the country to explain to Iranians that such an attack is directed against the regime, not against the Iranian people. This was always true, but it has become even more important to make this case emphatically, when the gulf between the Islamic revolution of 1979 and the citizens of Iran has never been clearer or wider. Military action against Iran's nuclear program and the ultimate goal of regime change can be worked together consistently.[127]

Such views carried some weight in certain policy-related communities in Washington, and resurrection of the strategy of 'regime change' of what was now portrayed as a discredited Iranian regime struck a chord with the Iranian leadership who even more vigorously hoisted Ahmadinejad's flag of defiance. The Leader's emphatic endorsement of the election result, coupled by the use of detention and force against protestors, and against the background of external pressure, had sealed the fate of the Green Movement. The show trials that were staged in the weeks following the election provided the means for discrediting the opposition and intimidating the public but also the removal of the top echelons of the Green Movement. Cajoling such prominent Mousavi allies as Shahebedin Tabatabae to say in court that "Mousavi started the face-off with the government by insisting elections were rigged", was meant to silence the opposition, but going further to suggest that Mousavi "was delusional from the start and it was his idea to bring people to the streets" would portion the blame for the disturbances on an unhinged character who could not possibly be trusted to lead a government.[128]

It came as no surprise that by early 2010, little organizational life was left in the protest movement. Indeed, the hundreds of arrests and death of several protestors during the massive and at times violent protest rallies marking Ashoura (a day of mourning in the Shiism marking Imam Hossein's martyrdom in AD 680) in December 2009, in which a nephew of Mousavi was assassinated by plain clothes security men, left little doubt of the regime's strategy. To drive the message home, a senior cleric and ally of Khamenei (Ayatollah Ahmad Khatami) demanded that the "judiciary needs to act firmly and there is no room for tolerance".[129]

Despite the gallant efforts of sympathetic critics of the nezam in exile who had issued a 'manifesto' for reform of the Islamic republic, no room for dialogue remained. The manifesto itself, released in early 2010 by the prominent intellectuals of the reform movement, Abdolkarim Soroush, Mohsen Kadivar, Ataollah Mohajerani, Akbar Ganji and Abdolali Bazargan (son of the republic's first prime minister), was designed to provide a 'positive theoretical base' for the revolutionary movement which overthrew the Shah in 1979, according to Soroush.[130] In it the signatories demanded the immediate resignation of Ahmadinejad followed by fresh presidential elections, abolishing the vetting and veto powers of the Council of Guardians, release of all political prisoners, putting on trial those who had been involved in torture and abuse of citizens' civil rights, the removal of barriers to political activity, lifting of restrictions imposed on the independent media, establishment of an independent judiciary, freeing universities from political meddling, and the removal of IRGC influence from all political and economic activities.

The death of Ayatollah Montazeri – the spiritual voice of the opposition movement – on 20 December 2009 provided another pothole for the movement to negotiate, depriving it of a powerful advocate in the regime's powerbase, the Qom religious seminaries. Montazeri played a crucial legitimizing role for the opposition movement and, as is clear from his last major intervention (in a letter issued to the clerical leaders [Marjas] and establishment in September), he also provided the justification for opposing the ruling establishment. He began by stating:

> The goal [of the revolution] was not simply to change the names and slogans but then keep the same oppression and abuses by the previous regime.... Everyone knows that I am a defender of theocratic government... although not in the current form. The difference lies in the fact that I intended the people to choose the jurist and supervise his work.... I now feel ashamed before the attentive people of Iran because of the tyranny conducted under his banner.... What we now see is the government of a military guardianship, not the Guardianship of the Islamic jurists.

His most powerful comments appeared under point three of the letter, by the end of which he was urging the clerical leadership to speak up and not allow their silence to be interpreted as acquiescence:

> Those incidents and atrocities that occurred after the presidential election, seen and heeded by the honourable Marjas and respectable scholars, should

sound the alarm for them and for the clergy. Actions such as the violation of human rights, oppression, and so on – all of these indiscretions committed in the name of religion took place with the assent of a small group of subservient clerics who are in favor of the government. What followed was a peaceful objection involving numerous classes of people who were critical of recent events. They acted within their legal and religious rights, based on the 27th article of the constitution. Instead of wisely and positively acknowledging the voice of a people seeking justice and the restoration of their violated rights, the authorities labelled the multi-million strong masses as insurgents, anarchists, and foreign agents. They then proceeded with a clampdown of the utmost violence, beating defenseless men and women, detaining many, and creating some martyrs on the streets and others in their horrifying prisons. Relying on their military and security forces, and by drawing firearms on defenseless people, the government has both martyred and imprisoned the innocent.... During the clampdown, the government detained politicians, political activists and gifted citizens of the country, each of whom had devoted years of invaluable service to the Islamic Republic. Based on pre-determined plans and against all religious and legal regulations, the authorities began a plot against them by forcing false confessions and displaying them in unlawful, dishonest and theatrical trials. As a result, the entire world ridiculed the legal system of Islam. As a result, the entire world has ridiculed the legal system of Islam.[131]

Montazeri's untimely death and the incarceration of Mousavi and Karroubi under house arrest further dampened the mood and the act of incarceration in itself came to symbolize the nation's predicament: The people had to go home, silently, and wait for another day to return to the streets.

Lame duck president?

But in focusing on the post-election political crisis engulfing the Islamic republic, we should not lose sight of the many domestic and external challenges (discussed earlier) that continued to plague the government. The socioeconomic situation remained perilous (inflation, unemployment, corruption remain serious handicaps), the crippling impact of the combination of US-UN-EU sanctions on Iran's financial and non-oil trade sectors was not removed (indeed intensified in the post-2009 period), soft oil prices challenged the spending power of the government leading to the inevitable problem of budget deficits. Regionally, the post-election crisis adversely affected Iran's regional appeal and also the legitimacy of its voice as the region's only authentic and popularly supported, and therefore legitimate, Muslim state. Not only were its allies on the defensive – as Karim Sadjadpour put it: "Hezbollah is now in the awkward position of being a resistance group purportedly fighting injustice, while simultaneously cashing checks from an Iranian patron that is brutally suppressing justice at home"[132] – but also its voice in relation to wider Shia issues was being morally challenged by 'quietist' Najaf, the traditional bedrock of Shia thought in the Muslim world. Ironically, Khamenei's efforts to blunt American pressure had had the opposite effect: Weakness and uncertainty at home had made Iran vulnerable abroad. Ahmadinejad was expected to put this right.

The summer of 2009 was a watershed for the Islamic republic: First, the relationship between state and society had changed, and while an eerie political silence had been imposed on the streets and cyberspace, social forces appeared able to operate in fora and spaces beyond the regime's grasp. Society was fighting to throw the state off of its back, and the more that state pressured the people, the more they pushed back through subtle acts of resistance. Second, at a fundamental level, the relationship between the forces that had made up the Iranian power elite had changed and previously strong bonds were either severed or suspended. The zero-sum game played out by the elite had made compromise supremely difficult to achieve. As Mozaffari noted,

> Now, it is no longer a matter of election fraud. The issue is not Ahmadinejad as a personality, or the role of the Guardians Council vetting body, or who is the supreme leader. The entire structure of the Islamic republic is under question and the era of public political apathy is over. The protest movement has already weakened the Islamic regime considerably. No matter how the ruling elite manages the situation, the days of the Islamic republic in its current form are numbered. It won't happen tomorrow, but the new will of the people may yet sweep away both the ayatollahs and the IRGC.[133]

There was the very real danger that if the political establishment had failed to re-establish order, then it would have left the country open to intervention by the Guard – constitutionally assigned as the guardians of the Islamic revolution – to become involved and, in the interest of nezam and revolution, hold the balance of power.[134] An overtly militarized regime would not have been good for Iranians or the neighbouring region. Failure of power at the heart of the Islamist republic, therefore, could have taken the country in two directions:

> Iran is at a crossroads.... One road is complete militarization and control of the people and being completely cut off from the rest of the world like North Korea, and another road is being the dictatorship it is but opening up to the rest of the world and moving forward with the rest of the world in technology, in athletics and many other respects, which would in turn naturally provide a little bit more freedom for the youth each step of the way.[135]

Given the domestic context for his second term, and pressure from the outside (Obama's apparent iron handshake), once he was re-established in office,

Ahmadinejad's administration was swift in stifling any space for protest. And apart from direct repression, his team set about emasculating virtually all the organizations and parties associated with the old reform movement and the new Green Movement. So in April 2010, the administration outlawed the largest reformist party (the IIPF) and the longstanding left-leaning Mujahedeen of the Islamic Revolution, which had developed links with the reform camp from the mid-1990s for "violating the sovereignty of the country, spreading accusations and lies, undermining national unity, and planning the breakup of the country".[136] These were grave charges indeed and were intended to put into the judiciary's way the leadership of these organizations, as had already been the case with the jailing (six-year sentences each) of three prominent reformists of Mostafa Tajzadeh, Davood Soleimani, and Mohsen Mirdamadi (secretary general of IIPF) in the same month. Perhaps as many as 200 activists and reformist leaders had already been arrested in June 2009 and the pressure mounted from then on. An eye-witness account of the prevailing political conditions related that "in the 10 months since the poll, the prevailing atmosphere has grown queasy with fear and suspicion. Months of arrest, detentions, harsh sentencing, forced confessions, reports of people being raped or beaten to death in detention, and televised show trials have cast such fear that some Iranians have begun comparing the atmosphere to the one that prevailed in the Iraq of Saddam and the Baath Party".[137]

Reinforcing such accounts of repression were such government acts as banning the country's most popular elected person, former president Khatami, from traveling abroad, partly to degrade him and also in fear of this charismatic figure becoming an exile opposition figure. This was not as fanciful as it appeared for links with the outside world had been a worry of the Leader for some time and in the state's post-election narrative of successfully defeating the velvet revolution the links with the networked and wealthy diaspora had become a major focal point. Severing the purported links between the 'insiders' and 'outsiders' was a priority and thus "dozens of individuals in the U.S. and Europe who criticized Iran on Facebook or Twitter said their relatives back in Iran were questioned or temporarily detained because of their postings".[138] Many were questioned at the airport on arrival in Iran and were required to show their Facebook accounts to prove that they had not posted pro-opposition messages.

Furthermore, the nature of his presidential victory and his obvious total dependence on the Leader's protection fuelled Ahmadinejad's resentment of the establishment as a whole and the Leader's decisive role in shaping state policies in particular. The president hated being seen as a puppet, and the more the Leader defended the election results the more vulnerable Ahmadinejad appeared. This partly accounts for his open hostility towards the Leader from 2010, as with his abrupt dismissal of the country's foreign minister, Manouchehr Mottaki, in December of that year during his official tour of East Africa, and his refusal to obey the Leader's order to remove from his office his close friend and confidant, Esfandiar Rahim Mashaei. By appointing Mashaei as his chief of staff, Ahmadinejad basically gave his confidant even more authority as his gatekeeper.

Ahmadinejad's efforts to further assert his cabinet authority was tested again in April 2011 over the political tensions between the minister of intelligence in his second administration, Hojjatoleslam Heydar Moslehi, and Mashaei. Ahmadinejad's unilateral action to demote Moslehi to the position of 'intelligence advisor' to the president was not only roundly condemned by conservatives but brought a rare direct intervention from the Leader who pointedly instructed the minister not to resign and the president to reappoint Moslehi to his ministerial post.[139] Ahmadinejad's eleven-day long refusal to carry out his presidential duties in protest to the Leader's interference in the cabinet's affairs further deepened the chasm between the two. In this period, Ahmadinejad's disdain for the clergy's role in politics and the economy became more evident and by the same token their concerns about him and his associates became more pronounced. The intra-elite crisis acquired such dimensions that in 2011 and in true Orwellian tradition the Leader's allies alluded to the existence of what they called a 'deviant current' at the heart of Ahmadinejad's administration, which had to be purged. This resulted in the arrest and imprisonment of several of his close aides and the irreconcilable rift between him and the Leader. In August 2012, intra-conservative tensions had reached the point of no return and resulted in parliamentarians, former ministers and former officials imploring the Majlis and the Leader to intervene, 'in the interest of the nezam', to limit Ahmadinejad's abilities to make decisions in the last year of his presidency.[140]

Ahmadinejad's second term did not start well, as we have seen. His dependence on the traditional conservatives and also the clerical establishment, which he had come to despise, had increased, and he could not shake off the suspicion that he had won the presidency through fraud. For these reasons, coupled by the deeper securitization of the state following the 2009 protests, Ahmadinejad started his second term even more aggressively than his first. His first targets were the conservatives and in particular the conservative-dominated eighth Majlis, which had been his core institutional base of support in the run up to the presidential elections. By suggesting that the parliament had become an irrelevant body in running the country's affairs, his allies were raising a question asked a decade earlier about whether Iran would in fact be better served under a presidential system and without the Majlis' interference in the executive's grave task of running the only revolutionary Islamic state in the world. Reformists and principlists alike took exception to the assertion that Ayatollah Khomeini himself had placed the executive branch above the other two pillars of the nezam, the judiciary and legislature.[141]

Other factors contributed to the executive branch's disenchantment with the legislature, including the Majlis' probing into economic deals involving companies or trusts belonging to the IRGC. In two instances following Ahmadinejad's re-election in 2009, the Majlis had questioned the efficacy of transferring control of major assets to the IRGC, and then at knocked-down prices.[142] The first related to the transfer for $2 billion in a privatization scheme of the Middle East's largest zinc and lead mine, at a fraction of the government's own real valuation of $6 billion. The second case was that of the country's telecommunications monopoly to a Guard-affiliate company for $8 billion, giving the IRGC control of the country's communications infrastructure.

Majlis' nervousness echoed the wider concerns with Ahmadinejad's plans to cut the billions of dollars paid out in subsidies every year to keep the prices of basic necessities (electricity, fuel and petrol, bread and other staple food stuffs) below the market rate. While the elite was fully aware of the negative impact of subsidies on the economy, such a move could also cause social chaos and reignite mass protests, which had only recently died down. The regime as a whole appeared ill-prepared to manage the political fallout of such a radical economic policy, particularly as it already had its eye on the government's interference in the country's fragile banking system, which was requiring banks to lend money with little due diligence and at artificially low interest rates. "So the banks on the one hand are unable to attract depositors because they can't pay interest enough to match at least the inflation rate… and at the other end, the money they have lent out they are not able to recoup", argued the noted economist Salehi-Isfahani.[143]

Despite the political and economic crisis engulfing his administration, Ahmadinejad pressed on and until the end of his term remained unrepentant, sticking to the line that Iranians had never had it so good as during his presidency. Far from acting as a lame-duck president, he continued to develop policies, actively interact with the public and also state institutions. He had tried to take control of key ministries (in particular intelligence, defence, foreign affairs) often regarded as more loyal to the Leader than the president, and even transform intelligence from a ministry to a bureau (and therefore under direct charge of the president). In May 2012, notably, he even attempted a major cabinet restructuring by proposing to merge eight ministries into four, an act that the parliament deemed illegal without a legislative process, and even took strong positions against some of the Majlis' own proposed legislation. Most notably, the president opposed the tightening of the vetting process for elected office under discussion in the Majlis in late 2012 and early 2013 as unconstitutional. This bill had proposed that anyone running for president would have to be 45 to 75 years of age, thus barring from such office senior figures like Ayatollah Rafsanjani, and have had at least eight years' experience in government service. In addition, candidates would have to receive the approval of twenty-five members of the Assembly of Experts as well as documented approval of one hundred members of the Majlis, and to have attained a master's degree or the equivalent from a seminary level of education.[144]

In the last analysis, though, the populists who had promised the world in the end delivered little. The political system was in crisis, the country was internationally isolated and under intense financial pressure, and the clamour for change would just not die down. By the end of Ahmadinejad's term and a century after Iran's constitutional revolution, which had given birth to the modern Iranian state, the country was still searching for a viable model of governance and in this it was back fighting old battles "and grappling with how to achieve a democratic state".[145]

2013: clocks go forward or back?

As has been demonstrated in this chapter, elections matter in Iran, in shaping the political balance of power in the country and in determining the country's direction of travel. As we have seen, the eventual winners of the 1989, 1997 and 2005 elections all managed to put their own unique stamp on the country, and each government made a major impression on the country's social, political and economic affairs, and to a certain extent on its international relations. Unquestionably, Iran's presidential elections, more than any other form of electoral representation, also show the importance of agency in the shaping of the country's policies.

The 2013 elections will be remembered, apart from the swift victory of Hassan Rouhani, for the rejection of Hashemi Rafsanjani and Esfandiar Mashaei as candidates, the two problematic candidates for the Leader. While the first former accepted the rejection of his candidacy without much fuss, creating any controversy,[146] the latter had threatened, supported by a strong complaint from the outgoing President Ahmadinejad, to wage a legal battle to have the Guardian Council review (i.e. reverse) its decision – something that had occurred only once in previous elections. Surprisingly, that final move never happened, and both Mashaei and Ahmadinejad remained quiet, accepting the final decision of the GC and indeed the election's surprising outcome. But Rafsanjani and Mashaei did not provide the only shocks: Another surprise was the rejection of another insider candidate, namely Manouchehr Mottaki, former minister of foreign affairs between 2005 and 2010. Having in mind his experience in foreign policy and close ties with the conservative camp as well as Ayatollah Khamenei, he would have expected to stand a good chance in the elections and probably receive more votes than other candidates such as Jalili or Velayati. Ali Fallahian, former ministry of intelligence (1989–97), Elias Hazrati and Mohammad Kavakevian (members of Parliament) were among the 678 rejected applications, but none of them generated such a controversy as Mashaei and Rafsanjani did. Although the name of the former reformist president Mohammad Khatami was mentioned as a possible candidate, he explicitly declined to participate in favour of Aref's candidacy as the leading, indeed only, reform candidate.

From the eight candidates finally accepted by the Guardian Council, three had considerable foreign policy experience, above all relating to nuclear negotiations. This, together with the hypothesis that the final televised debate on foreign policy defined the outcome of the election, demonstrated how important the regional and international environment had become for the country and for every Iranian. Ali Akbar Velayati was minister of foreign affairs for sixteen straight years, during the presidencies of Khamenei (1981–89) and Rafsanjani (1989–97), including the difficult years of war against Iraq. Hassan Rouhani was secretary of the national security council between 1989 and 2005 and accordingly served as the chief nuclear negotiator with the EU-3 group during Khatami's presidency; and Saeed Jalili was head of the nuclear negotiation team in the protracted talks with the 5+1 group and since 2007 was secretary of the national security council. Arguably, Velayati, as personal foreign policy adviser to the Leader, would have most faithfully represented the foreign policy thinking and decisions of the Leader, which would have theoretically facilitated a more constructive approach in the nuclear negotiations. Despite an agreement reached in April 2013 among Bagher Qalibaf (also a former presidential candidate in 2005) and Gholam Haddad Adel (Majlis Speaker between 2004 and 2008, and Ayatollah Khamenei's relative by marriage) and Velayati that two would withdraw in favour of the most popular candidate during the last week of campaign, only Haddal Adel did so, which left the conservative vote divided between Velayati and Qalibaf.

Another candidate, Mohsen Rezaei, had stood for the presidency in 2005 and 2009. In 2005 he withdrew a few days before the elections, speaking out about 'manoeuvres' aimed at undermining his candidacy. In 2009 he condemned the results but did not take part in the pro-Mousavi mobilizations, content with the outcome of the Council of Guardians' limited investigation of the vote. Although Rezaei is considered to have had a big following among the Revolutionary Guard, the results in 2009 and 2013 have shown that such a base had moved its allegiance to another candidate (Ahmadinejad). Rezaei's unsuccessful bids for the presidency also showed that IRGC leadership was in itself an insufficient tool for translating military stature into votes.

As already noted, the only candidate considered as a 'reformist' was Mohammad Reza Aref, a former minister and also vice president in Khatami's administration. Following the 2009 post-electoral protests, many reformist politicians were imprisoned and given life bans from political activity. Aref thus was one of few from the reform camp to be allowed to take part in the contest. Aref's chances of success in the presidential race were always seen as being small, but his presence did give the elections a wider base at the same time as giving the reform camp a voice and a reason for engaging with the electoral process.

Hojjatoleslam Rouhani's election success was not preordained and the conservative establishment certainly did not place him as a leading candidate. Indeed, BBC Persian service analyst, Hossein Bastani, citing local sources, argued that support for Rouhani in the Leader's office was scant, alleging that

> [T]he ballot box (no. 110) that was sited at the office of the Supreme Leader's, and which thus contained the votes of Ayatollah Khamenei and members of his entourage, held fewer than 20 votes for Rouhani. This was said to compare with 200 votes and 124 votes, respectively, for candidates Saeed Jalili, a former nuclear negotiator seen as a close ally of Khamenei, who came third in the national results, and Mohammad Bagher Qalibaf, the popular mayor of Tehran, who came second.[147]

That said, while Ahmadinajed's victory in 2005 and the controversial conditions surrounding his re-election in 2009 silenced Nateq-Nouri until 2013, when he resurfaced on the eve of the presidential poll he veered towards Rafsanjani and Khatami and supported Rouhani's bid in the presidential race.

Rouhani's victory, arguably, benefited from the confluence of several rather distinct factors. First, Rouhani got a boost from reformist Mohammad Reza Aref's withdrawal from the race on June 11th, just three days before the election. But Aref also went on to give his explicit backing to Rouhani, which boosted Rouhani's credentials amongst the reformists considerably. Second, in what appeared to be a surprising move, the two former presidents Hashemi Rafsanjani and Khatami warmly endorsed Rouhani as their preferred presidential candidate. Rouhani's appeal, they said, would go well beyond the reformist community and make him an attractive candidate for the more conservative sections of society and even some clerics in Qom.[148] Third, and perhaps most importantly, Rouhani also enjoyed the goodwill of the Leader. Given that he had been the Leader's representative on the country's supreme strategic body, the supreme national security council, and had longstanding links with the Leader, he had Ayatollah Khamenei's confidence. The other factor that propelled Rouhani to the front was the absence of unity on the conservative side. The conservatives' inability to coalesce around a single credible candidate meant that their support base was divided and fragmented. As the three leading conservatives (Qalibaf, Jalili and Velayati) competed for the endorsement of the Leader, they undermined each other's positions and the conservative cause. Interestingly, opinion polls did not rate them as popular candidates in any case so they were unlikely to swing voters behind themselves but their politics also showed them to be out of touch with the aspirations of the majority of Iranians.

Despite the apparent popularity of the reformist candidates, opinion polls did not give them a commanding lead and, based on opinion polls, few observers expected an outright winner in the first round of the elections. There were flashes, however, as the IPOS poll[149] signalled rising level of support for Rouhani following the widely watched televised debate. Thus, from just 8.1 per cent on 6th June (before the last debate) Rouhani's support rose to 14.4 per cent on 10 June. The 10th of June was the day that Aref pulled out of the race so allegiance to Rouhani would have risen as a consequence. But his popularity rating began to climb swiftly to 26.6 per cent on 11 June and to 31.7 per cent on 12 June. This was the last day in which opinion polls were conducted and proved to be an indicator of the direction of travel. Interestingly, the popularity of his principal rival, Qalibaf, plummeted following the debate. He had fashioned himself as a defender of the youth's interests and experienced enough to help promote the country's national security. His poll rating dropped from a high of 39 per cent on 6 June to 24.4 per cent on 12 June. In the course of a few days, Rouhani had emerged as the leading candidate and on the eve of the poll atmospheric indicators pointed to him emerging as victorious. He did win and as Table 2.8 shows, not only did he manage to win in the first round of the elections but he did so with a wide margin. Worth noting is that the conservative vote totalled 12.3 million, far short of Rouhani's 18.6 million. Rouhani presented his victory as a triumph against extremism.

TABLE 2.8 Presidential election, 2013

Candidate	No. of votes	Percentage
Rouhani	18,613,329	50.71
Qalibaf	6,077,292	16.56
Jalili	4,168,946	11.36
Rezaei	3,884,412	10.58
Velayati	2,268,753	6.18
Gharazi	446,015	1.22
Voter turnout	36,704,156	72.70

Source: Ministry of Interior.

Hassan Rouhani emerged as the lead and victorious candidate of the republic's eleventh presidential elections. With an official turnout of 72 per cent – less than the 84 per cent announced in 2009 – the 2013 presidential elections managed to fulfil the first of the goals established by the political class, namely the re-legitimation of the political system, recuperation of the population's trust in elections and especially in election results, which had been so publicly and massively contested in the summer of 2009. His clear victory gave Rouhani the legitimacy he needed for engagement at the international level, as well as the mandate. The rate of congratulating telegrams pouring in from across the world provided further evidence of support for his presidency following Ahmadinejad's confrontational policies. Rouhani, however, was conscious of the narrow margin of his victory and the limitations that this would place on him. It was clear from July onwards that he would need the backing of the reformists, as much as the conservatives – who still controlled the Majlis – for pushing through his foreign policy priorities and for dealing with the country's myriad of domestic problems. He thus sought consensus building, backed by the Leader, as his main strategy. His slogan of 'Government of Hope and Prudence' had raised expectations but it was clear that compromises with the conservative establishment would require him to limit the extent of reforms that could be introduced.

Horse trading has had a lasting effect and while some progress has been made, in socio-cultural areas his administration had found prudent, or impossible, to lift social pressures imposed by the judiciary and the religious establishment. The point to note is that Rouhani has been at the heart of the Iranian power elite since 1980. He has been secretary and representative of the supreme defence council (1983–88), commander of the Iranian air defences (1985–91), deputy commander of Iran's armed forces (1988–89), national security adviser to the president (1989–97) and secretary of the supreme national security council (1989–2005). This is in addition to his role as an MP, member of key parliamentary committees as well as deputy speaker of Majlis. So he can be summed up as an 'establishment rebel', if that is not a contradiction in terms. He is a product of this system and has been with it all his life. But at the same time his open-mindedness and willingness to improve relations with the outside world have served well in the nuclear negotiations and also in building support for his domestic economic agenda. His general popularity at home has cast him as an advocate of 'controlled' social freedoms as well, which he has used to great effect to keep the young people with him.

While President Rouhani has been clear about what needs to be done domestically and in foreign policy terms, and although his largely technocratic cabinet appointments have given clear indication of his pragmatist instincts, nevertheless, he is tied to the principles that the Leader has for so long espoused.[150] Rouhani has been painfully aware that he cannot change the power dynamics of the regime overnight. Yet the longer he waits, the easier it has become for the conservatives to regroup and to challenge his government. This they have done in the course of parliamentary questioning and the introduction of legislation once it became clear in April 2016 that their grip on the Majlis would be lost to pro-Rouhani parliamentarians of the tenth Majlis. By lighting a number of slow-burning fuses under legislative equivalent of improvised explosive devices, the conservatives hoped to cripple the administration and tie the new Majlis up into so many knots that they would find it impossible to serve the policy agenda of the executive.[151]

Political power and nuclear politics

The most direct political fallout of the JCPOA can be seen in the struggle for the control of Iran's representative institutions, and in this regard there is no institution more important than the parliament. The control of this institution following the nuclear deal became the domestic political football to fight over. Often the very public intense negotiations with the world's most important powers instilled a sense of pride in the besieged Islamic republic and pumped Iranians' sense of self-importance and international relevance. That the mighty United States eagerly sat around the same negotiating dinner, lunch, and breakfast tables with the political leaders of the Islamic republic showed to the world – as far as the regime was concerned – that Iran was central to regional diplomacy. The very public negotiations apparently also provided vindication for the Leader's hitherto hard-line position on dealing with the United States only on Iran's terms – that is, for the United States to accept the Iranian revolution, recognize the Islamic republic as a credible and legitimate regional power, not interfere in its internal affairs, and end the obstruction of its rise as a major Middle Eastern if not Asian power.

It is debatable, however, that unhooking the sanctions chain improved in any perceptible sense the regime's domestic popularity. The popularity of the president and his team was certainly assured by the success of the negotiations, but this success provided – more than anything – vindication of the people's own crafty calculations in the presidential race of eight candidates and their wise decision to elect this particular person as their presidential candidate of choice to lead them and negotiate Iran's way out of its painful isolation. This success showed the power of the middle ground in Iran and the urban masses' ability to decisively use the institutional tools of the regime at any given opportunity to instil change. If anything, therefore, for the hardliners the success of people power was going to pose a greater challenge for the regime than anything else. So the February 2016 elections, and majority control of the (fifth) eighty-eight-seat Assembly of Experts, which is responsible for the appointment and monitoring of the Islamic republic's Supreme Leader, became the targets of factional struggles. Just as the reform and centrist camps rubbed their hands with glee at the prospects of being able to cash in on the 'political dividend' from the JCPOA and planned to ride the popularity of Rouhani's negotiating success to a parliamentary majority, so the security establishment worked behind the scenes and with the tacit approval of the Council of Guardians (the final vetting station of self-registered candidates) to block en masse reformist and centrist self-nominees for election to the parliament. Rouhani's allies sought to maximize the return on a successfully negotiated agreement with the international community, which led to the lifting of sanctions on the country, by taking control of the legislative and other such elected organs of the state in which the voice of the people matters. Thus, an unprecedented number of candidates put themselves forward as potential candidates for February 2016's Majlis elections.

The next big test for Rouhani's coalition presented itself then and a record 12,000 individuals applied for candidacy (compared with 5,500 in 2012), but the Council of Guardians disqualified over half of them. This caused serious concern amongst the reformist and centrist camps about the intentions of the hardline elements in the regime closely aligned with the Council, the Revolutionary Guard and the Leader's office. According to Seyyed Hossein Marashi, a member of the Reformist Policymaking Council, of the 3,000 reformist candidates who initially registered, only 30 were approved to run. Marashi "criticized the disqualifications and said they contradicted the statements by the supreme leader and stand in opposition to the political system of the country".[152] This, he said, "is the biggest number of disqualifications in [Iran's] history". The president entered the fray and announced at a news conference on 18th of January, marking the lifting of sanctions on the country, that he would act: "the primary reports I've received [about the vetting process] did not make me happy at all. I will use all my power to protect the rights of candidates".[153]

While 1,500 of the disbarred candidates were reinstated under pressure from the government, few of these were reformists, leaving in the race a total of 90 reformists in a larger list of 233 pro-reform candidates. The conservatives' assumption of numerical superiority in the list of declared candidates did little to encourage the emergence of a coordinated conservative list. In fact, conservative lists proliferated as key sub-groups mobilized to take control of the conservative camp. Ali Larijani, Majlis speaker, was quick to announce a new coalition of Followers of the Velayat (Leadership), followed by Mohammadreza Bahonar's Conservative Majority Coalition, the neoconservatives-linked Yekta Front and formerly Ahmadinejad-supporter Paydar Front, and senior cleric-led (Ayatollahs Mesbah-Yazdi and Ayatollah Yazdi) Council for a Conservative Alliance.

To add salt to injury, 80 per cent of the 800 candidates for the Assembly of Experts (most of whom were pro-Rouhani candidates) were also barred from standing for lack of sufficient religious knowledge, which in the end left some 77 pro-reform candidates in the election to the assembly. In a sign of rising tensions within the establishment over these important elections, Ayatollah Rafsanjani, himself a member of this assembly, quipped, "Where did you [the Council of Guardians] get your qualifications? Who allowed you to judge?", for which he received an immediate slapping down by another senior cleric (the Friday prayer leader of Mashhad, Ayatollah Ahmad Alamolhoda) for "pleasing the enemy and paving the way for [their] influence".[154]

The entrenched conservative and security-linked forces, those who had thus far materially benefited from the sanctions, and those who opposed the negotiations with the 'Great Satan' as counter-revolutionary and dangerous for the value-based Islamic regime – saw in the nuclear deal an existential threat.[155] These groups, who are peppered in the establishment, drew closer together despite their own ideological differences, to contain the danger of reformists marching again by intimidating into silence the known members of the reform camp and also independent and pro-reform journalists. They mobilized to ensure that Rouhani's peace dividend would not give a reinvigorated reform camp success at their expense. Their initial strategy was intimidation and tighter control of cyberspace through which Iran's youthful population communicated and socialized.[156] The judiciary and the IRGC establishment, still under the control of hardliners and ideologues, used their powers to cow the opinion makers into compliance with their strict interpretations of acceptable social and political exchanges. In this, they enjoyed the support of the Leader who had said in September 2015 that the country's security and judicial authorities should be alive to the "political and cultural" infiltration of the country by the United States. Statements of this nature were repeated at rallies and gatherings, arguably providing the justification for the security authorities to go after political and social deviants in order to prevent the Islamic republic's moral corruption. Thus, those suspected of incitement, insulting the Islamic republic, denigrating Islam, promoting Western values, displaying behaviour inconsistent with Muslim culture, were systematically persecuted from 2014 onwards – when it had become clear that the nuclear negotiations would be concluded successfully and that the Majlis would bless the outcome.

So, the Guard's own website, Gerdab, announced in the middle of the delicate international negotiations in autumn 2015 that the Guard's cyber unit in Qazvin Province had identified 170 individuals said to be "managers of groups active in mobile social networks" who were taken into custody by the Guard's own Intelligence Organization.[157] For maximum effect, this announcement was also carried by the Fars news agency, which is known to act as the mouthpiece of the Revolutionary Guard. The Fars report stated that the detainees were picked up for acting "against moral security".[158] They were responsible for distributing "indecent and immoral" material though texting and transferring images that "encouraged people to commit obscene acts". The arrested individuals were accused of "insult[ing] ethnic minorities, officials and distinguished national figures" in their texts and circulations. To legitimize this act, the Fars news agency echoed the Guard's own statement that these individuals had been handed over to the authorities for prosecution, implying that they were transferred to the judiciary for attention. But in practice this had not been the case, and the judiciary's own official spokesman Gholamhossein Mohseni Ejei, declared a day later, that his office had "asked the Judiciary officials in Qazvin and found out that the recent report regarding the arrest of people involved in immoral websites is untrue".[159]

Less than a month later, it emerged that five journalists, all of them known for their links to the pro-Rouhani and pro-reform camps, were also arrested by the Revolutionary Guard's Intelligence Organization operating in plain clothes in Tehran for allegedly being "members of an illegal network linked with the governments of the US and Britain who were active in Iranian media".[160] They were accused of being "members of an infiltration group". They were part of the nineteen journalists who have been detained in recent years over violations of religious mores or national security, which makes Iran the third worst country in the world for detaining journalists. Institutional intimidation did not end with the arrest and harassment of journalists but extended, as in previous periods, to the forceful closure of news and reporting outlets. Thus, the reformist daily newspaper *Bahar* was ordered to cease publishing in January 2016 on the grounds that it "propagandized against the state and published material harmful to the foundation of the Islamic Republic".[161] Expressing his alarm at this state of affairs, the respected Committee to Protect Journalists Middle East and North Africa Program Coordinator, Sherif Mansour, went on the record to suggest that "Iranian authorities are clearly trying to intimidate the press ahead of parliamentary elections, and in the process they are undermining the legitimacy of the vote".[162] It is also worth drawing attention to the scale of restrictions that President Rouhani may be trying to overcome by noting that Iran was ranked 173rd out of 180 countries in the 2015 *Reporters without Borders* press freedom index.

The intra-elite political wrangling following the vetting of candidates eventually resulted in 55 per cent of those who had registered themselves as candidates being allowed to stand. This outcome meant that the candidature of some 6,229 individuals for the Majlis vote had been approved. So on election day, as many as 21 candidates were competing for each of the 290 parliamentary seats being contested in the country's 207 constituencies – a record! Having forced the Council of Guardians to raise the number of eligible candidates (to over 6,000), it would appear odd that on the eve of the vote the total number of candidates had dropped rather dramatically, with a fifth of the candidates (1,385 individuals) withdrawing from the race.[163] This kind of tactic, however, is not unknown in Iranian electoral gambles in which some act as stoking horses largely to strengthen the chances of more prominent candidates. With 4,844 candidates competing, the competition for each seat had dropped from 21 per seat to 17. The elections themselves followed a similar pattern to earlier ones, with the establishment urging a high voter turnout to show the world, as the Leader put it, the popularity of the Islamic republic. Not leaving the election to chance, the Leader-associated elite members openly advocated the election of individuals loyal to the conservative-leaning faction. Thus, at the important Friday prayers of the week before the Majlis and Assembly of Experts (19th of February) in Tehran, Mashhad and Ahvaz, the prayer leaders asked the faithful to vote for those candidates "who had death to America tattooed on their foreheads", those who were "champions of the fight against the United States", "those loyal to the Faqih".[164]

Despite some 250 political parties registered with the interior ministry, organized politics in the Islamic republic continued to remain in the domain of factions, and in the 2016 February elections for the parliament and Assembly of Experts, this was no different. The parliamentary election, in fact, was organized through established lists of candidates on the basis of which as much as 47.7 per cent of the voters would cast their vote for an entire list and as many as 70 per cent would cast their vote for those on coalition lists.[165] Sanam Vakil provides a good explanation of the workings of the political process in the February elections with this analysis:

> In the absence of political parties, candidates form lists of loose political alliances. These alliances can but do not necessarily bring together contenders of similar ideological views. Lists often merge candidates with divergent political opinions and agendas. All of this results in unpredictable allegiances and the perpetuation of factional tensions that has been a longstanding facet of Iranian domestic politics. Factional affiliations are also not guaranteed. Indeed, in this election a number of conservative parliamentarians ran under centrist and reformist associations. Some examples include Ali Larijani, the speaker of the parliament and longstanding conservative, who supported the nuclear agreement with close ties to the Supreme Leader, ran as an independent. Kazem Jalili, a conservative who has called for harsh penalties against Green Movement leaders Mir Hossein Musavi and Mehdi Karroubi, ran as a reformist. Ali Motahari, who also ran on the reformist ticket, supports the release of Musavi and Karroubi from house arrest, but is a social and political conservative.[166]

In the last analysis, three grand coalitions contested these elections, along with a significantly high number of 'independents'. The coalitions – the reformist List of Hope, the conservative Principlists Grand Coalition, and the moderate conservative People's Voice Coalition – each led by a prominent figure (Mohammaed Reza Aref, Gholam-Ali Haddad-Adel, and Ali Motahari, respectively) competed across the country. But two main camps emerged, with a small number of prominent individuals (Larijani and Ali Motahari, for example) choosing to distance themselves from their natural conservative camp and the latter forming a separate parliamentary list of middle-of-the road conservatives, labelled the Voice of the Nation, which tried to form a bridge between the two poles. Also a number of independent candidates were hoping to squeeze in and become holders of balance of power in the event of a close election result. So, in these elections, the Principlists on one side and the Coalition of Reformists on the other competed for control of the Majlis. The prize: To help or hinder the president in his endeavours to reform the economy and to improve relations with the West. The former coalition, which was the biggest (hard-line) group in the campaign, encompassing loyalists to Ayatollah Khamenei, emphasized Islamic social and political values but also support for a free market economy which was not corrupt and was free of Western influence. The coalition also included such political groups as the Devotees and Path-Seekers of the Islamic Revolution, the Front of Islamic Revolution Stability, Islamic Coalition Party and the Association of Combatant Preachers. This faction, crucially, also enjoyed support from such vested interested parties as the Revolutionary Guard, the clergy, and the influential bazaar community.

The Universal Coalition of Reformists, on the other hand, was comprised of those hovering on the margins of the establishment. This coalition, dubbed the 'list of hope', was essentially an alliance of members of a number of fairly small political parties which had hitherto acted as pressure groups or civil society activists. The coalition included several parties known for their reformist leanings, including the Union of Islamic Iran People Party, Nedaye Iranian, Iranian-Islamic Freedom Party, Association of Combatant Clerics, Islamic Labour Party and Moderation and Development Party. Weeks before the election, the main pro-reform parties agreed on a joint list of candidates which was branded as the 'Alliance of Reformists and Government Supporters', thus emphasizing the importance of this coalition to President Rouhani's government.

The elections for the Assembly were particularly significant because this assembly will sit until 2024 and is therefore likely to be electing the next Leader of the Islamic republic. For the election of the Assembly of Experts, 166 theologians were cleared to compete for its 88 seats in this body's 31 national constituencies, out of 801 self-declared candidates. Due to disqualifications by the Council of Guardians, nine of the thirty-one constituencies had only one candidate for their seat and were therefore likely to be elected unopposed were it not for the interior ministry's intervention to change some boundaries to make the election competitive. In the largest constituency, Tehran, the Rouhani-Rafsanjani (reform-centre) coalition, won fifteen of the sixteen seats outright. Rafsanjani topped the list with over 2.3 million votes, and Rouhani came third with 2.2 million votes. In a coordinated approach, the reformist List of Hope supported Rafsanjani's People's Experts list and their joint effort bagged them an unprecedented fifty-two seats of the eighty-eight. The hard-line Ayatollah Ahmad Jannati came sixteenth with 1.32 million votes, but in a big blow to the conservatives his two allies, Ayatollahs Mohammad-Taqi Mesbah-Yazi and Yazdi (chairman of the Assembly since 2015) were both defeated. Ayatollah Mohammad Yazdi's list of The Society of Seminary Teachers did rather badly which contributed to his demise. As the Assembly's list was overly conservative-leaning in any case this was more of a symbolic victory for the reformists than actual, a point underlined by the election of the least popular candidate in Tehran, the very same Ayatollah Jannati, to the chairmanship of the Assembly on 24 May 2016.

The results of both elections were remarkable. Voter turnout of 62 per cent in the first round and 59 per cent in the second of the Majlis elections was certainly respectable. It meant that for the main election on 26 February, some 34 million eligible voters had taken part. In the first round the List of Hope secured eighty seats and the Principlists, sixty-four, with the balance being held by the, often reform-leaning, independent candidates who won seventy-three seats. The reformist list won all of Tehran's 30 seats and in the final tally, following the second ballot, the reform camp secured a majority of 121 seats, the conservatives a much reduced presence of 83 seats, the independents 73, and Motahari's People's Voice 11 seats.

Three facts make the tenth Majlis noteworthy: First, this marks the reformists' first parliamentary success since 2004 and returns them to the centre of politics as the biggest parliamentary bloc. Second, a record seventeen seats were taken by women candidates, with most of them in the reformist camp; and, third, the tenth Majlis was of the newcomers, with only 26 per cent of incumbents winning re-election.[167] The vast majority of the new members had little parliamentary experience and the fact that a considerable number of members were also not associated with any election list was to make this Majlis a less predictable one. This said, the combined success of the reformist-centrist coalition in both the Majlis and the Assembly of Experts elections has ushered in a new era in Iranian politics in which for the first time the 'moderate' forces have a numerical superiority in three of the most electorally contested institutions of the Islamic republic. This in itself does not translate into greater control of levers of power – which Ali Larijani's uncontested re-election as speaker of parliament on 31 May 2016 after Aref's withdrawal of his candidacy clearly illustrates. And Larijani's re-election to the position of speaker with an overwhelming favourable vote of 237 out of 276 cast shows that it will be hard for the Hope coalition to build binding partnerships with such a large group of newcomers who appear to owe little allegiance to any particular faction. But, in the broader consideration of Hassan Rouhani's team, having Larijani as a compliant conservative in charge might be a better outcome than a reformist speaker who would always be on the defensive and subject of attacks from the conservative camp.

These are the results of what the *Economist* referred to in 2014 as an apparent Iranian "rush to the centre".[168] The appeal of the reformists never disappeared following the suppression of the Green Movement in 2009 and Rouhani's electoral success, followed by the Majlis and Assembly of Experts success in 2016, have underlined the continuing relevance of these political groups to the masses' aspirations for a changed, better, Islamic republic. The masses' continuing engagement with the political process is partly a result of years of pent up frustration but can also be partly explained by Iran's dramatic demographic shift. Combining high educational attainment with a fast-becoming middle-aged population[169] seems to have a sobering moderating effect on the public and it is those candidates who can best speak to the aspirations of this socially restless population which can secure their confidence. The return of the pendulum to the centre ground of politics in Iran is a positive development for the country and can point to growing social stability, which is good news for the elite also who are still struggling to find consensus in how to deal with Iran's deep-seated economic problems.

It was noted earlier that the Rouhani administration's push from its first day in office was to secure a negotiated nuclear settlement, which was predicated on support from the country's highest echelons of power, and the 'cover' provided by Ayatollah Khamenei for the Iranian team's 'heroic flexibility'. Indeed, while Rouhani's road to negotiations was certainly unblocked by the electoral support he received from the majority of Iranian voters in June 2013, the Leader paved the road for the president's new diplomatic approach. For this support, Rouhani did have to pay a price. At home, socio-political restrictions have remained more or less intact, jail sentences remain commonplace for intellectuals and public figures (including journalists), and perhaps most visibly of all the leaders and sympathisers of the Green Movement have remained under house arrest, are in jail, or in exile. Structurally, the political system has not opened up, which is itself increasingly in danger of becoming hostage to the same securitization problems that shaped Ahmadinejad's administration. This may be so because abroad, and despite a call for détente, Tehran's dogged support for the Syrian regime, its use of Shia militias in neighbouring countries, and its policy of manipulating Iraqi, Lebanese, Syrian, and, to lesser extent, Palestinian politics to serve its 'resistance front', have done much to alienate Iran's GCC neighbours and their regional allies. This has deprived Rouhani of the calming conditions which would allow him to rebuild at home during a period of peace abroad.

For all the important external successes of a negotiated settlement of the nuclear crisis – in terms of not imposing any changes on Iran's foreign policy goals, or setting clear conditions for its reintegration into the regional dialogues about terrorism, refugees, political change in key Arab states, or depriving it of its armed non-state actors – managing the transition from isolation and pariah status was always going to be a quintessentially domestic matter. So, before 'the people' could get ahead of themselves, the judicial and security establishments inevitably intervened in order to prevent the erosion of the order they and the Leader had already imposed on society. Thus, after the success of the nuclear negotiations, the policy compromises struck at home have become increasingly problematic for the Rouhani administration to manage. Inevitably, the nuclear negotiations impacted on the political process at home.

Authoritarian state, democratic society

In the clientelist model, in which the patron arguably establishes the rules of the political game and from the outset controls the system through a patron-client relationship, political platforms take shape horizontally and 'bonds' emerge which, in the words of former president Rafsanjani, "operate in place of political parties".[170] Whether one defines the Islamic republic as a 'quasi-democracy' or a 'democratic oligarchy',[171] the structural tension between its elected (popular) institutions of power and its unelected (unaccountable) institutions of power does not bode well for the long-term longevity of the nezam in its current form. While a variety of opinion is on display and a wide mix of personalities do compete in any given election, the individuals and groups allowed to compete are by definition loyal to the nezam, and things go wrong, as in June 2009, only when the nezam itself gets things very badly wrong.

What is clear in analysing the political structures and processes of the Islamic republic is that while the structures appear rigid, political activity takes place around the structures and across them. Indeed, it is partly thanks to the rigid political structures of this Islamic republic that struggle for access to and control of elected bodies of the state become so important. It is through such vehicles that political camps compete with each other for power, the instruments for wielding that power (ministries and agencies affiliated to the state apparatus), and of course influence. Elections therefore become at once an indicator of popularity of particular trends and personalities and also the means for mobilizing the masses. Electoral success matters and it is here that we can observe the thickness of political platforms, gauge the rhythm of change, and determine the balance of power between political factions.

The rigidity of the political system also partly accounts for the country's shifting political alliances and, as has been shown, the emergence of often short-term and opportunistic coalitions around election cycles. Such coalitions, as we have seen, are rarely strategic and rarely lead to a sustainable convergence of left-reform and right-conservative wings. There are those who occupy the centre ground (for example Rafsanjani and Rouhani) and do try to provide a bridge between the big poles in the system. But their success is limited by the inevitable compromises that they must make in order to move their agendas forward. Election cycles, therefore, actually provide the rhythm for the political musical chairs that are played out in Iran.

Elections, however, do not make the Islamic republic a democracy or a pluralist political system. With the agencies of the nezam acting as 'gatekeepers', access to office is controlled and so then is also the outcome.[172] What the June 2009 protests also showed, apart from discontent about control by the unelected institutions of the state, is how unpopular the regime as a whole has become. The discontent is further linked to the state's deliberate meld of the private and public spaces. The state dictates mores and from deeming what might be appropriate clothing, to haircuts, use of makeup, style of social interaction, and contact between genders, such matters are monitored and abuse of any can lead to physical punishment, fines and even imprisonment. Popular resistance peaks near election cycles as the prospect of reformist candidates winning and thus able to change these restrictive conditions encourages activism.

Political activity of the type taking place in Iran tallies with some aspects of Yael Yishai's model of a 'nonliberal democracy', with obvious omissions. To clarify, Iran's system is not "a nonliberal democracy... in the procedural sense as the rules of the democratic game, including free elections and party competition" are not preserved.[173] Rather, Iran's nonliberal democracy puts emphasis "not on diversity but on unity, not on pluralism but on oneness.... Participation... is not an instrument for challenging authority but a means of elaborating and implementing the general will". It is in the latter sense that Iran' system can be said to contain elements of a nonliberal democracy.

Iran's is not a pseudo-democracy either, as is sometimes alleged, precisely because participation is a core mechanism of the political system's legitimation. When the regime messes with electoral processes, even though it itself defines the parameters of candidate participation, it immerses itself in a deep crisis. We can derive from Yishai's work the observation that in the Islamic republic, participation is enshrined as a right, and this is an important point. This is not a privilege to be manhandled by the country's political masters and when it appears to be, as in 2009, then the masses have sufficient political tenacity to challenge elite-level political abuses. Further, the premise of the republic's political system is that elections are not an instrument for challenging authority but rather, as Yishai has put it, the instrument for elaborating and implementing the general will. If the regime defies the 'general will', even though authority is said to lie with God's representative (the Faqih), then it is raising questions about its own credibility. Elections, in a country that already declares itself as having an optimum political system, also tend to shape the partisan nature of its politics. If political actors are by definition barred from challenging the fundamentals of the political system, then they will fight all the harder for control of the instruments which can guide policy. Thus, inter-agency battles rage for control and, equally important in a country like Iran, for the extraction of rent.[174]

Second, despite the securitized state of affairs since the late-1990s, the political system has proved itself to be remarkably flexible and also resilient. This is, paradoxically, partly a result of the multi-centred structure of the political order and partly because no credible alternative (opposition) movement has emerged from within to challenge the Islamic regime in its entirety. The reformists are agents of limited change, despite the conservatives' fear of them as loose cannons bent, albeit inadvertently, on unpicking the Vali-e Faqih order. The repeated attempts by the centre-left and democratic forces to reform the system through elections has arguably produced limited results, but pouring energies into reform measures while keeping the edifice intact has arguably also limited the horizon of political possibilities in Iran. Yet, it is crystal clear that the Faqih order itself is the core of the problem.[175] The tension between theocracy and democracy that events of 2009 brought to light will not be resolved so long as the Faqih system remains intact. It is reform of the parallel universe of power, the unelected power-wielding organs of the state and an overbearing, unaccountable and all-pervasive Leader, which needs attention and to which the 'green manifesto' of the five Iranian intellectuals had hinted back in 2010. Control of (physical and cyber) space becomes important in this regard and it is for the control of such spaces that the Leader and the security establishment press society to conform and at the same time maintain a watchful eye on personal behaviour and inter-personal exchanges. In the regime's mind, personal freedoms, as expressed in diversity of taste, can lead to expressions of resistance. In the authoritarian-dominated political order, in Iran non-conformity can, in itself, mean resistance.

Third, it is interesting that the regime has turned a pathological fear of regime change into a powerful political tool for control, and when necessary the silencing of dissent.[176] At the first signs of protest the regime sees hands of 'biganehgan' (those external to us, or simply put foreigners) agitating what they depict as the simple people. But the constant reference to Western conspiracies has worn thin and in an age of information overload the public no longer believes in the secret conspiracies to overthrow their political order.

So, fourth, for all its efforts to control the flow of information, the Iranian public remains highly networked and demonstrates its distrust of, or dislike for, sanctioned media outlets by using external and uncontrolled internal sources of information and analysis. Iran's clampdown on the Internet and social media networks makes it one of the worst cases of such state control in the world: 87 (with 100 the worst) in overall ICT freedom, 20 (with 25 the worst) in terms of obstacles to access, 31 (with 35 the worst) for limits on content, 36 (with 40 the worst) for violation of users' rights.[177] While Internet penetration has reached 50 per cent and Internet use around 40 per cent of the population, access remains difficult because the state monopoly keeps subscription rates high and speeds low. Despite 30 million smartphones in circulation, state-controlled servers keep a lid on their use for Internet access and online content. The state also exercises control in other direct ways: Facebook and Twitter remain banned for public use (despite the elite all openly using both social media networks), and mobile messages applications are constantly under surveillance with pressure of closure. Yet Iranians continue to challenge the state in these very arenas. It is for this reason that blogging is such a big pastime in the Islamic republic with Farsi being one of the biggest blogging languages in the world. While accurate figures are hard to come by, it is estimated that Iran may have in excess of 70,000 bloggers, many of them political bloggers.[178]

For a paranoid regime whose whole worldview is shaped by conspiracy theories and fear of regime change, to have its very foundations shaken by its own citizens has not been received well, particularly as the more it tries to control the electoral process and determine the outcome of elections, the greater its weakness appears. We are entering a new period of uncertainty for the region and given Iran's significant weight and influence in the broader Middle East, developments in this country continue to cast a shadow over everything else in the region. More than three decades on since the revolution, Iran's place in the world remains ill-defined, as does its role conception. Indeed, the very nature of the political regime that grew out of the revolutionary coalition is now being openly contested. Electoral politics, in terms of openly contested elections and high voter turnout, which have been the mantra of the Islamic republic and the public face of its legitimacy, are now the very forces that are straining the very fabric of the political system, which emerged from the ashes of the Pahlavi monarchy. The regime is finding that once people have the vote and are encouraged to exercise their right to vote, you cannot then dictate the outcome to them without major backlash. But the limits of Iran's contained democracy will likely be severely tested as the regime grapples with strategies for improving the country's economy and for reviving its role as a major player in the global political economy – all of which require opening up to the rest of the world, economically, socially and ultimately politically.

Notes

1 Theda Skocpol, *States and Revolutions* (Cambridge: Cambridge University Press, 1979).
2 Ervand Abrahamian, 'Iran: The Political Challenge', *MERIP Reports 69*, July–August 1978, p. 4.
3 Skocpol, op. cit, p. 17.
4 William Shawcross, *The Shah's Last Ride: The Story of the Exile, Misadventures and Death of the Emperor* (London: Chatto and Windus, 1989).
5 Ervand Abrahamian, 'Ali Shari'ati: Ideologue of the Iranian Revolution', *MERIP Reports 104*, March–April 1982, pp. 25–28.
6 Hamid Algar (trans) *Islam and Revolution: Writings and Declarations of Imam Khomeini* (Berkeley, CA: Mizan Press, 1981), p. 56.
7 Ibid., p. 79.
8 Asghar Schirazi, *The Constitution of Iran: Politics and the State in the Islamic Republic* (London: I. B. Tauris, 1997), p. 1.
9 The structure of the revolutionary state, noted Martin, "is of Western origin, and to some extent a continuation of the arrangements of the Constitutional Revolution". See Vanessa Martin, *Creating an Islamic State: Khomeini and the Making of a New Iran* (London: I. B. Tauris, 2000), p. 164.
10 Ramy Nima, *The Wrath of Allah: Islamic Revolution and Reaction in Iran* (London: Pluto Press, 1983), pp. 106–107.
11 Homa Omid, *Islam and the Post-Revolutionary State in Iran* (London: Macmillan Press, 1994), p. 67.
12 Ziba Mir-Hosseini and Richard Taper, *Islam and Democracy in Iran: Eshkevari and the Quest for Reform* (London: I.B. Tauris, 2006).
13 President Ali Khamenei speaking at Tehran Friday prayers on 22 January 1988. See *APS Diplomat*, 16–23 January 1988.
14 Mehdi Mozaffari, 'Islamism in Algeria and Iran', in Abdel Salam Sidahmed and Anoushiravan Ehteshami (eds.) *Islamic Fundamentalism* (Boulder, CO: Westview Press, 1996), pp. 229–47.

15 Ariabarzan Mohammadi, *The Path Dependent Nature of Factionalism in Post-Khomeini Iran* (UK: Al-Sabah Paper no. 13, December 2014).
16 Kazem Alamdari, 'The Power Structure of the Islamic Republic of Iran: Transition from Populism to Clientelism, and Militarization of Government', *Third World Quarterly*, vol. 26, no. 8, 2005, p. 1299.
17 Giovanni Sartori, *Parties and Party Systems: A Framework for Analysis* (Cambridge: Cambridge University Press, 1976).
18 Mehdi Moslem, *Factional Politics in Post-Khomeini Iran* (New York, NY: Syracuse University Press, 2002).
19 Bahman Baktiari, *Parliamentary Politics in Revolutionary Iran: The Institutionalization of Factional Politics* (Gainseville, FL: University Press of Florida, 1996), p. 63.
20 Mehdi Moslem, op. cit, p. 47.
21 Hassan Rouhani, *National Security and Nuclear Diplomacy (Amniyat-e Meli va Diplomacey-e Hastehyee)* (Tehran: Center for Strategic Studies, 2011).
22 Arang Keshavarzian, 'Contestation without Democracy: Elite Fragmentation in Iran', in Marsha Pripstein Posusney and Michele Penner Angrist (eds.) *Authoritarianism in the Middle East: Regimes and Resistance* (Boulder, CO: Lynne Rienner, 2005), pp. 63–87.
23 Ziba Mir-Hosseini and Richard Taper, op. cit., p. 17.
24 Those with criminal records, former senior officials of the monarchical regime, those who did not accept the constitution of the Islamic republic were to be excluded and all others would have to provide a full manifesto and policy outlines with their applications.
25 Kazem Alamdari, 'The Power Structure of the Islamic Republic of Iran: Transition from Populism to Clientelism, and Militarization of Government', *Third World Quarterly*, vol. 26, no. 8, 2005, pp. 1285–1301.
26 Khamenei had jumped the gun in December 1988, months before the constitutional amendments abolishing the premiership and creating an executive presidency were introduced, by declaring at the very public platform of the Tehran Friday Prayers that "there are… some problems and ambiguities (in the constitution) that will be corrected one day". *APS Diplomat*, 26 November–3 December 1988.
27 Rafsanjani's main opponent, Mousavi-Khoinia, was backed by Mousavi and Karroubi, who were to emerge as the leaders of the Green Movement in 2009. Ironically, Rafsanjani became their main defender in the nezam following regime attacks on them for leading and spreading 'sedition'.
28 Anoushiravan Ehteshami and Mahjoob Zweiri, *Iran and the Rise of its Neoconservatives* (London: I. B. Tauris, 2007).
29 It is estimated that as many as 30,000 individuals may have been executed at that time, in response to a religious edict issued by Ayatollah Khomeini that there was no room for apostates in his Islamic republic. Ayatollah Montazeri also alluded to this tragedy in his memoirs (published in 2001) and the Iran Human Rights Documentation Center's detailed report on the executions notes that estimates of those killed range from 1,000 to 30,000. See IHRDC, *Deadly Fatwa: Iran's 1988 Prison Massacre* (New Haven, CT: IHRDC, 2009). The insider's account is provided by Ayatollah Hossein-Ali Montazeri, *Khatirat-i Ayatollah Montazeri, Majmu'iyyih Payvastha va Dastnivisha* [Memoir of Ayatollah Montazeri, the Collection of Appendices and Handwritten Notes] (2001).
30 For details see Anoushiravan Ehteshami, *After Khomeini: The Iranian Second Republic* (London: Routledge, 1995).
31 See Michael Axworthy, *Revolutionary Iran: A History of the Islamic Republic* (London: Penguin, 2014), p. 274.
32 Mehran Kamrava, *Iran's Intellectual Revolution* (Cambridge: Cambridge University Press, 2008).

33 Ziba Mir-Hosseini and Richard Tapper, *Islam and Democracy in Iran: Eshkevari and the Quest for Reform* (London: I.B. Tauris, 2006), p. 27.
34 Ibid.
35 Mehran Kamrava, op. cit.
36 For details see Ehteshami, op. cit., pp. 54–69.
37 Ali Banuazizi, 'The Crisis of Legitimacy, Resistance, and Civil Society', *Iran Nameh*, vol. xiv, no. 1, Winter 1996, pp. 61–78.
38 The fourth Majlis' banning of satellite dishes in 1995 in order to curtail 'imported social corruption' is a classic example.
39 Unnamed official cited in *APS Diplomat*, 9–16 August 2015.
40 Amnesty International, *Iran: Violations of Human Rights 1987–1990* (London: Amnesty International, 1990); Report of the Economic and Social Council (prepared by Reynaldo Galindo Pol) to the UN General Assembly, *Situation of Human Rights in the Islamic Republic of Iran* (New York, NY: United Nations, 2 November, 1989). The true figure of the mass executions is arguably much higher.
41 Shaul Bakhash, 'Iran since the Gulf War', in Robert O. Freedman (ed.) *The Middle East and the Peace Process: The Impact of the Oslo Accords* (Gainesville, FL: University Press of Florida, 1998), p. 253.
42 Bakhash, ibid., provides a list of the regime's repressive measures in the 1992–96 period.
43 Haim Bresheeth and Nira Yuval-Davis (eds.) *The Gulf War and the New World Order* (London: Zed Books, 1991).
44 Michael Axworthy, op. cit., p. 323.
45 Said Amir Arjomand, *After Khomeini: Iran Under His Successor* (Oxford: Oxford University Press, 2009).
46 Ghoncheh Tazmini, *Khatami's Iran: The Islamic Republic and the Turbulent Path to Reform* (London: I. B. Tauris, 2009), p. 154.
47 International Crisis Group, *Iran: Struggle for the Revolution's Soul* (Brussels: ICG Middle East Report no. 5, August 2002).
48 Ali Akbar Mahdi, 'The Student Movement in the Islamic Republic of Iran', *Journal of Iranian Research and Analysis*, vol. 15, no. 2, November 1999, pp. 5–32.
49 Worth noting that two-time presidential candidate Qalibaf was a signatory of this threatening letter. See Anoushiravan Ehteshami and Mahjoob Zweiri, op. cit.
50 *Tehran Bureau* report, 1 August 2009.
51 Michael Axworthy, op. cit., p. 354.
52 IRNA, 20 April 2000.
53 Majid KhosraviNik, *Discourse, Identity and Legitimacy: Self and Other in Representations of Iran's Nuclear Programme* (Amsterdam: John Benjamins Pubs, 2015).
54 Michael Axworthy, op. cit.
55 Quoted in Stephen C. Poulson, 'Nested Institutions, Political Opportunity, and the Decline of the Iranian Reform Movement Post-9/11', *American Behavioral Scientist*, vol. 53, no. 1, September 2009, pp. 27–43.
56 Said Amir Arjomand, 'The Reform Movement and the Debate on Modernity and Tradition in Contemporary Iran', *International Journal of Middle East Studies*, vol. 34, no. 4, November 2002, pp. 719–33.
57 According to interior ministry data, Khatami secured his second term with 21.7 million votes in 2001, with 77.1 per cent of the total vote. His nearest rival, Ahmad Tavakoli, got 4.4 million votes (15.6 per cent of the vote). Voter turnout was 67.8 per cent.
58 Arjomand, *After Khomeini*, p. 111.
59 Siamak Namazi, 'The 6th Majlis Elections in Iran: What Happened and What Can We Expect', *Journal of Iranian Research and Analysis*, vol. 16. No. 1, April 2000, pp. 14–21.
60 It did, however, manage to raise the age of voting from 15 to 18 and impose the maximum age of 75 on candidacy.

61 Ali Gheissari and Kaveh-Cyrus Sanandaji, 'New Conservative Politics and Electoral Behavior in Iran', in Ali Gheissari (ed.) *Contemporary Iran: Economy, Society, Politics* (Oxford: Oxford University Press, 2009), pp. 275–98.
62 Quoted in Michael Theodoulou, 'Growing Frustration on the Path to the Future', *The Times*, 13 June 2003.
63 Quoted in Behzad Farsian and Anton La Guardia, 'Challenge to Mullahs who act as God's Emissaries', *Daily Telegraph*, 17 June 2003.
64 Said Amir Arjomand, 'Constitutional Implications of Current Political Debates in Iran', in Ali Gheissari (ed.) *Contemporary Iran: Economy, Society, Politics* (Oxford: Oxford University Press, 2009), pp. 247–74.
65 IISS, *Strategic Survey 2002/3* (Oxford: Oxford University Press for IISS, 2003), p. 170.
66 Ali Gheissari and Kaveh-Cyrus Sanandaji, op. cit., p. 277.
67 Interview with Ayatollah Nateq-Nouri, Khabar online, 22 July 2014.
68 Ali Gheissari and Kaveh-Cyrus Sanandaji, op. cit., pp. 280–81.
69 Kasra Naji, *Ahmadinejad: The Secret History of Iran's Radical Leader* (London: I. B. Tauris, 2008), p. 58.
70 Ahmadinejad was Tehran's mayor of course at the time of the elections.
71 The issue of the 6 million votes discrepancy in the figures of the Council of Guardians and the interior ministry remained unresolved after the Leader intervened to silence doubters of the authenticity of the results of the first round. But Rafsanjani and others have asserted that around 6 million unexpired and false birth certificates of the deceased circulate in the hands of the IRGC precisely to 'engineer' suitable electoral outcomes. See Naji, op. cit.
72 *Sharq*, 23 June 2005.
73 Anoushiravan Ehteshami and Mahjoob Zweiri, op. cit., p. 64.
74 Ibid., Naji, op. cit.
75 Petrol, chickens, red meat, onions, wheat, rice, tea, pain killers, surgical equipment, cement, steel and a whole range of strategic and everyday goods would periodically disappear due to mismanagement or deliberate hoarding.
76 Hesam Forozan, The *Military in Post-Revolutionary Iran: The Evolution and Roles of the Revolutionary Guards* (New York, NY: Routledge, 2016).
77 Mahjoob Zweiri (ed.) *The Eighth Majlis (Parliamentary) Election – Where Is Iran Headed?* (Amman: Center for Strategic Studies, University of Jordan, March 2008).
78 Reuters, 5 December 2008.
79 Radio Farda, 7 November 2007.
80 Ahmadinejad indicated in January 2008 that his government had reduced the budget text of around one hundred pages to just one and a half pages, thus helping parliament to save itself a great deal of time debating the proposal.
81 Hossein Aryan, 'Falling Price of Oil Compounds Iranian President's Problems', RFE/RL, 29 October 2008.
82 Mehdi Mozaffari, 'What Comes Next for Iran?', RFE/RL, 16 July 2009.
83 See Anna Fifield and Najmeh Bozorgmehr, 'Tehran's Poll Debate Grows Bitter as Clerics Turn on the President', *Financial Times*, 11 June 2009.
84 Ayatollah Khamenei was speaking at a ceremony marking the twentieth anniversary of the death of the founder of the Islamic Republic, Ayatollah Khomeini. See BBC news, 4 June, 2009.
85 John R. Bolton, 'What if Israel Strikes Iran?', *Wall Street Journal*, 12–14 June 2009.
86 See Margaret Coker, 'Saudis Could Counter Iran', *Wall Street Journal*, 12–14 June 2009.
87 Robin Wright, 'Tipping Point in Tehran', *Washington Post*, 14 July, 2009.
88 Golnaz Esfandiari, 'Four Candidates Approved to Run in Iran's Presidential Vote', RFE/LR, 3 July 2009.

89 The four were Mahmoud Ahmadinejad, Mohsen Rezaei (former IRGC commander), former Majlis Speaker Mehdi Karroubi and the republic's last prime minister, Mir Hossein Mousavi.
90 See 'Iranian Presidential Elections', *Policy Brief* (Durham: Centre for Iranian Studies, Durham University), Epiphany Term 2009.
91 IRNA, 15 April 2009.
92 Kayhan Barzegar, 'The List: Iran's Presidential Wannabes', *Foreign Policy*, June 2009.
93 Golnaz Esfandiari, op. cit.
94 See Kaveh Ehsani, Arang Keshavarzian and Noram Claire Moruzzi, 'Tehran, June 2009', *Middle East Report Online*, 28 June 2009.
95 Golnaz Esfandiari, 'Reformers Hope Iran's 'Silent Voters' Will Be Heard in June', RFE/RL, 28 May 2009.
96 Ibid.
97 Hamid Dabashi, 'People Power', *al-Ahram Weekly*, June 25–July 1, 2009.
98 'Iran: The Party's Over', *The Economist*, 15–21 November 2008.
99 Colin Freeman, 'Iran's Rivals Accuse Each Other of Planning to Rig Election', *The Telegraph*, 11 June 2009.
100 See Walter R. Mebane, Jr, 'Note on the Presidential Election in Iran, June 2009', University of Michigan, 29 June 2009, p. 9.
101 Kaveh Ehsani, Arang Keshavarzian and Noram Claire Moruzzi, 'Tehran, June 2009', *Middle East Report Online*, 28 June 2009.
102 These comments were made by none other than Mohsen Sazgara, one of the founders of the *Sepah*, who is now based in Washington. See Hossein Aryan, 'Dilemmas in the Midst of 'Coup'', RFE/RL, 19 June, 2009.
103 All references to Mousavi's statements are from *Rah-e Sabz*, which documented the crisis but then suspended its activities.
104 Aryan, op. cit.
105 See Anoushiravan Ehteshami and Mahjoob Zweiri, *Iran and the Rise of Its Neoconservatives: The Politics of Tehran's Silent Revolution* (London: I.B. Tauris, 2007).
106 Hamid Algar (trans) *Islam and Revolution: Writings and Declarations of Imam Khomeini* (Berkeley, CA: Mizan Press, 1981), p. 79.
107 Negar Mottahedeh notes that "with more than ten thousand #iranelection tweets an hour throughout the month of June [2009], the involvement of netizens in the crisis in Iran was so widespread that the hashtag #iranelection remained the highest-ranking global hashtag on Twitter for two weeks following the presidential election, dropping only momentarily after the unexpected death of Michael Jackson". *#iranelection: Hashtag Solidarity and the Transformation of Online Life* (Stanford, CA: Stanford University Press, 2015), p. 7.
108 Dilip Hiro, *Iran Today* (New York, NY: Nation Books, 2005), p. 314.
109 Robin Wright, op. cit.
110 This statement was issued on his website soon after violence broke out.
111 Hojjatoleslam Mohammad Ali Ayazi of the Qom Seminary Society Theologians, speaking to RFE/RL, 1 July 2009.
112 Ibid.
113 Noted in Martin Fletcher, 'Iran Clerics Declare Poll Invalid and Condemn the Crackdown', *The Times*, 6 July 2009.
114 Reuters, 1 July, 2009.
115 See *The Peninsula*, 2 July 2009.
116 IRNA and ISNA 17 and 18 July 2009.
117 Noted in the comments made by Mohsen Rezaei, the fourth presidential candidate. 'Interview with Mohsen Rezaei', *Tabnak*, 9 November 2009.
118 Reuters 21 July, 2009.
119 Reuters, 1 July, 2009.

120 Reza Aslan quoted in Samira Simone, 'Opposition Movement in Iran not Over, Experts Say', CNN, 1 July 2009.
121 *Financial Times*, 21 June 2009.
122 Quoted in Ali Akbar Dareini, 'Supreme Leader Confronts Resurgent Iranian Opposition', *The Independent*, 21 July 2009.
123 Jonathan Spollen, 'Referendum Call Outrages Supreme Leader', *The National*, 21 July 2009.
124 See www.khandaniha.eu for the full exchange between Grand Ayatollah Montazeri and Hojjatoleslam Mohsen Kadivar on political developments in Iran. 11 July 2009.
125 IRNA and ISNA, 17 and 18 July 2009.
126 ISNA, 18 July, 2009.
127 John R. Bolton, 'Time for an Israeli Strike?', *Washington Post*, 2 July 2009.
128 Farnaz Fassihi, 'Iran Judiciary Targets Reformers', *Wall Street Journal*, 26 August 2009.
129 IRNA, 27 December 2009.
130 The manifesto is reproduced in Ramin Jahanbegloo and Abdolkarim Soroush, 'Iran on the Edge', *New Perspectives Quarterly*, vol. 27, no. 2, Spring 2010, pp. 32–33.
131 'Grand Ayatollah Montazeri's Letter to Marjas, Islamic Scholars and Seminaries', Mowjcamp, 14 September 2009.
132 Sadjadpour quoted in Nicholas Blanford, 'Will Iran's Political Turmoil Shake Hezbollah?', *Christian Science Monitor*, 20 July 2009.
133 Mehdi Mozaffari, op. cit.
134 Ramin Jahanbegloo, 'A Harsh Crackdown Is Coming in Iran', *New Perspectives Quarterly*, vol. 27, no. 2, Spring 2010, pp. 29–30.
135 Paneta Beigi, quoted in Samira Simone, op. cit.
136 RFE/RL, 20 April 2010.
137 Katherine Butler, 'The Fear Factor', *The Independent*, 30 April 2010.
138 Farnaz Fassihi, 'Tehran Extends Crackdown to Members of Global Diaspora', *Wall Street Journal*, 4–6 December 2009.
139 For Moslehi's account of this episode, see Fars News Agency, 5 May 2016.
140 Fardanews, 15 August 2012; *Iran*, 13 August 2012.
141 As a side, Ahmadinejad's attacks on the Majlis had been received with such seriousness that it encouraged the convergence of elements of hitherto opposing camps into a loose coalition. The beginnings of this new partnership to counter Ahmadinejad's assault on the nezam's independent institutions of governance were evident in November 2010 when a leader of the principlist faction in parliament, the hardliner Ali Motahari, alluded to the formation of an "unwritten alliance" with the smaller reformist faction in the eighth Majlis. See *Sharq*, 2 November 2010. Motahari's relationship with the reformists continued through to the ninth Majlis and the two sides continued to coordinate in later elections as well, as in the 2013 presidential race and also the 2016 Majlis elections.
142 Michael Slackman, 'Elite Guard in Iran Tightens Grip with Media Move', *New York Times*, 9 October 2009.
143 Quoted in Mike Shuster, 'Iran's Economic Troubles Mount as Sanctions Loom', National Public Radio, 5 April 2010.
144 RFE/RL, 5 December 2012.
145 Ali Gheissari and Vali Nasr, *Democracy in Iran: History and the Quest for Liberty* (Oxford: Oxford University Press, 2006), p. 158.
146 Rafsanjani applied to stand knowing he would be rejected, but anyway he decided to apply to give the Leader the chance to reject both himself and Mashaei, reducing Ahmadinejad's room for reaction and saving at the same time the image of neutrality of the Guardian Council and the Leader himself. With his political sacrifice, he deserved the right to impose Rouhani (his closest ally) instead of Aref (closer to Khatami) in the final stage of the presidential race. If this hypothesis is true, then Rafsanjani's move would be a master piece of *realpolitik* that helped him not only to

survive the last eight years without falling from grace but also to return to the main elite circle in the Islamic republic with a considerable amount of power over the elective and non-elective institutions of the state.

147 Hassan Bastani, *How Powerful Is Rouhani in the Islamic Republic?* (London: Royal Institute of International Affairs, November 2014), p. 7.
148 See http://www.iransview.com/unified-iranian-reformists-behind-rowhani-the-worst-news-for-principalists/927/.
149 See http://ipos.me/.
150 Shireen T. Hunter, *Iran Divided: The Historical Roots of Iranian Debates on Identity, Culture and Governance in the Twenty-First Century* (London: Rowman and Littlefield, 2014).
151 One example of this strategy is the adopted bill tabled by an outgoing conservative member of parliament, Ahmad Tavakoli, instructing the government to cut cash subsidies to one-third of the population. While a similar measure had been mooted by government itself, and this measure would likely save the exchequer around $3 billion per year, the timing of its implementation was now being dictated by this piece of legislation and not through government planning. A result of this will be disgruntlement against Rouhani by the vast majority of the population set to lose this important cash subsidy. See Khatereh Vatankhah, 'Outgoing Iran Parliament Moves to Radically Cut Cash Handouts', *al-Monitor*, 26 April 2016.
152 ILNA, 16 January 2016.
153 IRNA, 17 January 2016.
154 Mehr news agency, 5 February 2016.
155 Nicola Pedde, 'The Nuclear Agreement: Tehran's Take', *Aspenia*, no. 68–69–70, 2015, pp. 141–48.
156 According to a poll taken by the Tehran-based Tabnak news site in mid-February 2016, more than 60 per cent of Iranians received their electoral campaign information from the Internet and particularly from such apps as Telegram and Instagram, and only 20 per cent from official (often state-controlled) media sources such as radio and television. https://www.tabnak.ir/fa/news.
157 Gerdab, 16 October 2015.
158 Fars News Agency, 16 October 2015.
159 IRNA, 17 October 2015.
160 Fars News Agency, 2 November 2015.
161 ISNA, 2 January 2016.
162 CPJ, 11 January 2016.
163 Agence France Presse, 25 February 2016.
164 Agence France Presse, 19 February 2016.
165 Tabnak, https://www.tabnak.ir/fa/news.
166 Sanam Vakil, 'Despite Election Triumph, Rouhani Still Faces Formidable Foes', RIIA Expert Comment, 1 March 2016.
167 In a clear message to the conservatives, Gholam-Ali Haddad-Adel, the Principlist leader and former Majlis speaker, and relative of the Leader by marriage, lost his Tehran seat.
168 *The Economist*, 'Iran: The Revolution Is Over', 1 November 2014.
169 Iran's population appears to be aging fastest in the region with the 60 to 74 age group projected to be the largest cohort by 2050. See Spengler, 'The Horizon Collapses in the Middle East', *Asian Times*, 9 October 2012.
170 *Hamshahri*, 17 November 1997.
171 *The Economist*, 'Iran: The Revolution Is Over', 1 November 2014.
172 Rouzbeh Parsi, 'The Usual Surprise? Iran's Presidential Elections', *European Union Institute for Security Studies*, June 2013.
173 Yael Yishai, *Civilian Society in Israel towards the Year 2000 – Between State and Society* (Jerusalem: Paul Baerward School of Social Work, 1998), p. 155.

174 Alamdari, op. cit.
175 Daniel Brumberg, *Reinventing Khomeini: The Struggle for Reform in Iran* (Chicago, IL: University of Chicago Press, 2001).
176 Arzoo Osanloo, 'Contesting Governance: Authority, Protest, and Rights Talk in Postrepublican Iran', in Steven Heydemann and Reinoud Leenders (eds.) *Middle East Authoritarianisms: Governance, Contestation, and Regime Resilience in Syria and Iran* (Stanford, CA: Stanford University Press, 2013), pp. 127–42.
177 Freedom House, *Iran: Freedom on the Net 2015*, http://www.freedomhouse.org.
178 Parisa Najafi Tonekaboni, 'Iranian Bloggers and Internet Censorship', International Society for Human Rights, http://www.ishr.org.

3
IRAN'S POLITICAL ECONOMY

Context

Today, Iran is a medium-sized economy with the potential to become a leading Asian powerhouse. Already the world's eighteenth largest economy, and with a well-educated population of some 80 million people, a GDP of $540 billion ($998 billion in PPP terms), large landmass and rich mineral resources, plentiful power sources (and one of Asia's largest generators of electricity with 233 billion kilowatt hours of electricity), Iran remains one of the developing world's truly promising economies. In terms of GDP and population, Iran is the second-largest country in the region and as such carries significant weight in the Middle East and in Asia. Table 3.1 highlights the weight of the Iranian economy before new multilateral sanctions weakened it.

Iran is also one of the world's great trading nations, as Table 3.2 illustrates. It is noteworthy that Iran is one of the few MENA states in the list of top fifty leading exporters. Typically, oil exporters dominate the list of MENA countries, but Iran has traditionally been a great trading nation and exporter of fine products (carpets, silverware, fine art, handicrafts) and foodstuffs (including such valuable items as saffron).[1] The oil states are also the most vulnerable to market fluctuations and external conditions, but few have also suffered so directly from external pressure (sanctions) as Iran has done since the revolution.

Despite the economy's many problems, Iran's potential as an emerging economy has resulted in it being listed by Goldman Sachs as a member of the Next-11 ('N-11') group of emerging economies to follow in the footsteps of the BRICS. For now, though, Iran remains one of the world's least globalized countries, occupying the 134th position in a list of 140 countries in the DHL Global Connectedness Index 2014: In terms of depth of globalization, the Islamic republic was at the bottom of the table in 2014 (140th place) and in terms of breadth it

TABLE 3.1 Iran's economy in regional context, 2010/11

Country	GDP (PPP) ($billion)	Electricity generation (bkwh)	Stock mkt capitalization (as % of GDP)	FDI inflow ($billion)
Egypt	501	147	21	−0.5
Iran	**835**	**233**	**19**	**4.2**
Israel	211	59	60	11.2
KSA	700	240	59	16.3
Turkey	1,300	211	26	16.0
UAE	378	98	26	8.0

Source: World Bank database.

TABLE 3.2 Leading MENA countries in world top 50 trading countries, 2012

Country	Exports ($billion)	Rank	Imports ($billion)	Rank
Egypt	29	46	69	28
Iran	**104**	**27**	**57**	**33**
Israel	63	37	75	27
KSA	388	10	156	21
Turkey	152	22	237	15
UAE	350	12	230	17

Source: World Trade Organization, *International Trade Statistics 2013* (Geneva: WTO, 2013).

occupied the 91st position.[2] It languishes near the bottom on several counts: It ranks 136/137 in press freedom, 90/140 in labour freedom, and 135/140 in financial freedom.

Iran's economy is weak in the twenty-first century, and as it struggles to establish a strong economic system at home it at the same time struggles to find its place in the globalized international division of labour. In this it shares much with Iran of the late eighteenth century. Then, Iran began its march towards modernity, under the direct influence of European powers. But the nineteenth century ended with many of Iran's economic problems unresolved: Public debt had been rising fast, against a devalued currency and flat world prices for raw materials. At the same time the economy was 'internationalizing', opening up to British, Russian and other European capital, which was being invested in the development of the country's infrastructure, food production, petroleum, and some manufacturing. In the twentieth century, the situation became more dynamic and in the aftermath of the constitutional revolution, which brought to an end the politically diminished Qajar dynasty, oil surfaced as an attractive source of income, and a national bourgeoisie began to emerge, founding "several relatively large industrial, commercial, and financial enterprises".[3] This was unprecedented for Iran's semi-agrarian economy, yet the rapid decline of the Qajars also disrupted progress and wreaked havoc with the economy, further opening up the country to Anglo-Russian penetration. Having partitioned the country into spheres of influence in 1907, Tehran had effectively become a pawn in a game of imperial power politics being played out by Britain and Russia.

During the Great War (1914–18) the Iranian economy suffered greatly from crop failure, famine and the collapse in global markets for its exports, but the redrawing of geopolitical maps after the war gave Iran hope of recovery, which it grabbed in 1925 under a new political order. The first Pahlavi king, Reza Khan, showed much ambition for the development and renewal of Iran and thus set about modernizing the economy, but he too had to balance his ambitions against external pressures, as characterized by the 1929 Wall Street Crash, which practically ruined the Iranian economy.[4] Nevertheless, under his rule a new era had begun. The much-vaunted technical progress was made possible through the strong arm of the state under direct control of Reza Shah – not pretty but effective. Given the power structures that he had created around him since the mid-1920s, his forced abdication in 1941 removed the central pivot of the state and directly added to the socioeconomic chaos that followed the occupation of the country by the Allies and its economic decline. What followed was "hyper-inflation, shortages of food and other necessities, a ravaged infrastructure, and a virtual stand-still in investment".[5]

Iran also started the century as the world's first quintessential oil state, having seen oil produced as early as 1903, and the first international shipment was made in the run up to the Great War in 1912. After the war, oil formed the main plank of the economy and on the eve of the Second World War was accounting for some 13 per cent of government income and 62 per cent of the country's foreign exchange. By the late-1950s, oil was responsible for 15 per cent of GNP, 61 per cent government revenues, and 59 per cent of Iran's foreign exchange contributions.[6] The economy's fate was thus attached to that of oil, which after the Second World War had become the most desirable raw material and main source of fuel and energy for the industrial world. Iran, thus, had been placed in the fast stream of international capitalism.

Iran's economic development in the post-Second World War period

If Reza Khan's reign created the modern system, then the Qajar period was by definition pre-modern. Under the Qajars, there was not a national economy to speak of as Iran was a socially and geographically fragmented polity, and its socioeconomic structure lent itself to the flourishing of social communities of rich and poor. As a consequence, "Iranians were not loyal to their nation, or to any economic grouping; instead, they were loyal to their family, clan, local community, or religious sect".[7] Thus, upon taking power Reza Khan set about undertaking wholesale modernization of the state, society and with these also the economy.

The 1930s marked the birth of Iran's new economy. From the start, this was a state-led enterprise: "economic modernization centered around the shah's person. Partly out of distrust for the abilities of private Iranian citizens, and partly out of admiration for Ataturk's statist mercantilism, Reza Shah made the government the repository of all economic initiative".[8] As Limbert notes, Reza Shah's modernization programme increased government spending tenfold at crucial stages of economic development.[9] Through taxation and a known fixed income from oil production, the state created "electric power plants, roads, telecommunications facilities, government office buildings, and textile, cement, and food-processing factories".[10] The driver for Reza Shah was self-sufficiency, which of course also became the bear bug of the Islamic regime some half a century later.

In the rush to modernize and expand, government paid for the building of schools, ministries, roads, railroads, power-generation plants, factories, and Iran's first institution of tertiary-level education – Tehran University. The state also had to pay the salaries of all these new employees! Thus, the state led the creation of the modern economy of Iran, and increasing oil revenues (accrued to the state) after the war kept it in control of the mixed economy's commanding heights. The state did not create Soviet-style state enterprises, but with the introduction of formal seven-year (and later five-year) 'development plans' after the war, it embarked on a strategy of channelling resources to prioritized sectors. To help national development megaprojects, such as road and rail infrastructure development, basic industry factory building, irrigation, telecommunications, public utilities and services were prioritized.[11]

After the Second World War and the eventual departure of the Allies, the new king began making strenuous efforts to rebuild the much weakened economy and did so very much in alliance with the West, which of course fuelled tensions and political crises at home between his pro-Western allies and the Islamist and nationalist forces. Crisis of governance, 1941–53, was overcome with the victory of the monarchists in the fateful coup of August 1953 against the nationalist government of Mohammad Mossadegh. The critical events of 1953 and 1962 (White Revolution and the emergence of Khomeini as a radicalized cleric) proved to be the precursors to the mass uprisings of 1978 and 1979, but between 1953 and 1973 major macroeconomic changes had begun shaping Iran's economy. First, despite criticisms of the 1954 Agreement between Iran and the Consortium of Western oil companies following the 1953 coup, it is fair to conclude that it gave the government much better terms on the extraction of Iranian oil by foreign companies. As Mostofi notes,

> [The Agreement] at that time was more favourable than any other agreement of its kind in the Middle East and contained many elements that enabled Iran to reach its ultimate objectives, albeit in the course of twenty years. Furthermore, it ended an impasse and economic stagnation. In a comparatively short time the Iranian oil industry regained its rightful place among the producing nations and in twenty years increased its export ten fold.[12]

Crucially, the oil agreement facilitated more rapid capital accumulation and state investment in basic industries, health and education and infrastructure. Oil income, making up some 54 per cent of government revenues in the mid-1960s, also enabled the regime to co-opt the middle classes and situate them within the state's strategy of modernization. Relative autonomy of the state linked to the accumulation of state-controlled oil revenues provided the means for the regime to literally shape society, while bypassing social classes.[13] Oil, finally, also locked Iran into the global political economy as an emerging capitalist state with a close alliance with the West in the Cold War and a source of reliable and cheap energy.

Oil drives change

The four development plans until 1973 (i.e. before the oil price revolution), which followed their introduction in 1949, had a catalytic effect on the country and transformed the economy from a largely agrarian one to a semi-industrial one. But of particular importance to the story of Iran's economic transformation has been the role of oil income, which, having gone up by more than 100 per cent between 1955 and 1973, generated $12.3 billion in revenues in the 1949–73 period (which was less than the revenue in every single year between 1974–79). Oil revenues, argues Amuzegar, "helped finance nearly 85 per cent ($8.9 billion) of the Plan Organizations'… $10.5 billion allocated domestic investment during 1956–1973".[14] An organic relationship, thus, had been born between oil and the state, in which oil revenues acted as the financial lungs for the state's efforts to breathe new life into the Iranian economy.

The state had become dependent on oil revenues for the bulk of the country's national income and expenditures, and the fiscal autonomy derived from the control of oil income would enable it to act in new ways and increasingly immune from pressures from below. After the coup, the Shah quickly emerged as the all-powerful supreme authority in the country and used his superior vantage point to launch his ambitious and transformational 'White Revolution' in 1963. This new relationship between the monarch, the state and oil was to have far-reaching consequences for the country and its socioeconomic makeup, which first institutionalized rentierism as the form of Iran's political economy and at the same time led to the de-politicization of social forces which reduced formal opposition to policy changes.[15]

The absorption of oil income was also important to Iran's development strategy, which until the mid-1960s had followed an ISI (import-substitution industrialization) strategy. Oil income was used to encourage the development of local industry and manufacturing (assembly plants in practice), as well as the creation of such basic, feeder industries as steel, cement, bricks, petrochemicals and plastics, power (hydro and nuclear), and desalination.

The state also had its sights on the private sector and, through a series of incentives from the mid-1970s, encouraged the growth of investment in the country's increasingly buoyant but protected national economy. Still, empirical analyses suggest that the state's share in national investment grew exponentially: In 1959 the public sector had accounted for around two-fifths of the country's total investment, which by 1974 had increased to three-fifths (of a much bigger economic pie).[16]

For all the economic progress that had been made since the war, though, the decade of the 1970s fundamentally changed Iran's political economy. The key driver of this change, of course, as will be shown, was unexpectedly high oil income accrued in a very short period of time.[17]

As Table 3.3 shows, oil production began to increase fairly rapidly in the course of this decade, only having reached the 2 mb/d production mark for the first time in 1966. The expansion in oil output in a short period of time is significant, but what is more telling is the income being generated by oil exports from the early 1970s.

Data shows that while Iran's oil exports steadily began to increase from 1971, the income generated grew by a much bigger margin: From $3.7 billion in 1972 to $21.0 billion in just two years. Table 3.4 also highlights the emergence of another structural problem for the Iranian economy: Namely the near total dominance of Iran's exports by oil. As will be shown below, the ratio of oil exports to total exports rose to around 95 per cent by the end of the decade.

Iran, thus, joined the ranks of the Persian Gulf's 'capital surplus countries', growing the country's international interdependence and its deeper immersion into the fast-integrating global economy. But unlike the smaller Gulf Arab states, Iran was able to absorb a high proportion of its accrued income and as a consequence its investment capital enabled it to dramatically 'renegotiate' its place in the international division of labour and move from the 'periphery' of the world system to its 'semi-periphery' and closer to the interconnectivity of the 'centre' of global capitalism. Transnational corporations also took a keener

TABLE 3.3 Crude oil production and exports, 1970–79 ('000 b/d)

	1970	1971	1972	1973	1974	1975	1976	1977	1978	1979
Exports	3.309	3.979	4.498	5.277	5.369	4.671	5.214	4.867	4.447	2.407
Total	3.879	4.540	5.023	5.861	6.022	5.350	5.883	5.663	5.242	3.168

Source: OPEC database.

Note: Figures have been rounded for convenience.

TABLE 3.4 Value of total and crude oil exports, 1970–76 ($billion)

	1970	1971	1972	1973	1974	1975	1976
Oil exports	2.3	3.5	3.7	5.6	21.0	19.6	22.9
Total exports	2.4	3.8	4.0	6.2	21.5	20.2	23.5

Source: OPEC database.

interest in Iran and began winning hundreds of multibillion dollar contracts from the mid-seventies onwards. Thus, by 1975, 162 firms with foreign partners were already operating in the country, distributed as follows: Forty-five from the United States, twenty-two from Germany (FRG), twenty-one from the United Kingdom, nineteen from Japan, twelve from France, eight from Switzerland, five from Denmark and the remaining thirty-three from an assortment of other large and small countries.[18]

State-society relations under the monarchy

Additional income helped fast-track the economy's development and facilitated the transformation of the economy at a rate much faster than anticipated by the planners. Hence, noted Campbell in 1977, the economic plans of the previous two decades were dwarfed by those of the 1970s: "large sums have gone into investment in new basic industries and infrastructure for further expansion. Iran, which had no steel industry in the mid-1960s, now plans to be producing some 20 million tons in the 1980s, bringing it to the level of France or Britain today".[19]

To understand the nature of forces shaping the Iranian state today, we first need a clear view of state-society relations in pre-revolution Iran and the social structures that the Pahlavi monarchy developed. This capitalist state, unique in form and structure amongst the group of emerging economies in the 1970s commonly referred to as newly industrializing or semi-peripheral, had emerged through a two-pronged process: A struggle by the state against the traditional bourgeoisie, and their merchant (*bazaar*) and middle classes allies (with close links to the clerical establishment) on the one hand, and rapid integration of Iran into the global economy on the other. To fully appreciate the dynamics of power in Iran, we must dig deep into the roots of the state that became pregnant with revolution in the 1970s.

A key 'gene' of the old order was the Pahlavi regime's 1960s 'White Revolution', which introduced a series of fundamental socioeconomic reforms. The White Revolution did much irrevocably to change the social structure of the country, accelerate urban migration, and also to test the relationship between the ruling establishment and Iran's Shia (religious) hierarchy. The White Revolution (launched after a favourable referendum in January 1963) was founded on the principle of modernization of Iran's economy and society, and the disenfranchisement of the landed gentry in favour of massive redistribution of land holdings, privatization of state-held industrial units, female empowerment, improved healthcare and education. Though land distribution was not completed when the monarchy collapsed, nevertheless these and other socio-cultural initiatives formed the core of the reform programme, the overwhelming consequence of which was dramatic social change. For example, as a result of land redistribution, which was intended to improve agricultural productivity by giving farmers a bigger stake in the land, a significant proportion of the landed gentry was forced to look for new ways of capital accumulation and soon joined the ranks of Iran's growing group of entrepreneurs. Some took their lead from the government and established substantial agri-businesses, but many eventually joined the core of Iran's fast-growing comprador bourgeoisie – state dependent and active in commerce, finance and industry. In Heyat's words, "after land reform, previous land owners did not disappear but were transformed into agricultural, industrial and commercial capitalists and some of them became government employees".[20]

Massive improvements in the terms of trade for the country's most precious asset, oil, from 1971 onwards helped to accelerate the pace of socioeconomic change, in both relative and absolute terms. As already noted, Iran's oil receipts jumped from a healthy but rather modest $2.4 billion in 1970, to $5.6 billion in 1973 to $20.1 billion only a year later, climaxing at nearly $22.0 billion in 1978. Iran was transformed from a debtor to a capital surplus country overnight. Indeed, Iran's revised (due to the influx of significant additional unit of resource) fifth development plan (1973–78) provides a good illustration of the scale of oil income-driven change being introduced. The revised plan calculated total fixed investments and current expenditures of some $123.0 billion (in 1975 dollars) for the five-year period, 80 per cent of which was expected to come from oil revenues. The original fifth plan had calculated $32.2 billion worth of investment and expenditures and an annual GNP growth rate of 11.4 per cent.[21] Graham argues that the revised budget and massive expenditures created an uncontrollable boom which set the economy on the course of destruction. Total fixed investment increases against the original plan of 53 per cent in the industry and mines sector, of 72 per cent in agriculture and natural resources, of 161 per cent in transport and communications, of 130 per cent in housing, of 72 per cent in energy, and of 90 per cent in other sectors caused massive disruption.[22] Pesaran further contends that the same asset (oil) also diminished the urgency of developing and promoting the country's non-oil export industries (which would have helped Iran diversify the economy), and weakened the government's resolve to address the problems associated with the country's ailing tax system.[23] The increase in state expenditures raised inflation to over 20 per cent, created bottlenecks at ports and thus increased scarcity and made imports of critical industrial inputs more expensive, increased speculation in land, housing and such essential materials as cement, steel and bricks, created new demand for imported foodstuffs and luxury goods, and ultimately fuelled discontent against unfulfilled promises.

Nevertheless, the injection of additional funds into the economy accelerated the process of modern industrialization introduced from the late 1950s. Thus, in the ten years following 1965 industry grew at an annual average rate of 15 per cent and by 1977 there were approximately 250,000 manufacturing establishments in place, employing some 2.5 million people.[24] In essence, the revised plan intensified the process of socioeconomic change and also the concentration of wealth and power.[25]

The political economy of the country was being sketched by an elite-engineered social alliance, which determined not only Iran's macroeconomic orientation but also the social pyramid of the country in terms of its class structure and the relationship between the state and the economic elites of the country. In this process the state "developed into a rentier capitalist state, controlling the emerging social classes".[26] The Pahlavi compact was the basis for the consolidation of a state-dependent comprador bourgeois class which would be expected to help realize Iran's ambition of becoming one of the developing world's leading economies by the 1980s. The bases for this transformation were arguably being laid in the late 1950s and Iran's return to the international markets as a credible and cheap source of oil and as a safe home for transnational capitalist development. IMF data suggests that amongst the most promising Asian countries of the 1960s, Iran was the most attractive to foreign capital. Remarkably, in that period Iran had attracted more direct private investment than Asia's other leading developing economies combined. Furthermore, as is evident from Table 3.5, while the other leading developing Asian countries were heavily dependent on foreign loans for their development, Iran was already building a strong relationship with foreign private capital.

Moreover, OECD data shows that in the 1960s Iran led Asia in the securing of export credits (which is a source of foreign long-term capital): A total of $643 million in the eighteen-member Economic Commission for Asia and the Far East region (ECAFE), against the other major recipients of South Korea ($521 million), Philippines ($338 million), India ($250 million), and Indonesia ($240 million).[27]

The flames of the ambition to become a leading NIC were further fanned by the steep rises in oil prices between 1973 and 1977,[28] during which the heavy-handed monarchy revised upwards all of Iran's economic targets. In the 1970s, the protective state set about nurturing the comprador class and its associated modern and largely urban-based middle class, and in so doing reengineered Iran's traditional socioeconomic structures. The modern middle classes grew with the size of the bureaucracy and the regime's economic ambitions, making the state the country's most important employer. Compared with just 102,000 managers, professionals, and skilled administrators employed by the private sector in 1976, the state employed some 1.67 million people.[29] As Nomani and Behdad's detailed calculations show, in 1976 no more than "477,000 (5.4 percent) of the employed workforce could be considered in the middle class, and no less than 78.7 percent of this small middle class were employees of the state".[30] The capitalist class by

TABLE 3.5 Foreign private investment and long-term loans, 1960–69 ($ millions)

	Direct investment	Loans	Total
Iran	592.30	71	663.2
South Korea	66.60	1,188	1,255
Taiwan	184.60	488	632.9
Thailand	278.50	820	1,098

Source: IMF, *Balance of Payments Yearbook* (various annual editions).

comparison numbered 182,000 in that year, with nearly 80 per cent of this social group being based in the urban economy.

The quantitative expansion taking place in the Iranian economy during this period is illustrated in Table 3.6. The dramatic rise in (oil) revenues accrued to the state in less than five years in the first half of the 1970s is best observed in terms of the local currency (rial)

The massive injection of funds inevitably introduced some fundamental structural problems for the economy – with absorption capacity, skills shortages, and serious bottlenecks being just three of them. At the height of the boom, for instance, cargo ships had to wait over 100 days before they could dock and unload their cargo, which in 1975 alone cost $1.5 billion in surcharges and penalties paid to shipping lines. Perishable goods were discarded as soon as they were unloaded and industrial inputs often corroded on the dockside. Without the injection of spare parts and intermediate goods into Iran's largely assembly-based industrial and manufacturing sector units production and also productivity suffered, bringing the whole system to a grinding halt in the second half of the 1970s. By 1977 the economic crisis was so pervasive that the regime thought it prudent to pass the blame for the chaos and the inevitable inflation in consumer prices on to the bourgeoisie, effectively kicking a leg of support from under itself just a few months away from the first sign of unrest. Though there might inevitably have been an element of feel-good factor amongst the lower and the middle classes seeing businessmen harassed by newly appointed 'prices vigilantes' and publicly humiliated in front of monitoring tribunals, in arresting and heavily fining a number of prominent entrepreneurs for price fixing and hoarding of essential commodities, the regime also exposed its financial underbelly by in effect encouraging capital flight in its gravest hour of need. This in practice further eroded its already thin base and also alienated the one social group capable of financially helping to fix the problem.

In Iran's case, the Shah, and many close members of his family and entourage sat atop the country's power pyramid, using the state as the vehicle for accumulation and manipulation.[31] In Iran's 'triangle of fortune', "the court stood at its peak and the native and Western industrialists occupied its corners".[32] Unlike Latin American or the industrializing Asian countries, the military played virtually no role (beyond support for the monarchy) in Iran's economy or political

TABLE 3.6 GNP and oil price growth rates, 1971–74 (rials and %)

Year	GNP	Growth rate	Oil revenues	Growth rate
1971	962.7	20.6	152.1	74.4
1972	1,183.1	22.6	182.9	20.2
1973	1,763.3	49.0	477.5	161.1
1974	3,020.4	71.3	1,297.4	171.7

Source: Plan and Budget Organization, and Central Bank of Iran (various years).

power relationships – a reality which would be a critical factor in the revolution itself and indeed the emerging post-revolution power settlement. In pre-revolution Iran, the monarchy had gone out of its way to ensure that the military would never pose an existential threat to the king and had effectively neutralized it through pampering it with financial and military-related rewards on the one hand and controlling its senior echelons on the other. As such, in the brewing struggle between the regime and its opponents the military – for all its resources and powerful network – was unable to behave as an intermediary. It was also unable to intervene directly and take power itself in the name of national interest, as has happened on numerous occasions in Pakistan and Turkey next door to Iran, despite being charged to govern by the Shah when martial law had been introduced in 1978.[33]

Another distinguishing feature of Iran's economic system compared with the other semi-peripheral countries was the continuing role of the state. Theoretically, the growing presence of foreign capital and foreign economic penetration, leading to greater integration into the world economy, should have kept the state weak and marginalized.[34] Iran was arguably similar to South Korea in bucking this trend and just as under President Park Chung Hee the South Korean state remained in charge of charting the economy and the role of foreign capital, so in Iran's case, and largely due to the rentier nature of the economy, the state (the Shah) remained firmly in control of the economic drivers of the country and was able to filter the bourgeoisie's relations with foreign capital. The similarity is striking: In Iran the state set the economic plans and priorities and dispersed the funds for development; in South Korea the rapid economic growth starting the early 1960s was "a government-directed development";[35] but unlike South Korea the private sector was not the principal engine of growth; it was the state.

The flip side of Iran's transformations was the 'proletarianization' of the peasant class, through which a substantial portion of this community found it impossible to finance its new holdings (equipment and seed were expensive and not always available) and in resignation joined the army of day labourers in bulging towns and cities.[36] Eventually, these day labourers became the foot soldiers of the revolution.

Consolidation of dependent capitalism under the monarchy

In addition to the domestic impact of the oil boom, changes in Iran's international position in this era also took place, making Iran more exposed to external forces, which by the mid-1970s included a recession in the West and Western anxiety about the impact of high oil prices on global stability. On the other hand, as a consequence of Iran's industrialization its role in the international division of labour also improved, further fuelling the pace of change at home. Commensurate with its growing economic muscle and the largely internationally supported strategy of its leadership, Iran was soon being identified amongst a handful of developing countries with the capacity to emerge as a newly industrializing country.[37] Critical theorists also considered Imperial Iran as uniquely placed to break free of the periphery and join a small group of what Immanuel Wallerstein called the semi-peripheral countries.[38] Iran's moment of 'dependent development' had arrived, in what Peter Evans articulated as the alliance of multinational, state and local capital, and Fernando Henrique Cardoso further characterized as 'associated-dependent development'.[39] Though these concepts were developed in the context of Latin American political economy, outside Latin America Iran emerged as one of only a handful of countries to which the dependent developed model became applicable. In this kind of system the state plays a central role and unquestionably also in Iran's case the state was the preeminent actor in the economy and the main feature of the country's political economy. Thus, by the end of the 1970s, the state had "emerged as the largest capitalist [entity]… and owned all heavy industries… all major transportation networks and agro-industries and tightly controlled the banking system".[40]

But it had not always been like this and until the early 1970s the state had acted in support of the private sector – "far from conflicting with public investment, private investment is dependent on it".[41] In fact, right up to 1968, private sector investment had consistently exceeded public sector investment.[42] But in the course of the revised fifth development plan (1973–78), the investment ratio between the public and private sectors was almost completely reversed: 66.1 per cent public sector and 33.9 per cent private sector. The trend had become irreversible and by 1974 the state had overtaken the private sector in terms of gross fixed capital formation. The dependent capitalist state, we should note in passing, became the second gene that the Islamic republic inherited from the monarchy.

The state, thus, became the "economic prop of the ruling regime",[43] and through state mechanisms the monarchy proceeded to adjust Iran's traditional import substitution industrialization approach to an export-oriented one, and it was in this context that foreign capital engaged with Iran in a serious way, in banking, insurance and other financial services, industry and agriculture. Though Iran did not fully adopt ESI, by Middle East regional standards, Iran's economy had evolved into one of the region's largest, most integrated, and most sophisticated. Indeed, even before the oil boom had taken full hold – in 1973 – Iran was already responsible for 24 per cent of the region's exports and 21 per cent of its imports. As many as 77 of Iran's total of 183 major foreign investors for the period from 1956 (when data series were standardized) to 1974 (the critical stage of Iran's economic revival) had arrived after 1970. Iran in turn invested its surplus income in Western institutions at the discretion of the Shah, using the country's national wealth to reward his allies in the US and in Europe.

So, for all its problems and shortcomings, by the middle of the 1970s Iran had by far the largest and most diversified economy in west Asia and its local markets were amongst the most lucrative in Asia. By the mid-1970s Iran's per capita income was nearly twice the regional average, with its GDP growing faster even than the industrial countries.[44] While in 1972 there were around 40 large industrial units that employed more than 5,000 workers each, by the late 1970s there were 12,000 large establishments operating in the country with 1,000 of them employing over 5,000 workers each. Value added in manufacturing had grown by 14 per cent per annum in the four years following 1968 and by an average of 15 per cent per year in the 1973–78 period.[45]

Iran's purchasing power facilitated its rapid integration into the new world economy of transnational capitalism. Iran's moving up of the international division of labour also of course in turn raised the stakes in the survival of its leadership. The Pahlavi state thus fully exploited the country's advantages for regime survival but also went further and exploited its international role for geopolitical gain and regional assertiveness, going as far as becoming Washington's main regional ally and the main pillar of American-crafted 'twin-pillar' security architecture in the strategic Persian Gulf. In becoming a 'sub-imperial' power, Iran further deepened the chain of interdependencies between the regime and the capitalist core, increasing in the process also Iran's military dependence on the West. Between 1973 and 1979, Iran had ordered well over $20 billion in armaments, including the highly sophisticated US-made hardware F-14 Tomcat fighter and the Boeing early warning AWACS aircraft, being Asia's only customer for these. So when revolution occurred the total losses of foreign transnational corporations were estimated to be around $80 billion, with dozens of big-ticket orders being cancelled by the successor regime.[46] Iran's geopolitical elevation also added to the anger of those who saw Iran's regional security and international economic roles as doing the West's bidding and merely reinforcing their interests in west Asia and the Muslim world.

But the massive social experiment in Iran ran out of time in 1978 and the eruption of anti-Pahlavi protests brought a swift end to the monarchy. Iran's modernization and Westernization under the two Pahlavi monarchs, however, was responsible for the shape and nature of the state that emerged. A state-led, indeed state-dominated, dependent capitalist system had been established. Iran's society was in transition, with new, old and longstanding social groups struggling to establish a firm base. All were keenly aware of the emerging orbits of economic power around the monarchy and the Pahlavi-dominated state. In an environment in which neither European-style feudalism nor colonialism had been present to shape class structures, a milieu of social groups had coexisted, making social stratification and relationships complex and opaque. The outgoing modernizing monarch had disrupted existing social patterns and in the process endangered the interests of influential pre-capitalist and/or marginalized elites. Disarticulated capitalism, moreover, had produced hybrid social groups whose survival and prosperity often depended on the state and the forces in control of the commanding heights of the economy. As the revolutionary wave grew, many of the establishment fragments would eventually find themselves exposed to uncontrollable pressures from long-forgotten quarters lodged in the religious cities of Qom and Mashhad and Iran's country-wide network of merchants – the bazaaris. The pressure from below had become irresistible.

Pahlavi modernity, moreover, had driven a wedge between the power elite and the cultural elite, the latter being still in the realm of the traditional segments of Iranian society and close to the clerical establishment. The struggle between 'mosque' and state, which had been one of the underlying features of political discourse in Iran since its 1905–11 Constitutional Revolution, again became a dominant current running through the new revolutionary struggle. The other critical current was the national obsession with 'independence' of action and a thirst for a national(ist) leadership dedicated to the realization of Iran's aspiration for greatness through self-sufficiency in economic and political realms. The revolutionary desire for total autonomy and delinking from the US-dominated capitalist orbit, as enshrined in Iran's post-1979 constitution, was of course as much a backlash against the Shah's dependent capitalist model as a deep-seated resentment of foreign interference in Iran by Western powers.[47] Both sentiments were nevertheless to be reflected in Iran's post-revolution constitution, helping to shape the outlines of an emerging economy that deliberately sought to control the relationship between itself and the wider international system, and also went a long way towards imposing constraints on capital accumulation by keeping 'strategic' sectors of the economy in state hands.

The Pahlavis dragged the Iranian economy into the modern age and, as a consequence of the centrally driven strategy of rapid economic development and infrastructural investment, transformed from an agrarian society into a semi-industrial one. By 1979 Iran was poised to take the next step in its economic development, but the flawed nature of its development strategy and the authoritarian ways of its monarch had widened social cleavages to such an extent that pressures of modernization caught up with, and soon overwhelmed, the authoritarian regime, brushing the whole social experiment aside. The marginalization of domestic (traditional) bourgeois forces in the consolidation of dependent development had meant that these socially rooted social groups had little or no stake in the survival of the Shah and when the structural limitations of the economic system pressed against the regime, it was unable to muster national support in countering them. As the metropole powers also shied away from supporting the Shah after 1978 the political limitations of the dependent development model were also reached.

But progress, significant economic progress, had been made. Authoritative analyses of the Pahlavi era, including Pesaran's own work, have shown that

TABLE 3.7 Value of petroleum exports in relation to total exports, 1973–79 ($billion)

	1973	1975	1977	1979
Petroleum exports	5.6	19.6	23.6	19.2
Total exports	6.2	20.2	24.3	19.8

Source: OPEC, *Annual Statistical Bulletin* (various annual editions).

despite social and economic disparities, the standard of living of the majority of Iranians improved substantially in the Pahlavi period.[48] Oil revenues helped transform the country's well-managed economy into a financially well-endowed one by the late 1970s. Karshenas, for example, has underlined the point about improvements in Iran's per capita growth, arguing that between the 1950s and mid-1970s,

> The Iranian economy showed impressive growth rates paralleled only by a few other major economies in the MENA region or Asia. Starting from per capita GDP levels in the 1950s which were already much higher than the average for the MENA region as a whole, the Iranian economy grew at a faster rate than the MENA average, such that by the mid-1970s per capita GDP in Iran was nearly double the MENA average.... In fact, by 1975 the GDP per capita in Iran was far above any of the newly industrializing countries in the Far East.[49]

The picture for the 1975–90 period proved to be very different which was one of rapid decline. Thus, "by 1990 GDP per capita in Iran had declined by half, to levels prevailing in the 1960s".[50] And, in comparison with two NICs that Iran had outperformed in the 1970s, by 1990, "Korea had achieved per capita income levels twice those prevailing in Iran and Turkey had overtaken Iran". Iran had bypassed its geo-economic destiny.

The revolution removed the scaffolding holding up the economy and the loss of foreign capital and access to Western markets and technologies severely diminished Iran's ability to compete internationally. On the event of the revolution, Iran had fallen off the radar and, interestingly, the other NICs rapidly overtook it, with Hong Kong, South Korea, Taiwan, (and Brazil) accounting for 74 per cent of all manufactured goods exports from the less developed countries.[51] Domestically too the monarchy had left behind a dependent capitalist economy which was almost totally dependent on oil rent for its survival (see Table 3.7). The phenomenal rise in incomes masks the country's almost total dependence on oil exports for its national income.

But the fall of the monarchy had more far-reaching consequences for the economy as it not only removed from Iran the monarch and his political regime but also the comprador bourgeois class which was attached to the monarchy. Thus, in one fell swoop Iran had lost both the conductor and the orchestra, and with it the means to keep the economic wheels turning at home and maintaining Iran's position abroad. The revolutionaries had inherited a high maintenance super car with no trained drivers or mechanics!

Iran's economy under the Islamic republic

To understand the new economy one will need to situate it in the role that oil has played and also the repeated shocks that the country has experienced: Revolution, war, sanctions, and mismanagement have all played their part in shaping the post-revolution national economy. In the post-war period corruption in state institutions compounded the problems facing the economy. With oil came rentierism, a relatively autonomous state, and an etatist political economy. The revolution was a product of the state in which it gestated, and so while it gave birth to a wholly unique state-type, inevitably it carried within it the many socioeconomic genes of the old order. But, as already noted, the 1979 revolution changed many things in Iran. It changed the country's ruling class and its governance structures and institutions; it redrew the country's relations with the outside world; and it fundamentally redrew the country's economic priorities. A snapshot of its trade partners (Table 3.8) illustrates well the revolutionary state's changing global economic priorities and relations.

The points to note are as follows. First, the dramatic disappearance of the United States as what had been an essential source of industrial and related imports left an immediate void in the country's industrial structure. Second, the non-US Western core countries managed to keep their position as suppliers to Iran, which remained the case well into the 2000s. Finally, there was a significant rise of developing and centrally planned economies as exporters to Iran. Thus, barely a decade after the revolution, the latter two groups were accounting for 36.25 per cent of Iran's total imports, compared with around 20.0 per cent in the late-1970s.

Indeed, the process of 'de-Westernization' of Iran's trade partners accelerated after the 1990s and by the early twenty-first century one could detect a significant rise in the place of Asian countries in Iran's economic partnerships. Abedini Moghanaki and Shariatinia catalogue this strategic shift in Iran's economic focus by showing that into the twenty-first century, with reference to 2013 for example, just five Asian countries absorbed 69.5 per cent of the country's entire non-oil exports, with China accounting for 24 per cent of Iran's total non-oil exports of $31.3 billion.[52] By contrast, twenty years earlier, Germany, Italy and Switzerland had accounted for 40 per cent of Iran's non-oil exports.

TABLE 3.8 Geographical composition of Iran's imports (%)

	1971	1976	1983	1986	1988
Major OECD	74.3	68.7	47.6	46.4	41.9
USA	24.0	16.6	1.1	0.4	0.9
FRG	18.3	17.9	17.4	17.3	19.0
Japan	11.9	16.3	16.3	13.3	9.3
UK	9.5	7.7	5.5	6.8	5.2
Italy	6.0	5.3	5.2	7.5	4.4
France	4.6	4.9	2.1	1.1	2.3
Global South	9.6	16.1	17.7	19.9	19.3
CPEs	5.8	4.7	12.2	11.6	16.9

Source: IMF, *Direction of Trade Statistics* (various annual editions).

Ironically, the modernizing monarchy had left in its wake a country financially fairly well endowed, with a largely autonomous state that was well placed to take advantage of the new international division of labour following the transnationalization of production and transfer of manufacturing offshore. But this economy was dependent on the West and the wider international economy for its very survival, its development. More fundamentally, the rapid growth of the economy between 1959 and 1978 had, by and large, taken place under an enduring ISI strategy and "in a highly protected domestic economy". Furthermore,

> The paradoxical result of this strategy was to make the economy increasingly dependent on oil export revenues in order to finance the growing needs of the industrial sector for imported intermediate and capital goods. The problems associated with the distorted and inflexible industrial structure that had developed during the pre-revolutionary period was felt acutely in the 1980s, when three decades of rapid growth in oil exports revenues finally came to an end.[53]

However, the strategy of the new regime did not facilitate the badly needed restructuring of the economy, which had become evident as early as the mid-1970s. Indeed, with investment in new industrial units by both private and public sectors dropping from a high of 46,992 million rials in 1977 to just 5,533 million rials in 1983, the economy was in steady decline as a result of the disruptions caused by the revolution, which the war merely compounded.[54] As a result, in the decade following the revolution, the country's dependence on oil exports remained as high as it had been under the monarchy (see Table 3.9), with devastating consequences when oil prices collapsed to under $10 per barrel in 1986.

The revolutionary critique of Iran's economic development strategy under the monarchy pushed efforts to sketch an alternative political economy for the country – redistributive and as far away from the capitalist core as possible.[55] This vision of a post-Pahlavi state was being articulated, and enshrined in the constitution, by a group of revolutionary leaders who had come of age in an era of anti-imperial struggles and radical-populist rhetoric which had seen 'de-linking' from the imperial orbit as a shortcut to equitable development. Not only did they want 'independence' but they also wanted an 'Islamic economy',

TABLE 3.9 Value of petroleum exports in relation to total exports, 1982–90 ($billion)

	1982	1984	1986	1988	1990
Petroleum	20.2	16.7	6.3	9.7	18.0
Total	20.5	17.1	7.2	10.7	19.3

Source: OPEC, *Annual Statistical Bulletin* (various annual editions).

no matter how ill-defined. At its heart, in Iran such notions as social justice, redistributive economic policies, and anti-privileges would emerge as the new narratives. These would then shape the elite's national economic strategies and the republic's approach to its global relationships.

Land reform ('land to the tiller') measures introduced in the early 1980s reduced the size of holdings, wreaking havoc with production, and at the same time so many industries were being brought under state control. So, not only was industry in trouble but also agriculture. Nevertheless, the revolutionary regime needed an economic development plan, and in the context of the constitutional conditions set for the economy of this Islamic republic, the proposed economic strategy was founded on three approaches: To reduce the country's dependence on oil income; strive towards self-sufficiency (khod kafayi); and develop commercial links with the Global South and non-aligned countries.

The revolution, clearly, effected some fundamental changes to the political economy of Iran. At its heart, the new Islamic state aimed to be a welfare state, based on its core values of delivering social justice. The pursuit of this principle inevitably led to the central government holding considerably more economic power than during the monarchy. Indeed, in pursuit of this objective and in response to the flight of the country's comprador bourgeoisie and abandoned businesses, the state became the main economic power by bringing under its control a substantial proportion of the previously privately owned manufacturing and services industries, mines, banks and insurance houses, infrastructural and transportation industries, and much more.[56] Azad notes that just months after the victory of the revolution thirty-seven banks and ten insurance houses were nationalized; foreign trade was nationalized soon after and the post-revolution provisional government took steps to bring capital flows and the foreign exchange rate under its control as well.[57] Very quickly, as much as 70 per cent of the country's capital was brought under state control and in this process Iran's political economy resembled more a state capitalist model not dissimilar to China, Venezuela and Russia.

The strategic economic sectors remained under the control of the state, and the market became much more regulated. These developments were of course consistent with Article 44 of the constitution, which explicitly gave the state control of 'mother' and large-scale industries. The Islamic republic was in effect trying to combine a state capitalist model with arguably a 'new socialist' model that considered redistributive strategy as a social priority and, despite continuing reliance on hydrocarbons as the engine of the economy, also a renegotiation of the country's position in the international capitalist system. So, despite the overwhelming presence of the state in the national economy, the petti-bourgeoisie and the traditional (bazaar) mercantile bourgeoisie continued to prosper and their continuing presence, as well as the massive growth in the assets accumulation and yawning social inequality, underline the reality that Iran has remained a capitalist country and market forces have continued to influence, if not shape, the Islamic republic's economic strategy. It was the founder of the Islamic republic himself, after all, who declared in 1985 that "we promise… as long as there is Islam there will be free enterprise also".[58]

Post-revolution developments in Iran underline the view that populist regimes are themselves prisoners of the old order and rarely do they have a truly transformative socioeconomic impact. They, in the last analysis, leave the social fundamentals unaffected and also leave relations of production intact. Iran's revolutionary regime proved to be no exception; it expropriated the means of production from the comprador bourgeoisie but was from the outset caught in the power struggle between the victorious social groups engaged in a competition for the control of the state. This was so because significant disagreements existed amongst the *ulama* (Shia clerical establishment) themselves not only about their role in government, the place of the bazaar in the new environment, or the nature of the republic's economy, but more fundamentally because the "economic views of the ayatollahs frequently reflected their classes of origin and continuing family ties. Those from landlord or wealthy merchant families manifested the preference… for maintaining an economic system that would protect their interests, and ayatollahs from less-affluent families generally expressed more concern for redistributing wealth toward the poor".[59] Roxborough's observation that the "weakness and lack of cohesion of social forces in society leave the way open for the petty bourgeoisie or a bureaucratic apparatus to substitute itself for the bourgeois", rings true in post-revolution Iran.[60] Thus, argues Jafari, Iran was transformed into a 'state capitalist' system dominated by an expanding bureaucracy and para-statal organizations: In post-revolution Iran the "state affected class formation… because of its central role in capital accumulation. A new bourgeoisie – the millionaire mullahs – grew in the interstices between the state sector, the *bonyads* [foundations] and the bazaar".[61]

War and the economy

Unquestionably, the eight-year long war with Iraq did exasperate the crisis which had befallen the revolutionary economy.

But the war also skewed the new regime's economic policies and priorities. Clearly, war inhibited the new regime's options and room for manoeuvre, imposing in the process a huge burden on the economy and wider society. First, its reliance on the oil sector intensified, forcing it to shelve one of the cornerstones of the new regime's strategy of reducing reliance on oil exports and therefore dependence on the international economy. Oil income was needed in order to mitigate rising budgetary costs caused by the war, rapidly depleting foreign exchange reserves (which was compounded by the freezing of Iran's overseas assets), and the country's worsening balance of payments situation. Second, the war damaged the economy very directly, as follows, in both actual and opportunity costs. The damage sustained by the country's oil production and export infrastructure was substantial: Oil fields were flooded, Abadan refinery and Khoramshahr port complexes were reduced to lumps of metal, waterways were blocked, off-shore loading terminals and pumping stations (Kharg and Sirri islands, Gureh) were severely damaged. Perhaps as much as $87 billion of additional oil revenues may have been lost.[62]

As a consequence, the country's increasingly scarce financial, manpower and technical resources were being diverted to cover the escalating cost of the war. Also, the introduction of rationing, as part of a 'coupon economy' conflicted with market forces and the market allocation of resources, increasing cost of distribution, if not production, but also availability of essential goods and consumerables, and also foodstuffs. As many as 67 cities and towns and a further 3,891 villages were damaged and hundreds of thousands of people were displaced. In this regard, former President Rafsanjani is quoted as suggesting that "between 60% and 70% of the country's income was spent on the war".[63] This perhaps amounted to some $1 trillion in direct and indirect damages, calculated Ghaffari, with Mofid suggesting that total direct damages were $644.3 billion. The cost of the war, thus, far exceeded the country's entire oil income generated from its outset in the early twentieth century. Not surprising then that proposed expenditures of around $15.3 billion on development, as outlined in the country's first development plan, were abandoned.[64] To make matters worse, the collapse of oil prices, to as little as $8 per barrel in the mid-1980s deprived the government of its one sure source of revenue. Resultantly, oil revenues dropped from their post-revolution high of $20 billion in 1983 to just $6.6 billion in 1986.[65]

To put the price paid for the war in context, it has been calculated that Iran's real GDP was the same in 1988 as it had been in 1975 – thirteen years earlier – and per capita GDP in 1988 was equal to what it had been in 1970 – eighteen years previously.[66] Private investment had shrunk to a quarter of what it had been in 1977.[67] Unemployment at the end of the war had reached 16 per cent and inflation was running at an annual rate of 32.4 per cent. In the decade following the revolution, notes Amirahmadi, "Iran made less than $145 billion from oil exports as compared with $410 billion that it lost in direct economic damage".[68] The much vaunted 'Islamic economic' necessity of redistribution was shelved soon after the start of the war and this core principle of the Islamic state's political economy was sacrificed to the altar of growth economics, with the focus shifting to conventional understanding of economics and a recognition that the government's main priority should be to encourage growth and investment.[69]

In this context the regime unveiled its first five-year development plan (1983–88), which also provides clues to the long-term orientation of the Islamic republic.[70] A point of reference for the need to create a planned economy was revealed in 1983 and a report published by the Plan and Budget Organization calculated that the war had already cost the public sector alone $90 billion in damages. This initial plan was therefore designed to manage the losses being incurred by the war. Given the economy's deep crisis it was not surprising that this plan failed to deliver on any of its targets or planned outcomes. Factional in-fighting did not help matters either in which conservative forces close to the clerical establishment doggedly opposed the further centralization of the economy, as they saw it, which to them was against Islamic norms in any case.

In this context, economic exhaustion and ongoing factional disputes over the republic's economic strategy, towards the end of his premiership, Mousavi signalled a change of course in the direction of economic reforms to reduce the state's involvement in the economy. Thus, his government announced that it was aiming to give the private sector a greater role in the economy by giving it a greater share of the economy. In April 1989, in the last days of his government, Mousavi's ministerial team announced what was billed as a comprehensive privatization strategy leading to the transfer of ownership of all "non-essential and non-strategic" sectors of the economy to the private sector,[71] and in July his government was talking of using foreign borrowing to meet the country's post-war investment needs.[72] Even though a denationalization plan had been made as early as 1985 it took a further four years before the political conditions would allow the introduction of such dramatic changes in what had been an etatist state-revolutionary development strategy.

The war indisputably had a devastating and lasting impact on the political economy of the young Islamic republic and imposed costs from which it has arguably not yet been able to recover. The war may have disguised another tendency, if not intensified it, and that was the changes in the scale of private sector involvement in the country. Valibeigi notes that while in the early years of the revolution the number of permits issued to the private sector for the establishment of industrial units increased from 188 per year in 1974–78 to 367 per year in 1979–83, "the average size of investment in a new industrial unit in 1976 was 229.3 million rials, the average size of investment per new industrial unit established in 1983 was only 6.6 million rials… the magnitude of this reduction is so substantial that it can be considered as a major structural shift in the scale and type of private investment".[73] But in addition, the economy also suffered from what Amuzegar sees as ideologically driven resorting "to public ownership, price control, industrial regulation, import substitution, and overall economic regimentation designed to produce an elusive self-sufficiency".[74]

However, the long view shows that despite its many immediate and unresolved structural problems, the economy did not collapse, inflation, though high (20 per cent in the mid-1980s), was contained, food and other essential goods and services were made available, and an effective and transparent system of support for war victims was put into place.[75] Perhaps most interestingly of all, the private sector – though shrunken – had continued to thrive, accounting for 68.4 per cent of the employed population in 1986.[76]

The nineties: challenging taboos

The war had taken a heavy toll on Iran, not only exhausting its coffers but also leaving its national economy in tatters. The end of the war led to much soul-searching about the new direction of the country, and debates regarding social and economic development, foreign policy, and even cultural policy were taking place in the media and in Tehran's corridors of power. By autumn 1988 factional tensions over economic policy had become so overt and confrontational that Ayatollah Khomeini had to intervene to calm down matters. In trying to maintain the balance between the proponents of continuing tight controls and those wishing to open the economy to the private sector, he said, rather cryptically, that "academic argument should be given a high place in Islam and be encouraged rather than suppressed in the interest of dogmatic interpretations and authoritarian outlooks".[77]

Much energy was spent on the country's economic reconstruction strategy and inevitably on the need to change the country's relationship with foreign capital. The sitting government of Dr Mir Hossein Mousavi, the left-leaning premier, was adamant that economic policy should not weaken the corporatist direction of the economy. He said in September 1988 that "under no circumstances must our independence be compromised [by the activities of the domestic or foreign private sector]".[78] Arguments over economic principles had spilled over to affect economic policy and while Rafsanjani and President Khamenei were already hinting, in the autumn of 1988, at the changes being necessary in order to break the deadlock between institutions and competing political factions, it was not until Ayatollah Khomeini's death that structural change was finally possible. So the end of the war provided the conditions for the dramatic changes in economic policy.

The direction of travel following the war was explained thus: "the concentration of affairs within the state was a necessity during the war, a necessity which does not exist any more".[79] The emergence of a new executive president intent on opening the country to the rest of the world made the policy changes possible. There was a degree of urgency in this and an awareness of the crisis facing the country: "No one in the ruling class understood better than Rafsanjani", argues Jafari, "that the economic precipice facing the Islamic Republic meant it could not be business as usual if it were to survive".[80]

President Rafsanjani was quick to set about tackling the country's economic problems and in this challenge many of the ideological taboos (resisting foreign direct investment and foreign borrowing, limiting trade with the West, etc.) that had constrained the country's potential. His 'cabinet of reconstruction' had one goal in mind: To remove the structural barriers in the way of Iran's economic progress. "To increase the country's production... we should inject the capital which is at present accumulated in the private sector", Rafsanjani had said in December 1988, while still the Majlis speaker.[81] The strategy for the post-war economy was introduced by the newly created office of a new executive president whose task after the war was to improve the country's economy. The five-year plan (1989–94) focused on recovering economic ground lost and injection of additional resources into the moribund sectors of the economy. It, therefore, set itself the task of liberalizing the economy and privatization of the multitude of assets accumulating in the hands of the state and para-statal organizations. The post-war government made it clear that it recognized that in the post-Cold War order "economic considerations overshadow political priorities".[82]

In this endeavour he also had the backing of the IMF and the World Bank, which had outlined the need for the reforms and the engagement of the private sector to deal with Iran's structural problems. But addressing these problems did not seem easy.[83] The administration began to work on a number of fronts simultaneously: Putting up for privatization some 800 publicly owned enterprises, rationalizing the (multiple) exchange rate system, energizing the Tehran Stock Exchange and encouraging share ownership, showing a smiling face to foreign capital, easing trade restrictions, facilitating export expansion, and trying to liberalize labour laws. The stock market, which had only 56 listed companies in the 1980s, increased its listing to 200 in the first two years of the Rafsanjani administration, and the value of stocks traded reached 65 billion rials in 1991, the highest recorded since the establishment of the Tehran bourse in 1967.[84] Some 13.3 million shares were being traded in 1991, with as much as 50 per cent of the new shares going onto the market comprising shares being disposed of by the state-controlled National Iranian Industries Organization.[85] Equally dramatically, in January 1992 the administration announced the plan to privatize the country's auto sector and compensate the original (pre-revolution) shareholders of the automakers for their losses. All told, ten such companies were returned to the private sector, along with four major heavy industrial complexes: The Ahvaz Rolling Mill, Arak Aluminium Rolling Mill, Arak Steel Company, and Iran Marine Industries.

In a direct challenge to the conventional wisdom in Tehran, the government announced plans for absorption of over $20 billion in foreign capital investment (later raised to $27 billion in foreign investment and finance), and even set up the country's first free-trade zones (three in the Persian Gulf) to facilitate economic partnerships between foreign and local capital – as a 'bridge' between local and foreign investors. Both private sector importers and exporters were given financial incentives (such as the return to the exporter of 11 per cent of the foreign exchange from exports) and administrative support to bid for domestic and international contracts, and encouraged to do so in partnership with foreign firms. Though unsuccessful in the end, this was nevertheless a concerted effort to open up to the world and to restore the economy's receptiveness to external engagement, an effort to recover at least some of the ground lost since the revolution, as shown in Table 3.10.

Rafsanjani's efforts to liberalize the economy did not go unopposed, however, and the camp close to the former PM Mousavi mobilized to block the reforms in

TABLE 3.10 Trade openness (%)

	1975	1980	1985	1990	1992	1994	1996
Iran	76.0	29.7	16.0	45.5	40.9	52.6	32.4
MENA	75.6	86.3	74.8	88.4	89.2	86.5	93.2

Source: Data compiled from World Bank and Economic Research Forum databases.

the Majlis and in direct appeals to the Leader. The level of disbelief was captured by a local banker who expressed his shock in the following way: "Can you imagine a revolutionary government allowing outsiders to dictate economy policy? Next thing you know they would be dictating politics to us as well. We might as well say goodbye to the last 15 years".[86] While there was consensus for reconstruction of the economy when it came down to it there was no agreement over the strategy – the dichotomies of the revolution reared their head and pulled the elite in different directions, forcing President Rafsanjani to rely on the conservative factions to politically and institutionally marginalize the left-leaning camp.

The reforms themselves also had a mixed outcome. On the plus side, the government did revive market forces and manage to open up the economy to more competition and entrepreneurship, and at the same time transfer state-held assets and businesses to the private sector. The government also took steps to shield the underprivileged with the opening of price-controlled cooperatives (Refah) stores across the country. Its controversial but internationally approved policy of population control also proved to be effective in mitigating future economic pressures on households and the state. On the negative side, as cash was not plentiful, many of the privatized enterprises ended up in the hands of the many foundations (*bonyads*) controlled by elite members – this was, at best, 'pseudo-privatization'.[87] In its analysis of government policy, the *Economist* wrote that Iranians regarded privatization as "a bad joke. The few profitable bits of government enterprises that were put on offer – seldom more than a third of any company – were quickly gobbled up by friends or relations of the new elite. Other offers, potentially available to anybody, turned out to be indigestible: Wildly overstaffed state-owned firms that required new private owners to apply restrictive labour laws to the letter".[88]

This did not amount to the transfer and control of assets previously owned or controlled by the state to the private sector. Indeed, even where the private sector was a beneficiary, it still needed state support (in terms of using ministerial contacts for securing assets being offered to the public, finance for its acquisitions, access to soft loans, elite-linked partners to shield it from future state interventions, minimizing tax commitments) to ensure control of the enterprises being offered. So, by the end of his presidency, 86 per cent of the country's GDP still came from the state-controlled sector and the remaining 14 per cent also included the share of the powerful foundations which worked closely with the state.

Furthermore, liberalization of trade increased imports substantially, proving to be calamitous to local industry as cheap imports flooded the country and in many instances forced closures. The country's foreign debt ballooned from near zero in the 1980s to over $20 billion by the early 1990s, putting additional strains on an overstretched treasury reeling under soft oil exports income. The problem was compounded by the exchange rate instability and the collapse of the rial against the dollar. This exchange rate crisis forced the government to slash imports – from $28 billion in 1991 to under $16 billion in 1993 – hurting consumers and also industries dependent on intermediate goods and imported materials for production. The exchange rate crisis also complicated the government's strategy of setting a semi-floating level for the rial and the reintroduction of multiple exchange rates, which reopened the door for the thriving money lenders to indulge in currency manipulation and hoarding of foreign currencies.

Deregulation raised the inflation rate – to around 20 per cent – and with it unemployment, which led to unrest and at least seven mass protests, including one major public rebellion (in Qazvin in 1994) and large demonstrations in other cities including Tehran in 1995.[89] By the end of Rafsanjani's first term in office, as much as 31 per cent of the per capita GDP of $706 was being spent on foodstuffs, and a high of 46 per cent in rural areas.[90] Inflation, and the doubling of fuel prices in 1995, led to more protests – unheard of since the revolution. As one commentator put it: "reform policies have many victims.... The paradox here is that the victims are the core supporters of the regime".[91] So it was that Hanke concluded that by the end of his term in office Iran's 'Misery Index' had increased from 34.41 to 48.28, having reached a high of 64 in 1994.[92] By the end of the plan period (1996) stagnation and high inflation had set in, with rising unemployment, widening socioeconomic disparities, a weakening national currency, and centralization of capital: "the budget of the 404 biggest public companies amounted to 38.3 percent of the GDP. These firms' shares in the general budget had increased from 53 percent in 1989 to 67 percent in 1996, while their borrowing from banks had risen from eight percent of all banks lending to 30 percent".[93]

President Rafsanjani had made strident efforts to address the economy's weaknesses and to remove the blockages to the strengthening of the private sector as the mainstay of the economy, but in the last analysis pressures from within the elite not to unpick the etatist system, pressures from below not to allow market forces take hold of prices of essential goods and services, and outsiders' unwillingness to provide Iran with sufficient debt relief to compensate for soft oil prices in the early to mid-1990s, combined to make his strategy untenable. His administration had become a victim not only of factional in-fighting and ideological turf wars but also of policies of a US administration, which chose the containment of Iran and Iraq as the centrepiece of its Gulf strategy. In the words, of one European diplomat at the time, the purpose of US policy "is to bring the mullahs to their knees by tightening the economic noose".[94]

Iran's vulnerability to external pressures has been a constant source of anxiety for the elite and yet the nature of Iran's political economy (dependent development) and its century-old addiction to oil exports for its economic prosperity has meant that the country remains exposed to directed sanctions. Indeed, as will be shown, such sanctions came to challenge the viability of the economy in its entirety in the 2010s. One expectation of the time was that Iran's non-oil exports should stand at $48 billion by 2016; in reality the figure was around $40 billion and not far short of plans. But despite this the structural problems remained unresolved. This is largely because the successive five-year plans did not fully deliver on their key objectives of growth, diversification, privatization, or national development. Ironically, President Rafsanjani was accused by forces which would later form the core of the reform movement of 'Westernizing' the economy and turning it over to capitalist forces.

Khatami: torn between economics and politics

President Rafsanjani's successor, Hojjatoleslam Mohammad Khatami, came to power in 1997 with a messy economy in front of him and few tools for dealing with it. He, in any case, had come to power with somewhat of different agenda to the economics-focused programme of his predecessor. For him, lack of opportunity, unemployment, inflation, and red tape presented the greatest barriers to economic prosperity, the solution for which lay in limiting the control of the economy by state-run monopolies. But his political problem was how to liberalize the economy and remain loyal to policies which could ensure social justice. Furthermore, for Khatami the bonyads were also very much part of the structural problems. They were part of the economic problem because they had unfettered access to resources, had large budgets and were largely free of legislative control. But bonyads were a political problem as well, for they were largely unaccountable and free to make major investment and commercial decisions without reference to national economic plans.

Nevertheless, he continued with the liberalization strategy charted by the previous administration and having retained Rafsanjani's economic policy team he kept alive the promise of marketization of the economy. But Khatami also turned post-war policy on its head: By prioritizing a political reform strategy over economic policy, he effectively dodged the tough decisions required to deal with the economy's structural problems. Sure, he too had a five-year plan to offer, with the promise of privatization, but his administration's priorities were distinctly more political, reflecting his electoral campaign for more political freedoms and liberalization of public space. The plan talked about the need to promote the rule of law, deregulation and privatization, and the promotion of non-oil exports.[95] The tools for achieving these objectives were never fully adopted and as a result policy instruments remained somewhat blunt.

The Khatami administration also followed a novel approach to economic reforms by aiming to improve the market conditions for competition. In this it set about providing the means for the expansion of entrepreneurship and creating the conditions for competition. In an effort to free capital, Khatami sought to create direct competition for the state-controlled enterprises from the private sector. So as early as 1998, it began loosening permits for business development and thus extended licenses to private investors entering all the important sectors, including the banking and insurance sectors, construction, transport, telecommunications, postal services, and such major projects as power plant construction.[96] His administration heavily promoted non-oil exports, and with this aim in mind during his first term in office, he took several important legislative steps in favour of free trade: He removed non-tariff barriers, eased export regulations, abolished export taxes and levies, and promoted free-trade zones as havens for investment and trade partnerships. The policy of trade and investment liberalization was so central to President Khatami's economic strategy that in his second term in office as many as seventy-five foreign investment permits were granted, and over $11.0 billion in direct foreign investments were secured.[97] Integration of Iran's economy into the global capitalist system was thus encouraged, even endorsed by Khatami's core leftist allies, and with this the first tentative steps towards (re)internationalization of the Iranian economy were being taken.

In 2004, however, in the twilight of Khatami's presidency, a mini-earthquake of sorts happened when the Expediency Council, under the chairmanship of Ayatollah Rafsanjani, rescinded Article 44 of the constitution, which had enshrined control of the commanding heights of the economy to the public sector. This, argues Azad, "heralded a new era of economic liberalization and market reform in Iran... [allowing] for the privatization of 80 percent of state's assets".[98] These rapid and potentially dramatic economic changes alarmed the conservative right to intervene as soon as politically possible. And the conservative-dominated seventh Majlis, which was formed in 2004, sought to revise one of the centrepieces of Khatami's reforms, namely the terms of the country's new foreign investment law. Their speedy parliamentary intervention, in September 2004, swiftly backed up by the Council of Guardians, effectively torpedoed the arrival of major investments from Turkish firms in (mobile) telecommunications (Turkcell) and transportation (TAV) and ended the liberalization of two lucrative sectors.

Khatami's term is notable for another economic change: The establishment of a national fund for the future generations/strategic investments which by the end of his presidency had accumulated some $20 billion in reserves against soft oil prices throughout his presidency. But what proved impossible at this stage was the reform of the country's elaborate subsidies system which was costing the exchequer $13 billion a year in energy subsidies and a further $1.6 billion in food-related subsidies (cooking oil, rice, wheat, sugar) but was securing the regime's foundations in society.

Despite the unsteady process of market reforms and privatization, it is worth noting Azad's comment that during the sixteen-year presidency of Rafsanjani and Khatami some $1.8 billion worth of state-held enterprises were transferred annually to the private sector. The de-nationalization of the Iranian economy appeared to be in full swing before the voters brought to power the country's most ardent populist as its new president. One reason for the popularity of Ahmadinejad's populism and his attack on corruption was precisely the negative impact of the marketization of the economy and the high levels of inequality which had begun in the Rafsanjani period. Thus, by the end of Khatami's term in office, the share of the wealthiest tenth in the national income was 33.7 per cent, and that of the poorest tenth only 2 per cent of the national income.[99] The poorest 20 per cent of the population received just 5.1 per cent of the national income. The third five-year development plan, which covered the period to 2005, set itself the task of reforming the tax system, introducing fiscal and budgetary reforms, and alongside further privatization and government downsizing to also further extend the social welfare net. But economic growth targets were never achieved, which meant that job creation remained well below the planned targets and sense of misery and helplessness gripped the country.

Ahmadinomics takes hold

The opening up of the economy continued with the election of Mahmoud Ahmadinejad who brought forth the country's fourth development plan (2005–10) with a stated ambition to accelerate privatization.[100] In this task he was assisted by the Leader himself who in a decree in August 2006 ordered the transfer of banks, mines, transport and other manufacturing industries to the private sector. But in practice, as his populist instincts took over and he consolidated his grip on the instruments of power, Ahmadinejad proved to be less committed to a process of privatization that would transfer assets of state-owned/controlled businesses to the market or the private sector. Indeed, where privatization did take place he was keen, particularly during his second term in office, to use this process to further empower the bonyads and the businesses associated with the Pasdaran. In the most celebrated case the government oversaw the transfer of control through floatation of Telecommunications Company of Iran, which led to a 51 per cent control of the TCI by a three-party consortium consisting of Pasdaran-affiliated companies for the sum of $7.9 billion.

Ahmadinejad's first term in office also coincided with unprecedented high oil prices, of over $100 per barrel, which gave him ample opportunity to grow his base support and help the well-being of his rural and lower middle-class supporters. As Table 3.11 shows, the steady drop in oil exports was more than compensated for by high oil prices: While 2.5 million barrels per day of oil exports in 2007 earned the exchequer $66 billion – a very high sum in itself – exports of just 1.3 mb/d, with the drop caused by the intensive sanctions, still raised $62 billion in income for Ahmadinejad's administration. The government was still fairly cash-rich and able to keep to its basic financial commitments but unable to invest or incentivize growth. Pressures on oil exports and on Iran's ability to trade freely with the rest of the world began to extract a heavy cost from 2012 onwards.

TABLE 3.11 Oil production (and exports) and income during Ahmadinejad's presidency

	2005	2007	2009	2011	2013
Production (mb/d)	4.2	4.3	4.2	4.4	3.5
Exports	2.6	2.5	2.0	2.5	1.3
Income ($)	53	66	56	115	62

Sources: BP, *BP Statistical Review of World Energy 2015* (London: BP plc, 2015); OPEC, *Annual Statistical Bulletin* (Vienna: OPEC, various annual editions).

Note: Figures have been rounded up for convenience.

However, oil income levels of over $50 billion had been unprecedented in the history of Iran's oil exports, and it is worth underlining the petrodollar cushion that Ahmadinejad had been given by a comparison with the administrations of Rafsanjani and Khatami. In the former case (1989–97), annual income from oil exports never reached $20 billion, and in the case of Khatami (1997–2005), the figure reached the high watermark of $34 billion in the last year of his presidency.[101] Overall, the annual income from oil exports during the eight years of the 'reform era' averaged around $20 billion, which was a very modest sum when set against the country's growing population and the billions of dollars needed for the insatiable economic subsidies regime.

Ahmadinejad's administration justified its lavish expenditures to help the poor through reference to returning to the ideals of the revolution, and also his electoral mandate to bring Iran's oil riches to the ordinary people – to every Iranian's dining table, as he had put it.[102] The 'justice shares' programme, transferring shares from several bonyad or state-controlled companies, was typical of the trend: Turning 40 million Iranians into stock holders. But economic policy has never been free of politics and the pressures of Iran's economic isolation began to mount after 2010 and the failure of progress in the nuclear talks. As a consequence, the steady ratcheting up of the triple sanctions on the country – those imposed by the European Union, the United Nations and the United States – forced the administration to take drastic action. The government could no longer sustain the state's economic portfolio and had no choice but to raise funds through privatization. Thus, in its so-called 'golden year of privatization' (2010), the government sold off fifty large companies in such lucrative and important sectors as transportation, telecommunications, energy (electricity, fuel), steel production, and financial services, worth around $110 billion.[103]

The government had already gone much further than its predecessor, but the announcement in 2008 that the National Iranian Oil Company, the beating heart of Iran's economy, would gradually transfer as many as forty-seven energy-related firms under its control (worth roughly $90 billion) to the private sector marked a clear departure from the previous sensitivities about the keeping of strategic sectors of the economy in state hands. By the end of 2010, 275 state-controlled companies, worth some $630 billion, had been de-nationalized, which is historically unprecedented in Iran. Apart from the staggering sums involved, it is also of importance to note that around one-third of this had actually gone to the private sector, with the third sector (cooperatives, bonyads and para-statal bodies) picking up around $340 billion of the businesses.[104] This was not a privatization programme in the strict sense of the term but rather a straightforward scheme of transferring billions of dollars of assets from the state to semi-state organs. It was de-nationalization instead of privatization. But then we had been here before: In the Rafsanjani period privatization was a major policy tool for the restructuring of the economy. Unlike earlier economic reform efforts, however, this time the size of the bureaucracy expanded as fast as the transfer of assets to the private or semi-private sector. Privatization did not shrink the size of the bureaucracy and if anything actually expanded the government's wage bill.[105] With over two million employees, the republic's bureaucracy in comparative terms is one of the largest in the world today, and given that the bureaucracy has moulded and grown in response to the political conditions of the country, it has evolved into an inefficient and politicized beast resembling the patronage-based predatory (as opposed to a developmental) model prevalent in sub-Sahara Africa.[106]

Ironically, having managed to encourage an inflow of foreign investment, of around $12 billion, during his first term in office, the Ahmadinejad government enthusiastically embraced the 'resistance economy' – pulling up the drawbridge – to counter the effects of sanctions. Resistance economics, at its heart, was the republic's return to the tried and tested strategy of import-substitution industrialization in which sanctions provided the cover for the country to cut imports and boost domestic manufacturing and industrialization. Apart from the inherent flaws of ISI as an economic development strategy in the twenty-first century, in this particular case lack of access to the latest manufacturing techniques and technologies, little experience of product innovation, absence of venture capital and even a credible credit system for privately owned industries (which because of restrictive conditions since the revolution have remained relatively small) to invest in plant, the resistance economy resulted in what was ultimately marginal increases in the production of some basic goods, high prices for inferior commodities, and further concentration of industrial activity in the hands of state-controlled enterprises. This was, in principle, a mirror image of the self-sufficiency drive of the 1980s, when 'khod kafayi' was the country's revolutionary strategy. This time, however, the emphasis was on enhancing the country's economic sovereignty, which was picked up by the next government as part of its strategy of reintegration into the world economy.

Ahmadinejad also took other bold steps and took the knife to the revolutionary regime's sacred cows. It, for example, set about revising the country's labour law in order to allow for easier hiring and firing of employees and also removed the minimum wage – one of the regime's most important employment-related policies – to help the private sector. At the same time, the government began overhauling Iran's welfare and subsidies system, aiming to limit and focus the welfare provision. Third, it dared to attack a cornerstone of the regime's popular legacy by drastically cutting subsidies on foodstuffs, energy and much more. The government had little choice. Unprecedented high oil income could no longer shield the country from the double blow of the government's mismanagement of the economy and the effects of international sanctions resulting from its intransient posture in the nuclear negotiations. As a consequence, in the words of a credible report, Iran's economy was 25 per cent smaller in 2013 than its pre-2012 growth trajectory indicated.[107] Iran was finding itself short of investment to the tune of $300 to $400 billion a year and had seen investment in industry drop by 10 to 15 per cent a year during Ahmadinejad's presidency. At the end of Ahmadinejad's term in office private pay had dropped by 35.4 per cent, and government employees who make up the bulk of the workforce had lost around 50 per cent of their income: "at least half the population suffered a dramatic loss of income. In one week in October 2012 the currency plunged by 40% against the dollar.... At its lowest point the rial was down 75%. Unemployment has rocked. Car production, which used to account for 10% of GDP and employ 1m people, fell by about 70%".[108] Ahmadinejad's term, the *Economist* noted, exposed Iran to the "triple whammy of oil dependency, sanctions and inefficiencies covered by years of reckless state spending".[109]

Ironically, Ahmadinejad's petrodollars-flushed populism found greater momentum with the intensification of sanctions and a result of this unhealthy mixture led to a deepening of cronyism and massive corruption. Information about corrupt practices and financial excesses, often sanctioned by the government itself, had filtered onto social media outlets during Ahamdinejad's presidency, but the scale of corruption only came to light after his departure from office. While corruption was not a new phenomenon in the Islamic republic, apparently practiced by all state institutions and para-statal organizations, the scale of it under Ahmadinejad shocked society and was estimated at $17.8 billion during his second term in office.[110] Transfer of funds in many billions of dollars to private bank accounts, inflated salaries of state employees, secret fund transfers, awarding of lucrative contracts without a transparent bidding process, land and property acquisitions through the grey market, and much more has come to light since 2013. One such scandal in fact engulfed Rouhani's own administration when news of substantial payments and salary hikes for senior employees of ministries and the financial and insurance sectors in particular was leaked in 2016.[111] With monthly average wages being $400, it did come as a shock when payslips of high officials revealed monthly payments, in some cases, of over $50,000 per month.

In Ahmadinejad's world, populist etatism had merely reinforced clientelism. Yet Ahmadinejad was adamant that the "Iranian economy is so strong that it could live without oil revenues; our people could get accustomed to that and I think that things will change in the near future".[112] But change only began to occur with his departure from office in 2013, by which time, according to Rouhani's first vice president (Eshaq Jahangiri), Ahmadinejad's administration had squandered $159 billion of the Khatami-established Foreign Reserve Fund.[113] In terms of overall achievements and global comparisons also, Iran's record in this period is a distinctly underwhelming one. Transparency International's data, Table 3.12, paints a depressing picture.

TABLE 3.12 Comparative governance and development indicators, 2013

Corruption index	Competitiveness	Press freedom	Judicial independence
25 out of 100	4.22 out of 7.00	136.60	3.8 out 7.00
144th out of 177	66th out of 142	175th out of 179	66th out of 142

Source: www.transparency.org.

The data does not support the regime's rhetoric about itself. So, in terms of corruption, Iran was ranked 144th, in terms of press freedom, 175th, and judicial independence, 66th in the world in 2013. In terms of 'accountability' also, the Islamic republic scored badly, with −1.573. Under Ahmadinejad, Iran's 'misery index' worsened considerably, reaching an unforgiving 142.47 in 2012. At the end of Ahmadinejad's term, in the World Bank's Doing Business rankings, Iran was placed 145th out of the 183 countries, and in terms of tax revenues the country was 163rd in the world. The Heritage Foundation, which granted has a certain predisposed approach towards economic freedom, ranked Iran 171st in its list of 179 countries, and in terms of globalization (measured by the KOF Globalization Index) the country was ranked 162nd out of 181 countries. The EIU placed Iran 150th in the world in terms of quality of life.

It was time for radical solutions, which ironically were to be sought in the diplomatic arena in the first instance and through a concerted effort by the Rouhani administration to resolve the country's nuclear dispute with global powers as the precondition for dealing with the economic chaos left behind by Ahmadinejad. Within two years of coming to office, Rouhani had negotiated away the stiff multilateral sanctions and thus dared to usher in a new and promising era for Iran. But the complexity of the multilateral and unilateral sanctions regime would mean that an economic dividend from the nuclear deal would take some time to materialize, if ever in the form that the architects of the nuclear agreement had envisaged.

A new golden age?

The lifting of EU, UN and US multilateral, and many US unilateral, sanctions on Iran on 16th January 2016, as part of the JCPOA was marked by President Rouhani as ushering a new golden age for the country. In tweeting on the 17th of January that "the legs of Iran's economy are now free of the chains of sanctions, and it's time to build and grow", the president was effectively seeking to renegotiate the Islamic republic's economic relations with the rest of the world. With these words the gates to "the last gold mine on Earth", as one Iran-based Western diplomat put it, had been opened. Rouhani's ambition for the country was a big one: "under the new conditions", he said, "we want to export 30 percent of what we produce in Iran".[114] To realize the new opportunities Rouhani sought to tackle Iran's restrictive and cumbersome economic regulations. The new economic policy, announced in July 2014, aimed at ending 'stagflation' by kick-starting the economy by reducing red tape, diversifying the economy away from oil exports, reforming the financial services sector to encourage more investment, providing a stimulus package for the private sector involvement, reducing inflation by cutting cash and energy subsidies, stabilizing the currency, stimulating domestic demand, and encouraging more activity in the country's free-trade zones (FTZs).[115] The strategy also received a favourable review from the World Bank, which had excused itself from Iran since 2007, as "comprehensive... encompassing market-based reforms".[116]

A key component of the strategy was to build on efforts made by previous (Rafsanjani and Ahmadinejad) administrations to loosen further the country's foreign investment rules. In effect, Rouhani aimed to revolutionize the country's political economy by seeking to flood the country with foreign investment.[117] A new foreign investment law was required, which now promises not only tax breaks of up to 100 per cent to foreign investors, but also the right to send corporate profits overseas unhindered. The law also guarantees the protection of investments in case foreign investment laws were changed at some point in the future. This level of change sat somewhat uncomfortably with the tenets of the doctrinaire 'economy of resistance' first proposed in 2010 by Ayatollah Khamenei, formally proposed in 2012 by Ahmadinejad, and finally adopted by the Rouhani administration in 2014 as the method for countering sanctions and resisting the West's purported infiltration strategy. But in the new era even the premises of the resistance economy had to change. Majlis Speaker Ali Larijani summarized the debate regarding this matter by making a clear pitch for the strengthening of the private sector. Speaking at a major national event in February 2015, he argued that "there is no ambiguity in the general policies of the resistance-based economy; the problem lies in how such policies should be implemented. It's inaccurate to think that the Expediency Council's formulation of policies to create a resistance-based economy has come as a result of sanctions". In a clear critique of Rouhani's predecessor, he went on to suggest that "sanctions might have opened the wound of our ailing economy, but our economic problems are old. That's why only policies put forth by a resistance-based economy can address them.... Before sanctions, unemployment was high; today 44 percent of our graduates are jobless. We must try to tackle these issues. State employment is the worst solution. Responsibilities should be delegated to the private sector so that the economy is run by the public".[118]

A year later, on 22 March, Rouhani's chief of staff, Mohammad Nahavandian, spun the notion again in pursuit of his government's economic policies, by adding that opening Iran to foreign investment would in fact help build a resistance economy. So in order "to increase the resistance of Iran's economy, we should expand ties with neighboring countries and the world. If Iran is an active member of international organizations, the chance of getting hit by new sanctions and economic restrictions will be limited".[119] Integrate in order to insulate, as a strategy, would only make sense in the context of an economy that is still driven by state-capitalist forces and in which the struggle between the etatist forces of the nezam and those in alignment with the private sector remains unresolved. The prize, for both sides, would be unhindered capital accumulation, but the price for this – in terms of political and social opening of the country – is not one that any party is yet able to pay. Furthermore, the debates about the virtues of the resistance economy go to the heart of Iran's longstanding dilemmas about its place in the world and about its role in the new global economy. Post-sanctions, the issues were not only about survival but also about prosperity and Iran's place in the international division of labour.

Nevertheless, with the lifting of sanctions, arguably, the prospects for Iranian entrepreneurs looked rosier than it had for a generation. Despite the soft oil prices, of under $30 per barrel in early 2016, which had hit the Iranian economy hard, the world's leading economic powers were queuing up to cultivate one of Asia's last untapped markets (of nearly 80 million people, a strong, educated and dedicated workforce, and endowed with vast natural resources that went well beyond hydrocarbons). Russia, in anticipation of 'implementation day', had negotiated a $20 billion energy and trade agreement with Iran in 2014, so it was the turn of others to capitalize on the opening up of the Iranian economy. China, Germany, France, and Italy led the charge and others, Britain and also the United States, followed, all looking for lucrative trade, industrial and manufacturing, and mining and drilling opportunities.

So virtually following the announcement of lifting of sanctions, word circulated that Tehran had struck a deal worth an estimated $27 billion (list price) with Airbus to purchase 118 new aeroplanes, which a week later had gone up to the purchase of 160 short- and long-haul passenger planes.[120] Meanwhile, Germany announced that it intended to reintroduce state Federal export guarantees for companies that intend to do business with Iran. Germany's Daimler announced at the same time that it had signed letters of intent with local partners Iran Khodro Diesel and Mammut Group to arrange a "comprehensive re-entry" into the country: "there is a huge demand for commercial vehicles in Iran and we plan to quickly resume our business activities in the market there".[121] In fact, visiting Western business leaders and diplomats have found huge demand for all their products and services. But the East was not far behind in trying to 'cash in' on the potential economic bonanza in Iran at the time that the rest of the world was dramatically slowing down.

The arrival of China's President Xi in late January 2016, thus, was designed to set bilateral relations on fire in terms of deals being proposed and agreed. This visit of a Chinese leader for the first time in fourteen years was to cement China's strong bilateral relations with Iran and secure for the China Railway Construction Corporation the tabled proposal for a 3,200-kilometer high-speed train link between China's Xinjiang province and Tehran. Xi's visit was also expected to finalize the agreement for the construction of two multibillion dollar Chinese-built nuclear power plants in Iran. Chinese businesses took full advantage of the sanctions to replace US and European competitors in this large Middle Eastern market and have tried to consolidate their gains. As a result, China now buys 40 per cent of Iran's oil exports and is currently the country's top source of capital and technology. It is estimated that as many as 100 Chinese companies have a presence in Iran, and China is expecting the $40 billion Silk Road fund to bring Iran closer to Beijing and in so doing counter the influx of competition.[122]

Xi's visit resulted in seventeen new investment projects and the exchange of a twenty-five-year strategic partnership agreement to boost trade to a massive $600 billion by 2026 from its current level of $52 billion.[123] Rouhani followed the profitable visit of President Xi with a high-level (150-delegation) tour of Italy and France to negotiate trade and investment deals and also to cultivate the dormant political ties between Iran and these two European countries. In Italy, the president reached mega-deals totalling $18.4 billion according to local sources.[124] Accordingly, "among the deals signed… were a $4 billion contract for oil services group Saipem, up to 5.7 billion euros in contracts for steel firm Danieli, up to 4 billion euros of business for infrastructure firm Condotte d'Acqua, 4 billion euros for rail and road company Gavio and 400 million euros for planes from Finmeccanica".[125] In France, two days later, the president added to the historic Airbus deal a long list of French investments in Iran – in airport construction and as operators, in joint car production between Iran Khodro and Peugeot-Citroen (of 200,000 units a year from 2017), in rail transport, shipping, health, agriculture, and water resource development – worth an estimated $16 billion.[126] European seriousness about opening a new chapter in the EU's relations with Iran was underlined by the high-level visit of the EU's High Representative, Federica Mogherini, in April 2016 with seven other EU commissioners. The parties agreed to

"encourage the expansion of economic relations between EU and Iran, recognizing the importance of macro-economic issues, trade, finance and investment in achieving sustainable growth and development. They intend to engage in a macro-economic and finance dialogue including on the following initiatives:

- Improve and enable financial as well as encouraging banking cooperation between the EU and Iran. The EU can assist if required in addressing Anti Money Laundering and Countering Financing of Terrorism (AML/CFT) issues;
- Explore the prospect of extending the third country lending mandate of the European Investment Bank (EIB) to Iran, to enhance the availability of finance for investment in Iran and possible blending (of loans with grants);
- Cooperation in a variety of sectors with a focus in particular on encouraging regulatory and industrial policy dialogues and creating mutual opportunities, including textiles, tourism, raw materials, construction and any other areas to be mutually determined;
- Building on EU expertise in the field of SMEs support to foster business and in particular SMEs favourable environment in Iran and share information on the 'Enterprise Europe Network';
- Exchange of Iran and EU business missions in the second half of the year;
- Consider development cooperation on strengthening the private sector and SMEs in Iran;
- Facilitate and encourage EU-Iran business sector presence in each others' markets through a variety of measures".[127]

In addition, the EU agreed to "support and assist Iran to become a member of the World Trade Organization" and help Iran in areas of transport, science and technology, agriculture, and tourism.

So it should be noted that the return of European corporations will have the greatest impact and will at the same time also change the dynamics of Iran's economic relations with China, Iran's main economic partner during the previous decade. For while Ayatollah Khamenei has praised China for its reliable friendship for over twenty years and has recognized Beijing's willingness to stand by the Islamic republic during the tough sanctions period, businesses have been less forthcoming with praise, as they had to accept strict Chinese conditions on their doing business with Iran. Apart from complaints about the inferior quality of many of the imported Chinese products and the Chinese corporations' role in putting out of business Iranian production in some critical sectors (which had survived even the sanctions), Chinese practices were said to be controlling and debilitating. Thus, the projects director of a major industry, Marzieh Shah-Daei of the National Petrochemical Company, has publicly declared that with the lifting of sanctions Iran's petrochemical manufacturers were turning to the European banks and finance houses for finance, in place of Chinese investors who were charging high commissions and fees. Chinese investors, moreover, were said to be forcing Iranian clients to source 50 to 70 per cent of the equipment needed from China: "this is while we can get 70% of the equipment needed inside Iran".[128]

State-society relations under the Islamic republic

It is clear that the immediate task of the revolutionary regime was to stabilize the economy and as Iran's dependent bourgeoisie had already followed the Shah into exile, the state had little option but to bring under its control vast sectors of the economy – industrial, financial and insurance services, agricultural, extractive activities. The nationalizations brought under state control around 85 per cent of the country's major production units and facilitated the expansion of the emerging foundations, which over time became so dominant in the national economy.[129] Thus, eight years into the life of the republic, "an estimated 60–70 percent of the entire domestic economy and 90 percent of foreign trade were directly or indirectly in state hands".[130]

Iran's essentially middle class–led revolution ousted the old elite and put in charge of the state and the country's substantial resources an inward-looking petty bourgeoisie and traditional middle class who used access to the power of the state for private wealth and over time for capital accumulation. As noted by Nomani and Behdad, the "expropriations, nationalizations, war mobilization, and the extensive control of the state over the market in the [first ten years of the new regime] accelerated *embourgeoisement* of the selected few among the petty bourgeoisie".[131] What the war effort in particular facilitated was state and state-linked corporate control over means of production, and state command over the distribution of external surpluses (oil rents). A system of clientalism was created "where allegiance to the state was to become a function of the resource allocation process".[132]

Those with political connections, often developed through their blood or marriage ties with the clerical establishment, joined well-paid posts in the state bureaucracy, or else used the same means for managerial positions in the many state-owned or operated enterprises. They formed the core of the post-revolution ruling elite, often referred to as 'the *aghazadehs*' (the sons of the clerical elite). They are in this position because of the rapidly changing relationship 'between politics and social classes' as Roxborough would have it.[133] Roxborough further argues that the "weakness of any domestic bourgeoisie in [developing] countries has enabled the elites which have come to occupy state power to transform themselves into new dominant classes".[134] In Iran's case, clientelist relationships facilitated this process. The predominant role of the middle classes in the revolution, coupled by the wholesale departure of the comprador class in 1979–80, provided the social space for state-linked groups to create networks and use the political levers of power for accumulation and thus take the tentative steps towards emerging as the new dominant classes. But social struggles have remained as the traditional merchant classes and those small entrepreneurs with links to the religious or the political establishment allied themselves with the modern middle classes to block the neoconservative-Revolutionary Guard partnership to consolidate itself as Iran's first post-revolution dominant, indeed ruling, class. This social struggle continues and in election cycles one can see the competing forces at play, often camouflaged by political factions.

In this context, Iran's factional politics can arguably only be understood as the ultimate struggle between middle class and petty bourgeois forces for the establishment of a new ruling class.

The process of transformation, however, was rapid, and as the Iranian economy shrank – in 1981 the GNP was only 64 per cent of what it had been in 1977 – it also exposed the many new avenues for capital accumulation by the petty bourgeoisie, making some "monopoly capitalists all at once".[135] As the war economy deepened and the combination of (US) unilateral and multilateral sanctions kicked in, the role of the state became even more central. At the same time, though, state capital budget had shrunk by 30 per cent by 1989,[136] and the scramble for a share of the smaller pie by many more people – the population grew from 34 million to 60 million between 1976 and 1996 and had stood at 68 million in 2007 – intensified. This process deepened social cleavages and competition for the many levers of social and economic power that were to be found only in the state machinery. Even more alarming, by 1991 GDP per capita had dropped to just 62 per cent of the 1977 figure,[137] increasing relative poverty on a huge scale. Amirahmadi estimates that in the ten years after the revolution some 3.1 million people were added to the work force and due to the economy's poor performance fewer than 1.9 million new jobs were created in that time, thus increasing the competition for access to opportunities for employment.[138] A damning assessment of Iran's economic performance states that in the late 1980s,

> None of the economic goals enunciated at the outset had been reached, or even approached. The country's dependence on the external world... was... greater than ever. Economic diversification, and the reduction of oil's contribution to the economy and the government budget, still remained a distant goal. Agriculture's role in Iran's economic development was anything but crucial, and its self-sufficiency was further than ever from being realized.... In the meantime, corruption, bribery, smuggling, black-marketing, drug addiction, violent crime, and moral degradation were on the rise.[139]

Richards and Waterbury note in regard to Iran's economy that against such failures one must note "the increase in consumption per capita of various foodstuffs, the apparent narrowing of rural-urban income gaps, increases in enrolment ratios, and declines in infant and child mortality. The only way to explain the combination of falling incomes per capita and increasing consumption of food is to posit an increase in the equality of income distribution, in food".[140] It seems to the authors that the simplest description of Iran's economic condition after the revolution could be summed up in two words: "shared poverty". As such, by the 1990s, Iran's social pyramid was even steeper than in the Pahlavi era, with just 20 per cent collecting more than 50 per cent of the national income and the bottom 10 per cent being in receipt of less than 1.5 per cent of the same.[141] In post-war Iran, around 60 per cent of the economy was under state control and a further 10 to 20 per cent was controlled by just five large foundations directly tied to the Leader's office.[142] Despite the state-sponsored social support systems, as many as 10 million may be living under the absolute poverty line and as many as 30 million (some 40 per cent of the population) in relative poverty.[143]

Social and economic mobility ladders outside of the state machinery often proved to be very short indeed and as realistic opportunities of gainful employment were largely to be found in the state-run or -controlled sector, those in control were able to exercise greater patronage. As 'gatekeepers' the insiders began exploiting their position for political, and often, financial gain. Economic paucity, thus, also encouraged corruption, nepotism and favouritism, in place of a meritocracy. Furthermore, absence of a proper tax regime inhibited the distribution of resources across social groups and helped further polarize social relations. President Rouhani's minister of economy, Ali Tayyebnia, has noted that Iranian leaders fully recognize that increasing oil revenues had tended to side line the need for Iran to develop a modern taxation system, going further to note that lack of a comprehensive economic database, widespread tax exemptions, complicated and ambiguous regulations, along with a general failure to uphold the law, are keeping tax revenues minimal.[144] These and other reasons have brought tax revenues below 7 per cent of gross domestic product, according to the National

Tax Administration. So, "reforms of the tax code, including creating more targeted incentives, increasing tax base and removing discriminations, will go into effect from the start of the next Iranian year (starting March 20, 2016)", according to the minister. The ministry itself acknowledges that over 43 per cent of the Iranian economy is tax exempt, including many non-governmental and state-controlled companies that have thrived due to the exemptions. According to outgoing head of the tax administration (Ali Askari),

> [E]xemptions... benefit a broad spectrum of the economy... for instance, the agriculture sector, which comprises 10% of GDP, is free from paying tax. Tax exemptions are enjoyed by 33% of 22.9 million guild members. They do file returns, but don't pay a penny in tax. Tax exemption rates are different in each province. For instance, around 15–16% of the guilds in Tehran are exempt from paying tax, while 45% of guild members in Sistan-Baluchestan Province don't pay taxes.

He further acknowledged that his agency had failed to tax the grey economy "that makes up around 20% of the country's GDP".[145] In terms of new job opportunities, also much remains to be done, in quantity and quality. With a total workforce of some 24 million people, this is a country in which around 8 million are engaged in agriculture, 1.2 million still earn their living in the carpet-weaving industry, and another 5.2 million are employed in the traditional, low-tech, handicraft industry – a total of 14.4 million workers.[146] With low wages as a factor in poverty, economic vulnerability remains a serious problem and this has become more evident since the lifting of sanctions in January 2016. As a World Bank assessment notes raising the poverty line from $2.0/2.5 to $3.0/3.5 "could put 4%–6% of the population – 4.5 million people in poverty. This suggests that many individuals are vulnerable to changes in their personal disposable income and to the persistent rise in the cost of living".[147]

So the struggle to strike a balance between state and society has been ongoing and acute partly because the collapse of the Pahlavi order was accompanied by the departure of the dominant comprador bourgeoisie and the professional middle classes who owed their livelihood to the monarchical regime. Rapid capital flight squeezed the already fragile economy, and to prevent total economic collapse, the revolutionary state stepped into the shoes of the old private sector and, in search of stability, facilitated the growth of the state bureaucracy many fold. The establishment of numerous parastatal organizations, charities, and foundations (bonyads) after the revolution – in part due to nationalization of many industries and in part for populist ideological reasons – further concentrated economic power and decision-making in the hands of new proto-state organs and state institutions.[148]

These foundations, economically powerful and politically distinct, grew in importance and in the process evolved into semi-autonomous entities with independent influence and extensive networks. With the growing base of the foundations, their directors and managers acquired access to sources of capital (concentrated in state-controlled banks) and dozens of revenue-generating semi-monopoly enterprises. Easy access to the revenues of these industrial and commercial units enabled the senior functionaries of such entities to become wealthy figures in their own right. The process enabled their embourgeoisement, and the long arm of the state provided them with sustenance. As Suzanne Maloney has observed, "in conjunction with this financial muscle has come political influence; by virtue of intricate personal and institutional ties with the government, the *bonyads* have become pivotal actors in the enduring rivalry among the ideologically oriented factions within the clerical establishment". More crucially, in terms of the consequences of the changing political economy of Iran for the social power base of the Islamic republic, she notes that "more broadly, the evolution of the *bonyads* as a semi-autonomous centre of power redistributes the relationship among the various social groups [especially the traditional merchant class] whose support is key to the government's survival".[149] She notes that as many as ten rather large charitable organizations, foundations and public bodies of this nature have emerged since the 1980s, controlling estimated assets in excess of $20 billion. One of the most important, the Foundation of the Oppressed, was estimated to have as many as 800 companies under its control, employing some 700,000 people, and controlling assets worth over $10 billion in the late 1990s. The Foundation of the Oppressed has business interests in agriculture, commerce, construction, mining, transportation, entertainment and recreation, cinemas, and many others.

Thus, as the balance of relationship inextricably shifted in favour of the state, so the struggle between the state-rooted ruling factions and the non-state bourgeois fragments and middle classes (who have been struggling for survival in many cases) intensified, arguably spilling over into direct confrontation and open violence in the years following Ahmadinejad's first presidential election victory in 2005. External forces, ironically, also played their part in strengthening the state-linked groups to further strengthen the autonomy of the state while also consolidating the grip of these forces on the economy. Sanctions, thus, have had a direct impact on the political economy of Iran, on the one hand making para-statal organizations more powerful and on the other hand encouraging domestic production to compensate for banned imports and helping innovation in many fields.

Sanctions and the economy

Sanctions have been a feature of the Iranian economy since the revolution, and they have over time come to affect not only the conditions of the economy but also the country's socioeconomic system and class relations. Iran has had to live with sanctions for a generation and no single country has been more persistent in imposing sanctions on the Islamic republic than the United States. In the 1990s Iran paid a heavy price for Western sanctions but these were never effective enough to force or encourage it to change course or adjust its economic policies to moderate their impact. Particularly after the 2002 revelations regarding the extent and intensity of Iran's nuclear programme something changed and pressure began to mount considerably after 2005.

Binding UN sanctions, introduced under instructions by the Security Council, were augmented by a combination of new sanctions from the US and the EU. The United Nations, which took responsibility for Iran's nuclear file in 2006 on advice from the IAEA Board of Governors, imposed a series of sanctions on the republic in order to control Tehran's access to military-related technologies, dual-use technologies, and strategic arms transfers. UN's blacklisting of key individuals and companies close to the regime badly disrupted Iran's international networks and as a consequence increased the premium on its ability to conduct its (open and clandestine) business overseas. This also provided the perfect cover for the state-linked organs and individuals, most trusted by the regime, to extend their interests. Most notable of course was the IRGC. As Forozan shows, the Guard explicitly focused its energies on securing contracts and projects worth over $1 billion and the logic used for creating and consolidating control of such large, corporatist, monopolies was that the Anbiya's commercial activities in lesser projects would damage the private sector.[150] Thus, as foreign companies abandoned this market due to increasing sanctions, the vacuum in the economy was filled by the Guard, which

> Kept Iran's oil-dependent economy running, but also ensured a monopoly in the energy sector for IRGC affiliates. For instance, the IRGC owned Khatam al-Anbiya was awarded a no-tender contract to develop the South Pars gas field in the Persian Gulf, the largest in the world. Other IRGC firms provide ancillary services in these sectors. Any competition was swiftly annexed by the Corps itself. The Oriental Oil Kish, Iran's first private oil drilling company is an example. Effectively, the IRGC monopolised the oil and gas industry by stifling private sector participation. Telecommunications is the largest non-oil sector in the Iranian economy. This too is controlled by the IRGC. The Telecommunication Company of Iran (TCI) has a monopoly over fixed-line infrastructure, and until recently, was the largest Internet Service Provider in the country. The IRGC-linked Mobin Trust Consortium (MTC) owns 90 per cent of the TCI's shares. TCI's subsidiary, the Mobile Communication Company (MCI) has the largest market share of mobile services in Iran, and is valued upwards of US$4 billion. The TCI also controls bandwidth allocation for data services, ensuring IRGC dominance in the telecommunications industry. The bulk of the IRGC's economic clout comes from its presence in large-scale development in the country. This sector is also dominated by Khatam al-Anbiya, which along with its subsidiaries, executes contracts in large development projects such as dams, highways, railways, mining, offshore construction, pipelines, and even parts of the Tehran Metro.[151]

In November 2011 the US introduced sanctions on Iran's oil transactions and also third parties processing Iran's oil revenues, and just eighteen months later deepened these by blacklisting a number of Iranian and foreign enterprises for acting as conduits for Iran's oil-related business activities. The EU, until the mid-2000s Iran's main trading partner, had already followed suit with its own sanctions. In addition to asset freezes and travel restrictions, from 2012 it also took three dramatic steps: It froze the assets belonging to the Iranian Central Bank and barred any trade with it and other Iranian bodies in precious metals (January), imposed a ban on all Iranian oil imports (July) which accounted for 20 per cent of Iran's oil exports and refused to extend insurance cover for Iranian oil shipments, (in March) barred Iran from the global banking transactions system (SWIFT) thus stopping in their tracks all of Iran's financial (banking) transactions, and finally (in October) it imposed a ban on all gas-related transactions and went so far as severing all links with Iranian banks and financial houses. Iran's economy was stranded.

The US-EU sanctions, coming atop the earlier UN ones, effectively paralyzed the Iranian economy, which was already reeling under pressures arising from the ill-advised and arbitrary economic policies of the populist Ahmadinejad administration (2005–13). The US and the EU began to use sanctions more instrumentally and in coordinated action drove Iran into imposed isolation, depriving it of oil income, access to the international banking sector, hard currency, and many other goods and services. The post-2010 sanctions, therefore, were qualitatively different, designed specifically to cause serious pain at the macroeconomic level, limit the regime's policy options, and challenge its ability to shield society from the corrosive effects of sanctions. The results of these sanctions were immediate and devastating: Iran's oil exports dropped dramatically in a matter of months – from 2.2 mb/d to little more than 750,000 b/d in May 2013 – costing the Iranian exchequer an average of $6 billion per month, or around $26 billion in total oil revenues in 2012, which of course crippled the subsidy-based economy and hampered the government's ability to meet its basic expenditure commitments.[152] As Table 3.13 shows, Iran's global access had also been curtailed with a handful of countries accounting for the bulk of its trade. In the absence of options, the UAE (Dubai in reality) became Iran's main access point for much of its imports, which in turn tied the government's hands even further.

TABLE 3.13 Iran's trade partners, 2012

Exports (%)					
China	India	Turkey	South Korea	Japan	% of total
22.1	11.9	10.6	7.6	7.1	59.3
Imports (%)					
UAE	China	Turkey	South Korea	Japan	% of total
33.2	13.8	11.8	7.4	NA	66.2

Source: IMF, *Direction of Trade Statistics Yearbook* (Washington, DC: IMF, 2013).

Economic growth was brought to a halt and in fact caused the economy to shrink by a massive 5.8 per cent in just one year. Associated problems included the national currency's collapse, which lost 75 per cent of its value against the dollar in a matter of months, scarcity of basic foodstuffs and amenities, a vibrant black market for all consumerables, more widespread corruption, collapse of manufacturing, and of course a rampant inflation of over 40 per cent. With unemployment hovering at around 28 per cent, social misery continued to mount, with young people under 25 accounting for around 70 per cent of the recorded unemployed. The middle class – the mainstay of modern Iranian society – was shrinking fast and at the same time the regime's 'downtrodden' base was being savaged by high prices, unemployment and at the same time the withdrawal of many subsidies. Speaking to a domestic audience about the situation before the 2015 nuclear deal, Foreign Minister Zarif put it in stark terms: "if it were not for the deal, officially known as the Joint Comprehensive Plan of Action, Iran's oil sales would have come to a halt".[153]

Efforts to address the economy's structural problems have been made from time to time – liberalization of the economy and privatization of state assets took place in the 1990s, and reform of the state subsidies system was initiated in the 2005–13 period – but these largely failed because of intense political pressure by entrenched interests and also because the regime never, as Clawson put in 1988, made the decision to "either make room for market forces or increase state control of the economy. Any middle path would combine the worst of both".[154]

But, despite the pressures of war and sanctions, the successive governments have tried to make a positive difference, and even resurrect the welfare agenda of the founding fathers, which has arguably been part of the republic's revolutionary psyche. As such, the regime has been keen to develop the country's living conditions as a priority. Thus, in such key sectors as education, housing, energy, roads, and health, it can point to significant successes. Indeed, it is remarkable how much progress Iran has made in these fields, given the difficult conditions the country has faced since 1980. Data gathered from national sources, IMF, UNICEF, and the World Bank show that at the end of the 2010s, thirty years after the revolution, some 4.4 million people were enrolled in tertiary education, with nearly 190,000 individuals training to become physicians, and a further 1.6 million were enrolled in engineering and hard sciences programmes; and, with a nearly equal gender balance, 13.2 million children were enjoying formal schooling, with some 60,000 schools serving the country's rural areas. Ninety per cent of the rural communities now had access to clean piped water, and the government's active agricultural support programme was facilitating the production of basic foods such as wheat and rice in the country. Over 35 per cent of government expenditure has tended to go on education, social services and health, with health taking 2 per cent of GDP, education 5 per cent. There are ninety-two institutions of higher learning serving the country and a further fifty-six research institutes. There is a national social security and pension system in place that covers over 75 per cent of the population and also a social welfare net to support the low-income social groups. On average around 20 per cent of the budget has gone on social welfare since the mid-1990s. Life expectancy is 73, immunization coverage is 99 per cent, and total adult literacy rate stands at an impressive 85 per cent.

After the sanctions

In the week following 'implementation day', Iran had agreed to trade and investment deals worth nearly $1 trillion. How would its economy cope with this level of foreign trade and investment and, if all the agreements reach implementation, what would the economy of the republic look like? Inevitably this high level of foreign involvement will dramatically change Iran's business relationships as well as its business culture, will inevitably challenge the para-statal organizations' hold on the economy, and consequently redefine the country's state-society relations. If this process is taken to its logical conclusion then, ironically, the republic's new masters will have taken the country back on the trail that the Shah had cleared for the country. With the ambition of turning the country into an industrial power, they will be making Iran a new outward-looking Asian economic giant and perhaps also the Middle East's first successful example of transition to a post-oil economy. The strategy of turning Iran away from its outmoded import-substitution industrialization development strategy towards an export-substitution industrialization (ESI) one is always laced with danger, but as the economic prize is huge and as this is the only viable option for an economy of this size, it is hard to see how else Iran would build a post-oil economic base to satisfy its national needs and to meet its regional and international ambitions. So the question remains, can Iran's political system and its pyramid of power cope with this level of change and accept Iran's integration into the international economic system?

For some, the process of change will be acceptable as they see Iran's rise in the context of a wholly new global division of labour in which the centre of gravity of world economy will have shifted away from the United States and towards Eurasia, Iran's own neighbourhood. So it is in this regard that President Rouhani has put so much emphasis on rebuilding economic ties with the European Union and further developing them with China, India, Russia and others in Asia. But despite the rhetoric, Iran remains mindful of the importance of the United States to the global economy and the positive role that its corporations can play in accelerating Iran's development, so while Eurasia has tended to feature more graphically in Iran's economic recovery plans, changes to the US' rules of engagement (in terms of the lifting or qualifying the crippling unilateral US sanctions on Iran) will provide the catalyst for new economic links between Iranian and American business interests. In this context, Iran has arguably accepted the terms of the capitalist order and its place in the new international division of labour.

Opting fully for the neoliberal economic narrative, former defence minister and now key advisor to President Rouhani, Akbar Torkan, has spelt it thus: "the administration has a preference for direct investment as opposed to portfolio investment as that would lead to transfer of technology and expertise to Iran, which in turn boost[s] productivity".[155] First Vice-President Eshaq Jahangiri maintained that the country "should gain its real position in the world's economic [meaning production] chain. Iran's economy should be linked with the world's economy in such a way that cutting ties with Iran would become impossible and costly for other countries".[156] This being the case, then the implications of such an admission (submission as others would have it) are enormous, for while Iran's executive leaders cut commercial deals in the post-sanctions environment and remove the barriers to entry for foreign commercial interests, the republic's political persona (as exemplified in its political economy) continues to show a counter-hegemonic posture and the narrative of resistance to the 'arrogant powers'. Iran's new place in what Hinnebusch has referred to as the "transmission belts of global neo-liberalism",[157] will require massive structural changes in Iran: An overhaul of its socioeconomic and state-society relations, with major impact on the country's political order. The practical and theoretical implications (for neoliberal economics and radical political economy) of this are enormous.

For the opponents of the neoliberal approach, Rouhani's apparent acceptance of the global economy's rules of the game will mean subjugation to the still-US-dominated system of global production and exchange. The Islamic republic will slowly but surely be fully absorbed into the fast-moving system of trade, investment and exchange as a market and as a new manufacturing base for transnational corporations. In rushing to revise its foreign investment laws to attract as much as $50 billion a year in direct foreign investment, the government has already acknowledged that Iran will need to adapt its laws to comply with international norms and legal frameworks. This in itself will change the conditions for capital growth in the country and the arrival of foreign capital in these quantities, pouring into the key sectors of the economy will impact local business conditions and encourage entrepreneurship. This will not necessarily lead to democratization per se, but must necessarily encompass compliance with Western-established norms of transparency, rule of law, and compliance if Tehran is to be successful in raising the country's place in the global division of labour. So, unlike other examples from the Global South where globalization precipitated less freedom and more authoritarian control, in the Islamic republic the reverse may materialize, in that as the arrival of foreign capital loosens the grip of para-statal entities on the economy, this process may force changes in the civil legal codes, encourage the growth of the Westward-looking middle classes, and facilitate the revival of the country's weak but surviving national bourgeoisie. It could, arguably, reduce the Bonapartist grip ('change from above') of the state on society and thus eventually rebalance state-society relations in favour of the latter.

Taking the long view, it does remain a problem that Iran's economy and social relations continue to be influenced, indeed shaped, by raw material exports. In a classic developing country condition, and despite some success at diversifying Iran's trade (exports) mix, hydrocarbons dictate the health of the country. Over a hundred years after the discovery of oil the economic fate of the country continues to be tied to hydrocarbons and global demand for black gold. Three basic drivers continue to make this so:

- First, hydrocarbons continue to dominate the global energy mix of this century as they did the twentieth; and the more moderate the prices the less likely that renewables can replace crude oil and natural gas – particularly where extraction costs remain relatively low.
- Second, given the abundance of hydrocarbons reserves on its territory (13 per cent of the world's crude oil reserves and 18 per cent of its natural gas reserves), it makes perfect economic sense for Iran to exploit hydrocarbons to drive its national economy and use the accruing petro-dollars to grow the economy and help its development. It is not surprising that so much of the government's income continues to derive from the hydrocarbons sector: Rent from oil reduces the pressure to raise direct and indirect taxes, gives the government freedom of action in resource allocation, and allows it to direct economic activity.
- Third, given the realities of supply and demand, Iran finds it very difficult to push the economy to diversify from hydrocarbons when even minimal investments in the hydrocarbons sector can add to the value of its exports and thus raise national income levels. But as oil income alone drops on a per capita basis – oil exports of $90 billion in 2010 translated into a per capita income of just $3.3 per day when the population had stood at 75 million, around the World Bank's poverty line indicator[158] – it is proving to be an insufficient engine for domestic wealth creation and any diversification (or industrialization) which does take place, petrochemicals and refined products for example, is itself dependent on hydrocarbons as the key raw material. Yet, diversification is taking place, as rises in Iran's non-oil exports show, and the more that Iran can raise its non-oil exports level the less dependent its trade balance will be on oil exports and the less sensitive to oil prices its economy will become.

The strategic advantages of ending the economic sanctions are to be found here and that is why the government is also urgently seeking to raise foreign investment in sectors beyond hydrocarbons and related industries. Success, however, will depend on the effectiveness of its open-door policy and consensus at the elite level that this, rather orthodox model, is the right development model for the Islamic republic.

To this we can add another macroeconomic problem: Namely the environmental challenges faced by the country which have been compounded in recent years by neglect as much as by demographic change, urbanization, a weak agricultural sector, flawed planning (building up a hydropower industry with little regard to the implications of dam building for the country's major river systems and tributaries, for example), and lack of investment in environmental improvements.[159] The environmental crisis has clear socioeconomic as well as political implications for the country and public awareness is forcing the regime to take such problems as pollution, lack of clean water, deforestation, desertification, and drought much more seriously than hitherto. Environmental problems could be costing Iran between 5 and 10 per cent of its GDP, according to international sources accessed by David Michel.[160] To make an environmental policy work, the government will need to secure local buy-in and engagement with local communities, as there is always a human and financial cost attached to prevention of further degradation on one side and environmental improvement measures on the other side. To redress the neglect of previous decades, the government will also have to cede power and authority to local actors and interested parties for the implementation of improvement strategies, both of which will of course carry a political cost.

After the Rafsanjani administration's unsuccessful efforts to relink Iran fully to the capitalist international order, it is during Rouhani's presidency, and as a consequence of the forward momentum generated by the lifting of multilateral sanctions, that the Islamic republic is again attempting to relocate itself in the global trade and production chains. This time, there appears to be little substantive populist or ideological opposition to the reintegration course of action. The government can fully rationalize the need for attracting foreign capital and for inviting Western corporations and banks to assist in Iran's new economic development strategy (the highlights of which are employment generation, technological innovation, industrialization, development of agriculture and a strong and outward-looking services industry), but the broader implications of this strategy for a regime still vulnerable to revolutionary and ideological groupings in the republic are yet to be digested fully. We are still dealing with a regime which sees itself as revolutionary, different and also better than others, and whose founding fathers have neither abandoned their roots (as in the case of China post-1989) nor been unseated (as in the case of the Soviet Union in 1991). The 'state class' which came into being through state's nationalizations and etatist policies of the 1980s has been entrenched further following the intensification of sanctions in the 1990s and 2000s. Though by no means a 'class for itself' this divided state bourgeoisie needs to determine whether it is in its longer-term interest to integrate more fully into the global system or to try to defend its domestic position by limiting the reach of global capitalism into the Iranian economy.

Notes

1 Algeria (35th), Iraq (29th), Kuwait (24th) and Qatar (23rd) all featured in the list in 2012, even appearing above another of the region's major economies (Israel).

2 Pankaj Ghemawat and Steven A. Altman, *DHL Global Connectedness Index 2014: Analyzing Global Flows and their Power to Increase Prosperity* (Bonn: Deutsche Post DHL, 2014).
3 Charles Issawi, 'General Introduction: 1800–1914', in Charles Issawi (ed.) *The Economic History of Iran, 1800–1914* (Chicago, Il: University of Chicago Press, 1971), p. 19.
4 Nikki Keddie, *Modern Iran: Roots and Results of Revolution* (New Haven, CT: Yale University Press, 2006).
5 Jahangir Amuzegar, 'The Role of Oil in the Economic Development of Iran 1949–1973', in Baqer Mostofi and Keith McLachlan (eds.) *The Development of the Iranian Oil Industry 1954–1973* (London: School of Oriental and African Studies, 1991), p. 23.
6 Charles Issawi, 'Epilogue: The Iranian Economy, 1914–70', in Charles Issawi (ed.) *The Economic History of Iran, 1800–1914* (Chicago, Il: University of Chicago Press, 1971), pp. 373–86.
7 M. Reza Ghods, *Iran in the Twentieth Century: A Political History* (Boulder, CO: Lynne Rienner, 1989), pp. 3–4.
8 M. Reza Ghods, ibid., p. 101.
9 John W. Limbert, *Iran: At War with History* (Boulder, CO: Westview Press, 1987).
10 John W. Limbert, ibid., p. 13.
11 Julian Bharier, *Economic Development in Iran: 1900–1970* (London: Oxford University Press, 1971).
12 B. Mostofi, 'Preface', in Baqer Mostofi and Keith McLachlan (eds.) *The Development of the Iranian Oil Industry 1954–1973* (London: School of Oriental and African Studies, 1991), p. x.
13 Afsaneh Najmabadi, 'Depoliticisation of a Rentier State: The Case of Pahlavi Iran', in Hazem Beblawi and Giacomo Luciani (eds.) *The Rentier State* (London: Croom Helm, 1987), pp. 211–27.
14 Jahangir Amuzegar, 'The Role of Oil in the Economic Development of Iran 1949–1973', in Baqer Mostofi and Keith McLachlan (eds.) *The Development of the Iranian Oil Industry 1954–1973* (London: School of Oriental and African Studies, 1991), p. 35.
15 Afsaneh Najmabadi, op. cit.
16 E. Melikaf, *Development of Manufacturing in Iran, 1962–74* (Keele: PhD thesis, Keele University, 1979).
17 Masoud Ghaffari, *Political Economy of Oil in Iran* (London: Institute of Islamic Studies, 2000).
18 Farhad Daftary and Maryam Borghey, *Multinational Enterprises and Employment in Iran* (Geneva: International Labour Office, 1976).
19 John C. Campbell, 'Oil Power in the Middle East', *Foreign Affairs*, October 1977, pp. 93–94.
20 Z. Heyat, *Iran: A Comprehensive Study of Socio-economic Condition* (CA: Eastern Publishing Society, 1983), p. 58.
21 H.J. Budig and M. Süer, *Middle East and North Africa Markets Review 1973–74* (London: Gower Economic Publishing, 1973). The authors noted, rather glibly, that the "social effects of such rapid modernization, however, are yet to be seen". p. 135.
22 Robert Graham, *Iran: The Illusion of Power* (London: Croom Helm, 1979).
23 M. Hashem Pesaran, *Iranian Economy during the Pahlavi Era* (Cambridge: University of Cambridge Department of Applied Economics Working Paper no. 9418, October 1994).
24 See Heyat, op. cit., p. 64.
25 Even before the boom had kicked in, forty-five families were believed to own around 85 per cent of all privately owned industrial units in the country.
26 Ahmad Ashraf, 'From the White Revolution to the Islamic Revolution', in Saeed Rahnema and Sohrab Behdad (eds.) *Iran after the Revolution: Crisis of an Islamic State* (London: I.B. Tauris, 1995), p. 31.

27 Data from the OECD's *Geographical Distribution of Financial Flows in Less Developed Countries* (Paris: OECD, various annual editions).
28 As is shown later, Iran's oil income climbed from $5.0 billion in 1973–74 to over $16 billion a year after that, standing at $19.46 billion in 1977–78.
29 Farhad Nomani and Sohrab Behdad, *Class and Labor in Iran: Did the Revolution Matter?* (Syracuse, NY: Syracuse University Press, 2006), p. 97.
30 Farhad Nomani and Sohrab Behdad, *Class and Labor in Iran: Did the Revolution Matter?* (Syracuse, NY: Syracuse University Press, 2006), pp. 97–98.
31 Marvin Zonis, *The Political Elite of Iran* (Princeton, NJ: Princeton University Press, 1971).
32 Mohsen M. Milani, *The Making of Iran's Islamic Revolution: From Monarchy to Islamic Republic* (Boulder, CO: Westview Press, 1994), p. 61.
33 It was also significant that US President Jimmy Carter's personal envoy to meet with the Iranian military, General Robert Huyser, had arrived in January 1979 (just days before the Shah's final departure from the country) in order to encourage the high command to support the provisional government being put in place. See General Robert E. Huyser, *Mission to Tehran* (London: Andre Deutsch, 1986).
34 Richard E. Barrett and Martin K. Whyte, 'Dependency Theory and Taiwan: Analysis of a Deviant Vase', *American Journal of Sociology*, vol. 87, 1982, pp. 1064–89.
35 Edward S. Mason, Mahn Je Kim, Dwight H. Perkins, Kwang Suk Kim, and David C. Cole, *The Economic and Social Modernization of the Republic of Korea* (Cambridge, MA: Harvard University Press, 1980).
36 A political by-product of the White Revolution was the rise in influence of a certain Ayatollah Khomeini, who from 1963 joined the ranks of the opponents of the Pahlavi monarch.
37 Brazil, South Korea, Taiwan, Singapore were other countries being included in this group at that time. Different lists also had Turkey, South Africa, Israel, and Hong Kong attached to them.
38 Immanuel Wallerstein, *The Capitalist World-Economy* (Cambridge: Cambridge University Press, 1979).
39 Peter Evans, *Dependent Development: The Alliance of Multinational, State, and Local Capital in Brazil* (Princeton, NJ: Princeton University Press, 1979).
40 Ahmad Ashraf, 'From the White Revolution to the Islamic Revolution', in Saeed Rahnema and Sohrab Behdad (eds.) *Iran after the Revolution: Crisis of an Islamic State* (London: I.B. Tauris, 1995), p. 31.
41 Robert Looney, *The Economic Development of Iran – A Recent Survey with Projections to 1981* (New York, NY: Praeger, 1973), p. 20.
42 Anoushiravan Ehteshami, *After Khomeini: The Iranian Second Republic* (London: Routledge, 1995).
43 H-G Muller, 'Remarks on the Role of the State Capital Sector and National Private Capital in the Revolutionary Process of Capitalism in Iran up to the End of the 1970s', in G. Barthel (ed.) *Iran: From Monarchy to Republic* (Berlin: Akademie-Verlag, 1983), p. 74.
44 Massoud Karshenas, 'Structural Adjustment and the Iranian Economy', in Nemat Shafik (ed.) *Economic Challenges Facing Middle Eastern and North African Countries: Alternative Futures* (London: Macmillan, 1998), p. 204.
45 Melvyn J. Else, *Iran: Business Opportunities for the 1980s* (London: Metra Consulting Group, 1978).
46 James F. Petras and Morris H. Morley, 'Development and Revolution: Contradictions in the Advanced Third World Countries – Brazil, South Africa, and Iran', *Studies in Comparative International Development*, vol. XVI, no.1, Spring 1981, pp. 5–43.
47 See Anoushiravan Ehteshami, 'The Foreign Policy of Iran', in Raymond Hinnebusch and Anoushiravan Ehteshami (eds.) *The Foreign Policies of Middle East States* (Boulder, CO: Lynne Rienner, 2002), pp. 283–309.

48 M. Hashem Pesaran, *Iranian Economy during the Pahlavi Era* (Cambridge: University of Cambridge Department of Applied Economics Working Paper no. 9418, October 1994).
49 Massoud Karshenas, *Structural Adjustment and the Prospects of the Iranian Economy* (London: SOAS Department of Economics Working Paper no. 57, September 1995), p. 2.
50 Massoud Karshenas, ibid., p. 3.
51 GATT, *International Trade, 1985–1986* (Geneva, GATT, 1986).
52 Mohammad Reza Abedini Moghanaki and Mohsen Shariatinia, 'Global Power Transition, Sanctions and Iran's Export Orientation', *Iran Review of Foreign Affairs*, vol. 5, no. 1, Spring 2014, pp. 5–28.
53 Massoud Karshenas, op. cit., 1995, p. 4.
54 Mehrdad Valibeigi, 'The Private Sector in Iran's Post-Revolutionary Economy', *Journal of South Asian and Middle Eastern Studies*, vol. XVII, no. 3, Spring 1994, p. 15.
55 Evaleila Pesaran, *Iran's Struggle for Economic Independence: Reform and Counter-reform in the Post-revolutionary Era* (London: Routledge, 2011).
56 Ali Rahnema and Farhad Nomani, *The Secular Miracle: Religion, Politics and Economic Policy in Iran* (London: Zed Books, 1990).
57 Shirzad Azad, 'The Politics of Privatization in Iran', *Middle East Review of International Affairs*, vol. 14, no. 4, December 2010, pp. 60–71.
58 See *The Middle East*, April 1985, p. 52.
59 James Defronzo, *Revolutions and Revolutionary Movements* (Boulder, CO: Westview Press, 1996), pp. 271–72.
60 Ian Roxborough, *Theories of Underdevelopment* (London: Macmillan, 1979), p. 144.
61 Peyman Jafari, 'Rupture and Revolt in Iran', *International Socialism*, no. 124, September 2009, http://www.isj.org.uk/index.php4?id=585&issue=124.
62 Kamran Mofid, *The Economic Consequences of the Gulf War* (London: Routledge, 1990).
63 Cited by Masoud Ghaffari, *Political Economy of Oil in Iran* (London: Institute of Islamic Studies, 2000), p. 615.
64 Economist Intelligence Unit, 'Iran', in *The Middle East and North Africa 1985* (London: The Economist Publications, 1985).
65 OPEC database.
66 Hooshang Amirahmadi, 'Economic Destruction and Imbalances in Post-revolutionary Iran', in Hooshang Amirahmadi and Nader Entessar (eds.) *Reconstruction and Regional Diplomacy in the Persian Gulf* (London: Routledge, 1992), pp. 65–108.
67 Eliyahu Kanovsky, *Iran's Economic Morass: Mismanagement and Decline under the Islamic Republic*, (Washington, DC: Washington Institute for Near East Policy, Policy Paper no. 44, 1997).
68 Amirahmadi, op. cit., p. 69.
69 Kaveh Ehsani, '"Tilt but don't Spill": Iran's Development and Reconstruction Dilemma', *Middle East Report*, no. 191, November-December 1994, pp. 16–21.
70 Kamran Mofid, *Development Planning in Iran: From Monarchy to Islamic Republic* (Wisbech: MENAS Press, 1987.
71 BBC, *Summary of World Broadcasts*, ME/W0077 A1/1, 16 April 1989.
72 Comment of Minister of Economics and Finance (Mohammad Iravani) in an interview with the monthly magazine, *Eqtesad*, July 1989.
73 Mehrdad Valibeigi, op. cit., p. 15.
74 Jahangir Amuzegar, 'The Iranian Economy before and after the Revolution', *Middle East Journal*, vol. 46, no. 3, Summer 1992, p. 423.
75 Patrick Clawson, 'Islamic Iran's Economic Politics and Prospects', *Middle East Journal*, vol. 42. no. 3, Summer 1988, pp. 371–88.
76 Ali Rahnemi and Farhad Nomani, op. cit.
77 Ayatollah Khomeini's intervention in November 1988 was prompted by a senior aide to provide a definitive direction for the post-war economic policy. *APS Diplomat*, 5–12 November 1988.

78 *APS Diplomat*, 10–17 September 1988.
79 Majlis Speaker Rafsanjani addressing a public gathering in Tehran. BBC, *Summary of World Broadcasts*, ME/0341 A/2, 22 December 1988.
80 Peyman Jafari, op. cit.
81 Quoted in *The Echo of Iran*, 5 January 1989, p. 15.
82 Then-Foreign Minister Ali Akbar Velayati cited in Hooshang Amirahmadi, 'Iranian Economic Reconstruction Plan and Prospects for its Success', in Hooshang Amirahmadi and Nader Entessar (eds.) *Reconstruction and Regional Diplomacy in the Persian Gulf* (London: Routledge, 1992), p. 137.
83 Kaveh Ehsani, '"Tilt but Don't Spill": Iran's Development and Reconstruction Dilemma', *Middle East Report*, November-December 1994, pp. 16–21.
84 See Anoushiravan Ehteshami, 'Iran', in Tim Niblock and Emma Murphy (eds.) *Economic and Political Liberalization in the Middle East* (London: British Academic Press, 1993), pp. 214–236.
85 Ibid.; Business International Limited, *Iran: A Manual for Foreign Business. Opportunities and Operating Conditions to 1994* (London: The Economist Group, 1991).
86 Unidentified banker cited in Vahe Petrossian, 'Iran's Problems Come to a Head', *Middle East Economic Digest*, 3 December 1993, p. 5.
87 Kevan Harris, 'The Rise of the Subcontractor State: Politics of Pseudo-privatization in the Islamic Republic of Iran', *International Journal of Middle East Studies*, vol. 45, no. 1, February 2013, pp. 45–70.
88 Barbara Smith, *A Survey of Iran: Children of the Islamic Revolution* (London: *The Economist*, 18 January 1997), p. 13.
89 *Christian Science Monitor*, 14–10 April 1995.
90 *Gulf States Newsletter*, vol. 19, no. 499, 14 November 1994, pp. 8–11.
91 Unnamed Tehran-based academic cited in Lamis Andoni, 'Second Revolution Brews in Iran', *Christian Science Monitor*, 14–20 April 1995.
92 Steve Hanke, 'Can Iran Find a Master of Its Economy?', *Wall Street Journal*, 23 May, 2013. The MI is a composite of inflation, unemployment and interest rates minus the annual change in per capita GDP. The lower the figure, the lower the 'misery' level is said to be.
93 Azad, op. cit., pp. 65–66.
94 Cited by Amberin Zaman, 'Rafsanjani feels Friendless', *The Middle East*, January 1994, p. 12.
95 John Grimond, 'God's Rule, or Man's? A Survey of Iran', *The Economist*, 18 January 2003.
96 Harris, op. cit.
97 Evaleila Pesaran, op. cit.
98 Azad, op. cit., p. 67.
99 World Bank data base, http://www.devdata.worldbank.org.
100 Nader Habibi, 'The Economic Legacy of Mahmoud Ahmadinejad', *Middle East Brief*, no. 74, June 2013, 9pp. Published by Brandeis University's Crown Center for Middle East Studies.
101 Data compiled from OPEC, *OPEC Annual Statistical Bulletin 2005* (Vienna: OPEC, 2005).
102 Sara Bazoobandi, *Iran's Domestic Political and Economic Challenges* (Jeddah: Gulf Research Center, November 2012).
103 Azad, op. cit.
104 Ibid.
105 Najmeh Bozorgmehr, 'Iran's Bloated State Grapples with Excessive Overstaffing', *Financial Times*, 27 February 2014.
106 Niheer Dasandi, *The Politics-Bureaucracy Interface in Developing Countries: Characteristics, Determinants, and Impact on Reform* (Singapore: UNDP Global Centre for Public Service Excellence, 2014).
107 Oliver August, 'Special Report Iran: The Revolution Is Over', *The Economist*, 1 November 2014.

108 Ibid, p. 11.
109 Ibid, p. 13.
110 The case of Babak Zanjani has exemplified the depth of corruption. Sentenced to death for corruption in 2016 his case has revealed the murky interactions between state functionaries and 'trusted' businessmen who facilitated transfer of funds and acquisition of goods and services for the regime and its functionaries. Zanjani accumulated $2.8 billion through his shady dealings of over $9.3 billion. See Iran Human Rights Documentation Center, 'Infographic – Government Corruption in Iran', http://www.iranhrdc.org/english/news/features/1000000600-infographic-government-corruption-in-iran.html.
111 The conservative media, such as Vatan-e Emrooz website on 30 June 2016, exploited this scandal to undermine Rouhani, but the truth of the matter is that as many as 3,000 officials had been drawing exorbitant salaries – often over $30,000 per month – for years and the regime had known about it.
112 *Iranian Diplomacy*, 20 October 2012.
113 *Etemad*, 21 October 2015.
114 Reuters, 26 January 2016.
115 M. Javad Ardalan, 'Comments on the Iranian Economy', The Iranian British Chamber of Commerce, Autumn 2014.
116 The World Bank, 'Iran Overview', 29 September 2015.
117 As he declared to the Majlis on 17 January, "government policies in the post-sanctions era will focus on attracting foreign investment, expanding non-oil exports, and making the best use of financial assets". IRNA, 17 January 2016. The government has set itself the target of attracting $50 billion in annual direct foreign investment between 2016 and 2021.
118 IRNA, 17 February 2015.
119 IRNA, 22 March 2016.
120 Reuters, 29 January 2016.
121 Philip Pullella, 'Iran Sanctions: Islamic Republic Rapidly Resumes Global Trade in the Wake of Nuclear Deal', *The Independent*, 18 January 2016.
122 Philip Pullella, ibid.
123 Reuters and Associated Press, 23 January 2016.
124 Reuters, 26 January 2016.
125 Ibid.
126 Reuters, 29 January 2016. As a sweetener France's Total group also agreed to buy 200,000 barrels of oil a day from Iran.
127 'Joint statement by the High Representative/Vice-President of the European Union, Federica Mogherini and the Minister of Foreign Affairs of the Islamic Republic of Iran, Javad Zarif', EU Commission Press Release Database, 16 April 2016.
128 'Iran Attracts Billions of Dollars of Foreign Investment', *Iran Daily*, 1 February 2016.
129 Anoushiravan Ehteshami, *After Khomeini: The Iranian Second Republic* (London: Routledge, 1995).
130 Jahangir Amuzegar, 'The Iranian Economy before and after the Revolution', *Middle East Journal*, vol. 46, no. 3, Summer 1992, p. 423.
131 Farhad Nomani and Sohrab Behdad, *Class and Labor in Iran: Did the Revolution Matter?* (Syracuse, NY: Syracuse University Press, 2006), p. 204.
132 Maryam H. Panah, 'State and Society in the Islamic Republic: The Impact of Post-revolutionary War', *Journal of Iranian Research and Analysis*, vol. 16, no. 1, April 2000, p. 88.
133 For a broader comment on importance of the relationship between politics and social classes for understanding social change in developing countries, see Ian Roxborough, *Theories of Underdevelopment* (London: Macmillan, 1979).
134 Ian Roxborough, *Theories of Underdevelopment* (London: Macmillan, 1979), p. 142.
135 Farhad Nomani and Sohrab Behdad, *Class and Labor in Iran: Did the Revolution Matter?* (Syracuse, NY: Syracuse University Press, 2006), p. 204.

136 Hooshang Amirahmadi, *Revolution and Economic Transition: The Iranian Experience* (New York, NY: State University of New York press, 1990).
137 Jahangir Amuzegar, *Iran's Economy under the Islamic Republic* (London: I.B. Tauris, 1993).
138 Hooshang Amirahmadi, *Revolution and Economic Transition: The Iranian Experience* (New York, NY: State University of New York press, 1990). Amirahmadi estimates that by 1989 disguised and registered unemployment had stood at around 41 per cent of the total work force.
139 Jahangir Amuzegar, *Iran's Economy under the Islamic Republic* (London: I.B. Tauris, 1993), p. 312.
140 Alan Richards and John Waterbury, *A Political Economy of the Middle East* (Boulder, CO: Westview Press, 1996), p. 242.
141 Jahangir Amuzegar, *Iran's Economy under the Islamic Republic* (London: I.B. Tauris, 1993).
142 Nikki R. Keddie, *Modern Iran: Roots and Results of Revolution* (New Haven, CT: Yale University Press, 2006), p. 273.
143 Radio Zamaneh, 29 May, 2010.
144 IRNA, 16 December 2015.
145 *Financial Tribune*, 18 January 2016.
146 Statistical Centre of Iran, *Annual Report 1392* (Tehran, 2014).
147 Wold Bank, *Iran: Overview* http//www.worldbank.or/en/country/iran.
148 As many as ten rather large charitable organizations, foundations and public bodies of this nature have emerged, controlling estimated assets in excess of $20 billion. One of the most important, the Foundation of the Oppressed, was estimated to have as many as 800 companies under its control, employing some 700,000 people, and controlling of assets of over $10 billion in late 1990s. The Foundation of the Oppressed has business interests in agriculture, commerce, construction, mining, transportation, entertainment and recreation, cinemas, etc. See Suzanne Maloney, 'Agents or Obstacles? Parastatal Foundations and Challenges for Iranian Development', in Parvin Alizadeh (ed.) *The Economy of Iran: The Dilemmas of an Islamic State* (London: I.B. Tauris, 2000), pp. 145–76.
149 Suzanne Maloney, ibid, p. 148.
150 Hesam Forozan, *The Military in Post-Revolutionary Iran: The Evolution and Roles of the Revolutionary Guards* (New York, NY: Routledge, 2016).
151 Samanvya Hooda, 'Iran's Economic Renaissance: Will the IRGC Profit? – Analysis', *Institute for Peace and Conflict Studies*, 5 June 2016.
152 See 'Ouch! Tehran is Hurting', *The World Today*, vol. 70, no. 6, December 2014, pp. 32–33.
153 *Financial Tribunal*, 1 February 2016.
154 Patrick Clawson, 'Islamic Iran's Economic Politics and Prospects', *Middle East Journal*, vol. 42, no. 3, Summer 1988, p. 388.
155 *Financial Tribunal*, 1 February 2016.
156 Tasnim, 15 February 2016.
157 Raymond Hinnebusch, 'Globalization, Democratization, and the Arab Uprising: The International Factor in MENA's Failed Democratization', *Democratization*, vol. 22, no. 2, March 2015, p. 336.
158 David Ramin Jalilvand, 'Recent Developments and Challenges in Iranian Oil and Gas Sector', *Orient*, vol. 54, no. iv, 2013, pp. 67–73.
159 Introduction of gas-fuelled public transport (taxis and buses) is a credible step forward but does not change the pollution equation without a public transport-first urban strategy and with so many polluting cars on Iran's roads.
160 David Michel, 'Iran's Environment: Greater Threat than Foreign Foes', (Washington, DC: USIP Iran Primer, 28 October 2013). http://iranprimer.usip.org/blog/2013/oct/28/iran%E2%80%99s-environment-greater-threat-foreign-foes.

4
INTERNATIONAL RELATIONS

Introduction

Earlier it was argued that Iran is a civilizational state with deep cultural roots and a long imperial history, and despite many external shocks and setbacks over two millennia of dynastic rule a strong sense of continuity has been instilled in the country in which twentieth-century revolutionary turmoil did not dent the sense of historical legacy, self-importance and self-worth, as critical influences on its worldview and policy choices.[1] Indeed, in many ways, these national sentiments may have been reinforced.

History not only shapes Iranians' approach to change, but it also acts as precedent, thus giving the state the scales by which to weigh its policies and the yardstick by which to measure the success of its actions. It further weighs its actions not only from a historical perspective but also in terms of the regime's ideology: Its Islamist ideology of resistance and purported struggle for justice. "The character of the nation", argues Fuller, "has direct impact on the kind of domestic – and foreign – policy that it will conduct".[2] In this sense, the combination of a long history, geopolitical weight and pan-regional presence has always given Iran a role in Eurasian relations. Add to this hydrocarbons income and a unique interpretation of political Islam and one can begin to appreciate the unique character of the Islamic republic.

To understand Iran's international relations, you must study its character, the construction of its personality, and, in the last analysis, the role of (political) agency in its foreign policy. In Fuller's words, "nations have unique personalities or cultures, developed over a period of time by the unique melding of factors that produce a distinctive culture and operating style".[3] Iran appears as a country on a mission and its direction of travel, given its Islamist superstructure and radical oratory, generates much interest – indeed also apprehension and concern – in regional capitals and Western countries. The Islamic republic in this regard is an 'enigma' – a calculating rational actor with limited goals in realist terms for some and a regime of power hungry 'mad mullahs' intent on disrupting the status quo for others. True, the revolutionary republic transformed the ideological underpinnings and orientation of the country; it transformed Tehran's approach to alliance building and partners; and it rotated Iran's geopolitical weight in some new directions, but at the same time many features of the monarchical regime also remained intact. So it is not surprising that much controversy continues to surround scholarly work on Iran's foreign policy, which at its heart is still being shaped by a combination of regime-type ruling the country and the external geopolitical circumstances. As such, to unpack the extent of continuity and change in Iran's international relations has become a permanent pastime for observers, yet there exists little consensus as to the enduring features of the country's foreign policy over the long run (since the 1950s) and its relations with the rest of the world.

How much of what Iran does is by design – a grand plan – and how much is a knee-jerk reaction to acute regional threats and challenges? The volatility and complexities of the region in which Iran finds itself have arguably added another layer of difficulty for those trying to make analytical sense of Iran's international relations. But in the clamour and the loud conflicting geopolitical noises out of the MENA regional order, it is too easy to lose sight of agency – the reality that, in Salimi's words, "ideas about who 'we' are serves as a guide to political action and basic worldview… this conceptual lens through which foreign policymakers perceive international relations tends to set the norm for what is considered by them as 'rational' foreign policymaking".[4] In essence, role conception and policy are buried in values as well as self-perception.

Before the revolution, realpolitik and a strong streak of realism drove the monarchy's external relations and policies. From the mid-1950s the 'executive' monarch took a greater interest in the operational aspects of policymaking and by the mid-1960s had come to dominate the machinery of government.[5] The Shah and a group of advisors and associates shaped and articulated the priorities of the state and closely followed their implementation by the foreign ministry. Noteworthy is the fact that from the mid-1960s, ministers rarely made policy, and ambassadors and military commanders reported directly to the monarch, often without their own bosses being privy to such exchanges.[6] Under the banner of nationalism, from the 1960s the Shah closely associated the state's foreign policy with the monarchy's interests and used the country's ancient civilization to legitimize the pursuit of what Halliday referred to as expansionist policies.[7] Secure at home after the suppression of the clerics' short-lived uprising in the early 1960s, the Shah set his sights on restoring to Iran what was said to be its rightful place amongst the world's great countries. Receiving support in this endeavour from two other 'civilizational' states of China and Egypt from the early 1970s underscored for the cash-rich Shah Imperial Iran's natural place in the community of states. Assertiveness, fuelled by petrodollars and illusions of grandeur, was being programmed into the Shah's foreign policy and his regime inevitably took it upon itself to determine not only the security of the region being vacated by Britain but also the shape of the neighbouring South and Southeast Asian regions.

As already noted, after 1979 ideology, as a fountainhead of policy, emerged as a new and formidable force in shaping the Iranian republic's international relations. Ideology as a self-defining set of principles has shaped the regime's worldview, the identification of friend and foe, and the image of itself as a unique (revolutionary) Islamic state charged with defending, and, where and whenever possible, uniting the Muslim world against adversarial powers. The political forces that the revolution gave birth to have provided the focus of much analysis of the regime's social structures and the 'power elite' which emerged in the wake of the hostage crisis. The narrowing of the political base helped refine the outlines of Iran's new foreign policy, and closer analysis of the new power elite raised the interest in the domestic sources of Iran's foreign policy.

Interest has grown in recent years so the application of what has become closely associated with the constructivist school of international relations has found in the case of Iran a rich seam to mine. Deeper engagement with such issues as identity formation, role of ideas and values in policymaking and place of subjective sources of knowledge as policy drivers provides very interesting analytical variations to the zero-sum schools which have seen Tehran as either a mad but calculating regime or a hard realist conniving one in which pragmatism masks opportunism and hegemonic ambition.[8] While an analysis of the role of ideas – ideationalism – does not necessarily contradict the conclusions of other approaches, it nevertheless does make for a more nuanced and perhaps deeper analysis of the drivers of Iran's international relations. Thus, an important feature of Iran's foreign policy is the weight that domestic factors have acquired in determining the country's international relations.

The 'black box' of international relations – the domestic context for foreign policy – has emerged as a critical variable in the analysis of the Islamic republic's external policies.[9] In this realm at least there is considerable difference between the monarchy and the republican regime, for unlike the Pahlavi period since the revolution domestic politics has played a critical role in the shaping of the regime's international relations, despite it retaining the geopolitical features of the *ancien regime*'s external policies. A focus on agency is therefore essential in this instance, for the ideas and ideals of the Islamic republic and those of its elite (as much as the empowered voices coming from below) provide what Selbin has called 'the mediating link'[10] with structural conditions – the 'given' of the international system that revolutionary regimes have to contend with. Moreover, such revolutionary regimes' internationalism, which in this case was articulated in religious terms, is a direct response – challenge – to the status quo and a critical driver of such regimes' desire to bend the global order to their own will.[11]

The modus operandi of revolutionary regimes is to drive change: They burst onto the international scene often in an attempt to change the prevailing order rather than conform to it. Revolutionary regimes are therefore inherently destabilizing internationally and as a consequence tend to be disruptive of what they regard as old patterns of relationships, so normatively we should expect the republic's foreign policy to be challenging and even hostile to the dominant order. When such forces emerge in a state with massive geopolitical weight and confidence derived from a rich civilizational culture, then things really get interesting.

Historical features of Iran's international relations

As the gateway between Europe and Asia – the ancient heartlands of the civilized world – Iran has been a geopolitically significant country for centuries, whose landmass has respectively acted as a barrier, bridge, or container for major powers. Positioned at one of the most critical points on the Eurasian landmass, it has since medieval times played a major role in the shaping of regions. It has both benefitted from its geography – building extensive ties with imperial China for example – and also suffered from it, as with the devastating Moghul invasion that began in early 1220. Since ancient times Persia has campaigned against or exploited links with Asian and Mediterranean powers, but the most dramatic changes to its standing occurred with the arrival of European powers – and their commercial and political machines – in the Middle East and West Asia. Indeed, the Portuguese introduced Persians to Europe, in 1507, and exposed this traditional society to the tremendous power of the expanding maritime European empires that were beginning their deeper penetration of the East. The Persians were of course already fully familiar with the growing power of the continental giant to the north and had already exchanged blows with the czars over spaces in what is now the Caucasus and Central Asia. Before the arrival of the Portuguese much of Iran's exposure to the emerging powers of Europe, and its understanding of them, had been filtered through Iran's exchanges with the Ottomans to the west and Russians to the north, but after the 1600s everything changed.

Although the encroachment and pressures of emerging European powers increasingly squeezed Iran, and often at the mercy of their greater and more mechanized firepower, the Safavid kings (1502–1722) played a significant role in giving the country many of its identity pillars.[12] One was, in contradistinction to the Sunni Caliphate next door, the formalization of Shia Islam as the country's official religion; the others were the place of a strong central state, the importance of centralized military power for national security, a deeper sense of cultural nationalism, and a revitalized sense of territorial awareness. In this period Iran rivalled the Ottomans in many fields, but it was subsequent to the Safavid defeat by the Sultan Selim and loss of Iraq and eastern Anatolia in early 1500s that Iran witnessed the steady territorial expansion, and consolidation, of Ottoman rule beyond Asia Minor.[13] Sultan Selim's defeat of the Mamluk dynasty in 1517 and assumption of its territories by the Ottomans gave them control of virtually all Muslim holy sites – from Baghdad and Damascus to Jerusalem, Cairo and, of course enhanced the legitimacy of the Caliphate through their control of the

Hejaz and the holiest Muslim sites in Mecca and Medina. Ottoman consolidation effectively checked Iran's presence in Anatolia and the Levant. Over the centuries Safavid elites watched from the sidelines the Ottomans' exchanges with the increasingly proactive European powers and the steep process which made this Muslim empire more of a European actor than an Eastern one.[14] The Persian Empire was, during these struggles, either sidelined or thoroughly exploited by one or more of the powers involved.

However, in the Qajar period and the power plays of the Great Game, Iran experienced thorough exposure to European pressures. As Farmanfarmaian notes, "pressures were being exerted from three directions: The north from Russia; the east from British India and the new buffer state of Afghanistan; and the west from the Ottomans and the British in the Persian Gulf. For the Qajars, the focus of both their internal and foreign relations, therefore, was on resistance to external penetration".[15] Fearful of Russia, the Ottomans, and Britain, the Qajars tried to build an alliance with the other major European power, France. Indeed, even before the 'politico-military' Franco-Persian Treaty of Finkenstein (1807) had been concluded, Napoleon Bonaparte was reaching out to his Qajar counterparts. Thus, from the Russian front Napoleon writes that "Part of the Russian army, especially the cavalry which was on the frontier [with Persia], has been recalled and is being directed against me. Benefit from these circumstances".[16] In practice, though, this would prove to be little more than a fair-weather partnership for, as Amini notes, if "Napoleon had been interested in Persia and its destiny, it was merely to intimidate Britain and Russia by turns".[17] Thus far, its experience of the new emerging global powers had not been positive and was not to change either, for the Czars exacted the greatest pain, in 1813 and 1828, in forcing Iran through treaty to cede vast tracts of territory in the Caucasus to Russia against overwhelming military odds in Iran's favour. Before the 1828 Turkomanchai Treaty, which cost Iran much of the Caucasus, the country had also been engaged in a bloody campaign (1821–23) in the north and west with the Ottomans.

Capitulation in war was followed by a regime of commercial concessions to European companies and individuals by the Qajar kings, which were indeed akin to mortgaging the country's resources (and future) to foreign forces, and this was done in return for an immediate cash gratification and promise of more. But equally profoundly felt was the belittling of Iranian talent and voices in externalizing the country's foreign relations. The final symbol of impotence was to be the 1907 Anglo-Russian Convention that conveniently divided Iran into their spheres of influence: Russian in the north and Britain in the south. The 1919 Anglo-Persian Treaty completed the country's humiliation by effectively turning Iran into a British protectorate, putting the latter in charge of the country's trade, finances and the armed forces – the three key pillars of power in early-twentieth-century Iran.

Avery's historical contextualization of Iran's concerns with independence and autonomous action is well made: "penetration of Iran's way of life by foreigners was, and to a considerable extent still is, the cause of serious concerns in the mind of the people" of this country and in the end foreign concessions were seen as being little more than the exploitation of Iranians and, as in the case of the infamous Tobacco Concession of 1890, "an assault on the nation's privacy, as well as, on its pocket".[18] Few things resonate more strongly with Iranians than the sense of humiliation following these concessions. The final stand against the Tobacco Concession, of course, which was abrogated in 1892, gave birth to a national awakening that culminated in Iran's Constitutional Revolution of 1905 and the eventual demise of the Qajar dynasty a few years later. But the salient point is that for "Persia under the Qajars, its geopolitical importance and its need to protect both its borders and its resources, reflected a continuum that defined Persian identity and Persian foreign policy, and which continues to do so even under the country's rubric as the Islamic Republic of Iran".[19]

Despite the eventful 200-year period following Nader Shah Afshar's conquests in the Indian subcontinent, it was in the twentieth century, with fires of war burning around it, that Iran's place in the community of nations became of immediate importance to the major powers.

Arguably, the end of the Qajar dynasty in 1925 and the subsequent establishment of the new Pahlavi monarchy under Reza Khan marked the emergence of Iran as a modern territorial state with an emerging national interest and a new set of priorities.

Iran's international outlook, and deep suspicion of foreign powers, is partly shaped by this rich history and the destructive role that European powers played in emasculating this proud country. The prominent Qajar monarch Nasser ed-Din Shah himself is reputed to have recognized the negative impact of European interventions, expressing the wish "that never a European had set foot on my country's soil".[20] Suspicion of the motives of major powers was the first lesson that history taught Iran's modern rulers; the other big lesson was the damage that indecisiveness, tinged with incompetent and subservient leadership, can cause the country.

More broadly, the struggle to retain Iran's separate identity under external pressure – invasion, devastation, and domination by foreigners – has made a deep impression on the country's culture and its drive for 'independence'. This was the case under the Pahlavis and has remained so under the Ayatollahs. As is evident, in explaining Iran's foreign affairs, the framework must be "multi-level and multi-causal, as well as contextual".[21]

International relations of a modern state: the Pahlavis

For the Pahlavis, securing the country's territorial integrity was paramount, and for this reason the Pahlavi monarchs looked to build a strong centralized state and military force able to defend the country. They also banked on alliances that would strengthen the country's security pillars and its central administrative systems. Suspicious of British and Russian/Soviet powers, Reza Khan looked to Germany, as a strong European power with no history of aggression against Iran, for support. His son, Mohammad Reza Pahlavi, having experienced Soviet bullying during and after the Second World War – including blatant continuing occupation of Iranian territory after 1945 – sought partnership with the rising star of the faraway power, the United States of America. Although the United States did not avail itself of this friendship well, implementing the Anglo-American-engineered coup against Premier Mossadegh, nevertheless a grateful Mohammad Reza Shah sought to build an increasingly close partnership with Washington after the events of 1953. This partnership turned Iran into a Cold War 'frontline' state and a significant pawn in the strategy of containment of the Soviet Union. The Baghdad Pact, until Iraq's sudden departure in 1958, sealed the new geopolitical arrangements, which positioned Iran as the centrepiece of the Pakistan-Iran-Turkey-Iraq alliance.[22] But the Pact's limp response to the fall of the monarchy in Iraq did not instil confidence in the alliance and, despite the restructuring of the alliance into a new organization (CENTO), Tehran's belief in the inherent weaknesses of such a multilateral security structure pushed it ever closer to the United States as the only credible guarantor of Iran's security.[23] This relationship, however, as will be shown later, developed its own unique problems for the monarchy.

Having taken a front-row seat at the start of the Cold War, in the 1950s and 1960s Iran had to contend with, from the margins, the changing regional power relations, centred on the Arab region. Though not a direct player in the ensuing 'Arab Cold War' of the 1958–71 period, the Shah was keenly aware of the impact of the Arab Cold War on the regional balance of power and as a consequence also on Iran's own well-being. Nasser's pan-Arab revolutionary wave from Egypt contributed to the undoing of the monarchy in neighbouring Iraq in 1958 and the creation of an Arab nationalist coalition, which for a while threatened other monarchical regimes in the region.[24]

Tehran had to stand by and witness the demise of colonial power in the region, the emergence of new states and spaces in place of colonial occupation, and a rapidly changing regional dynamic that cut a security crisis along the two axes of Arab-Israeli conflict and inter-Arab conflict. Iran was external to both dynamics yet part of the strategic theatre in which the forces were in play. And even then it was clear that Iran, for all its strategic assets, remained an unintegrated regional state and as such was vulnerable to forces beyond its control. Pressure from the Soviet Union to curb Iran's ties with the West manifested itself through political probes against Iran. Then, the rise of Arab nationalism and its changing relationship with the established Arab states exposed it to new forces rising to the west and south of the country, forces which clearly were beyond its control. And finally, the weakening grip of the European resident powers on the MENA region, which stretched into the 1970s, forced Tehran to chart a more independent path in its regional relationships – and to be more assertive once it was clear that the country had accumulated a relatively high degree of diplomatic, economic and military assets.

Thus, what Iran wanted under the Shah, according to Campbell, was "strength, modernization, independence of policy, a regional role, and greater respect from the rest of the world".[25] Oil income provided the means for independence of action, as an influential report at the time notes, but also increasingly in possession of considerable soft power:

> In the full flush of its oil wealth after the 1973 oil price increases, Iran became a source of credit to the less well-off Arab states, as well as to a number of African countries. Substantial financial assistance was promised to Egypt, $11 million to Jordan and $150 million to Syria. A loan of $10 million was to be provided to Afghanistan during 1976 and a considerably higher sum was earmarked for Pakistan.[26]

Greater sums in loans and credits were also offered to India, in addition to the $630 million contribution Iran offered in 1976 towards the creation of a major iron ore mine in Kudremukh. The monarch also began to talk about a 'commonwealth of Indian Ocean states' aimed at reducing the presence of the big powers in this important ocean and making way for the local powers such as Iran. This was consistent with Iran becoming a regional commercial and diplomatic hub, as well as the strategy of building a 'blue water' naval capability as part of a wider military build-up that would enable Tehran to project power (and force) beyond Iran's immediate neighbourhood. Acquiring naval access to Mauritius' port facilities in 1972 provided a further concrete example of Iran's ambitions to project power. In this light, Ramazani concludes, from the mid-1960s Iran had begun to use the "unprecedented increase in Iran's capabilities and a favorable environment" to grow an appetite for a greater external presence, thus reaching out to and multiplying its links with a widening circle of states.[27] Arguably, the country's rapid socioeconomic development in the run-up to the unprecedented oil price rises of the 1970s had enabled the Shah to mobilize the country's resources in pursuit of a greater regional and international role. Alikhani explains that in the late-1960s the Pahlavi king must have looked around and seen in the crises engulfing the region an opportunity for his own country to climb the ladder of greatness, to become a 'second Japan': "The Arabs reeled under the shock of their defeat by Israel in 1967. Turkey suffered from military intervention in her political system, and Pakistan tottered on the verge of collapse. By contrast, Iran stood out as a haven of stability and initiative".[28]

The moment to test its greater influence came after Britain's announcement in 1968 that it was disengaging from territories and military commitments 'east of Suez'. Britain's formal departure provided the impetus for Tehran to place a bigger footprint on the region. So, despite creating a real security dilemma for the littoral Gulf Arab countries and Sheikhdoms who had thus far either relied on British protection or had negotiated a modus operandi with its powerful representatives, Britain's departure also presented opportunities for the bigger and more established countries, such as Iran, Iraq and Saudi Arabia, to make a move for greater influence. An early sign of things to come was Iran's mobilization to occupy three strategic Persian Gulf islands thus far shared with its neighbours in the Trucial States and Iraq's robust reaction leading to Baghdad's severing of its diplomatic relations with Tehran.[29] Iran's larger footprint was not a welcome development for the small Sheikhdoms struggling to find their way towards statehood, particularly when in 1975 Tehran and Baghdad put their bilateral difference aside and proposed a Gulf security pact. By the mid-1970s Iran had established itself not only as the main pillar of Gulf security but also as an ally of both Egypt and Israel, having already forged a close military partnership with Israel, the Arabs' nemesis. Iran's power appeared supreme and its distance from its Arab hinterland, so vividly felt in the 1960s, was ending.

Britain's withdrawal also helped Tehran to draw ever closer to the undisputed superpower of the age, the United States, and with oil income steadily rising, a security partnership evolved that was militarily strong enough to become a pillar of regional security. The evolution of the relationship is admirably sketched by Gary Sick:

> With the United States bogged down in Vietnam, with U.S. domestic opinion firmly opposed to any new military ventures abroad, with the withdrawal of the British from their strategic role east of Suez, and with oil of the Persian Gulf beginning to be recognized as a key factor in Western security, there was an inescapable logic in asking a strong regional power to accept a security role that the United States was simply incapable of undertaking at the same time…. The shah accepted this new relationship with alacrity.[30]

Iran's resurgence as a regional actor required that it took greater responsibility for the fate of the region and played a greater role. In this vein, for its immediate region, Tehran advocated a policy of 'regional security being the responsibility of regional states themselves'. Thus, responding to the news soon after the British withdrawal that the United States was to keep its naval presence in Bahrain, the Shah declared: "We have declared before that we would not want to see any foreign presence in the gulf, England, the United States, or China – our policy hasn't changed".[31]

Having accelerated the pace of the country's economic recovery in the 1960s from its low-point in the 1940s and 1950s, the 1970s marked the golden age of the Pahlavi dynasty in which oil wealth fuelled the Shah's vision of grandeur. He charted for Iran the path towards the 'Great Civilization' and a major role in both Asia and the Middle East.[32] Unveiling a breathtakingly large nuclear power generation programme in 1974 of twenty power plants generating 20,000 MW of power in just twenty years, which included major partnerships with the United States, France and Germany, became a centrepiece of the drive towards the gates of the great civilization. All things being equal, the success of this programme would have given Iran all the nuclear-related industrial and manufacturing capacity of the developed countries and would have made the country one of the largest nuclear states of Eurasia by the late twentieth century.

Iran also increasingly acted as a powerbroker, peacemaker, intermediary, security guarantor, and, ultimately, as the voice of the most powerful cartel in the world, the OPEC bloc of oil exporters. Looking at the empirical data and the qualitative indicators of Iran's regional role, ironically on the eve of the revolution Iran's position could not have appeared more secure.

Iran in the mid-1970s was a pivotal country. It was producing 10 per cent of the world's oil output (equating to 18 per cent of OPEC's) and accounting for nearly 20 per cent of OPEC's total exports. It was using its petrodollars to extend its soft power to Afghanistan and Pakistan to the east, and it was enjoying acceptance as a regional player with influence in the Levant, and its good relations with the oil producers of North Africa to engage with the changing political dynamics of inter-state relations there. On the hard side of power projection, the Pahlavi regime saw a rapid and intensive build-up of the country's armed forces, tripling the size of the armed forces in less than ten years (from 1970 to 1979), raising the country's military expenditure to over $10 billion a year in the later years, enabling its armed forces to increase the size and sophistication of the hardware at its disposal: Number of main battle tanks rose from around 900 to 1,985, combat aircraft from 150 to 445, and military helicopters from 140 to 684. Its new MBTs were imported from the US and UK, the latest M-60s and Chieftains; the air force was provided with dozens of F-4 Phantoms and 80 of the brand new F-14 Tomcat; the navy was supplied with six powerful destroyers, hovercrafts and advance fast patrol boats. With a military machinery second only to Israel's in the region, it had also begun exercising its military muscle in assistance of its allies – in Iraq (with the Kurds), Oman (against the Dhofar rebellion), Saudi Arabia (to provide military transport support for movement of Saudi forces to the Arab-Israeli theatre), secretly providing spare parts for the Turkish military after its occupation of Cyprus, or in support of the US' military deployments in Vietnam.

While Imperial Iran was essentially a status quo power, its rise to eminence in the course of the 1970s had enabled its leaders to also pose some challenges to the dominant powers. With a heightened degree of arrogance, the Shah embraced the status accorded him as an international statesman and used his position as leader of OPEC to repeatedly chastise the West for what he characterized as its foreign policy excesses, mocked its economic vulnerabilities to the oil producers, and gloated about the West's weaknesses in the face of the Third World's rise. He seemed to have had good cause to do so as he had, in the 1960s, already fought several diplomatic battles with the Western-dominated consortium of oil companies running Iran's oil industry for a greater share of the oil income. After the 1973/4 oil price rises, therefore, he was easily characterized by the Western media as the villain of the peace and a megalomaniac who displayed illusions of grandeur. He was, as he himself said, seen as the "robber baron" by the Western media.[33] But, more significantly, he was increasingly viewed suspiciously by some (particularly economic) policy circles in the West who saw in his strategy of raising oil prices a direct threat to the stability of the entire international economic system.

In some ways, the Shah was only at the beginnings of using oil and power politics (exploiting his close relations with the United States and friendly ties with both the Soviets and China) as the basis for articulating a new foreign policy of 'both East and West' for Iran when crisis hit. Before it was hit by what Milani has called "the crisis of wealth",[34] the monarchy had, perhaps for the first time in over 150 years, carved for Iran an international niche and substantial diplomatic space. In Halliday's words, "from having been, at the beginning of the century, a wholly passive factor in international affairs, Iran has now become a significant actor, whom other states, larger and smaller, must take into account".[35]

Yet, and because of the narrow foundations of the imperial edifice, the country would become instantly vulnerable to direct pressure from within and indirect neglect from without. Pressure, inevitably, arrived in 1977, thanks to the sudden and unexpected drop in oil prices following the announcement by Saudi Arabia that it was unwilling to implement the oil price hike agreed by OPEC in December 1976.[36] The Shah's efforts to redraw the country's relations with the West on its terms had backfired spectacularly, and the monarch now found himself dangerously exposed, for not only could he not push ahead with his ambitious national development plans, but also he was found to be totally vulnerable to even indirect external pressure. Ironically, in trying to control their unruly ally whose appetite for petrodollars had become a zero-sum game over the stability of the world economy, the United States had, perhaps inadvertently, prepared the ground for the collapse of its most 'trusted' and reliable regional ally anywhere. In so doing, they had also at the same time raised the importance of their partnership with the Kingdom of Saudi Arabia – another oil monarchy but uniquely traditional and non-Western when compared with Iran, and also unlike Iran embroiled in battles of identity and influence in a radicalized and increasingly polarized Arab order.

Meanwhile, for Iran, the link between economy and foreign relations had been firmly established. By the end of the 1970s, moreover, oil had come to characterize Iran's position in the world and also shape, if not determine, the country's role conception. While after the revolution the Islamic regime appeared determined to break the somewhat organic links between oil, the state's political economy, and the international partnerships that oil had spawned, with the pressures of war and also isolation – to say nothing of crippling sanctions – the Islamic republic found itself returning to the world of 'oilonomics'. Oilonomics in turn would soon re-emerge as a feature of the country's foreign affairs.

International relations of the Islamic republic

The Islamic republic's foreign policy has been a cause of concern internationally and source of much discussion relating to the role of revolutionary states in critically significant global regions. Much of the debate has revolved around the operationalization of the dual notions of Islamic internationalism and revolutionary counter-hegemonism as the key features of republic's foreign policy. Therefore, to understand Iran's foreign relations, one needs to adopt a holistic approach, considering not only the foreign policy determinants of the state but also the political economy of Iran, and the process (system) of foreign policymaking. Pertinent also is the fact that a revolutionary state, such as the Islamic republic, which emerges in a strong state and with considerable geopolitical weight, becomes at once the object and subject of international relations. Its policy choices define it and shape responses to it. So, it is in this regard that Rahnema and Nomani draw attention to the conditions shaping the republic's approach to foreign policy and the uniqueness of its offering – the determinants of its foreign policy. But the authors also, rightly, focus on what they see as pressures that arise from "different interpretations of the international role and obligations of Islam as an ideology"; "the domestic political environment"; the influence of historical factors on the population's consciousness; and, "a realistic sense of survival".[37] Together these form the analytical framework for capturing the republic's international relations. These 'rules' are at the heart of foreign policy analysis literature but clearly different case studies privilege some 'variables' over others – the domestic political context over the regional or international conditions, for example. More formally, as Halliday has argued, when looking at states like the Islamic republic, one must see foreign policy as a product "not just of personal and bureaucratic process within the state but of interests, and clashes, of state and class alike. Ideology and norms are central, not as the constitutive domain of politics, but rather as part of the process of legitimation and coercion".[38]

Now, taking the drivers in turn, the constitution of the Islamic republic is quite clear on the guiding principles of the country's international relations. In article 2 it declares that the Islamic republic rejects all forms of oppression, and in four short articles under 'Foreign Policy', it outlines the republic's principles as follows: In article 152 it expects the Islamic republic to defend "the rights of all Muslims, non-alignment with respect to the hegemonic superpowers"; article 153 forbids it to succumb to foreign control of the country's key resources and its culture; and in article 154 it announces that the republic "has as its ideal human felicity throughout human society, and considers the attainment of independence, freedom, and rule of justice and truth to be the right of all people of the world. Accordingly... it supports the just struggles of the *mustadafun* [down-trodden] against the *mustakbirun* [oppressors] in every corner of the globe".[39] In this regard, Iran has been a revisionist and counter-hegemonic state since the revolution, and in its terms of reference has been leading a 'counter-domineering camp' which has marshalled national and international forces to stand up to 'global arrogance'.[40] The so-called resistance front which Iran leads in the Middle East is a product of this self-declared role.

In Iran's case, institutionalized foreign policy decision-making has been a strong feature of its international relations, but in sharp contrast to the 'strong-man' system of the Shah, in the Islamic republic elite factionalism has emerged as a key domestic determinant. But factional differences rarely escalate to challenge the dominant discourse or the survival of the regime and this is so for two main reasons. First, the Leader has come to play an active and decisive determining role in framing discussion and formulation of strategic decisions. And second, the elite as a whole tends to keep factional battles contained and does not as a rule deliberately escalate differences to threaten the efficacy of the state narrative, though it should be added that in 2009 and following the outcome of the presidential elections it came very close.

So, having considered the drivers of foreign policy, we can proceed to provide a systematic account of the country's foreign policy behaviour. The forces identified by Rahnema and Nomani converge to shape and determine Iran's foreign relations, but as they rightly note, in reality the republic's foreign policy has been conducted in the absence of an overall Islamic theory of foreign policy, which could give a regime like Iran's a structural steer as well as a modus operandi.

Universalism and denial of the division of Muslim communities into sovereign states as international actors, export of revolution as a necessity demanded by God, and strict adherence to the path of Islam against the non-Muslim state (neither East nor West, in other words) have tended to be applied selectively, unpredictably, even cynically, in the pursuit of the Islamic regime's material interests. In this context, one of the hardest tasks of the republic has been the juxtaposition of regime/Islamic interest with national/state interest. In managing this complex relationship some analysts see policy confusion and inconsistency in Tehran. But others point to this reality:

> The regime exists because of the revolution, so maintaining the leadership's and the Iranian population's commitment, or at least adherence, to the Islamic Revolution's ideology becomes an existential challenge for the regime. This does not mean Iran's governing philosophies are inflexible. Certain core ideological principles, however, not only shape the regime's worldview but also create redlines defined by the supreme leader that foreign and domestic policies cannot violate.[41]

It has to manage its state policy in the context of regime survival strategy, which after all is the most important redline of all for the ruling regime: "despite all the foreign threats and antagonistic policies against the IRI since the revolution... the major challenges to the IRI's survival have been internal issues", argues Sadeghinia.[42] As put eloquently by one of its own officials, a former deputy foreign minister (Abbas Maleki) says: "Iran's foreign policy objectives are... generated from her particular geostrategic and economic position". From this realist base he proceeds to clarify that Iran's "specific post-revolutionary context makes her more determined to pursue political independence and reject being pigeonholed as a supplier of raw materials to the global economic system". Revolutionary Iran, from this perspective, would be seeking to renegotiate the terms of the country's entry into the international division of labour, arguably in ways similar to that of the Pahlavi regime that tried to do so in the 1970s – to reduce Iran's dependence on hydrocarbons exports and to move the country up the value chain and towards foreign-investment-generated industrialization.

Political independence was also a major concern of the Shah's foreign policy, being acutely aware of the power of the Soviet superpower in the north and the pressures of the Cold War bearing down on such frontline states as Iran. So why is the Islamic republic's approach any different, or is it? Maleki breaks down the search for political independence as a driver of the republic's foreign policy into four policy areas: "maintaining of our territorial integrity and security, safeguarding of our evolving political system, providing our people with basic welfare, and pursuing a foreign policy that acknowledges our Muslim identity as a nation and operates within the context of values generated by Islam".[43] None of these, one can argue, would be inconsistent with the principles underpinning the Shah's foreign policy goals. Yet the conduct of this regime has been anything but that of the Shah.

Ghods, on the other hand, maintains that after 1979 Iran's foreign policy was all about establishing its new place in the world:

> Iran's foreign policy was primarily one of negative equilibrium. All military agreements with the United States were rescinded, and all U.S. military stations and surveillance posts in Iran were disbanded; the hostage crisis minimized U.S. influence in Iran. Relations with the Soviet Union were correct, but cold. The Islamic Republic pursued a variety of third-power options. Economic and political relationships with China, Japan, Western Europe, and North and South Korea were strengthened.

Iran managed to re-emerge as a regional player but "this time, Islamic ideology was a cornerstone of regional foreign policy", giving Tehran the means to form an alliance with the Shia of Lebanon and with Syria in response to Gulf Arab hostility towards it.[44] Clearly, the post-Pahlavi regime pressed the country in a very different direction compared with its predecessor, ending its most durable alliances with the West, particularly the United States, severing its strategic partnership with the Western-constructed regional organs, and confronting regional countries that, up to the revolution, had been its allies. Bakhash makes the case that "the Islamic revolution and the ideas and ideology to which it gave birth have significantly reshaped Iranian foreign policy".[45] Thus, relations with Israel and Egypt were cut and those with the *ancien regime*'s Arab allies (Saudi Arabia, Jordan, and Morocco) were curtailed. Some radical Arab parties, like Syria and the PLO, emerged as new friends but other radical states, like Iraq, were shunned.

Tehran's new foreign policy may have had an ideological underpinning to it, but as its policies towards the region's two Ba'athist powers of Iraq and Syria in the 1980s demonstrate, its policies were also dictated by geopolitical imperatives, and thus a considerable degree of pragmatism guided its policies. Bakhash further notes that the principles of the Islamic republic's foreign policy can be divided into five key components, of which three are particularly significant and relevant to the discussion here.[46] The first is that, like the Pahlavis before it, the leadership has continued to regard Iran as a regional power with regional interests and also international aspirations. Tehran regards itself as a legitimate regional actor by virtue of history, but also its mass revolution and popularity of its stance in support of the vulnerable and deprived. Its Islamic foundations, it claims, coupled with its superior political system, provide it with the moral legitimacy to intervene in the region 'in defence of Muslims' and in support of their perceived causes and values. Indeed, Iran's political elite claim to do no more or less than is expected of them in the IRI's constitution.

Second, given the conditions of its birth – an eight-year long devastating war (1980–88) which was fought in near-complete isolation – Tehran's foreign policy has been shaped, above all, by security concerns. The Iranian elite has a dim view of the West and has tended to see the West's pursuit of its interests in the Middle East as counter to its interests and part of a rather zero-sum game of chicken played out in the MENA subsystem. In this way of thinking, Iran has seen dangers and conspiracies behind every Western action, even when Western action has aided its security: As in the removal of the Taliban in Afghanistan and the Ba'ath regime in Iraq. Tehran sees ulterior motives for these actions. The fact that US/Western troops were ensconced on Iran's borders subsequent to 9/11 might have fed the sense of siege in Tehran and the fear that the West was adding to its forces stationed in Bahrain and other GCC states as part of a broader encirclement strategy for an inevitable confrontation with the Islamic republic. Iran's leaders have said so on more than one occasion.

Third, as already noted, the Islamic republic has followed a 'counter-hegemon' foreign policy since its birth – neither East nor West – in which it has, intermittently, sought to build closer relationships with non-aligned or non-US-oriented great and regional powers. 'Looking East' has been one fruitful strategy which emerged as early as the mid-1980s and which Ahmadinejad pursued most vigorously after 2009 as a counter to biting Western-imposed sanctions. Another plank of this strategy in the early twenty-first century was the pursuit of closer links with the populist South American states such a Venezuela and Bolivia. It is worth noting, however, that the Shah also had cultivated links with Asian powers and had developed good links with both India and China in the 1970s, as well as partnerships with many of the pro-Western Asian countries, such as Taiwan, South Korea, the Philippines, and Singapore, as part of the strategy of diversifying its alliance network.

The international relations of Iran since 1980 have developed in long cycles, punctuated by the force of the key events in the history of the republic and also the influence of its popularly elected presidents after 1989. Indeed, since then and the creation of the executive presidency, the latter's role has become even more significant, though on most strategic issues the executive's policies have tended to be moderated by the Leader and the real or imaginary 'redlines' that his considerable office has drawn. Policy is derived through a complex interplay of individuals and institutions, of political factions and interest groups, intense discussion amongst primary and secondary elites in many fora, and a process of informal (opaque) exchanges that help tip the balance in a particular direction. Such recognized power centres as the presidency (in control of the executive wing of the state), the Leader's office, national security council, the Majlis, and the security establishment play a formal role in formulation and execution of policies. But public opinion, the media, political groups (parties, associations), and religious occasions also play a role in the articulation of policies and in turn influence upwards perception and reception of policies being implemented.

As has been shown elsewhere in the book, the establishment of an executive presidency in 1989 in fact led to the creation of a more influential and politically involved Faqih. While the Faqih has set some of the republic's parameters, the strategy and conduct of Iran's international relations has been in the hands of the executive and the mandate arising from his electoral success. Neither is the state a wholly autonomous actor when it comes to foreign affairs nor the Leader an absolute power. So, in looking at the policy choices of the regime, articulated by its four presidents since 1989, we can discern obvious differences in policies, priorities, diplomatic language and posture, as well as worldviews. While all four (three clerics and one non-cleric) have been presidents of the same republic, through their influence in society these actors successfully redefined the context for the formulation of Iran's foreign policy and thus were able to pursue different agendas with different objectives.

The war years

When the war broke out in September 1980, the revolutionary regime was still in its infancy and barely able to contain the sub-national, political and ideological energies unleashed by the revolutionary process of 1978–79. Further, the new body politic was not well positioned to rapidly articulate a new foreign policy strategy, and the repeated assassinations of its emerging leaders reduced the regime's ability to create a critical mass of foreign advisers and strategists. Junior or inexperienced individuals were being tasked to take over senior policy roles. The mini-civil war that was raging in Kurdistan alongside an urban guerrilla war waged by left-leaning armed groups across the country sapped the regime's energies and limited its scope for policymaking. Until late 1981, foreign policy was in a process of transition. Although relations with the United States had been severed following the hostage crisis, the moderate wing of the revolutionary elite continued to try to keep relations with the rest of the world on an even keel, trying to deal with multiple crises: Iraq's aggression and its support from the Soviet Union and moderate (pro-US Arab) states, Afghanistan's occupation by Soviet forces, impact of Egypt's peace with Israel on Iran's relations with the Arab world, growing sanctions against it, and of course the continuing confrontation with the United States. The so-called 'liberal' (social democratic) wing of the revolutionary coalition found it impossible to deal with these crises and by choosing to focus on stabilizing relations with the US, it effectively exposed itself to annihilation by the more radical (clerical-dominated) wing of the coalition which Khomeini ultimately supported.

Following rapid changes in the political makeup of the elite after 1981, Ayatollah Khomeini was able to look beyond balancing the radical clerical and moderate social democratic wings of the revolutionary coalition and introduced a degree of coherence to the new entity's international role, providing ideological context for its role perception. He set about providing a focus for the new republic's foreign policy priorities, at the heart of which stood the 'neither East nor West' strategy.[47] In this worldview, not only should the Islamic republic "remain independent of the superpowers, but it must seek to promote just Islamic societies in other regions".[48] The Islamic republic must be trans-Iranian/pan-Islamic to be true to its revolutionary values. While the principles had been established in the constitution, as already noted, the policies themselves took shape under crisis conditions: A war with Iraq to the west, occupation of Afghanistan by the Soviet Union to the east, and general hostility from the West. To oppose the Soviet occupation of its neighbour formed one plank of its policies, leading Iran to create a large Shia coalition of Mujahedeen to fight the Soviets; the other was the removal of the Iraqi dictator from power and through this the drive for the liberation of Jerusalem – as the clerics put it. Fighting in the 'imposed war' became a patriotic and Islamic duty and Iran alone, in the campaign against Iraq, would fight 'global arrogance' on its very doorstep. The attacks on Shia establishments in Iraq and the deportation of 200,000 Shia Iraqis on the grounds of alien nationality to Iran provided an added moral dimension to Iran's cause. For Iraq, the purpose was to package Iran's revolution in sectarian terms, of Shia mobilizing against the Sunni. Tehran found this sectarian narrative hard to shake off then and much harder to avoid in the decades following the end of hostilities with Ba'athist Iraq.

Clearly, the revolution's own ideology, as exemplified in the constitution, had played its role in delinking Iran from the West (and its previous allies in the Middle East) and pushing it towards the non-aligned community of states, but the outline of its relations with the outside world only began to sharpen in the context of the bloody and long war that Iraq started in order to gain strategic advantage while containing the threat from Iran.[49] But the war did not start without a context and, arguably, this was provided by geopolitical uncertainties following the revolution. Analysts have demonstrated that Baghdad had shown a degree of willingness in the year following the establishment of the Islamic republic in February 1979 to accommodate the Islamist regime as a positive addition to the anti-imperialist and pro-Non-Aligned Movement (NAM) camps, but was rebuffed and instead faced Tehran's calls to Iraqis to rise up and overthrow their ruling Ba'ath regime.[50] By the end of 1979 relations had begun to deteriorate substantially and Iraq, reluctantly, it is said, chose the option of limited war as the best way of deflecting Iran's threat: "given the growing evidence that the

Iranian regime was set upon destabilizing the Ba'ath, Iraq came gradually to realize that it might have to resort to armed force".[51] From Baghdad's perspective, limited war would have had many other advantages beyond the weakening of Iran, which included Iraq's domination of the Arab order, control of the Persian Gulf sub-region and greater influence over the vulnerable monarchies, improved relations with the West, and last but not least, changing the terms of the 1975 Algiers agreement regarding demarcation of their shared waterway in its own favour.

If the revolution changed the character of Iran as a state, then the Iran-Iraq War defined its relations with the outside world. The war proved to be a sobering experience for the idealists of the revolutionary regime who had expected a strong response to Iraq's invasion from the international community. They were shocked by the UN's response to the conflict and saw a clear bias in the Security Council's deliberations on 28 September 1980, which led to the first (resolution 479) of the nine UNSC resolutions on the war. The Security Council called for the immediate cessation of hostilities and, with UN mediation, the settlement of their dispute through peaceful means. What was striking from Tehran's point of view was the delay in convening a Council meeting – a week after Iraq's invasion – when all the key players were already in New York for the General Assembly, and then to issue a resolution which not only did not name or condemn the aggressor but did not even call for the withdrawal of Iraqi forces from Iranian territory. This matter, relates a witness to the proceedings, "made a profoundly negative impression on the Iranian delegation led by Prime Minister Rajaie... [who] castigated the Council for inactivity and bias".[52]

Iran's suspicions of international bias against it were reinforced yet again when only two years later, in July 1982, with Iran getting the upper hand on the battlefield, the Security Council called (resolution 514) for a return to the internationally recognized borders. Even the 18th July 1987 resolution (UNSCR 598) leading to the end of hostilities, which Iran reluctantly accepted a year later as the basis for peace, was not neutral in Tehran's eyes. Sir Anthony Parsons, who had been the United Kingdom's UN Ambassador (1979–82) at the start of the war, noted that, to Iran, resolution 598 "had the same pro-Iraqi coloration as its predecessors". He went on to say:

> As the Iranian government perceived the situation, they were being ordered to lay down arms and withdraw from the territory they had won at appalling human cost, with no certainty from the language in paragraph 6 that the 'impartial commission' would even meet, let alone 'identify' Iraq as the 'aggressor' [a core Iranian demand throughout], nor that financial reparations would be agreed in their favour, the language of paragraph 7 [the Secretary-General to assign a team of experts to study the question of reconstruction] being equally equivocal. It was therefore no wonder that Iran, without actually denouncing the resolution, should have equivocated.[53]

Added to Iran's frustrations was lack of access to military parts, hardware and weapons systems themselves from the West, which of course was of its own making as Tehran had deliberately severed the country's military partnerships with the West. So, in the immediate term, it had little option but to resort to the cannibalization of its remaining advanced Western-supplied hardware, the stockpiles of which were vast at this stage thanks to the Shah's extravagant procurement strategy, followed by imports of Soviet-made arms through Soviet-allied networks and good offices of such countries as Libya, Syria and North Korea. Its counterpart, on the other hand, was enjoying a massive arms bonanza, the costs of which were apparently underwritten by the neighbouring Gulf monarchies. Arms supplied by its traditional ally, the Soviet Union, followed several substantial arms deals between 1981 and 1983: Surface-to-Surface Scud missiles, T-62 and T-72 MBTs, MiG-23 and MiG-25 fighters poured into Iraq's armoury. Iraq also enjoyed military support from beyond the Soviet orbit, from such countries as Egypt, Brazil, Chile, as well as from several Western countries. France, for example, became a major supplier of advanced military aircraft (Mirage F-1 and Super Etendard) and anti-ship missiles to the Iraqi armed forces (which were used to great effect against naval targets); Italy and Spain supplied naval vessels and military vehicles respectively.[54] The practical outcome of the unequal military relationships was that by the mid-1980s, Iraq's military holdings had actually grown while Iran's had depleted at an alarming rate. As Karsh shows, by 1985, Iraq's holding of MBTs had gone up by 150 since 1980, of combat aircraft by 168, and of artillery pieces by a massive 2,700.[55] For Iran, despite clandestine military imports, MBT numbers had shrunk by 735 and combat aircraft by as much as 365 over the same five-year period; only its stock of 1,000 artillery pieces had remained the same. Iran's scepticism grew worse by the deafening silence of the West against Iraq's deployment of chemical weapons on the battlefield from 1983 and its use of Scud missiles against Iranian urban centres, including the capital.[56]

Not surprisingly, Iran's whole experience heightened the sense of isolation and also betrayal already in evidence in Tehran and thus bolstered the hand of anti-Western rejectionists in the newly forming elite. It also strengthened the sense of victimization by Iranians and the view that, as had been the case at the time of Imam Ali and his sons, right would prevail over might. They, the Iranians, were victims of global arrogance. The war reflected "the tenacious unyielding nature of the Islamic republic which prided itself on its unique moral rectitude, and accepted losses as acceptable adjuncts to the process of self-reliance and spiritual purgation on which it had launched itself... established ways were defunct, compromise debilitating, and will-power and sacrifice sufficient for Iran to prevail".[57]

The war therefore firmly shaped, if not defined, the republic's foreign relations. The war, conceived as a limited campaign by the Iraqi side, also helped shape the Iranian regime's narrative, setting it on a new approach to foreign affairs, which focused on dividing the outside world into two camps of friend and foe. Regionally, Iran placed the Arab monarchies on the front line of its opponents, a view which was reinforced by the monarchies' poorly disguised and often open support for the Iraqi regime.[58] Thus, Saudi Arabia became the proponent of 'American Islam', Bahrain's monarchy became an occupation force suppressing Bahrain's majority Shia population, Kuwait became the target of subversion and acts of violence for its support for Iraq's war effort, and all of the Gulf Arab regimes, bar Oman's, were characterized as illegitimate. The war provided the new Islamic republic the opportunity and justification for loading its revolutionary message on strong rhetoric and also on real barrels of guns. The war provided the justification for Tehran to challenge sovereign frontiers and borders as artificially created barriers to Muslim unity that only it could overcome. But, as Halliday notes, from its early days, the republican regime was also rather selective in implementation of its internationalist commitments and in the course of the 1980s the 'export' of the revolution became more symbolic than actual.[59] This trend, however, did not end Iran's 'international militancy', and therefore its use of, or backing for, terror and political violence across the globe.

At the same time, the regime was conscious of its vulnerability to Baghdad's pan-Arab narrative and its strategy of delegitimizing the Islamic republic as a legitimate regional actor. So it keenly pursued relations with other anti-Western Arab republics. In this regard the war spurred Iran on to consolidate its new partnership with Syria, the Mashreq's most influential and powerful actor and a prominent 'front-line' state against Israel (Iran's post-revolution adversary). Syria's support for the revolution and opposition to Iraq's invasion created the right mindset for the two countries to draw closer. Before the start of the war, Tehran had already reached out to the PLO and clearly the interests of Tehran and Damascus also converged over extending support to the PLO, in addition to the countering of Iraq's influence in the Arab region, and creating a coalition of radical forces (excluding Iraq, of course, which was increasingly positioning itself as a moderating force and defender of the Arab monarchies threatened by Iran) to confront the US and Israel.[60] For Tehran, Syrian friendship was a gift, for it offered Iran a bridgehead in the Levant and the Arab heartland, a counter-narrative to Baghdad's (which wanted to couch the war in Arab-Persian/Sunni-Shia terms), indirect access to the Gulf Arab states through Damascus' links, and also a means to secure access to the Soviet Union (Syria's external patron) and its military hardware which was soon finding its way to Iran from Syria.[61] Syria also gave Iran a powerful Arab ally in its efforts to counter US influence in the region and build a multipolar environment in the Middle East.[62]

Syria's secular nature, a Ba'ath-led anti-Islamist regime, mattered less to Tehran than its geopolitical importance and the fact that its inner core elite was dominated by a religious sect close to Shias. Syria, also, was to become the gateway for Tehran to extend its reach into Lebanon and its substantial Shia communities. Iran had, for generations, close links with Lebanon, and the Shia communities of both had interacted closely and unhindered by ethnic differences. Indeed, many of Iran's anti-Shah revolutionaries had undergone guerrilla training in Lebanon (often with the PLO), the radicalization of whose Shia communities had begun in the 1970s, with their mass eviction from southern Lebanon by Israel-backed Christian militias and in 1978 by Israeli forces directly following their invasion of southern Lebanon. Over 300,000 Lebanese Shia were displaced and livelihoods ruined.[63] The Shia organization Amal emerged in 1975 in the Lebanese civil war and as they suffered under Israeli attack, they keenly watched the clerical-led anti-Shah revolution in Iran as offering an opportunity to change the dynamics of Lebanese politics, and so enthusiastically set about establishing local committees in support of the Iranian revolutionary forces. The solidarity of their respective experiences, coupled with the links that Islamist and secular revolutionary Iranian groups had already established with the PLO in the course of the 1960s and 1970s,[64] provided the basis for the Islamic republic's leaders setting their sights on Lebanon as a base for the expansion of its revolutionary influence. Revolutionary Iran's anti-Zionist and anti-Israel stance provided further reasons for their interest in the Levant – Syria and Lebanon in particular. US military presence in Lebanon and Israel's military invasion of its small and vulnerable neighbour in 1982 provided the incentive for the strengthening of the Iranian-Syrian alliance and also for the Islamic republic to develop, organize and mobilize Shia networks in Lebanon, Syria's 'backyard', as new paramilitary forces to confront Israel.[65]

Amongst the Shia groups a loose grouping, mirroring Iran's Islamic Revolution Guards Corps (IRGC), emerged after Israel's invasion in 1982 and was quickly in evidence in Beirut's southern neighbourhoods and amongst the remaining Shia communities of south Lebanon.[66] Working alongside Iran's IRGC forces already in the Bekaa valley, this new militia was to emerge as Lebanon's most potent paramilitary organization, to become known as Hezbollah from 1985, and thus in a very short time Iran had found a useful military and socioeconomic force as a policy instrument in a country of huge strategic importance, both geographically (a 'front-line' Arab state) and also as a nerve centre of ideas in the Arab world. Hezbollah celebrated the alliance and unambiguously attached its colours to the mast of the Islamic republic. In their 'open letter', announcing Hezbollah's establishment, they declared:

> We, the sons of Hizbullah's *umma*, whose vanguard God has given victory in Iran and which has established the nucleus of the world's central Islamic state, abide by the orders of a single wise and just command represented by the guardianship of the jurisprudent (*waliyy al-faqih*), currently embodied in the supreme Ayatullah Ruhallah al-Musawi al-Khumayni… who has detonated the Muslim's revolution, and who is bringing about the glorious Islamic renaissance.[67]

From here the Iranian revolutionaries could showcase their new Islamist paradise to the Arab world, but Lebanon also acted as a microcosm of the difficulties the Islamic republic might face as it 'exported' its revolutionary brand, for within a short period of time Shia communities not affiliated to Hezbollah or the Iranian political model mobilized to confront Iran and its ally. Thus, in the spring of 1988, as unseemly as this was for Iran, a bloody turf war was raging in southern Lebanon between the two Shia organizations of Hezbollah (with around 5,000 fighters) and the more established Amal (with 30,000 fighters). With scores killed on both sides and Amal confronting Hezbollah in and around its stronghold of Nabatiyeh, it was reported that as many as 10,000 pro-Amal demonstrators stormed the IRGC's offices in Tyre and tore down Ayatollah Khomeini's photographs chanting, "We say loudly we do not want to see Iranian Revolutionary Guards here. We say loudly we do not want Hezbollah here.... No to the Party of the Devil and no to the Party of Dollars".[68] Not even a month later, the two militias were again at war, this time for control of the Shia-dominated southern neighbourhoods of Beirut. Their clashes left more than 400 people dead and 1,200 wounded and required the deployment of over 4,000 Syrian troops to keep the peace.[69] In the face of opposition to its activities, Iran's support for Hezbollah deepened and over time, particularly when Syrian interest in Amal waned, it built up Hezbollah as the most effective militia in the Lebanese theatre.

Iran had all the ideological, religious, and political reasons for deepening its presence in Lebanon, and Syria provided it with the means for doing so. As noted above, Syria in itself was of great strategic importance to Iran whose value was underlined by its Ba'athist regime's rejection of the West, its religio-cultural proximity to Iran's own, and the fact that it was home to as many as eighteen key religious sites of importance to Shias.[70] The importance of religious affinity as a driver of Iran's interest in drawing closer to secular Syria cannot be underestimated and it is in this that the 'paradox' of Islamist Iran and socialist Syria as allies can be explained. After Hafez al-Assad's overtures to Iran in 1979, the clerical elite of the Islamic republic found the lure of unfettered access to Islamic, particularly Shia, revered religious sites on Syrian soil an irresistible pull. In terms of significance, sites in Syria mirror those in Iraq for Shiis: The martyr Imam Hussein's sister and daughter of Imam Ali (Zeinab) and Hussein's two daughters died in Syria as prisoners of the Umayyads; Imam Hussein's daughter (Sekinah) is buried here and also as many as six of Ali's close companions. Syria is replete with significant Shia sites and places, and Iran invested in many improvement and development projects to boost religious tourism. These sites are dotted around the county and include several significant projects directly financed by Iran in places that have since become known for different reasons – like Raqqa which in January 2014 became the headquarters of the staunch anti-Assad and anti-Shia jihadi group Islamic State.

Despite Iran's strategic gains in Syria and Lebanon in the 1980s, as it was still the war that had shaped the alliance network of the Islamic republic, these, by definition, remained rather limited. On the contrary, Tehran's dogged pursuit of the war, in the face of major international efforts to bring it to an end, and against Arab demands to end it for the sake of Muslim unity, had exposed the revolutionary regime to accusations of complicity with the very forces that it purported to confront. Thus, said King Fahd of Saudi Arabia in January 1988: "Iranian rulers are adopting a policy whose aim is to harm all states in the region.... This approach serves the ends of international Zionism which constantly seeks to spread discord in the Islamic nation to undermine it".[71] This was the kind of language Tehran had often used against the Arab states.

The war also had another sobering effect on Tehran: The realization that its own behaviour had generated a strong and dangerous backlash, encouraging the creation of hostile coalitions capable of mobilizing very effectively against it. The then-parliamentary speaker, Hojjatoleslam Rafsanjani, who had recently also been appointed as the acting commander-in-chief, articulated this growing awareness thus: "Time is not on our side any more. The world – I mean the anti-Islamic arrogant powers – has decided to make a serious effort to save Saddam and tie our hands".[72] Basically, to blunt Tehran's main foreign policy goal! Thus, 1988, with regard to the elite taking stock of its military and political policies, proved to be decisive, for not only did its resistance to accepting the 1987 SCR 598 ceasefire resolution prove to be militarily expensive – between February and April, Iraq rained 190 missiles at Iranian cities killing or injuring thousands, the backbone of Iran's navy was crushed by the US Navy in a matter of hours in several short engagements in April, and perhaps most crucially of all Iranian forces lost control of the strategic and hard-fought-for Faw peninsula to Iraqis in just 36 hours in the same month[73] – but its attempts to securitize relations with its southern neighbours merely strengthened their resolve to stand behind the Iraqi regime and to orchestrate adding pressure on Iran to change its behaviour in the sub-region.

Following Saudi Arabia's very public severing of diplomatic relations with the Islamic republic in April 1988, as an exiled senior Iranian cleric explained, in May Tehran had now realized, following recent military setbacks, that its international isolation resulting from hostage taking, terrorism and intimidation had to end in order to make headway in efforts to normalize relations with the West, starting by freeing French hostages held in Lebanon by pro-Iranian groups.[74] Indeed before Iran's acceptance of SCR 598 Rafsanjani publicly unveiled what he called a new plan for restructuring Iran's foreign relations, adding on national television that "one of the wrong things we did in the revolutionary atmosphere was to constantly make enemies. We pushed those who could be neutral into hostility, and did not do anything to attract those who could be friends. It is part of the new plan that in foreign policy we should behave in a way not to needlessly leave ground to the enemy".[75]

Ending the war, ending the hostage crisis, and renewing relationships became the keys to opening a door to the West and the new pragmatist president, Rafsanjani, was at hand to take the republic in a different, and accommodationist, direction. But this was not the end of the matter, and his strategy was not going to be adopted without a fight. This was highlighted by the Rushdie affair following Ayatollah Khomeini's fatwa in February 1989, just months before his death, which legitimized the murder of Salman Rushdie, the author of the novel *The Satanic Verses* on the grounds of insulting Islam and the Prophet Mohammad in his novel. For Khomeini, this was a God-send, to help rid the republic of its "naïve foreign policy" following the war by "sell-out liberals". "As long as I am alive", he said as a last gasp of the regime's rejectionist stance, "I will not let the government fall to the liberals... I will not deviate from 'no East, no West' principles... I will cut off the influence of American and Soviet agents in all fields".[76] For Premier Mousavi, the main opponent of accommodation with the West, Iran's diplomatic isolation following the fatwa "will drive home the fact to government officials that they should not rely on Europe" for recovery. The distance between the ideological factions and the pragmatists (realists, more accurately) was profound, and despite heavy hits to the fragile economy – massive drops of 20 per cent in a week in the country's currency against its main foreign exchange (US dollar) in February, for example – he still saw "Iran's firm decision on the issue... [as ensuring] the independence and dignity of the country".[77] The Islamic republic was about values and about non-reliance on others.

This episode generated adverse consequences for those trying to rebuild relations with the West, leading to the European Community's recalling of their heads of mission from Tehran in February and the breaking off of diplomatic relations with the United Kingdom in early March, the home country of Rushdie, which was a reminder of the fact that Iran's foreign policy would remain hostage to the balance of forces at home and to the power of factional politics being played out in the country's vast, often competing, revolutionary and state bureaucracies. The Rushdie affair also captured the volatility of Iran's foreign relations and the ease with which crises could emerge to derail policies and international relations. Mousavi's response to Rafsanjani's earlier criticism of the cost to Iran of needlessly alienating potential friends internationally came just weeks before the end of his time in office. In a statement issued by the Iranian ministry of foreign affairs, the outgoing government declared that "the Foreign Ministry considers itself not just the executor of the foreign policy of the Islamic Republic of Iran. Rather, in a wider horizon, it sees itself as the executor and protector of the foreign policy of Islam against infidelity and thus regards defence of dear Islam and its values a divine and legal task".[78]

Combined with the trans-Islamist tendencies, which had guided the republic's foreign relations, change of direction would also have had to contend with the ever-present Third Worldist (anti-imperialist) echo which had also emanated. The latter had tended to shape Iran's foreign relations in the war years and had led to unusual partnerships that now may have seemed incongruous. One such partnership was with the Democratic People's Republic of Korea (DPRK), which the outgoing President Khamenei celebrated in May 1989 during a state visit to Pyongyang as an alliance of progressive anti-American countries threatened by Washington: "this threat is particularly aimed at you [DPRK] and us.... If big countries threaten progressive countries, then progressive countries should threaten them in return".[79]

The domestic environment, and indeed mindset, that the new executive president would inherit would have to be very different if his strategy of international accommodation was to make any progress. So, his ability to change direction was tested by the republic's chosen foreign policy orientation. In the last analysis, and despite domestic and regional pressures, the end of the war had changed the security dynamics of the sub-region sufficiently to help open new doors of diplomacy for Iran, and consequently change the conditions of decision-making at home. Changing conditions in which decisions had to be made also helped change the mindset of the decision-makers, who themselves were also adjusting. In a dialectical process, new leaders responded to the new realities and in turn reinforced the strategy of opening up. The trick was to balance the imperatives of the revolution with the needs of a post-war society.

The pragmatists take charge

In many ways, the ground had already been prepared for experimenting with a different foreign policy approach, for trying to mend fences. Taking hostages for political reasons and using terrorism as a diplomatic tool would be shelved, and Tehran would refrain from projecting power through interference in other countries' internal affairs in favour of restoration of diplomatic and economic relations with the outside world. In the endeavour to become a good citizen, Iraq's invasion of Kuwait on 2 August 1990, soon after Rafsanjani's election, helped much in the new executive government's efforts to recover lost reputation. Iran condemned the invasion, complied with UN resolutions, refused to line up against the West and used this episode for vindication of its eight-year 'resistance' against Iraq. Iran now stood as the only country which had warned against Saddam Hussein and had in fact sacrificed itself for the containment of the Iraqi Ba'athist menace. Iran's refusal to rush to the aid of Iraqi uprisings in the south (Shia majority) and the north (Kurdish regions) following Saddam Hussein's defeat in the Kuwait campaign also helped project its declared policy of non-interventionism and neutrality, despite hard line backlash against the president for betraying the trust of Iraqi Muslims.

But the end of its own war with Iraq changed the conditions for Iran's foreign relations, which of course also benefited from the profound political changes at home. The emergence of a centrist executive presidency intent on improving Iran's external relations facilitated the drive towards accommodation with neighbouring countries. The domestic leadership changes coincided with some rather dramatic regional and international, systemic, transformations as well – the end of the Cold War, the outcome of the Kuwait war which considerably diminished the Iraqi threat to Iranian national security – which "brought home to Iran in a dramatic way the revolutionary changes that had occurred in the international political system and the necessity of Iran to adapt its policies to these changes".[80] Pragmatism was also reinforced externally. From 1989 onwards, the Rushdie crisis notwithstanding, Iran set about restoring broken or strained ties with regional and major powers, with the president and his foreign minister actively engaging with other countries through foreign travel and visiting dignitaries to

Iran.[81] While terrorism as a domestically driven instrument of foreign policy remained, the restoration of diplomatic relations with Jordan, Morocco, resolution of outstanding issues with the European countries, and the ironing out of tensions with the neighbouring Gulf Arab countries took centre stage. Even economic overtures to the United States were made, including an unprecedented offer, in 1995, to a US oil major (Conoco) of a lucrative ($1 billion) off-shore oil and gas exploration contract.

Unfortunately for President Rafsanjani, the election of Bill Clinton in the US halfway through his first term in office created new obstacles for his foreign policy agenda.[82] First, Clinton's chosen secretary of state, Warren Christopher, had first-hand experience in dealing with the Islamic republic and remembered well the humiliation of his country when it took fifty-two of its government personnel hostage in Tehran. He had written in 1985 that the hostage crisis was an episode of great domestic and foreign policy importance to the United States, which also showed that with regard to the violation of its international obligations, "the host government condoned and then embraced what the terrorists had done, and thus made their crime its own – an almost unprecedented act and one of extraordinary repugnance".[83] To Christopher, the Islamic republic was an "international outlaw" nation that sponsored terrorism and was now also determined to acquire weapons of mass destruction. Its policies showed that it was intent on doing harm to the US and its regional interests: "When I was in the Middle East, I found that to be a common judgment among many of the leaders that I met with, that Iran was greatly feared at the present time because of their support for terrorist groups, which they have not in any way disavowed".[84]

Second, the Clinton White House was increasingly concerned by what it saw as Iranian clandestine efforts to acquire a nuclear weapons capability, which was being partly fuelled by less than secret Iranian negotiations with China and Russia for the construction of nuclear power plants in the country.

Third, Clinton had made Arab-Israeli peace the priority of his regional policy and as his strategy of regional peace began to produce results in 1993 and 1994, the administration and its Israeli ally saw in Iran's behaviour and its leaders' condemnation of the peace process a real obstacle to regional security. They were also keenly following Iranian revolutionary guards' extensive presence in Bosnia (in support of the Muslim population of the former Yugoslav region) and also in Sudan (in support of the Islamist Islamic National Front which had taken power in 1989). In Sudan, particularly following President Rafsanjani's trip to Khartoum in December 1991 leading to the exchange of an economic and defence cooperation agreement, Iran was providing direct military support as well as financing Sudan's arms purchases from China.[85] The US had direct interests in both territories and was itself actively involved in these theatres during Clinton's presidency.

Rafsanjani was not fully able to shake off the country's past image or end its organs' interference in other countries' internal affairs. For example, in its enthusiastic support for Algeria's Islamist militants, Iran managed to alienate the key

Arab interlocutor country that had brought the hostages crisis to a satisfactory end a decade earlier and found the government of Algeria deporting seven of its diplomats in the country in 1992 in protest to Tehran's endorsement of the Islamist challenge to the ruling secular regime. Equally, it incurred the wrath of the important non-Arab Muslim country next door, namely Turkey, when the propagation bureau of the Qom theological schools condemned Turkish government's decision to ban headscarves at universities as an "anti-Islamic act in line with global arrogance's schemes against the sanctities of Muslims".[86] Ankara's public rebuke was unequivocal: "It is impossible to accept outside efforts to become party to Turkey's internal affairs.... Turkey until now has been responsible enough to refrain from passing judgement or taking a stand on Iran's own regime and internal developments".[87] Nor was he able to fully redefine Iran's relations with its southern neighbours, and despite repeated efforts after the liberation of Kuwait in February 1991 to advance the proposal for a sub-regional collective security structure to include all the Persian Gulf states, the GCC countries chose to deepen their defence partnerships with the Western powers and for good measure also established an all-Arab '6+2' (GCC+Egypt+Syria) security forum for the sub-region that excluded Iran but included Iran's most important Arab ally.

The GCC snub and American concerns about Iran's role in the sub-region and its military (naval) purchases put Iran's efforts to build a local security forum on ice – indefinitely. Thus, relations normalized in the course of Rafsanjani's presidency but never became warm enough to lead to a total overhaul or the introduction of confidence-building measures to address the fears and concerns of the two sides.[88] Gulf Arab countries remained suspicious of Iran, its role in the Gulf, influence in their countries, and as a competitor in global energy markets. Iran's policies did not in reality extend beyond the restoration of relations and, despite broader business and cultural exchanges (substantial trade traffic with the UAE, and opening of cultural centres, for example), the Gulf remained a zone of insecurity, which developments in the region following 9/11 and the subsequent war in Iraq in 2003 (which ended Sunni rule in Iraq) helped to deepen. After the Iraq war, and the revelations regarding Iran's nuclear-related activities, Rafsanjani's successor had an even harder job of persuading his GCC counterparts that Tehran could be trusted as a security and political partner.

Nevertheless, after a decade of anti-establishment behaviour, it appeared that Iran was returning to the diplomatic fold. Furthermore, with the Cold War over, Iran began to extend its reach to new postures, thus slowly emerging as an actor in multiple regions. Iran's efforts to return the hostages home also yielded results, culminating in what the European Union called at the 1992 EU summit in Edinburgh the start of a 'critical dialogue' with Tehran.[89] The European strategy of engagement with Iran stood in sharp contrast to the 'dual containment' of Iraq and Iran that formed the nucleus of President Clinton's Gulf strategy. So, from Tehran's perspective, engagement with the West had already borne fruit in terms of driving a wedge between Europe and the United States.[90] Of course, Iran may have had little choice but to seek economic partners in Europe; with

American doors still shut and China not the economic power that it is today, Tehran had banked on the Soviet Union and its Warsaw Pact allies to bail Iran out of its economic mess.

As late as June 1989, just two years before the demise of the Soviet state and with it its global political and economic strength, Tehran tried to establish extensive partnerships with its northern neighbour, on a scale bigger even than those struck by the Shah in the 1960s that gave Iran its first heavy industries, such as cement, steel and agricultural goods production. Rafsanjani's trip to the Soviet Union in June (21–22), when he was still Majlis speaker, was designed to put in place the structures and conditions for economic cooperation between the two countries, providing Iran with an alternative to its continuing reliance on the West for manufactured and capital goods and for a wide range of consumer products. The ten-year plan was to set up low-cost production facilities in Iran based on Soviet technologies and capital plants – the wholesale relocation of factories ranging from metal, cement production, electricity generating (thermal, nuclear, hydroelectric) plants, electrification of Iran's aging rail system, satellite technologies, gas processing, improving and increasing Iran's military production, and even space exploration.[91] This was to be a turning point, had it not been for the collapse of the Soviet super-state in 1991 and its demise as a military-industrial power for decades. After 1991, of course, a whole new window of opportunity opened up that encouraged the rebalancing of the country's focus eastwards. Assured of Iraq's demise as a security threat, the country's diplomatic machinery turned its gaze away from the Arab region and went into overdrive as it adjusted to the opportunities presented in Central Asia and the Caucasus following the demise of the Soviet Union.

Improvements in international relations

An authoritative survey confidently noted in 1992 that "the more militant days of the Iranian Revolution seem at last to have ended; conversely, the rise of Islamic Iran as a great regional power may have only begun".[92] Subsequent developments show that this prediction would prove somewhat premature on both counts, but it did correctly allude to the reality that if President Rafsanjani was to succeed in returning the country to the trajectory of development and growth, he would have to rebuild the country's material capacity, both economically and militarily. Recovery was the essence of reconstruction.

Regarding defence, several major arms transfer deals with the Soviet Union/ Russia and China were reached to replenish Iran's exhausted arsenal, including the transfer of advanced fighter jets, tanks, naval vessels, air defence and anti-ship missile systems.[93] At this time concern grew regarding Iran's rearmament drive and an effort to build a WMD programme, despite the IAEA declaring in 1992 that its team had "inspected different parts of Iran's nuclear facilities and have found nothing suspicious".[94] Circumstantial evidence – such as Iran's purchases of uranium from Namibia through a Swiss-owned company, a secret deal with

Argentina for enriched uranium, a new reactor core for the Tehran University nuclear research centre, and assistance with the completion of the Bushehr power plant – had emerged in the late-1980s that Iran was building a strong nuclear portfolio.[95] We now know, of course, that the decision to restart the nuclear programme was taken in 1987, a year before Rafsanjani's election to the presidency, with the directive to find partners for uranium enrichment and reactor construction from anywhere, but that it was his administration that pursued the programme strategically.[96]

Rouhani, the most authoritative primary source on Iran's nuclear programme, notes in his account of the development of the programme that he himself led a high-level team of nuclear technicians and scientists to Beijing in 1988 to explore nuclear cooperation with China. But the most direct assessment came from the CIA Director James Woolsey, who stated in 1994 that: "we believe that Iran is eight to 10 years away from building [nuclear] weapons, and that help from the outside will be critical in reaching that timetable.... Iran has been particularly active in trying to purchase nuclear materials or technology clandestinely from Russian sources".[97] Just a few months later, in January 1995, Russia announced that it had concluded a $1 billion contract with Iran to complete the construction of Iran's first nuclear power reactor at Bushehr and plans for the construction of a further four. The contract included the training of hundreds of Iranians as technicians and scientists in nuclear construction and research. In September 1995, under immense pressure from the Clinton administration, China had to back down from its 1993 agreement to build two 300-megawatt nuclear power reactors in Iran. But China did remain involved and helped build Iran's zirconium plant and uranium conversion facility in Isfahan, which would provide the cladding for nuclear fuel.

As noted, the emphasis on economic recovery placed a new premium on pragmatism and accommodation. In search of skills and investment capital for Iran's ailing industrial (including hydrocarbons) sectors, which would be on the front line of tackling the economy's serious structural problems, the administration of President Rafsanjani unveiled a strategy of economic liberalization (see chapter 3) which anticipated improvements in Iran's relations with the outside world, notably the West, as the basis for reconstruction of the war-torn economy. This strategy, at the same time, pushed oil to centre stage of the reconstruction efforts. Oilonomics had returned to shape policy and this time it was advocating pragmatism and an end to adventurism.

Rafsanjani's policies of the eight years following the war had, in effect, laid the groundwork for those seeking a renaissance of Iranian society and reforms to the republic's stifling public institutions. For these newly emerging reformist forces, economic prosperity was contingent on social and political freedoms and 'rationality' in policy. Ideology was, to a large extent, an increasingly irrelevant policy tool for the post-war executive elite and arguably a barrier to progress. In this period the concept of 'national interest' also re-entered the republic's lexicon, but the concept remained ill-defined and contested. Who drew up the national interest of a revolutionary and ideological regime, which institutions would drive it, and what was the national interest to be based on or anchored around? Do Iranian decision-makers act in the interest of the revolution or the state? There were no simple answers to these questions, and while 'pragmatism' became the term of choice to capture the policies of the Rafsanjani administration, it also hid more than it revealed about the Islamic republic. Was the regime a reformed political entity returning the country to a 'normal' state – non-interference, abandonment of radical violent groups, normalization of relations with other countries? And in this regard, was 'pragmatism' a shorthand for 'opportunism', the shelving of adventurism for now, or indicative of a deeper, more profound change? Different countries saw the process of change very differently.

In the West, Iran continued to be viewed with suspicion, and on the back of such diplomatic fissures as the Rushdie affair, the murder of opposition figures overseas, and continuing warm relations with radical Islamist groups (Hezbollah, Hamas, Islamic Jihad, for example), Rafsanjani's pragmatism could get Iran only so far with the Western powers. Closer to home, however, Iran found a much more receptive environment, which Rafsanjani's administration used to rebuild relations with neighbours and secured for itself an elevated place in such culturally and religiously important bodies as the multilateral Islamic Cooperation Organization. But, in looking east, his administration was instrumental in repositioning Iran as an emerging Asian power.[98] In the post-Soviet spaces of Central Asia and the Caucasus, Iran showed its nimbleness in adjusting to the post-Cold War order in Asia and moved to build economic and cultural links with the largely unknown countries of the former Soviet Union and to act as their bridge to the outside world.[99] Iran restructured what had become a defunct regional organization into the ten-member Economic Cooperation Organization (ECO) in 1992 encompassing all the Muslim republics of the former Soviet Union (plus Afghanistan and the two old members of Turkey and Pakistan) as a vehicle for regional cooperation. Headquartered in Tehran, with ECO Iran created the largest Muslim-only regional organization in the world, and with it an economic community of some 300 million people'.[100]

Initially motivated by a stabilization strategy, Tehran very quickly moved beyond concerns for its own security in the post-Soviet space to cultivating a central role for itself. It intended to be the regional power of choice to fill an imaginary vacuum that would follow the collapse of the Soviet empire, while forging links northwards in order to break free of the straightjacket resulting from an Arab-dominated MENA regional system.[101] Despite reservations about the ideological nature of Iran's Islamic regime, and a greater interest in the secular, prosperous and cash-rich Turkish republic, elites in the newly emerging republics soon developed a modus operandi with Tehran. From Armenia to Kazakhstan, Iran flexed its muscles and built partnerships, including through the creation of another regional grouping (the less-known Caspian Sea Cooperation Organization), and, in many of these newly emerging countries, openly competed with such rivals as Turkey and Saudi Arabia for cultural and religious influence and business opportunities.[102] In the course of two high-level visits to Central Asia (and Azerbaijan in the Caucasus) between 1991 and 1993, Rafsanjani successfully put in place the planks of cooperation, which included energy, construction, infrastructure development, agriculture, education, tourism and culture.[103] In its approach towards the post-Soviet spaces, Rafsanjani also successfully demonstrated Tehran's constructive and problem-solving attitude in its international relations.[104]

The pragmatic and cooperative trend in Iran's international relations during this period was further demonstrated in the way it sought consolidation of relations with the Asian giants of China, Russia and India – all featuring highly in Iran's look-east strategy. With each, Iran cultivated closer economic links, but with the first two countries the deepening of military ties played an equally important part.[105] With this strategy of 'de-containment' that Rafsanjani successfully deployed in Asia, the regime was able to counterbalance Washington's efforts to isolate it and used 'prudent pragmatism' (read: defensive realism) to make headway in Asia's politically turbulent environment following the Soviet collapse.[106]

In geopolitical terms, for all the communal tensions in the post-Soviet territories and the rudimentary nature of their economies and polities, for Iran these countries provided a profitable escape route from America's containment of the country and new spaces for Iran to develop as markets for its rather uncompetitive industries and products. This was best demonstrated in May 1996 when Rafsanjani had managed to assemble eleven heads of states to witness the opening of the Mashhad-Sarakhs-Tedzhen railroad, built with Iranian financial support. But chaos following the USSR's institutional collapse at the heart of Asia was also something to guard against. So Iran accepted Moscow's efforts to contain jihadism in the region and sought to focus on constructive engagement and clearing of the ethnic, communal, territorial, and clan differences rising to affect political dynamics of the Caucasus and Central Asia. This was in sharp contrast to its behaviour in the Middle East where it continued to act unilaterally and intervene at will in affairs of other states.

When Rafsanjani vacated the presidential office in 1997, Iranian society had begun stirring, with civic groups and latterly revolutionaries advocating an 'airing' of society after many years of social restriction. Public debates, echoed through the floor of the parliament, Friday prayers, and through the growing network of newspapers and periodicals, helped to broaden the base of a national dialogue about the future direction of the Islamic republic as it tried to come to terms with the prevailing post-Cold War, apparently unipolar, international order. With the regime assured that in the region its role and interests had, to a large extent, been secured, it responded positively to the demands for greater reforms, and it was in this context that a reformist cleric emerged as the champion of change in 1997's presidential elections. Confidence at the heart of the elite in the regime's ability to change and reform was a reflection of the confidence it felt internationally. Despite pockets of trouble, notably in neighbouring Afghanistan, and being subject of the Clinton administration's 'dual containment', the republic's regional status had never been better. Unlike the enemy next door, Tehran was free to pursue its international relations with little problem, and it was now Saddam Hussein's regime that was weak and vulnerable. Tehran's relations with its Arab partners (Syria, Hezbollah, Hamas and Islamic Jihad) had remained solid despite Iran's rebuilding of ties with the moderate Arab states, and indeed Hezbollah and Hamas had been rehabilitated in Arab capitals and sensitivities over Iran's relations with these organizations had markedly diminished.

Despite the rising tensions since 1992 with the UAE (and the GCC more broadly) over the three Persian Gulf islands under Iran's control, his administration tried hard to keep the channels of communications clear with the Gulf Arabs and appealed for a locally negotiated settlement of the dispute. Although his administration failed to prevent the internationalization of the islands dispute and had to contend with the matter being referred to the United Nations by the UAE, it had managed to heal the rift that had opened up between the republic and the Gulf Arab monarchies in the 1980s, while keeping away from the political crisis engulfing the GCC itself following the unexpected palace coup in Qatar in 1995 and the apparent support extended to the deposed ruler from the neighbouring countries.

Iran's relations with the European Union had improved markedly, too, and as 'critical dialogue' between the two sides gradually removed the obstacles to the restoration of political relations, the EU was now openly opposing the imposition of unilateral extra-territorial sanctions (the 1996 Iran-Libya Sanctions Act, ILSA) on the Islamic republic. This was inevitable, as by the mid-1990s the EU had emerged as Iran's main trading partner, taking 36 per cent of its exports and supplying 40 per cent of its imports.[107] At the same time, Iran had continued to develop its military links with Russia and also military and trade ties with China. Further, its relations with India and Japan were also improving. So by the late-1990s, Iran had secured for itself a credible set of global relationships to include Western powers as well as the emerging powers of Asia. In the Middle East, it was acting as a regional power and was by this time viewed as a regional actor in Central Asia as well. Iran had, by diplomatic indicators at least, entered a new age, and its policies and diplomatic posture reflected the change. Perhaps through dialogue the remaining tensions could be reduced, too, and it was then that the idealists surfacing as a force in their own right added 'coexistence' to the Rafsanjani administration's policy of accommodation.

Détente and the dialogue of civilizations

Under very different conditions then, the presidency changed hands from Rafsanjani to one of his trusted lieutenants, Hojjatoleslam Mohammad Khatami, a former minister in Rafsanjani's cabinet. He was elected as Iran's second executive president in 1997 with a massive mandate.[108] Though foreign policy did not feature much in the election campaign, Khatami nevertheless did raise expectations that his reformist administration would build on President Rafsanjani's efforts comprehensively to improve Iran's relations with the outside world. We saw in chapter 2 how his electoral success galvanized the masses (the middle classes in particular) and threatened to transform the country's political landscape, and how he used his electoral and social popularity to introduce new and radical policies. Well, armed with the same strong mandate, he set about deepening Iran's relations with the West and the rest of the international community. But he planned to do much more: To alter the Islamic republic's external role profoundly, readjust course further to align with the post-Cold War order and global accommodations, and to end revolutionary dogma as a policy instrument.

The 'philosopher president', as he came to be known, preached a message of peace and dialogue – of coexistence. As Organization of Islamic Conference (OIC) chairman in 1997, he spoke eloquently of the contributions of the Islamic civilization to the world but also warned of narrow-mindedness marginalizing Islam and Muslim countries in the fast-changing globalized world. In his last speech as OIC chairman in Doha in November 2000, he visited many of the same themes but went further and spoke of a new paradigm of international relations being sought by Iran (and by extension, the OIC which had endorsed Khatami's dialogue in 1997). Khatami's worldview remained rooted in the familiar principles of justice, freedom and democracy, but his prescription was the adoption of dialogue as a "new paradigm of international relations" whose strength was to be found in the "disintegration of the hitherto existing international division between the core and periphery".[109] Khatami's revolution was to close the distance between the Islamic republic and the West by turning the competing values paradigm with the United States and the West into a compatible values paradigm. By shortening this distance Khatami intended to build a bridge of trust.

Thus the principles of dialogue were raised again, at the United Nations, whose tribune he also used (at the United Nations General Assembly in September 1998) to emphasize that his administration had "accorded the removal of tension the highest priority in its foreign policy".[110] President Khatami further spoke of the need to improve relations with other countries irrespective of their past problems with Iran and as proof of his commitment to normalization and confidence building he advanced the agenda of a dialogue of civilizations, which was adopted as a United Nations initiative in the early 2000s. He had trailed some of the themes of the UN speech in an interview with the US' foremost international news channel, CNN, on 7 January 1998, in which he demonstrated not only the depth of his education and knowledge (including about America's founding fathers and the US' core values) but also recognition of Western ideas and ideals as positive and civilization-enhancing.[111] More specifically, his reflections on the republic's foreign policy made an impact, most notably his 'regret' for the US embassy takeover in 1979 and the burning of the American flag, the call to break the wall of distrust between Tehran and Washington. The fact that the Islamic republic had made anti-Americanism a feature of its anti-hegemonic role conception and core rhetoric of its elite was swiftly sidelined in Khatami's efforts to rebuild bridges. But he went even further and in the most erudite manner, unexpected of a revolutionary head of state whose country had turned antagonism and bellicosity into an art form, he spoke of the bond uniting different civilizations. At the UN's launch conference of 'dialogue amongst civilizations' in September 2000, he spoke of the strength in cultural plurality, of universal love: "believing in dialogue paves the way for vivacious hope; the hope to live in a world permeated by virtue, humility and love, and not merely by the rein of economic indices and destructive weapons".[112] Such talk was anathema to Islamist supremacists in whose binary world of good and evil Western civilization was spent and the East was too marginal to matter. But to the West, the tone and content of the new president was not just unexpected; it was seen as a breath of fresh air.

President Khatami's conciliatory tone would, inevitably, create difficulties for his administration at home, but during his first term in office, at least, he made rapid progress on implementing his coexistence and détente strategy. Khatami's Iran was to be shaped by international "dialogue and synthetic integration", in contrast to the previous era identified as 'antagonistic isolation'.[113] But could he avoid the skeletons in the regime's cupboards – from state-sponsored terrorism to subversion and militarization – so as not to fall foul of the international community again?

For all the domestic criticisms of its foreign policy, however, what was undeniable was the fact that, under Khatami, Tehran was attempting a qualitative leap in its conceptualization of the world – to move beyond the division of the world into good and bad. Through its dialogue of civilizations, its president was signalling his government's acceptance of the world as it was – the status quo – and the place of the ancient Persian/Iranian-Islamic country within it.[114] The new language of Iran's diplomacy and the skills of its president led to Khatami becoming the first Iranian president to visit a number of European countries at the head of high-level delegations. Thus, he was warmly received in France, Germany, Greece, Italy, the Vatican, and Spain. By 1998, having recovered from the Berlin judge's ruling on Iranian terrorism and fully buried the Rushdie affair,[115] the EU's 'constructive engagement' had been restored, and a year after his election, President Khatami's prudent foreign policy was being reciprocated by European leaders, who saw in his presidency economic opportunity but equally importantly a chance to make long-term improvements in the Islamic republic's relations with the West. The EU leaders continued to press Tehran on such issues as human rights violations, its support for what the EU regarded as terrorist groups, and opposition to what was then a lively peace process. European leaders were making an effort to bolster the hand of moderation in Tehran's ruling circles, despite US pressure to isolate the country for its support of terrorism (and support for Hamas and Hezbollah organizations), opposition to the Arab-Israeli peace process, intimidation of American regional allies, and an alleged WMD programme.

In the MENA region, Khatami articulated détente in terms of collaborative approaches to crises. He became the first sitting president to visit Saudi Arabia in May 1999, following his predecessor's path-opening visit to the Kingdom in early 1998.[116] Relations with the Kingdom improved considerably following Khatami's visit and his warm encounters with Crown Prince Abdullah, leading to the signing of a security agreement between the two countries. Improvements also occurred following Khatami's visit to Bahrain in May 2003 – the first Iranian leader to visit the country since the revolution. But these exchanges did not reduce tensions: With Bahrain, problems remained over Iran's support for the majority Shia community; and with the UAE, who saw in Iran's presence on the three Gulf islands occupation of its territory. Relations with the UAE had been so tense that in the rapprochement between Iran and the Kingdom, the UAE saw a direct threat to its own security and interests (in trying to recover the islands lost to Iran).

But what Khatami did not do was to change Iran's narrative on the Arab-Israeli conflict – support for the Palestinians as a religious and moral duty and condemnation of Israel as an alien implant in the Muslim Middle East continued. He stayed close to the regime's narrative of anti-Zionism and went out of his way to celebrate Iran's close relationship with the 'resistance front' of Syria, Hezbollah and Palestinian Islamist groups of Hamas and Islamic Jihad. Two years into his first term, for instance, he made a point of meeting with the four main Syria-based radical (secular and Islamist) Palestinian groups in Damascus to convey Iran's support for their case and to unite them in the fight against 'hegemony'.[117] But in a landmark development, Khatami also successfully courted Lebanon's non-Shia elite, and the arrival of Prime Minister Rafiq Hariri, an anti-Syrian and close associate of the al-Sauds, in Tehran in October 1997, was indicative of the regime's efforts to try to broaden the base of their relationships in the Arab world.[118] The Lebanese president's visit in November 2008 at the head of a strong delegation drew Iran closer to the political elite of Lebanon and therefore widened its base in Lebanon beyond association purely with the Shia organizations of Hezbollah and Amal.

In January 2001, many months before 9/11, he again emphasized the need to strengthen the Iran-Syria-Lebanon (Hezbollah) axis as a "precondition for stability" in the region, pushing it towards a formalized partnership.[119] He returned to the Levant in 2003, following the Iraq War, and in a skilful combination of hard and soft power, Khatami was able to fuse Iran's alliances in the Levant into a single community (of resistance) while also using the warm reception he received in Beirut in what was remarkably the first visit of an Iranian president to a country of such strategic importance since the revolution as evidence of the Islamic republic's popularity in the Arab world and amongst the 'front-line' communities facing Israel. In praising Hezbollah's role in pushing Israel back from Lebanese territory in 2000, he at the same time sought to strengthen the organization's standing as a credible Lebanese force prepared to defend the country's integrity and play its part in the development of Lebanon. Hezbollah was being given more room and also prominence in Iran's policies. Hezbollah was, as Khatami put it, a "Lebanese reality, part of Lebanon's defensive power",[120] it belonged to the people of Lebanon yet conveniently allied to Iran as well. Khatami's primary aim was to embed Hezbollah into the Lebanese state as a legitimate political and para-military actor with strong links to Iran but also with an independent will. In this way, Iran would reduce the burden of supporting Hezbollah without losing its patronage of this useful all-Shia organization at the heart of the Levant. Having a manoeuvrable ally such as Hezbollah in the Levant would show its benefits during Ahmadinejad's presidency, in confronting Israel militarily at the height of Iran's nuclear stand-off with the international community, and in mobilizing it in defence of Iran's most precious Arab ally in Syria following the Arab revolts of the 2010s.

In the north, too, Khatami tended to continue with the constructive policies of his predecessor, though it took him a little while longer to get going in the north. Conscious of the American pressure to, first, isolate Iran from what had become exciting new energy zones, and second – following 9/11 in particular – to bring these republics into the North Atlantic's security framework, Khatami built on détente to counter US' increasing influence and its anti-Iran message in these republics. He, thus, prioritized the four areas of energy cooperation, Caspian Sea integration, counterterrorism, and regional trade as follow-ups to Rafsanjani's strategy of extending Iran's cultural, economic and political influence in the post-Soviet Muslim spaces. Armed with the message of cooperation, he first tried to resolve the brewing problem regarding maritime borders of the Caspian Sea. His efforts at a Caspian Summit in April 2002, the holding of which was itself a minor miracle, to secure an equitable distribution of the sea between the five riparian states – a claim of 20 per cent of the Caspian's rich natural resources – against the majority's wish of dividing the sea and its riches according to each country's shoreline, proved unsuccessful, but nevertheless he did use the trip to Turkmenistan as a springboard for an extensive (nine-day) tour of the post-Soviet republics in spring 2002.

Travelling to Kazakhstan, Uzbekistan, Kyrgyzstan and Tajikistan, Khatami was warmly received by a succession of autocratic leaders who liked his message of tolerance but liked even more his position against the Taliban and jihadi challenges in Central Asia. His call for a 'global peace coalition' to counter radicalism also resonated warmly with these countries on the front line of shifting Eurasian geostrategic plates. But, at an intellectual level, much of the elite remained suspicious of political Islam that Iran itself purveyed and worried about its anti-American rhetoric affecting their increasingly warm relations with the Bush administration. In hosting Khatami, these leaders were keenly aware of the benefits of having the charismatic and popular Iranian president visit their countries, but they also recognized the importance of Iran as a geopolitical shortcut to the outside world as well as a key trade and energy partner. His success in securing economic agreements with the well-endowed Caspian states of Kazakhstan and Turkmenistan was notable, which included integrated rail transport links and trade of foodstuffs.

The inauguration of the weekly Almaty-Tehran railway service in March 2002 was a crowning achievement.[121] But also noteworthy was the fact that just days before Khatami's departure for the Caspian Summit, China's President Jiang Zemin had heralded in comments in Tehran the rebuilding of the Silk Road 'ties' in Asia – of convergence of Iranian and Chinese interests in Asia's heartland. Zemin – only the second Chinese head of state to have visited Iran since the revolution – was returning Khatami's trip to China in June 2000 at the head of a 170-strong delegation of ministers, industry leaders and high-ranking defence officials, which had helped consolidate the relationship successfully built by his two predecessors. Zemin's four-day stay led to a number of strategic partnerships in energy, defence, counterterrorism, transport, construction, and tourism and was highlighted by the Chinese president as building the basis for "an all-round cooperation among Tehran, Beijing, Moscow and New Delhi".[122] Notwithstanding the assertion that Iran "was pushed toward Asia more than it was pulled in that direction",[123] Zemin's visit left no doubt that the country was now an unmistakable link in China's most important chain of relationships, and in this regard also an Asian major power.

While Khatami's successes were important, and while he was able to keep both China and Russia on side in the course of courting the West and negotiating improvements in relations with the post-Soviet republics, he did, however, fall short of delivering on the country's three key priorities. First, despite repeated efforts, he was unsuccessful in his strategy of pressing the Central Asian republics to choose between Tehran and Washington as their primary energy and security partners. In the first instance, following 9/11, the US provided extensive security support for these countries that not only feared al-Qaeda but also their own home-grown Islamists. Iran, itself a proud and overtly Islamic state, not only suffered from an image problem but also, in practical terms, could not offer the security guarantees to persuade the secular leaders of these republics that it could be part of the solution to the challenge of political Islam in their countries. In the field of energy also, Tehran – suffering under sanctions imposed on its energy sector by the United States – could not provide the necessary technical skills and financial support for exploiting the region's energy riches. It could not, in the end, compete with existing energy routes – through Russia – or the building of new ones southwards (through Iranian territory to the Persian Gulf) out of the Caspian region instead of the more expensive – eastward and westward – options that eventually emerged. In the words of one observer: "I sense that Central Asian leaders recognize that deals with the U.S. will have a better financial payoff and they are more likely to bring in development assistance. It is easy to contrast the U.S. and Iran economically and decide which model you would rather emulate".[124]

Second, Khatami was unable to negotiate the demarcation of Caspian Sea boundaries, and although this issue did not affect Tehran's relations with the northern Caspian states, it did influence the decisions of Iran's immediate northern neighbours in turning towards the United States and Western energy companies for extraction and distribution of their hydrocarbons. Indeed, with Azerbaijan,

Iran's relations were increasingly securitized in Khatami's second term, and by the time Ahmadinejad took over as president a naval military build-up had begun and Baku had begun making territorial claims in Iran's own, much larger, Azerbaijan of over 24 million people.

Third, Khatami was not successful in using the ECO, which was rebooted by Rafsanjani in the early 1990s, as a vehicle for regional economic integration. In the 2000s, ECO languished in the shadow of the war on terror and as Central Asian states strengthened the security barriers around them. Closer economic cooperation, let alone integration, soon became untenable and intra-ECO trade suffered accordingly. Tehran continued to lower barriers to trade and investment and to attempt to harmonize customs regulations and environmental policies, to operationalize the ECO development bank, but ECO's contribution to international trade remained small – growing from 1.26 per cent of world merchandize trade in 1994 to just 2.34 per cent in 2012.[125] Iran appeared as a top-five trading partner of just two ECO countries (Afghanistan and Turkey) and its own contribution to ECO's total trade also dropped from 30 per cent of the organization's total in 1994 to just 18.6 per cent in 2012.

Adding to this was the crisis of governance in Afghanistan following the Soviet withdrawal in 1989 and Tehran's failure to prevent chaos and the rise of the Taliban to government in 1994 and counter Pakistan's overwhelming presence in this country. The Rafsanjani and Khatami administrations' neglect of Iran's eastern neighbour allowed the consolidation of anti-Shia Taliban as the government of Afghanistan and the arrival in that country of Osama bin Laden and his al-Qaeda network, which would in the end invite direct military intervention in that country by Iran's most implacable adversary – the United States. Turmoil in Afghanistan adversely affected the development of ECO and diminished Iran's effort to turn it into an effective regional economic organization. Problems mounted in Afghanistan following the defeat in summer 1998 of Iranian-backed reminisces of the Mujahedin fighters (the so-called Northern Alliance) by the hard-line Pakistan-supported Taliban who had appeared on the national scene as a puritanical Islamist force committed to cleansing Afghanistan of infidels and apostates (Shia populations) and the imposition of most narrowly defined Sharia law on the country. Their capture and occupation of Mazar-e Sharif, Iran's gateway through the pro-Iranian Hazara communities into Afghanistan, and their maltreatment of resident Iranian diplomats, brought the Afghan crisis home to Iran. Indeed, the crisis was so real that barely a year into his presidency Khatami found himself touring over 70,000 Iranian troops on the front line of a deepening crisis along Iran's eastern borders and in danger of being embroiled in what could easily have become a war with the irregular Taliban in Afghanistan, ostensibly to avenge the Taliban for the massacre of thousands of Hazara Shiis, eight Iranian diplomats and an Iranian journalist.

Pressure mounted at home for the government to act, to avenge the killing of its civilian citizens and unarmed Hazaras by the 'barbarian Taliban' (as the group was being referred to in Iran), and while Tehran waved the stick on television screens, it at the same time sought an urgent diplomatic solution to defuse the crisis. Remarkably, not only did the government seek United Nations Security Council intervention, but also former president Rafsanjani declared at public gatherings that Iran would not make any hasty decisions to go to war. Iran did occupy the moral high ground in the UN's condemnation of the Taliban's actions, but the continuing presence of the internationally outlawed Taliban (only three countries recognized the legitimate government of Afghanistan) on its doorstep until its defeat at the hands of US forces in autumn 2001 meant the weakening of Iran's influence in this critical state whose impact on Iran had been great: Its opium had numbed the minds of as many as 4 million Iranians, many of them young, and as many as 3 million of its nationals had fled their own country in the 1980s to live and work in Iran.

Khatami did not have it all easy, then. Indeed, further to the geopolitical constraints impinging on his presidency, he was exposed to several major shocks, which caused serious setbacks on the international stage as a consequence. These merely amplified Iran's strategic loneliness that he and his predecessor had tried so hard to overcome. The first was the return of a ghost from the past: The implication of Iranian leaders in acts of state terrorism during Rafsanjani's presidency, which had focused on the killing of opposition figures in Europe and elsewhere. One episode left a lasting legacy and the inevitable deterioration of Iran's relations with its main economic partner, the EU. It was in fact in April 1997, before his stunning election victory in the presidential race of that year, that a German judge's implication of the leaders of the republic in the assassination of four Iranian Kurdish leaders in a Berlin restaurant in 1992 led to the EU countries yet again breaking off their dialogue with Tehran, suspending all ministerial contacts, and recalling their ambassadors from Tehran. So, even before starting his presidency, Khatami had an urgent diplomatic crisis to manage and defuse. European diplomats did return in 1998 but did not push the boat out much for Iran until forced, which occurred in the course of their intervention in the nuclear crisis and the constructive role they played in liaising with Khatami's political allies in trying to defuse the crisis in 2003–04.

For political (factionalism and a hostile parliament continued to threaten his administration) and economic reasons (unemployment remained high, privatization had stalled, budget was in deficit, and the oil price had dropped to around $20 per barrel), Khatami had to put these setbacks aside and prevent a slide towards confrontation at home, if for no other reason than to ensure that there would be no derailment of the strategy of engagement and accommodation. He thus, until 2001, continued to try to secure successes in both material and moral ways for his engagement strategy.

The second major shock to his presidency was the terror attacks on the US in September 2001 that unhinged the regional order and exposed Iran to new pressures. This single act, and the fallout from it, was to shape the entire region's relations with the United States and in Iran's case its foreign relations as much as its domestic politics.

Iran and 9/11

Despite Tehran's incessant anti-US rhetoric, the attacks on US soil on 11 September 2001 and the massive loss of innocent lives actually shocked the regime and Iranian citizens alike. Khatami was able to ride the crest of emotion sweeping amongst Iranians and the West to remind the West that Iran, too, had suffered from terrorism and in sharing America's pain was a partner in fighting terrorism. The Iranian people instinctively and deliberately expressed sympathy for the victims of these crimes, holding candlelit vigils all over the country. But the elite responded with characteristic diversity. While isolated voices condoned the attacks, most rationalized the attacks in terms of a convenient distraction from the Palestinians' plight or a conspiracy to sully the name of Islam.[126]

The attacks also put Iran on the geopolitical front line of America's 'war on terror' as the Bush administration made plans to unseat the patrons of al-Qaeda in Afghanistan and to punish all others – which was soon to include Iran itself – who appeared as supporters of terrorism, harboured hostility towards the United States, or displayed the means (WMDs primarily) to threaten it and its interests.[127] Following 9/11, Khatami faced pressure from two competing currents: On the one hand, the demise of two intractable enemies (Taliban in Afghanistan in 2001 and Ba'ath regime in Iraq in 2003) at the hands of the US military fed the perception that these developments had opened up space for Iran to extend its influence. But on the other hand, the sense of encirclement as the United States' military comfortably settled in neighbouring countries had dented the optimism driving his policy of détente. It would not be long before the 'war on terror' reached Iran, so Tehran's celebrations proved to be short-lived, as just months after the removal of the Taliban from power, US President George W. Bush homed in on Iran and branded it a member of an 'axis of evil': States of Iran, Iraq and North Korea, and their alleged terrorist allies "constitute an axis of evil, arming to threaten the peace of the world. By seeking weapons of mass destruction, these regimes pose a grave and growing danger".[128]

Just three months later, National Security Adviser Condoleezza Rice fleshed out the Bush administration's views in stating,

> [Iran's] policies unfortunately belie the notion that engagement with it has helped. It has been engaged – I mean, Great Britain has relations with Iran. A number of our European allies have relations with Iran. Our problem with Iran is in policies that are so destructive to international politics – from the support of terrorism around the world to the support of terrorism in the Middle East and, frankly, the un-elected few in Iran who continue to frustrate the hopes of their own people, who repeatedly turn out and vote to throw off tyranny. There are an un-elected few who continue to frustrate the hopes of the people. And we're simply speaking the truth about the nature of Iran. Now, the truth is we've had some useful interaction with Iran around Afghanistan. Iran is Afghanistan's neighbor.

> We expect Iran to have good relations with Afghanistan, but they need to be transparent relations, they should be relations that are state to state, not relations that try to play into the complex and difficult politics of Iran. So I think that our view is that the behavior of Iran at this point would suggest that it is a state that while there may be some positive forces within it, those positive forces are not quite yet capable of changing the nature of Iran's behavior; Iran's behavior continues to be a major problem in international politics. And we watch the developments with great interest, but Iranian behavior puts it squarely in the axis of evil – whether it is weapons of mass destruction or terrorism or any of those things. It's a complicated situation, but I think the behavior speaks for itself.[129]

Détente now seemed like capitulation, at best appeasement, to Iranian conservatives who were deeply conscious of the strategic dangers facing the Islamic republic following President Bush's doctrine of intervention where terror was supported and where democracy was absent.[130] Iran's sense of insecurity following 9/11 and President Bush's axis of evil speech targeting Iran accentuated the sense of uncertainty, providing the first shock to the system and to Iran's calculations about its greater role in the post-Cold War order. Thus far, Iran had managed to adjust to the end of the Cold War by building relations with the European powers and complementing this through improved relations with Russia and the East. At the same time, it had also moved to develop economic ties with the newly independent Muslim republics of the former Soviet Union and to act as a bridge between the landlocked Central Asian states and the rest of the world. Isolating the United States by improving diplomatic and economic relations with the Eurasian countries seemed to make perfect sense for a country harbouring ambitions of major regional power status. The paths that President Rafsanjani had opened, in Russia, China and the European Union, his successor, capitalizing on his electoral legitimacy as the most popular president of the Islamic republic, assiduously widened and used effectively to improve Iran's international standing. However, the ways in which 9/11 created a new geopolitical web of interests and counterterrorism partnerships acted as a huge obstacle for Khatami's efforts to sustain and rebuild relations.

The paradox for Iran, as it adjusted to the reality of American pre-eminence in the post-9/11 international order, was that while it saw its own role enhanced in geopolitical terms, the very fact that it had emerged as a big player also exposed it to greater external pressures and particularly much greater American scrutiny.[131] The post-9/11 order, therefore, was both good and problematic for the Islamic republic. Enemies on its two longest land borders had been destroyed without a single Iranian shot being fired, but at the same time, US military and political presence in West Asia increased exponentially. Even as reminisces of Iraq's WMD capabilities were being reduced to dust in the course of the 2003 war, Tehran's own activities in the nuclear field were coming to light. Iran was finding itself as an ally of the West in the anti-Salafi Islam struggle, but at the same time on the US' list of terrorist states by virtue of its close association with the Hezbollah organization in Lebanon and support for Palestinian groups. Ironically, despite the two sides having a shared interest over the need to contain Sunni radicalism, to defeat overtly anti-Shia al-Qaeda terror network, and to remove from Iran's borders the menace of the Taliban, the US appeared as a greater threat to the regime's security than it had ever been in the previous twenty years.

The need to confront terrorism (war on terror), the campaign to prevent the spread of WMDs, and efforts to defuse Islamist radicalism were issues that now, more than ever, placed Tehran at the centre of American efforts to contain these triple threats to its national security, all of which seemed to emanate from the Middle East. And in the eyes of America's neocons, regimes such as the Islamic republic's were more guilty than most as the perpetrators of terror and instability in this strategic region.[132] Open calls in the United States for extending the war on terror, already underway in Afghanistan, to Iran spooked the political forces around President Khatami sufficiently to offer 'an understanding' with the US. But the conservatives huddled around Khamenei and, in evidence at Iran's many Friday prayer pulpits, had a different idea, many of whom continued to portray the September 11 terrorist acts equally as a US-engineered plot on American soil to protect Israel and thus justify attacks on the Muslim world and, at the same time, as proof that the 'Great Satan' was vulnerable and indeed a hated power around the world.[133]

US President George W. Bush's branding of Iran in January 2002 as a member of the tripartite 'axis of evil', just days after the revelations that the ship (Karina-A) apprehended by the Israel Defence Force on 3 January had in fact been carrying Iranian-supplied weapons for the Palestinians, sealed the fate of rapprochement and Khatami's calculations that US-IRI cooperation over the removal of the Taliban from power in Afghanistan and the establishment of a new government there would provide the conditions for coordinated efforts to improve regional relations.[134] Far from 9/11 improving the prospects for reconciliation, the US' continuing occupation of Afghanistan and its invasion of Iraq in March 2003 brought the war on terror close to Iran's own borders. The United States was now a resident military power, still enjoying a high degree of international sympathy for the terror attacks on its soil, so Tehran scrambled to reach out to Washington.

The offer of a 'grand bargain' with the United States to deal with the outstanding issues between them – over Iran's nuclear programme, Tehran's sponsorship of terrorism, its position on the Arab-Israeli peace process, its involvement in Iraq – was delivered to the US government in May 2003, providing the first strategic opportunity in years to change the dynamics of the region. Khatami had taken a leap of faith in search of reconciliation at a time that regional relations were again in flux. If this for Tehran was a first step in a choreographed dance of friendship with the United States, then it had gotten its footing badly wrong, for not only was the White House at that moment basking in its swift military successes and therefore not in a mood to cut a deal with one of its regional adversaries, but also it "could not be seen to be negotiating with a government now suspected of violating its NPT obligations when it had, just weeks before, invaded another state it had accused of being duplicitous".[135] Indeed, from 2002 onwards, concerns about Iran's violations of its NPT commitments, in the charged atmosphere of the time, would come to shape successive Iranian governments' relations with the major powers. The nuclear crisis, started during Khatami's presidency, defined Iran's relations with the West and Khatami's limited success to end the crisis during his term, brought to an end efforts to move Iran beyond its conditional partnerships with the Western world.

Nuclear politics takes over

References to Iran's pursuit of weapons of mass destruction had been made since the 1980s and most recently during Rafsanjani's presidency Western intelligence agencies often warned of Iran's suspicious activities in the nuclear field. An authoritative voice had observed in 1994 that for what it had experienced during the war at the hands of Iraqi forces, as much as for geopolitical, national security and domestic (political symbolism) reasons, Iran could be tempted to walk down the nuclear, WMD, path. This assessment was made at a time when Iran's geostrategic environment had stabilized and the Rafsanjani administration was making considerable progress in developing links with the regional states and the Eurasian powers (the EU in the west and China and Russia further east). Indeed, Rafsanjani himself admitted to Iran having considered developing a nuclear deterrence capability even before he had become president, stating in October 2015, after a nuclear deal had successfully been struck between Iran and world powers, that "our basic doctrine was always a peaceful nuclear application, but it never left our mind that if one day we should be threatened and it was imperative, we should be able to go down the other [weaponization] path".[136]

In the 1990s development of the nuclear programme would, essentially and of necessity, have had to have been a drawn-out process. Chubin, for example, had argued in 1994:

> Iran's program is not a crash one but is incremental, hands-on experience with research reactors, justified by access to technology and a sensible, very intelligent decision to avoid confrontation, to avoid giving the appearance of having a crash program. As far as capability goes, access to fissile material clearly would accelerate the program, and it is clear that Iran has at least some possibility of getting access to such fissile material, given its particular location, near the former Soviet Union.[137]

So despite the low-key approach, there appeared to be little doubt that under Rafsanjani, Iran had been focusing on mastering the nuclear craft, with Rafsanjani himself even traveling to Pakistan to negotiate with A.Q. Khan for the transfer of nuclear know-how and enrichment in particular from his organization. No wonder then that Rouhani refers to Rafsanjani's administration as "the nuclear government".[138] However, it appeared that by 1997 Rafsanjani's strategy of incremental progress had been so successful that it had advanced beyond explainable as a small research-based endeavour. Indeed, the programme had acquired a life of its own and thus was not a difficult decision for Khatami to accelerate the programme when he took over.[139] In the 2000s, the largely intelligence-generated concerns about Iran's programme, which had been registered as far back as a decade earlier – by the end of the Clinton administration, US sources had confirmed that Iran had a WMD programme, including an extensive strategic missile programme, and that it was pursuing these along a dozen distinct paths – had proved to be largely correct.[140] But nothing as concrete as the revelations in 2002 had been disseminated before, and, given the scale of the revelations and the international reaction, not surprisingly, the nuclear crisis came to chart the course of Iran's foreign relations for the remainder of Khatami's time in office.

Khatami's genuine attempts to reintegrate Iran into the international community were now overshadowed by concerns about proliferation. The scale of the programme made it difficult for his administration to dismiss the information now in the hands of the IAEA as unfounded, and the political balance of power at home (combined with the conservatives' embrace of the nuclear programme as a sign of Iran's scientific prowess) made any position but standing by the programme as a source of national pride an impossibility. Not for the first time in his presidency, Khatami's diplomacy was caught between the rock of international pressure to comply with international norms and the hard place of Iranian politics in which the national security establishment determined macro-level defence and security policies and priorities. With the programme celebrated as a major achievement for the Islamic republic and a model for the developing world to follow for the accumulation of scientific knowledge and practices without Western input, it proved impossible for Khatami to distance himself from it in order to find negotiating space. Khatami was implicated as a champion of the clandestine programme.

More broadly, the nuclear crisis would not only distract him from the urgent problems at home but also come to damage the government's continuing efforts to establish détente – which had become all the more pressing following the terror acts of 9/11. The kind of damage Khatami would come to suffer in in the wake of any nuclear-related revelations had been anticipated at the height of his popularity in 1999: "Clearly, it would be hard for a president who ran on a 'rule of law' platform, and who would like to reintegrate Iran into the international community", had mused Eisenstadt, "to justify the violation of international commitments [IAEA] and treaty obligations [NPT]".[141] This is exactly where Khatami now found himself and the challenge for Khatami was then, as posed by Eisenstadt, how to reconcile these divergent realities.

To recap, despite Western intelligence estimates that Iran had been working intensively on the country's nuclear programme, and calculations made in 1993–94 that it could be close to manufacturing a nuclear bomb in the early

2000s, no one was prepared for the revelations made by a largely marginalized opposition group in the summer of 2002 regarding the scale of Iran's clandestine nuclear programme. Armed with photos, names, documents and maps, the National Council of Resistance of Iran revealed to the world the shocking extent of Iran's activities, revealing for the first time the location of its secret centrifuges site (for uranium enrichment) near Natanz and that of its undeclared pressurized heavy water reactor project in Arak.[142] The programme itself, which Iran acknowledged had been accelerated in 1998, became much more public after 2002, when a string of revelations forced the Iranian authorities to acknowledge that they had in fact sought enrichment facilities, separating units, and nuclear weapons designs.[143] It was announced by the Iranian authorities in early 2003 that Iran's nuclear programme aimed "to complete the circle [cycle] of fuel for plants for peaceful purposes" and the head of the country's atomic energy programme declared that his agency had begun work on a uranium enrichment plant near the city of Kashan (the Natanz site), stating that "very extensive research [had] already started".[144] These two locations would become infamous internationally and the containment of both will in the end form the core of the successful nuclear negotiations conducted by Ahmadinejad's successor in 2015.

Worrying, from the West's perspective, was the revelation that Tehran had found a solution to the problem that Chubin had identified in 1994 – namely access to fissile material – domestically. If not a crash programme, then Iran's nuclear programme exposed during Khatami's presidency certainly appeared to be comprehensive. The fuel would come from the brand-new uranium conversion facility built in the industrial city of Isfahan. The Isfahan plant was to be complemented with another facility for producing uranium fuel casings. International concerns about Iran's nuclear ambitions were further heightened by additional announcements, particularly as only on 9th February Tehran had announced that it had successfully extracted uranium and was planning to process the spent fuel from its nuclear facilities inside the country. The Iranian president himself appeared on national television on the anniversary of Iran's Islamic revolution in February 2003 to congratulate Iranians on their nuclear achievements, enumerating Iranian scientists' research successes, and then underlining the statements already made by the head of the Iranian atomic energy organization regarding major additions to the programme's infrastructure. The nuclear programme and Iran's successes in enriching uranium, only one of ten countries to have achieved this feat, heralded Iran's arrival in the exclusive nuclear club and with this capability the chance to put to rest Iran's obsession with hegemonic domination by 'arrogant powers'. State narrative focused on Iran breaking scientific ground on its own and completing the nuclear fuel cycle without reliance on the outside world.[145] Completing the nuclear fuel cycle was a sign of modernity, rationality, and scientific rigour – all speaking to the narrative of progress and achievement, of self-sufficiency and what the regime would see as 'development with Islamic characteristics'. But the fear of the arrogant powers remained, and was in fact intensified following the revelations.

In the period to 2005, Iran's negotiating narrative under Khatami continued to underline Iran's rights under the NPT (to enrichment and all the other scientific benefits of nuclear technology for economic and medical betterment) but located this on its revolutionary platform of resisting pressure from the West. Indeed, Iran's leaders would later claim that their single-handed efforts to liberate the secrets of nuclear science from the major powers would facilitate development and scientific breakthroughs in the Global South. It would be atoms for all once the Islamic republic was in the nuclear club. The efficacy of breaking its NPT obligations in the process and even raising the theoretical possibility of WMD proliferation were issues not to be discussed, for above all, the programme provided evidence of Iran's independence and also its power.

Unquestionably, the nuclear controversy acted as a major shock to Khatami's détente diplomacy, providing the third shock in my analysis to his foreign policy. In the context of post-9/11securitized global order, the detailed revelations regarding Iran's nuclear programme, the clandestine aspects of the programme, and the extensive range of secret activities undertaken by the organs of the Iranian state inevitably pushed Iran to the top of the agenda of global concerns. For the United States in particular, Iran was the greatest source of threat to its security and that of its regional allies in the MENA region. President Khatami's détente, it seemed to outside powers, had created the space for Iran to make a concerted effort towards the acquisition of a WMD capability, the mastering of a national programme of nuclear fuel production, and possible delivery systems in its wide-ranging arsenal of surface-to-surface missiles (SSMs). Iran's engineers and scientists, it transpired, had been pursuing an intensive and multi-dimensional nuclear programme under the guidance of Iran's revolutionary guards – the ideological wing of the republic's security establishment. Iran was now at the top of the West's rogue actors, having already been singled out by the Bush administration's diehard neocons as being ripe for regime change. Administration insiders argued that the best way of addressing the proliferation problem in Iran was to get rid of its ruling regime.[146] There was little faith left in Khatami's dialogue with the West and having, apparently easily, disposed of Iraq's dictator, the temptation was strong in Washington "to roll the tanks eastwards", as an insider put it to me, "and test the Iranians".[147]

As far back as the introduction of the Clinton doctrine of 'dual containment' of Iran and Iraq in 1993, the United States and the (then fifteen-member) European Union have had their differences over Western policy options towards the two northern Gulf oil-rich states. Iran, as we saw, had been heavily engaged in encouraging European countries (and Russia) to break the American quarantine. The launch of Operation Iraqi Freedom in March 2003 and the fall of the Iraqi Ba'thist regime at the foot of US forces less than a month later, provided sufficient evidence for the European powers that Washington was prepared to engage in multiple theatres without the backing of the NATO alliance. Recognition of the United States' ability and willingness to act without the consent of the international community encouraged Tehran to solicit a diplomatic approach to the crisis from the EU, which itself was struggling very hard to mend the bridges at the heart of the Union following the very public and sustained opposition of Germany and France to the Anglo-American-led war in Iraq. It was in this context that the EU's 'constructive engagement' dialogue with Tehran came to be used as the platform for de-escalation.

The EU claimed that to avoid another war, it was taking effective action to bring the crisis to a negotiated end and thus the EU troika (Germany, France and the United Kingdom) announced just ten days before the 31st October deadline set by the IAEA board of governors that it had persuaded Iran to give a full account of its nuclear-related activities, halting its uranium enrichment activities, and to bring its entire nuclear activities under the IAEA regime of snap inspections. The EU was faced with the task of convincing the United States that the Tehran agreement was comprehensive and robust enough as to delay the referral of the Iranian case to the United Nations Security Council, which had always been Washington's preferred course of action. Despite the different European and American approaches, however, the West had left little doubt in Tehran that Iran's nuclear activities had shot Iran to the top of their agenda. Moscow's urging that Tehran should sign the NPT's Additional Protocol without delay was another sign that the international community was converging on Iran as an emerging international security problem.

Of particular concern to the IAEA were the sites being developed in Natanz and Arak, of whose existence the agency had first learnt through intelligence sources and not the Iranian authorities themselves. Iran's late notification of the two sites to the IAEA, though legal under the terms of the NPT,[148] reached the organization only in September 2002, a month after details of the Natanz and Arak facilities had been broadcasted. The IAEA's February 2003 inspection of Natanz revealed not only that Iran had been able to develop and advance the Pakistani-supplied technology to assemble and 'cascade' 164 centrifuge machines, but it also had assembled sufficient quantity of parts for installing a further 1,000 centrifuge machines for future use, and the potential on the site for housing as many as 50,000 centrifuges. Natanz, Iran told the IAEA, had been designed to produce low-enriched uranium for Iran's planned expansion of nuclear power plants and was therefore unable to generate weapons-grade highly enriched uranium.[149] The scientific community, however, expressed concern that the depth and extent of the Natanz plant implied a far more ambitious project.[150] Indeed, the IAEA's November 2003 report on Iran to its board of governors advised that "Iran has now acknowledged that it has been developing, for 18 years, a uranium centrifuge enrichment programme, and, for 12 years, a laser enrichment programme".[151]

It was further revealed in 2003 that Libya's secret negotiations with London and Washington over the abandoning of all of its WMD activities also yielded much valuable information about Iran's secret nuclear programme, shedding more light on the nature of its clandestine links with Pakistan and North Korea and the underground nuclear trade in parts of Asia.[152] It had thus emerged by late 2003 that Iran had established a multiple programme of research and development, based around a strategy of flexible acquisition. This was exactly what security observers had feared since the 1990s, for it was now evident that technically Iran could withdraw from the NPT by giving a three-month notice and then enrich uranium to weapons-grade level. The IAEA took this possibility very seriously, whose head noted that at the time of the revelations that "we were dealing with people who were willing to deceive to achieve their goals... [which], disturbingly, had been endorsed and carried out at the highest levels of the Iranian government".[153]

Glory at home had come at the price of a credibility gap abroad and a gaping security deficit. Trust, the cornerstone of the Islamic republic's value-based approach to international relations, had evaporated, and even the regime's protestations that the Leader had issued a fatwa (religious ruling) against the development and deployment of weapons of mass destruction now sounded opportunistic at best and disingenuous. Iranian leaders had, in Elbaradie's assessment, "oversold" the nuclear programme: "they had presented it domestically as the jewel in Tehran's crown, a scientific achievement for the nation. This made it tough to explain why they were suspending. Of course they neglected to point out to the Iranian public that the suspension [agreed as part of the terms of the October 2003 Tehran agreement] was a consequence of having deceived the IAEA for years".[154]

For all the razzmatazz surrounding the announcements of Iran's nuclear achievements, and despite the general support for the programme, public and elite opinion remained sharply divided over the costs and benefits of a nuclear programme now evolving under international pressure.[155] Amongst the public concerns still being raised were such issues as the affordability of the programme, the foreign policy fallout from it, and also that the focus on the nuclear programme was helping mask a whole host of socioeconomic and political issues.[156] What is interesting is that opinion was not divided purely along factional lines.[157] Thus, some conservative-leaning and reformist elements argued strongly that possessing WMDs was a national security imperative. Even secularists followed the realist narrative and supported the republic's nuclearization.

Developing a nuclear option appeared to be rooted in the geopolitical insecurity paradigm: As Iran's neighbourhood is insecure and inter-state relations are uncertain, with Israel and Pakistan in possession of nuclear weapons, it would make strategic sense for Iran to at least develop the option. Such senior clerics as Ayatollah Jannati declared in September 2003 from Tehran's Friday Prayers tribune that Iran, like North Korea, should leave the NPT instead of bearing the "extra humiliation" of added inspections and the signing of the Additional Protocol. While some were alive to the dangers of a nuclear arms race developing as a consequence of Iran's decision, this was not seen as a real threat because Iran's neighbours did not have the means or the will to go down the path of nuclearization. For other proponents of the nuclear programme, it provided many other R&D and scientific benefits apart from providing a renewable source of energy for the country for decades to come.

Sceptics too had a strong case to make. First, as Iran did not face an existential threat to itself and as its borders had been breached only once over the last 200 years, what conceivable justification was there for Iran to become a leading proliferator? Iran did not have any natural enemies to warrant the development of nuclear weapons. Second, pointing to North Korea and Pakistan, many remained sceptical of the value and extent of positive spinoffs arising from a civilian or military nuclear programme. In the same vein, they questioned the actual and opportunity costs of a comprehensive programme and pointed to the costs associated with assuring the safety of the facilities, environmental protection and removal of radioactive waste. Third, if anything, argued some advisors to the president, the deployment of nuclear weapons by Iran would adversely affect its relations with all of its neighbours, including Russia. So what would be the security benefits of such a programme when Iran would be exposing itself to counter-proliferation, a greater regional arms race that it could never win, and even hostile attack from Israel?

Iran now faced a classic security dilemma: Having hidden its nuclear activities from prying eyes for over ten years because of sanctions and for fear of attack by Israel or a joint US-Israeli operation, the exposure of its programme now made it all the more vulnerable to military intervention. If it now backed down under international pressure not only would it lose face and kudos, and end its posture of resistance to external pressure, but it would also suffer from a great legitimacy deficit at home, having justified the expense and secrecy of the programme as a national imperative and its achievements as a source of national pride. Yet, by not compromising, it could face referral to the Security Council and undo all its efforts to build confidence with the neighbouring states.

The Arab states, shocked by the extent of Iran's clandestine programme, were soon seeking even closer security cooperation with the United States. Khatami's strategy for the rest of his presidency, therefore, was to defuse the tensions through negotiations and thus prevent Iran's referral to the UN Security Council. Iranian leaders rightly recognized that once the file was transferred to the Security Council, Tehran would lose control and find itself at the mercy of world powers.[158] Iran's negotiating bottom lines were publicly explained by the former president, Rafsanjani, during Tehran's Friday prayers sermon on 3 October 2003: "our national security not be endangered, that our [Islamic] values and our sacred sites not be affected, that [military] secrets unconnected with the nuclear program not be revealed and that others fulfil their duty" to assist Iran with its stated civilian programme.[159] In this endeavour, Hassan Rouhani was given the leading role in explaining Iran's position, and in a high-level meeting with the director general of the IAEA in Tehran in October 2003, he assured the IAEA that Iran was ready to turn a new leaf – "the Iranian government has decided to engage in full co-operation with the IAEA" is how the Tehran declaration put it[160] – and by agreeing to implement the so-called Additional Protocol of the NPT would thus allow wide-ranging and snap inspections access to its technical team. This gesture, animated through the October 2003 and November 2004 agreements with the EU troika to suspend enrichment, proved to be the most significant breakthrough of the crisis until 2013 and the Rouhani administration's public commitment to end the crisis through negotiations with the six parties of the five permanent members of the Security Council and Germany (known as '5+1' or '3+3').

The Khatami administration's approach to the crisis is crisply explained by the country's chief nuclear negotiator at the time, and the person responsible for charting a policy line consistent with the state's main interests – to avoid attack and to keep the programme alive – while trying to accommodate as many of the country's elite interests as possible. In his authoritative book, *National Security and Nuclear Diplomacy*, among the many issues that Hassan Rouhani alludes to are the domestic problems faced by Khatami's administration, in which external pressures so quickly translated into an elite crisis that an issue of such national importance became the object of internal fights: "So", he argues, "the first sign of dissent at the decision-making level occurred only after the start of the [international] crisis".[161] Consensus in other words broke down only after the extent of the programme had become public through external channels. Being accused by hardliners of bringing shame onto the country and "everlasting disgrace" dramatically polarized intra-elite positions.[162] Added to this was the role that factional rivalries had come to play in the nuclear crisis: All the parties were acutely aware that maximum social credit would go to the faction that broke the deadlock and managed to cut a deal with the West (read: the United States), and for such social capital rivals would go out of their way to scupper a deal. This happened repeatedly during Khatami's presidency, but ironically continued into Ahmadinejad's term as the reform camp now did what it could to take the 'freeze-for-freeze' deal, which they themselves had spoken of being successfully negotiated with the EU in 2006 by Ahmadinejad's team.

So when in March 2004 the IAEA board of governors heard that Iran had continued to build centrifuge machines and was not making a full declaration of its past enrichment activities, and following European protestations on the matter, the window on a negotiated settlement appeared to be closing. President Khatami effectively said so in June 2004: "We have no moral commitment any more to suspend uranium enrichment. If the draft resolution proposed by the European countries is approved by the IAEA, Iran will reject it. If Europe has no commitment toward Iran, then Iran will not have a commitment toward Europe. We assume they are not respecting their commitments".[163] Yet both sides still hung on and the November 2004 Paris agreement is indicative of the efforts being made to find a path forward. The Paris agreement is important for a number of reasons. First, (temporary) suspension of enrichment was a precursor for more cooperation and not an end in itself. Second, the troika committed the European Union to work with Iran to improve its aviation industry, economic conditions, and even help prepare it for WTO membership. Third, the EU agreed to support Iran's efforts to develop its nascent nuclear industry and facilitate access to technical know-how in the field of nuclear industry. Fourth, and perhaps most importantly of all, the troika agreed to address one of Tehran's core concerns by providing Iran with what the document refers to as national security guarantees and suspension of support for the Iraq-based armed opposition group (Mojahedin-e Khalgh). Finally, the agreement pointed to a future of stability, in which the accord would become a basis for confidence building and normalization of relations with Iran. The Paris agreement carried in it foreign policy successes for Iran and also the basis on which to find a solution to the nuclear crisis. In terms of future developments following the difficulties encountered during Ahmadinejad's presidency, the agreement also showed European preparedness to work towards dialogue with Iran without prejudice.

From Khatami to Ahmadinejad

Khatami's multifaceted foreign policy strategy aimed to take the republic through the international doors that Rafsanjani had managed to open. At its heart, the ambition was to end Iran's international isolation, reduce the stresses put upon it by misunderstanding and miscalculation, to secure the means to improve social and economic conditions, and turn détente into permanent peace. Despite his efforts, two insurmountable forces limited his success. First, the domestic forces and interests wedded to the ideals of the revolution found in him such a threat to Iran's unique brand of revolutionary Islam that, in the course of his presidency, they mobilized to undermine his efforts at coexistence with the West. But the greater obstacle to his efforts was the changing international context. First, there was 9/11 and the direct and indirect challenges and opportunities that US intervention in the region brought and with the re-securitization of MENA inter-state relations. Following this was the fallout from Iran's nuclear-related activities which tied Iran's political elite to a protracted diplomatic standoff with the West and the wider international community at the expense of dialogue as a tool of confidence building. By the time Khatami had handed over to Ahmadinejad, Tehran had buried dialogue, détente. The essence of pluralism (working together with other parties irrespective of differences) had been substituted with singularism; it was back to 'we will do what we want and there is nothing that anybody can do about it'.

It was argued earlier that revolutionary states are inherently securitized and their fate and survival are intrinsically linked to their behaviour in the international (external) realm. In revolutionary Iran, however, the external was internalized from the start, and the hostage crisis and the Iran-Iraq War reinforced this condition. Therefore, while it is clear that Tehran has had a great hand in changing the regional dynamics, it has itself also been affected by the same. The external, in a revolutionary and ideological setting, influences the internal, and in Iran's faction-ridden political establishment in actual fact changes the domestic balance of power, too. The voters, who have played their part in shaping Iran's external orientation, are often the background to the power play at the elite level, and given that the boundaries of political action are predetermined (selection of candidates and the regime-set lists for election), it is not surprising that Iran's strategic priorities and the regime's strategic sentiments play themselves out in the course of elections. Furthermore, as the Islamic republic has not experienced a period of stability in its international relations, this partly accounts for the sense of paranoia present even in the mind of the reformist forces, but it is actually prevalent amongst the so-called revolutionary (pro-Khamenei) elites. So, in a sense inevitably, the regional came to shape the national in the aftermath of 9/11 and as the edge of war drew closer to Iran's own borders, its elite retrenched and fell back on the republic's revolutionary ideals as a first line of defence and a strategy of push-back (uncompromising unilateralism) as its second.

The fate of Khatami's dialogue of civilizations, arguably, was sealed by forces beyond his control. That massive factional swing could happen in a country presided over by the champion of dialogue and détente was anticipated following the 2003 Iraq War, some two years before Ahmadinejad's rise to power in fact, in the following way: "if the US finds resurrecting an Iraqi unitary state a protracted and problematic affair, is forced to maintain a large military presence right next door to Iran and intensifies its intolerance of Iran's nuclear programme" – which it did do – "Iranian conservatives", predicted a strategic assessment, "may close ranks against a prominent enemy and delay the process of reform".[164] Conservatives did close ranks, and insecurity tightened the grip of the security establishment in Iran and conservative forces close to the Leader – already nervous about the consequences of continuing reform – not only turned off the taps of reform but also helped to bring to power an overtly populist and ideological neoconservative whose whole purpose was to end détente and, in a throwback to the 1980s, implement an 'independent' foreign policy characterized by resistance against hegemony. The die had been cast for the policies of Khatami's successor.

Foreign policy of the neoconservatives

Ahmadinejad's presidential term started with the nuclear crisis coming to a boil as President Khatami ended the self-imposed moratorium on the country's uranium enrichment activities as his last executive act in July 2005. It is fair to say that from the beginning, Ahmadinejad's administration had to balance the nuclear programme against its blatantly populist socioeconomic measures. Iran's new negotiating posture under Ahmadinejad led in September 2005 to the IAEA Board's 'non-compliance' resolution which the new administration declared the IAEA resolution "illegal and illogical".[165] President Mahmoud Ahmadinejad had come to power in 2005, under somewhat questionable circumstances, aiming to adopt an altogether different foreign policy agenda. Representing a unique case of Iranian neoconservatism, Ahmadinejad drew his foreign policy inspirations from the revolutionary core of the republic, which in the wake of the nuclear crisis had become enmeshed with a heightened sense of nationalism.

Tinged with populist rhetoric, Ahmadinejad came to articulate a foreign policy that pressed the peddles of Islamism and anti-imperialism, but along with it also that of nationalism. His populism was not dissimilar to the twentieth century African and Latin American post-colonial narratives of state control and anti-imperialism. But it also had a unique Iranian aspect to it, to be found in his critique of the conciliatory approach of his predecessor to relations with the West and the outside world more generally. The devaluing of the revolution's principles was a crime committed by the previous government and a robust response to the pressures of the West for Iran to abandon its nuclear achievements. Thus, throughout the election campaign, and not so unopenly underlined by the Leader as well, Ahmadinejad criticized his predecessor for compromising the Islamic republic's standing and selling out, in the nuclear talks, Iran's core values. He in turn sought power, and legitimacy, from the republic's revolutionary legacy: Resistance, independence, steadfastness. Much of his rhetoric fell on a receptive national audience dissatisfied with Khatami's policies at home and unhappy with the unresolved status of the nuclear crisis. Ahmadinejad in fact posited his alternative strategy through a critique of Khatami's approach to the nuclear crisis, dismissing many of his experienced advisors and policy interlocutors, and aiming to undo much of what had been achieved under the 2003 Tehran and the 2004 Paris agreements with the EU3 was his agenda. Negotiating on Iran's terms, as he saw it, would form the first plank of his foreign policy, and from the outside this was seen as a step backwards. For interested parties which were directly involved in the nuclear talks, "the mood... rapidly turned bleak".[166]

The second external driver of Ahmadinejad's new foreign policy approach was the deepening of post-9/11 geopolitical crisis engulfing the region, particularly the consolidation of US' military presence in Afghanistan and Iraq and the logistical military chain which this had created in support of the US-led military campaigns in virtually every country bordering the Islamic republic. Ahmadinejad, with full support from the Supreme Leader, was intent on challenging the US' grip in such spaces as Iraq and to ensure that they would be sufficiently unsettled in both Iraq and Afghanistan as to deter them from taking aggressive measure against Iran. Within weeks of the Iraq War, it was also clear that Tehran would have a free hand in the affairs of its western neighbour, and despite the occupying Anglo-American forces, the makeup of the post-Saddam political forces would be such that Iran's influence would become paramount.

The third strand of his foreign policy approach was informed by a high degree of self-belief in the Islamic republic's emergence as a major regional and Asian power at a highly volatile moment in history. This belief was premised on Iran's virtuous role as a leading Muslim power and as the only country capable of changing, improving, the MENA region's relationship with the outside world on the Muslim peoples' own terms. The previous administration had already declared that "no one can deny that Iran is a regional power", so Ahmadinejad continued this narrative but with a sharper edge.[167] So he started his fight back against the West by a series of rather antagonistic assertions about Israel, its right to exist and the authenticity of the Holocaust. Iranian leaders had picked on Israel before, so while Ahmadinejad's stance on Israel appeared harsher than his predecessors (but nevertheless echoing Khomeini's comments), it was his blatant Holocaust denial that set him apart from his predecessors and indeed other Muslim leaders. Nevertheless, his anti-Zionist and anti-Israel stance gained him much popularity across the Muslim world. He set himself up as the unflinching supporter of Muslim rights in the Holy Land and the bravest proponent of Palestinian rights. From Indonesia to Bolivia, he became the most popular populist national leader. And like all populist leaders, he thrived on mass adulation and, ironically, the more unpopular he became at home the more he used overseas visits as a demonstration of his international popularity. These increasingly became occasions for Ahmadinejad to demonstrate Iran's growing soft power under his presidency.

Nuclear crisis deepens

The nuclear crisis that erupted in 2002 dominated the twilight years of the Khatami presidency and, despite his government's efforts in May 2003 (to mend fences with the United States) and November 2004 (to deescalate the nuclear crisis), Khatami handed to his populist and inexperienced successor the open file of the nuclear programme, at a time when the security problems engulfing the region were at their height. Given the national importance of the nuclear programme, from the beginning the new Iranian president, buoyed by the support of the Leader and the revolutionary guards, focused on the nuclear crisis as a symbol of the Islamic republic's virtues and values and demonstration of the country's independence and freedom to chart its own destiny unhindered by outside pressure.

Reversing some of Khatami's nuclear policies, the new administration announced in May 2005 that it was resuming uranium enrichment, which had been frozen under Khatami as part of the November 2004 Paris accords negotiated by Iran's chief nuclear negotiator, Dr Hassan Rouhani. In 2006 Tehran asked the IAEA to remove the seals from the Natanz facility for Iranian scientists to begin experimental enrichment, all on a very limited scale. But none of this meant that Iran was abandoning diplomacy, and remarkably Iran's new secretary of the supreme national security council and a confidant of the Leader (Ali Larijani) was continuing to explain to whom Tehran saw as reliable interlocutors that Iran remained "interested in direct talks with the United States... ready to discuss not only Iran's nuclear issues, but also Iraq, Afghanistan, Hezbollah, and Hamas... [to] assist with security in Baghdad and also help establish a national unity government in Lebanon".[168] Indeed, a lack of reciprocity by the West and their apparent haste to refer Iran to the Security Council under Chapter VII of the UN Charter (namely threats to peace and breaches of the peace) in July 2006 – a month before Iran could state its formal position on the question of suspension of uranium enrichment posed in June –seemed to have tipped the balance in Tehran in favour of pushing ahead with the programme.[169] The nightmare scenario of the previous administration had been realized: Iran had now been referred to the Security Council. The ensuing Security Council resolution, "of dubious legality"[170] and logic, was seen by the Iranian side as being politically driven and its timing designed to scupper the chances of success in the Larijani-Solana discussions. So, just days after issuing its twenty-one-page response on 22nd August to the EU-negotiated package of incentives to freeze nuclear activities in their tracks, the president announced that Iran was going ahead with the completion of the Arak heavy-water reactor complex and in October formally notified the IAEA that it had begun testing a new cascade of 162 centrifuges.[171]

As to why the conditions for negotiations deteriorated so rapidly we should turn our attention to the intense conflict raging in the region. On the one hand, in Iraq, US forces were now being challenged by both former Ba'athists and emerging Shia groups in government and in civil society closely aligned with Iran, and on the other, the Iran-sponsored Hezbollah and Iran-supported Hamas were waging an extraordinary military campaign against Israel which had put the apparently invincible Israel Defense Force on the defensive. Iran appeared to be pulling the strings in the two theatres of greatest importance in the region – the Persian Gulf and the Arab-Israeli front. This wider context provided the backdrop for the UN discussions regarding Iran's nuclear activities and consolidated the view in Washington, backed by its Arab allies it has to be said, that the Islamic republic was now the cause of all mischief in the Middle East. Iran may have already discounted a compromise with the West but it had not accounted for the hostile reaction received from virtually all of its regional neighbours (bar Iraq and Turkey). Iran's regional relations from this point on were to be determined by the logic of geopolitics, and the region's geostrategic conditions being shaped by US hands. Iran, in the region's new Cold War setting, was a challenge to the US and its interests in the region and should be subject to maximum pressure: The Islamic republic was not unfamiliar with pressure, but this was a new world for Tehran, in which the odds of a US attack on Iran following the Lebanon war were put at "50–50" by a state department official.[172]

Reflecting on the smooth transfer of Iran's nuclear file to the Security Council in 2006 Elbaradei puts his finger on the importance of geopolitics in shaping relations in saying "it was staggering to compare the difference in treatment of North Korea and Iran. North Korea had walked out of the NPT and made explicit threats about developing nuclear weapons (and would in fact test its first weapon less than six months later, in October 2006), yet the Americans were ready to join them in a direct dialogue, and Chris Hill [US special envoy to North Korea] seemed to be in Pyongyang every other day. By contrast, Iran, which remained under safeguards and party to the NPT, was penalized for possibly having future intentions to develop nuclear weapons, and the Americans refused to talk to them without precondition".[173] Inflexibility and the heated differences over the enrichment issue – the West wanted immediate suspension of all enrichment activities and Iran would only agree as part of the negotiations and alongside guarantees that it would not face 'aggression' (military attack or further sanctions) – paved the way back to the Security Council and the unanimously adopted resolution 1747 on 24 March 2007, imposing a range of sanctions on Iran and also calling on Iran to comply with the earlier resolution (1696 of July 2006).[174] Iran's response was to increase the number of centrifuges at Natanz and to subject all future agreements with the IAEA to Majlis scrutiny (and ultimately veto); yet wiser heads saw in resolution 1747's incremental mechanism "future political and economic threats to Iran" and even endangering "the national security of the country".[175] Security Council resolution 1803, passed on 3rd March 2008 with support of fourteen members and one abstention, turned the screw tighter by limiting Iran's (land, air, sea) communications links with the outside world, the access of its main banks and financial institutions to finance from overseas, and limits on its governmental personnel and institutions to function outside of the country.

Resolution 1835, passed on 27 September 2008, which reiterated the need for Iran to comply fully with previous demands of the Security Council was the precursor to the much tougher resolution 1929 (issued on 9 June 2010), which began imposing sanctions on Iran's main lifeline – its oil exports. Imposition of more stringent sanctions by the European Union and the United States following the passage of resolution 1929 totally handicapped Iran and left it as isolated as it had ever been since the revolution. Most telling sanctions included the EU's severing of its energy links with Iran, sanctioning of all Iranian banks (including the country's central bank) and denying it any financial mobility. The denial in March 2012 of access to the Brussels-based SWIFT (Society for Worldwide Interbank Financial Telecommunication), the world's biggest electronic payment system that handles most cross-border payments, in response to the international sanctions regime and a direct European Union order, effectively cut Iran off from the international economic system. SWIFT said in a statement that "disconnecting banks is an extraordinary and unprecedented step for SWIFT. It is a direct result of international and multilateral action to intensify financial sanctions against Iran".[176]

Meanwhile, enrichment activities had continued. Iran notified the IAEA in April 2008 that it was planning to introduce a new generation of locally designed sub-critical gas centrifuges (IR-3) as well. In 2009 it again notified the IAEA that it was building another enrichment facility (Fordow near Qom) to contain sixteen cascades with a total of approximately 3,000 (IR-1) centrifuges.[177] The government had accelerated the construction of Natanz, which became operational in February 2007. It should be noted that as of early 2008 Iran had completed the installation of eighteen 164-machine cascades at the Natanz enrichment plant, which were operating at full capacity, though obviously with the expected technical problems that such a sophisticated facility would face. The technical information showed that there had been nearly 3,000 (2,952 to be precise) operational centrifuges at this facility. But Ahmadinejad's declared intention was to grow the centrifuges to a massive total of 50,000. In total, it had converted 320 tonnes of uranium into UF6 between March 2004 and 2008.

The step change in Iran's nuclear activities after the 2005 elections is illustrated by the fact that a total 3,970 kilograms of UF6 had been fed into the operating cascades between February 2007 and May 2008, producing low-enriched uranium (up to 4.7 per cent U-235 according to Iran's own Atomic Energy Agency). Iran accumulated 600 to 700 kilograms of low-enriched uranium in just one year, 2008. Such a stockpile alarmed observers and was described by scientists as reaching a breakout capability – the brink of nuclear weapons status – since running 600 to 700 kilogram of low-enriched uranium through Iran's enrichment facilities again would provide enough fissile material for one bomb.[178] And the process continued into Ahmadinejad's second term, in which in less than a year (between December 2009 and February 2010) Iran had accumulated an additional 257 kilograms of low-enriched UF6.[179] Even more significant was Iran's declaration in 2010 that it intended to enrich uranium to the maximum permissible, namely to production of enriched UF6 to 20 per cent U-235. Subsequently, the IAEA confirmed that "between 9 and 11 February 2010" enrichment levels of up to 19.8 per cent U-235 were obtained at Iran's pilot enrichment facility.[180] Tehran was intent in driving home its nuclear advantage and, in the face of sanctions, by the end of 2011 not only had the Bushehr nuclear power plant become operational but Iran had increased its holdings of low-enriched uranium to over 4,500 kilograms and its stock of the higher 20 per cent enriched uranium to over 70 kilograms. Despite successes in the nuclear field, the pressure of the UN, US, and EU sanctions – most intensive in history according to the Obama administration – and clandestine subversion of the programme, forced a stock-taking in Tehran, and it was no surprise that Iran's nuclear diplomacy under Ahmadinejad, as a main feature of his foreign policy, became one of the critical aspects of the 2013 presidential election campaign.

Tehran acknowledged President Obama's message of compromise from the outset of his presidency in January 2009 but as not much more than an admission of guilt for the United States' mischievous behaviour towards Iran. In addition to mutual suspicion, by summer of 2009, political turmoil in Tehran following Ahmadinejad's re-election had so intensified the sense of insecurity amongst the elite that there seemed little room for negotiations. Also, as noted by Takeyh, Tehran's foreign policy establishment was in such turmoil following the rupture of the elite into the warring factions supporting Ahmadinejad's re-election and those who supported Mousavi's bid that no single and credible voice was coming out of Tehran: "Iran does not have a foreign policy right now. It has domestic politics, and its foreign policies are just a sporadic expression of that".[181] Furthermore, given Washington's rather sceptical view of the 2009 election process and the open and vocal American support for the protestors in Iran made making a compromise with a seemingly illegitimate president harder to pull off. Information released in late 2009 that Iran had yet another small, but secret and undeclared ('backup'), enrichment facility (Fordow near Qom) provided all the ammunition that the opponents of a deal needed to intensify pressure on Iran.

From Tel Aviv to Riyadh and the rest of the GCC, demands for Iran's nuclear programme being accounted for and curtailed were now resonating with world powers, yet Tehran appeared committed to a negotiated settlement of the crisis and, even as late as autumn 2009, had proposed direct bilateral talks with the United States regarding technical support for nuclear fuel transfer (out of the country of the 1,200 kilograms of low-enriched uranium accumulated) and also fuel and a modern replacement for Tehran University's aging research reactor.[182] The Security Council passed a fourth, and a much stronger, sanctions resolution in May 2010, in the midst of Iran's negotiations with Turkey and Brazil (as trusted honest-brokers) to defuse tensions by transferring the low-enriched uranium to Turkey. Needless to say, the new SC resolution killed off any chance of the trilateral approach bearing fruit.

However, a close reading of the evidence suggests that Iran could have arrested the escalation of the crisis and prevented the country from being subject to escalating and crippling mandatory sanctions. As has been shown, despite its own efforts and that of other countries (Austria, Brazil, China, Germany, Russia, South Africa, and Turkey) and inter-governmental organizations (IAEA, ICO, NAM) to find a negotiated settlement from its peak in 2002, the nuclear crisis continued to play a major role in shaping Iran's relations with the outside world. Much of the problem at the height of the crisis appears to have resulted from American suspicions, being fed by its own regional allies, of Tehran's ultimate intentions and the distrust in Iran's sincerity following the rhetoric and gesture politics of Ahmadinejad. But, at the same time, Tehran's own approach also had impacted the flow of negotiations. Tehran's own behaviour, it is asserted, "managed to transmute an issue of compliance with its non-proliferation obligations into one of nationalism and self-determination",[183] thus making compromise hugely more difficult.

Once the nuclear programme became a question of national pride and a totem of modernity, it was practically impossible for the populist gesture-politics president to propel the problem towards the negotiating table. Ahmadinejad had become a willing hostage of his own rhetoric, with grave consequences for the country, and had left his successor with a major problem to unknot domestically and in relation to being able to dislodge the programme from the grip of the Security Council. Noting Tehran's diplomatic and political mistakes after 2005, Mousavian, for example, points to foreign policy consequences of political changes in Iran itself, arguing that from being a "legal-political issue" during Khatami's presidency – and therefore a subject of negotiations ultimately – the nuclear crisis had become a "security-political-legal issue" under his successor, making it almost impossible to manage along the diplomatic track: An unstable triangle arguably, in which security would come to dominate – and therefore inhibit a negotiated settlement. Mousavian further draws an explicit link between executive changes in Iran and the policies that resulted in the referral of the country to the Security Council, from whence the issue was turned "into a totally security matter during the Ahmadinejad period".[184] The intrusive sanctions after

2010 did indeed pose a major national challenge and, by emasculating its national economy, did threaten the country's socioeconomic cohesion and security.

Populist Iran responds to encirclement

Ahmadinejad's confrontational posture towards the West and his inflammatory rhetoric were partly a result of the populist seam running through his administration and the sense of grandeur informing his worldview, but the regime's more aggressive stance was also partly due to the rather unhidden strategy of regime change being promoted in the United States. With American forces surrounding Iran on virtually every border, and its president marking out Iran as a threat to the post-9/11 order, it would have been untypical of Tehran not to take note and prepare a response. Iran's new strategy was shaped in the context of the ongoing wars on its borders, external pressures arising from its nuclear programme, the steady securitization of the regional system and, particularly importantly, the United States' declaration in its 2006 National Security Strategy that, in two dedicated paragraphs, marked Iran out as the greatest challenge from a single country facing the United States. In the words of the strategy document:

> We may face no greater challenge from a single country than from Iran... the regime continues to claim that it does not seek to develop nuclear weapons. The Iranian regime's true intentions are clearly revealed by the regime's refusal to negotiate in good faith; its refusal to come into compliance with its international obligations by providing the IAEA access to nuclear sites and resolving troubling questions; and the aggressive statements of its President calling for Israel to "be wiped off the face of the earth." The United States has joined with our EU partners and Russia to pressure Iran to meet its international obligations and provide objective guarantees that its nuclear program is only for peaceful purposes.... As important as these nuclear issues are, the United States has broader concerns regarding Iran. The Iranian regime sponsors terrorism; threatens Israel; seeks to thwart Middle East peace; disrupts democracy in Iraq; and denies the aspirations of its people for freedom. The nuclear issue and our other concerns can ultimately be resolved only if the Iranian regime makes the strategic decision to change these policies, open up its political system, and afford freedom to its people. This is the ultimate goal of U.S. policy. In the interim, we will continue to take all necessary measures to protect our national and economic security against the adverse effects of their bad conduct. The problems lie with the illicit behavior and dangerous ambition of the Iranian regime, not the legitimate aspirations and interests of the Iranian people. Our strategy is to block the threats posed by the regime while expanding our engagement and outreach to the people the regime is oppressing.[185]

To Tehran, this was more like rag to a bull and no longer mere idle threat; it was a declaration of intent, of efforts to orchestrate a velvet revolution in the country. Indeed, armed with the belief that the Iranian people were waiting for their American saviour, the Bush administration doubled its efforts to isolate Iran and even provided funding for the CIA for stealth operations to destabilize the country's economy and institutions.[186]

With the nuclear negotiations in an impasse and the US, though more vulnerable in the region, still intent on 'containing' Iran, it was not hard for Tehran to adjust course after 2006 and pursue a more aggressive and uncompromising international posture. Thus, Ahmadinejad embarked on building new international partnerships and deepening existing ones. Having successfully negotiated observer status for Iran in the Shanghai Cooperation Organization (SCO) in 2005, in declaring its desire to see the SCO emerge as a global counterforce to NATO and Western domineering, Tehran submitted its application for full membership in 2006. This was the first time since the revolution that Iran had voluntarily proceeded to negotiate entry into a political-security partnership with other major powers. This move was the end of the 'equilibrium' strategy and equidistance between the great powers; 'neither East nor West' was, perhaps out of necessity, increasingly about acceleration of the Eastward tilt which had been in evidence since the 1980s. Equally important, application to join was a dramatic recognition, in a proud and fiercely independent regime, of the need to find some cover from the onslaught of the United States.

In regional power politics terms, Ahmadinejad's success in positioning Iran at the heart of the regional resistance front had also exposed the country to mounting pressures from the moderate Arab camp (all the way from Morocco and Tunisia to Egypt, Jordan and Saudi Arabia) on the one hand and Israel on the other. For both, Iran's role in Lebanon and Palestine and Tehran's extensive links with Hamas (and to a lesser extent Islamic Jihad) and Hezbollah were unsettling. But for the Arab states in particular, Tehran's apparently overwhelming influence in Iraq had posed a new and unprecedented geopolitical and geo-cultural challenge. Iraq, they feared, had been turned from the eastern gateway to the Arab region to the motorway for the extension of Iranian influence and power to the Mashreq. By 2008 the Arab states had begun to regroup and Obama's electoral success provided them with more solid assurances that the United States would no longer substitute adventurism for foreign policy and that the new White House would reach out to them to find collective solutions to the region's many problems. They were now able to rely on the US without the mention of their superpower ally causing them embarrassment or anxiety.

Of course the Arab states and Israel, as much as the West, shared a big fear: The apparently unstoppable intensive and comprehensive nuclear programme that Ahmadinejad had so vociferously and proudly championed. For Israel, however, Iran's programme would be a direct high-level security (and, to some Israelis, an existential) challenge, and for the Arab states, a sign of Iran's drive for regional domination, if not hegemony. Put plainly, "the basic fact is that the Iranian nuclear program poses a serious and equal threat to all the GCC states".[187] Indeed, in the Persian Gulf context, Iran's apparently rapid progress in the nuclear field after 2007 had set the alarm bells ringing even more loudly. From the GCC states' perspective, the situation was deteriorating rather rapidly.[188] These fears had compelled senior GCC figures, such as the UAE's foreign minister, Sheikh Abdullah bin Zayed al-Nahyan, to formally raise the subject of Iran's behaviour with the US. One such occasion was with the Secretary of State Hillary Clinton on the margins of the donor's conference for Palestine in Sharm el-Sheikh in tones unheard of since the 1980s.[189] Iran was portrayed as an aggressive power intent on compromising the security of its neighbours.

Furthermore, pressure on Iran had been building up since the July 2008 Geneva meeting between Iran and the 5+1 group and their submitted package of incentives. The negotiating ball had been in Tehran's court in terms of a formal response since then and given the direct security aspects of the nuclear programme (and the fact that the regime had successfully turned the programme into a national symbol of state power and of technological prowess), it was not surprising that this matter did not feature as an election issue in 2009. But at the back of everyone's mind was the need for a response to the package of incentives on offer, and also the fact that the nuclear negotiations directly would feed into the diplomatic exchanges being mooted between Tehran and Washington. Internally and internationally, the nuclear programme would be a major issue, despite it not receiving much air domestically. As we saw, Ahmadinejad's first term in office ended with the IAEA no clearer about Iran's ultimate motivations for its broad nuclear programme as it was at the start of the negotiations process in 2003. Indeed, the last comment from the outgoing head of the IAEA was that his gut feeling was that Iran was looking to acquire a nuclear weapons' capability![190] The backdrop to the tenth presidential poll, therefore, was internal socioeconomic and political problems and also a complex set of potentially difficult international problems coming into sharp focus. Yet, following it, Tehran appeared poised to allow its influence to bear across the region.

The Islamic republic's '1969 moment'

This was but one aspect of Ahmadinejad's efforts to build new partnerships as his administration went out of its way to develop links in other parts of the world, notably with Latin American countries, mainly those opposed to the United States, and also African and Middle Eastern states interested in the strengthening of Iran's 'resistance front' against the US and 'Zionist conspirators'. Intent on demonstrating Iran's 'soft power', this government focused much of its efforts on challenging its self-declared main rival (Israel) regionally and internationally also while building strategic partnerships with anti-US countries – trying to build partnerships on the premise of shared enemies. Partnerships with anti-American governments of Venezuela and Bolivia were part of this strategy,[191] and the effort also extended to deepening relations with Nicaragua and Cuba. Often trade and investment plans – joint manufacturing, car production, tractor-assembly plants, joint ventures in energy and petrochemical production partnerships – underpinned what were essentially political exchanges. Thus, the Iranian president declared on an official visit to Brazil in November 2009: "Iran, Brazil and Venezuela can play a determining role in planning and establishing new orders in the world".[192]

Ahmadinejad turned a trip to Lebanon in October 2010 into a show of political force, praising Iran's ally (Hezbollah) and also making a point of visiting the border villages with Israel. The trip was summed by one Lebanese commentator as follows:

> He is coming for his own Iranian reasons. He wants to show the world that Iran is a regional power, and that Iran is a confrontation state with Israel. The fact that he will be visiting Bint Jbeil in the south, which Hizballah calls the capital of liberation, means a lot to him. First he wants to convey to his people that Iran is preponderant. He wants to show that Iran is a major power player that must be treated with respect and understanding, and must be engaged instead of confronted.[193]

He, further, resorted to using international platforms, such as the D-8 group of the most populous Muslim countries' (who met in Nigeria in July 2010, shortly after the imposition of new tough UN sanctions on the country), into attacks on the United States and for garnering support for Iran in the nuclear standoff. A year later, in November, Foreign Minister Mottaki toured four African countries of Burkina Faso, Ghana, Togo and Benin to cultivate closer political and economic links with these countries.

It was discussed above that the late-1960s appeared to the monarch as the golden opportunity for pushing Iran to extend its influence regionally and internationally. Arguably, the Islamic republic's 1969 moment may have arrived in the aftermath of the 2003 military intervention in Iraq. After Tehran's immediate fear that the Islamic republic may be the third target, after Afghanistan and Iraq, of US intervention in the region evaporated, and following the US' unwise rejection of Iran's offer of a 'grand bargain', Tehran sought to capitalize on America's mistakes and exposed position in Iraq to create an area of strategic depth for itself. Thus, after decades of limited success in extending its influence beyond its core allies, with the fall of the Ba'ath regime, weakening American influence in Iraq and beyond, strengthening of Iran's grip on Iraq, and the regional popularity of the country's 'resistance' strategy, it was tempting to see the nature of changes in the region as providing the Islamic republic with its first strategic opportunity to extend its influence across the Middle East and widen its Muslim hinterland.

By the time Ahmadinejad occupied the presidency Tehran was all ready to cash in the strategic benefits of the regime's 1969 moment. Two years after the Iraq War, and despite the escalating nuclear crisis with the West, the US (despite its overwhelming military might) was less steady on its feet in the region,

Iraq was at Iran's mercy, Tehran's allies in the Levant remained strong, while America's Arab allies appeared to be in complete disarray as a result of Bush's policies in the region. Crucially, income from rapidly rising oil prices – from less than around $25 per barrel in 2003 to $75 per barrel in 2006 and to $141 per barrel in 2008 – was again filling the coffers of state after years of low oil prices, which in turn emboldened Ahmadinejad and fuelled his foreign policy adventures.[194] Regular shows of its growing military might, in terms of advanced missile systems in particular, were to underline its real power strengths and its increasingly effective reach to deter and, if need be, attack its enemies.

No other event, however, more than the thirty-four-day war in Lebanon in 2006 provided the theatre for demonstration of Iran's hard and soft power. In every day of Hezbollah's month-long campaign against Israel, the longest of any Arab party against Israel, Iran flaunted its regional advantages against its Arab and Israeli adversaries. To Israel's astonishment, Hezbollah fired 3,970 (largely Iranian-supplied) rockets into Israel, pointedly exposing its urban centres to attack – 'no one is safe!' – fired radar-guided anti-ship missiles off the coast of Lebanon, resisted Israeli armoured incursion into southern Lebanon with strong anti-tank fire (including laser-guided missiles), and did not bend under the weight of the aerial bombardment of its bases in the south and in the capital.[195] Moreover, at first reluctantly, all Arab regimes had little option but to line up behind the Arab side (Hezbollah) and condemn Israel and its (Western) backers for the devastation wrought on Lebanon.[196] The war isolated Iran's adversaries, brought Arab regimes into line, squeezed Israel, and brought closer the Iran–Syria alliance. Hezbollah's defiance and its survival had turned its turbaned leaders into the most popular on the Arab street and Tehran, drawing on more than twenty years of political, economic, religious and security influence in Lebanon, used Hezbollah's war with the IDF to enhance Iran's reputation in the Arab world, and, by virtue of its close association with Hezbollah, also improved the standing of its resistance axis in relation to all other Arab parties with an interest in the Arab–Israeli conflict.[197]

Iran was on the right side of the struggle, and the demonstrated ability of its Shia protégé to sustain an intensive military campaign against the most powerful military force in the region raised Iran's standing in the Arab region. For the Arab regimes, however, the war and Iran's role in it underlined the growing strength of the Tehran-led 'Shia crescent' in the Arab region and the need to counter it.[198] Ahmadinejad's blusters and the regime's hand in Lebanon, Palestine and elsewhere during a period of Arab weakness encouraged the main Sunni Arab regimes to coalesce together and seek containment of the Islamic republic through a combination of dialogue (Qatar inviting Ahmadinejad to the GCC summit in Doha in December 2007), resistance (supporting Iran's adversaries in Iraq, Palestine, Afghanistan, Pakistan, Lebanon, and Sudan), balancing (strengthening the military partnership with NATO countries, particularly the United States), and pressure (pushing the US and its allies to isolate Iran, threaten military action and impose more sanctions on it). By the beginning of Ahmadinejad's second term the combination of regional and international reactions, and the bandwagoning of regional powers with the US, had visibly raised the pressure on his administration's ability to hold its confrontational line.

So, by mid-2010, the strategic landscape was beginning to look very different and Iran appeared to have squandered its strategic advantages through miscalculation and bellicose diplomacy. Iran's diplomatic isolation was being reinforced through a series of punishing economic sanctions, which intensified pressure not only on the regime's policy instruments but also on key corporations and individuals suspected of being involved in its nuclear programme. The sanctions also strained many of Iran's economic ties with European as well as other Asian countries. President Obama's approach of tight and punishing sanctions was working, and this strategy he had pursued on the basis that the Iranian elite was rational, calculating and therefore responsive to pressure and incentives. As he himself put at the twilight of Ahmadinejad's presidency: "I think it's entirely legitimate to say that this is a regime that does not share our world view or our values. I do think… that as we look at how they operate and the decisions they've made over the past three decades, that they care about the regime's survival. They're sensitive to the opinions of the people and they are troubled by the isolation that they're experiencing".[199]

In this tightening of the screw, Iran's access points were also hardened, as in the UAE for example, through which much of Iran's trade was traversing. So, just weeks after the introduction of a new round of sanctions in June 2010, the UAE ambassador to the IAEA, Hamad al-Kaabi, confirmed that its observation of the UN sanctions had "led to the shutting down of dozens of international and local companies involved in money laundering and proliferation of dual use and dangerous materials. Security forces have interdicted scores of ships suspected of carrying illicit cargo and seized numerous sensitive shipments that could be used for the manufacture of weapons systems, including specialised aluminium sheets, titanium, high-speed computers and sophisticated machine tools".[200]

As already noted, pressure on Iran continued to mount after 2010 when a new set of UN, US and EU sanctions were introduced to force Iran to change course in the nuclear field. To put the impact of sanctions in context, it is noteworthy that Iran's oil exports in 2012 averaged no more than 1.5 million barrels per day (mb/d), well below the 2.5 mb/d that Iran had intended to produce in its annual calculations. The International Energy Agency calculated in its March 2013 oil market report that Iran's maximum sustainable crude production capacity had dropped by 700,000 barrels a day since December 2011, to a production level of 3 million barrels a day. Data released in January 2013 showed that oil sales had declined by as much as 40 per cent in 2012, and budget projections for the Iranian financial year starting in March 2013 indicated that exports were not expected to remain at the same level in 2013. Projections for oil exports in 2013, the last year of Ahmadinejad's presidency, were for between 0.9 and 1.3 mb/d, meaning a catastrophic drop in exports in little more than two years. Oil exports had stood at 4.0 mb/d in 2010 and 2.2 mb/d in 2011.

By now Iran was suffering a loss of around $5.0 billion a month in revenue and, although some increase in its oil exports for a short period in 2013 did boost the Iranian treasury by an estimated $4.5 billion per month, the cost of keeping the economy going under these conditions had increased dramatically. Inflation and unemployment had gone, even though oil exports revenues of the Ahmadinejad presidency (2005–12) had reached the historically unprecedented level of $644 billion. By contrast, the country's income from oil exports in the entire Khatami period (1997–2005) had stood at $157 billion. Denial of ship insurance by the EU in 2012 meant that 95 per cent of super tankers (which are covered by EU companies) could no longer load Iranian crude without risk. Iran had to put scarce resources into leasing or buying its own super tankers to compensate for this loss. Sanctions had crushed the already weak national currency and its value against the dollar had more than halved by the end of 2012.

The currency's collapse made hard times harder, so the dollar went from 870 tomans in 2005 to 3,200 tomans in 2013, which means that a 1-million-toman monthly salary's value had dropped from $1,114 in 2005 to just $313 in 2013. Add to this the effects of inflation, and the erosion of real incomes is even greater. The Iranian population's purchasing power had dropped by 72 per cent between 2005 and 2013. With unemployment hovering at around 28 per cent, social misery mounted, with young people under 25 accounting for around 70 per cent of the recorded unemployed. Hyperinflation had become a real danger as prices rose by over 40 to 50 per cent on average after 2010. Finally, the country's GDP contracted by just over 5 per cent a year in 2012 and 2013, just as Iran was also enjoying historically unprecedented levels of oil income. But none of this detracted from the republic's 1969 moment, to which the president himself alluded during his last overseas trip (to Ghana). Ahmadinejad was asked, "you fought with the West, with your own supreme leader. What did you achieve?" to which he replied:

> Despite all the unfair pressures exerted on the people of Iran, we are making headway very fast. Since the day they imposed sanctions on us, we have gone nuclear. And now we are making use of peaceful nuclear energy. When they imposed sanctions on us, we became a country that has launched satellite into space. The pressures have caused problems for us, but they haven't been able to bring our progress to a halt.[201]

In reality, Ahmadinejad's mismanagement of the economy and the pressures of the sanctions arising from his inability to find a negotiated settlement to the nuclear crisis had seemingly squandered the regime's '1969 moment', by which time another geopolitical landslide, the post-2010 Arab uprisings, had exposed the republic's strategic vulnerability to a fragmenting, fragile and divided Arab order. Initially the uprisings were celebrated in Tehran as the triumph of true anti-imperialist and Islamist forces and the chance for extending its reach and brand of political Islam to the heart of the Arab world. Some observers also saw things Tehran's way; so George Friedman (founder of Startfor Global Intelligence), for example, noted that when "the Arab Spring is over, Iran could emerge with a sphere of influence stretching from western Afghanistan to the Mediterranean... a massive shift in the balance of power in the region, with Iran moving from a fairly marginal power to potentially a dominant power".[202] Closer observers of the situation interpreted the situation very differently, noting that "Iran is... perceptively losing the struggle for power in the ME".[203] The uprisings were certainly an opportunity for strategic gain for Iran as, in their eyes, fall of pro-Western dictators would loosen US' regional foothold, but matters did not fully go Iran's way.

The Arab uprisings

The anti-authoritarian uprisings across the Arab world, following the fall of President Ben Ali's dictatorship in Tunisia in December 2010, soon spread to the Levant and the Arabian Peninsula. The departure of Egypt's Mubarak and Libya's Qaddafi in 2012 stood in sharp contrast to the ongoing bloody encounters in Bahrain and Syria: The former being a Shia-majority country dominated by a small Sunni elite and close to Saudi Arabia; the latter, a Sunni-majority country ruled by a minority Alawi leadership closely aligned to Iran. The script could not have been written more starkly concerning how the peoples of these two hugely different countries ended up intensifying Sunni–Shia tensions but also worsening Saudi–Iranian relations in the process.

The impact of the Arab uprisings has been felt across the region. First, Islamist politics has been in the ascendant. At one level, the emergence of the Muslim Brotherhood, in the early stages of the uprisings, as the Arab region's most potent political force helped the reorientation of the region's most prominent Islamist 'national liberation movement', Hamas, away from Iran and towards the Arab heartland. Egypt, under the Brotherhood banner in particular, asserted an alternative revolutionary-Islamist discourse totally distinct from that of Iran. The rebalancing of non-violent Islamist forces, which continued to the end of the Morsi administration in Egypt in July 2014, had a direct effect on Iran's ability to continue to influence the political landscape of Palestine and, through that, the wider Arab world. Hamas' decision to shift its base from Syria in 2012 was another blow to the Shia alliance's ability to exert pressure on Israel and the moderate Arab states and a blow to the Iranian-Syrian alliance. Hamas, of course, did not moderate its policies as a consequence of these developments, but it did shift its loyalty to the detriment of the Iran-orchestrated Shia alliance until the fall of the Brotherhood government in Egypt. Despite meeting many of Gaza's needs and providing the bulk of Hamas' annual budget (perhaps as much as $500 million of its $540 million budget in 2010),[204] it, slowly but deliberately, re-oriented itself towards the Brotherhood-led political forces which had become dominant in the traditional 'Arab centre' for a time.

Furthermore, the prospects for a new Sunni Islamist bloc of states emerging in the aftermath of the Arab uprisings also increased. Emergence of a new coalition of 'democratic transition' Sunni states, supported by Turkey and Qatar, was, for a short period (2011–14) a distinct reality, potentially putting clear distance between these countries and Iran. The growing voice of Sunni Islamist political forces in Egypt, Tunisia, Libya, and of course Syria radically changed the discourse of politics in the Arab world and, in the process, facilitated the rise of these Islamist forces in proximity to Iran as well. Having had a presence in the Gulf Arab countries since the start of their modernization in the 1960s and '70s, the Islamists increased their presence sufficiently to be visible across the GCC countries. Being nearer to the Shia heartlands, of course, the growing voice and presence of Sunni Islamists in the GCC countries' institutions – as in Kuwait's National Assembly in 2012 – only intensified the tensions in Iranian relations with their immediate Arab neighbours.

Arguably, the intensity and spread of the Arab uprisings also increased the danger of sectarianism in the Middle East. Thus, the danger of sectarian violence returning to Lebanon has increased – a direct result of the crisis in Syria. The fragmentation of the Syrian state into confessional strongholds has become more likely as the violence has intensified, which has increased pressure on Iran to help defend and protect the Shia and Alawi enclaves of the country. Another major worrying trend since early 2012 has been the rising tide of Arab fighters from the Gulf volunteering to join and bolster the ranks of the Syrian opposition groups, from the al-Nusra Front and Daesh to the Free Syrian Army. These often-young Arab Sunnis are not only being radicalized but are also receiving combat training and will over time become battle-hardened fighters in their own right. This is a real and present danger not only to the Gulf monarchies themselves but also to Iran. The prospects of a new cycle of inter-communal violence have only increased, and, as a consequence, the danger of instability spreading to the GCC countries, as well as to Iran, has risen immeasurably. Yet a shared enemy and fear of a jihadi onslaught have done little to encourage dialogue between Iran and its neighbours.

Iran's alliance with Syria in the resistance front, which includes Hezbollah, has been in danger since the Syrian uprising. Hezbollah's position as a champion of radical but progressive change in the Arab world has been irrevocably tarnished, and indeed is being challenged in the Sunni world by its unyielding support for the Assad regime. Hezbollah has increasingly been seen, and indeed portrayed, as an Iranian lackey and a 'Shia only' organization whose interest is in pressing its sectarian agenda. Gone, then, is the organization's heroic legacy built in the fires of the 2006 war with Israel and its reputation on the Arab street as the only anti-Zionist and anti-Israel force in the Arab region capable of confronting the might of the Israeli armed forces. Hezbollah has remained a 'front-line' organization of importance, for sure, but in a most unexpected manner, the front line in the Arab world dramatically changed from the old and static Arab–Israeli one to a violent and dynamic Sunni versus Shia and Iran versus Arab 'front line'. Indeed, Hezbollah arguably found itself in the geopolitical wilderness: A bedfellow of not only its close ally, Iran, in supporting the Assad regime but also of its sworn enemy, Israel, which was equally averse to regime change in neighbouring Syria.

In addition, the geopolitical battleground shifting to Syria in the final years of Ahmadinejad's presidency tested Iran's ability, itself still under severe international sanctions, to provide sustained support for its allies. With Syria transformed into a pawn in the struggle for control between Iran and Saudi-backed states, Iran had few options beyond falling back onto the Arab Shia communities in particular to provide manpower and resources for the proxy fight against Sunni Arab states and the actual battle against the Sunni jihadis. For neighbouring Iraq, of course, Syria is a front line, for if Islamists come to power in Syria, "it's clear that they would have been helped by Saudi Arabia and other Sunni countries. This will impact Iraq because they will try and push Sunnis here to work against a government dominated by Shiites".[205] Iran, moreover, was also unprepared for the Saudi reaction to the crisis in Bahrain in 2011. Riyadh's decision to mobilize its security forces in support of the al-Khalifa dynasty in Bahrain left Iran adrift and heavy-footed. Riyadh's response to the crisis in Bahrain further widened the rift between Iran and Saudi Arabia.

In the last analysis, Ahmadinejad had become prisoner of his own rhetoric and staged patriotic hubris and the contradictions that his policy pursuits engendered. In the end, he had to blame the outside world for all his failures and the conspiracies of the 'Satanic-Zionist' axis chasing down his successes in the international arena. But only so much can be parked at the door of interfering outsiders, and ultimately the day of reckoning approached in the twilight of his presidency, when everything was ranged against his administration. This was to an extent inevitable and was a by-product of the structural deficiencies present. As Ansari surmised at the height of Ahmadinejad's power and popularity, "the international crisis, though sustaining relatively high oil prices, has itself, under the management of Ahmadinejad, ensured that the economy has not been able to stabilise; thus ironically reinforcing the problems that the government continually attempts to alleviate by turning up the heat abroad".[206] The more they stirred the pot abroad to cover up the mess at home, the worse the situation at home got. Thus, Ahmadinejad's failed policies at home and in the international arena generated a backlash and provided the context for the election victory of the centrist candidate in the elections, but the one person amongst all the candidates with a track record of successful negotiations with the West and the IAEA was Rouhani – who emerged as the choice of the people as president.

Rouhani aims to open up 'new horizons'

Unlike previous election campaigns, in 2013, foreign policy was a key focus by all the candidates. The majority of the eight candidates strongly attacked Ahmadinejad's policies and several (including the five from the conservative camp) went so far as to hold his administration responsible for the economic and political quagmire in which the country found itself. Hojjatoleslam Rouhani in particular was vocal in his criticisms of Ahmadinejad and the mistakes he had made, at the same time pointing to his own foreign policy approaches. During an election rally in Kurdistan in June, for example, he said, "I do not approve of the current foreign policy. We should try to have good international interactions to gradually reduce the sanctions and finally remove them". In the course of one of the heated televised debates, he put the blame for Iran's problems squarely at the door of Ahmadinejad's nuclear diplomacy, knowing full well that the policies of the previous eight years had been fully endorsed by the Leader himself: "All of our problems stem from this – that we didn't make the utmost effort to prevent the nuclear dossier from going to the UN security council. It is good to have centrifuges running, provided people's lives and livelihoods are also running".[207] Iran, he concluded, needed to open new horizons in order to fulfil its destiny and to meet the needs of its people.

A hint of his approach to international relations was evident in his reflections on Iran's nuclear diplomacy following the revelations about its secret nuclear achievements in 2002. In his book on the subject, he made explicit reference to what his approach to international relations would look like. Speaking as a quintessential realist, he argued, first, that the Islamic republic's foreign policy was not dissimilar from other states', all of which were struggling to survive. This in itself was an important admission of the limitations of ideological and material powers that Tehran could wield – contrary to its revolutionary slogans and rhetoric, the Islamic republic was not exempt from the rules governing the international system. But he went on to argue that the principle of international relations was every country's search for security and survival, and in Iran as elsewhere, "survival is the driver which shapes countries' foreign policy… and we too are searching for survival".[208] In Iran's overtly Islamic state, it will inevitably give values an important place which, admitedly, can and do cost the country's progress but values-based desires should not be pursued at the expense of the nezam's survival. As he was to say after his election: "We need to strike the right balance between idealism and realism. There are those who want to close the gateways to this country. We know that is impossible".[209]

The talk was, to quote phrases used by the president and the foreign minister, of "building confidence", "trust", pinpointing areas of "common interest", identifying "shared objectives", and pursuing "common interests" with neighbours and the international community. The aim was for détente, primarily with the West, the United States and a modus operandi with the United States, or at worst a mutually acceptable 'managed' system of competition between Tehran and the US. In an article in the *New York Times*, Foreign Minister Zarif provided a sketch of the Rouhani administration's philosophical approach to foreign affairs, explaining it thus: "Iran's foreign policy is holistic in nature. This is not due to habit or preference, but because globalization has rendered all alternatives obsolete. Nothing in international politics functions in a vacuum. Security cannot be pursued at the expense of the insecurity of others. No nation can achieve its interests without considering the interests of others".[210] This liberal interpretation of international relations, coinciding with the executive's desire to make amends, move the agenda beyond the nuclear negotiations, and the re-entry of Iran into the forum of decision-making states is particularly interesting as it lays out for the first time a post-revolution view of the world and an articulated view of Iran's potential role in an interdependent global order. For the regime conservatives and the so-called 'principlist revolutionaries', who correlate the Islamic republic's policies with such notions as 'soft war' and the need for constant vigilance against Western (American) cultural, economic and political invasion of the country, integration and collective security might as well be alien concepts – the very tools that would open up the republic to Western influence and subversion.

'To desecuritize issues' was how the new foreign affairs team explained President Rouhani's approach, and the primary strategic goal of his administration was to end Iran's isolation, the threat of which was weakening of the nezam to breaking point and, by securitizing the economy, was sliding towards a dictatorship. As Tabatabai articulates, "Rouhani speaks in favor of opening up Iran socially and politically not because he believes in pluralism and social participation but because he is convinced that a repressive political landscape will lead to conflict and endanger national security".[211]

To achieve this goal Rouhani's team focused on unlocking the nuclear box, which was only possible through direct negotiations with the West. Secondary objectives were to use the nuclear talks as a means of building confidence with the United States, recovering the trust with the EU, consolidating ties with its security and nuclear partner (Russia), and finally, improving relations with the neighbouring states. The team was clear that the key to improving Iran's diplomatic position was in negotiating an end to the nuclear crisis, and interestingly Rouhani's government set about building its strategy of engagement on the plank of electoral legitimacy and the power of the ballot box. Legitimacy gave the president authority as well as room for manoeuvre. As Foreign Minister Javad Zarif put it within months of taking office: "In our recent presidential election, which was a proud manifestation of the ability of an Islamic model of democracy to bring about change through the ballot box, my government received a strong popular mandate to engage in constructive interaction with the world, and particularly with our neighbors. We are dedicated to making use of this mandate to instigate change for the better".[212]

While 'change for the better' proved possible in the key realm of nuclear diplomacy, geopolitical tensions proved much harder to address constructively, and ironically the better Iran's relations with the major powers became following Rouhani's electoral success, the more problematic became its relations with the dominant Arab states.

Success of nuclear diplomacy

It is remarkable how quickly President Rouhani's administration managed to end the nuclear crisis and free Iran of its crippling economic and diplomatic isolation.

This was done in a coherent and courageous manner and was only possible because of the mandate that Rouhani had received form the people, and later from the Leader, to end Iran's isolation through a negotiated settlement of the nuclear crisis. Also, it had not been lost on Iran's centrists that its aggressive posture was adding to regional tensions and at the same time rewarding the hard line stance of regional rivals Israel and Saudi Arabia. While Tehran had expected (and feared) Israel's strong opposition to its nuclear programme from the beginning, the position of Saudi Arabia, as articulated by a senior Saudi prince (Turki al-Faisal), was perhaps more sobering to the Iranian elite. A highly articulate and experienced official in his own right, Prince Turki carried considerable weight internationally, so it was of some significance when he declared starkly at a NATO event in the UK: "We cannot live in a situation where Iran has nuclear weapons and we don't. It's as simple as that. If Iran develops a nuclear weapon, that will be unacceptable to us and we will have to follow suit".[213] He added later that "we must study carefully all the options, including the option of acquiring weapons of mass destruction. We can't simply leave it for somebody else to decide for us". Iran had been put on notice.

Thus, from early on, Rouhani and his foreign minister began signalling their readiness for dialogue with the major powers, including the United States, to end the crisis.[214] Their first act was to take control of the nuclear file by bringing it back into the foreign ministry and therefore under the control of the executive, instead of the country's national security council. Then, the Leader's endorsement of 'heroic flexibility' in diplomacy sanctified the direct negotiations strategy of Rouhani, leading in September, to Iran's proposal for the restarting of the seven party (6+1) talks. The change in attitude was clear, as a close observer of the nuclear crisis noted further to a meeting with the new Iranian foreign minister in New York:

> In New York back in 2013, Zarif told our group that acquiring what he called 'strategic' capabilities (meaning nuclear weapons) would make Iran less safe, rather than more. Iran, he said, is now a regional powerhouse in terms of its economy, natural resources, and conventional military power. If Iran were to acquire, or even appear to attempt to acquire, strategic capabilities, it would cause outside powers to interfere and make it a target. In retrospect, he was signaling that Tehran had shifted its strategy after Rouhani's election in 2013 – from steady pursuit of a nuclear weapon in defiance of the UN Security Council, to a willingness to scale back its nuclear program and put the weapon option on the back burner in return for sanctions relief and regaining a place in the international community.[215]

The talks began in earnest in October 2013 in Geneva. As was expected, Iran continued to talk tough, as in the government's strong letter to the IAEA criticizing its August report on Iran:

> The Islamic Republic of Iran has already made it clear, that based on the legal provisions such as those of the Agency's Statute and the Safeguards

Agreement, the BOG [Board of Governors] resolutions against Iran are illegal and unjustified. The issue of Iran's peaceful nuclear program has unlawfully been conveyed to the UNSC and the Council has taken a wrong approach by adopting the politically-motivated, illegal and unjust UNSC resolutions against Iran. Therefore, any request by the Agency stemming from those resolutions is not legitimate and not acceptable.[216]

But Iran's foreign minister had already signalled, according to one source, that Iran was prepared to make dramatic changes to its nuclear profile:

Tehran was prepared to take significant steps to reduce its stockpile of low-enriched uranium and limit the centrifuge program. In discussing the plutonium-production potential of the Arak heavy water reactor, then under construction, the technical specialists said they were prepared to take the necessary actions to convince the United States that Iran would not produce plutonium, the second path to the bomb. They also indicated some flexibility on how intrusive they might allow inspections to be, should an agreement be reached. Less than two months later, Iran and the P5+1 (China, France, Germany, Great Britain, Russia, and the United States) came to the Interim Agreement.[217]

A programme of talks was accomplished through Iran's insistence on a fixed schedule of talks (three to six months, Rouhani said in September 2013), and with a focus on what Iranians called 'goal-oriented talks'. Having already secretly met with US officials in Oman since March 2013 (during Ahmadinejad's presidency), Rouhani's about-face was warmly endorsed, which led to the initial round of the Geneva talks in October (15–16), itself paving the way for a more structured meeting, in November, to prioritise the key issues. Tehran had done its homework as, at the October meeting, Foreign Minister Zarif was said to have presented "an outline of a plan as a proposed basis for negotiation, which has been carefully considered by the [P5+1] as an important contribution. Members of delegations followed with in-depth bilateral and joint consultations on various elements of the approach".[218] This was unprecedented praise, for an unprecedented Iranian approach had agreed that "nuclear, scientific, and sanctions experts will convene before the next meeting to address differences and to develop practical steps".

Iran-US delegations also held a bilateral meeting even, which a member of the US delegation confessed as having been the most "intense, detailed, straightforward, candid" of its kind.[219] On 11th November, Tehran gave IAEA inspectors 'managed access' to its nuclear sites, just as the Geneva meeting was breaking up without an agreement over Iran's insistence that its right to enrichment should be enshrined in the final deal. A week later agreement towards 'an interim accord' was in sight, beginning with a suspension in Iran's enrichment activities and on 20th January 2014, the six-month long accord was enforced. The agreed extension of the talks for a further four months in July 2014 was indicative of the political tensions rising in Tehran and Washington and was a sign of the pressures under which the parties were negotiating. A month later (in August 2014), Iran responded to one of the key concerns of the IAEA by offering to redesign Arak to reduce the plutonium content of the plant. In November 2014, the parties extended the negotiations by a further seven months, and progress was still being made as Iran agreed in April 2015 to halve the number of active centrifuges in Natanz to 5,000.

Until summer of 2015 then an incremental de-escalation of tensions through the implementation of a series of measures had been put in place, all designed to build confidence and allow for negotiations to take hold.[220] In July, agreement was reached on Iran's nuclear programme, and the multilateral treaty was signed by six global powers and Iran. In return for the lifting of sanctions, Iran agreed to cut its stockpile of low-enriched uranium by 98 per cent, use no more than 5,060 IR-1 centrifuges, eliminate its medium-enriched uranium, limit enrichment to only 3.67 per cent until 2030, not build pressurized water reactors for the next 15 years, not enrich uranium in its second-generation centrifuges until 2025, give IAEA inspectors regular access to Iran's facilities, and either close or convert facilities which could serve proliferation.[221] In January 2016 the agreement came into force. At this point all diplomatic restrictions on Iran evaporated, and the visits of leaders of China, European countries, India and also the European Union's commissioners, between January and May of 2016 sent Iran's diplomatic corps into hyper-drive. While Tehran hosted many prominent heads of state following implementation day, its own political leaders travelled the world cementing the newly emerging, as well as the very important existing, ones.

Of course, not everyone was happy with the nuclear deal and its outcome, and the US' regional allies in particular remained sceptical of the successful implementation of the deal and its strength to check Iran's nuclear ambitions in the long run, as much as about the return of an unshackled Islamic republic able to cause mischief in the region without impunity. Perhaps this side effect of 'nuclear peace' raises more concern than the deal itself. In Tehran, too, questions have been asked about the deal. In academic circles, and engaging to the educated youth in particular, symposia and meetings have vigorously debated the costs and benefits of Iran's nuclear programme and also the tangible fruits of the nuclear agreement against the price (sanctions, isolation, loss of confidence in the country's honesty, etc.). What was the point of it all, particularly when set against Iran's gains, which are even fewer than was the case in 2009? Who will account for the lost Ahmadinejad generation?

On the other hand, from the other side of the political spectrum, the Rouhani administration has been accused of giving away the family silver in its 'ideological desire' to end the nuclear impasse at any cost. The security establishment in particular and its allies in the Majlis have been openly critical of the government and the foreign minister and, despite the political cover extended to the negotiating team by the Leader himself, talk of succumbing to Western charm and exposing the country to Western influences have become frequent accusations.

In August 2015, following the success of the nuclear negotiations, Rouhani's foreign policy line was again reinforced and the foreign ministry spokeswoman, Marzieh Afkham, underlined the importance of the nuclear deal as evidence for success of her government's foreign policy in these terms: "the promotion of stability and cooperation and the reduction of chaos" and the government's readiness to hold "fresh, sincere and profound" talks with all neighbouring and Muslim countries. Creeping eerily close to the Khatami administration's posture, she added that "Iran has proved that it adopts dialogue as a principle and it attaches significant importance to regional and international peace and stability".[222]

But, ironically, success on this front made Iran's regional adversaries even more nervous, for four main reasons. First, that the success of the negotiations will reinforce America's belief that it can work with Iran to counter extremism in the region; that Iran may emerge as the West's partner of choice in countering Sunni radicalism. Second, that dialogue with Iran will pave the way for their closer bilateral relations and thus put a distance between Washington and its traditional regional partnerships. Third, the nuclear deal, leading to the lifting of sanctions on Iran, will enable Tehran to regrow its economy, reassert itself as an oil giant, and also be even more brazen in asserting itself in the region. Finally, that with the nuclear crisis ended, the US may be less inclined to have a semi-permanent presence in the region. The sum of these fears, ironically, further alienated the Obama administration from its Arab allies and Israel, who saw in the nuclear deal grave strategic short-sightedness and cover for drawing closer to the Islamic republic. So, the further Iran and the world powers went in agreeing to a lasting deal, the more aggressive the core Arab states became in their relations with Iran. The nuclear deal further fuelled the region's geopolitical uncertainties.

Geopolitical uncertainties shape policy

Despite the eye-catching success of the nuclear negotiations, Iran's role in the region – deepening support for the Assad regime and its support for the Houthi rebels' uprising in Yemen against its UN-recognized post-revolution government – prevented Rouhani from making progress on his fence-mending exercise with the main Arab states, notably Saudi Arabia and its GCC partners, and Egypt. The crisis in Syria and Iran's brazen military and political support for the brutal Assad regime had left Iran bereft of a voice in the Arab world and at the receiving end of abuse from Arab elites as well as the increasingly vocal, well-organized and mobilized radical and jihadi Sunni groups freely operating in the territories of both of its allies (Iraq and Syria). The stronger Iran's support for its allies became, the bigger the hole around it. So, in all the regional and international discussions about Syria's future, taking place between 2012 and Russia's dramatic military intervention in autumn 2015, Tehran was conspicuously absent. Even in Iraq, where the West undertook a coordinated deployment of military and intelligence power in defence of the post-Maliki Iraqi government against Daesh's massive territorial gains, Iran was excluded. Indeed, Tehran was allowed at the Syria table in autumn 2015, at the insistence of Russia and tacit support from the United States; most regional partners opposed Iran's presence in the Vienna talks. With relations with Saudi Arabia securitized, Tehran appeared more isolated from the conservative Arab states than ever before.

So, the period post-9/11, and in particular the post-2011 uprisings era, has had a direct effect on Iran's regional policies. Iran has found it harder to sell itself as a champion of liberation when its state machinery has devoted itself to the preservation of the blood-stained Syrian dictator who has massacred hundreds of thousands of his own people and has stood by while a third of his country's citizens have become refugees. Tehran finds it equally difficult to package Hezbollah as a resistance bulwark when the militia has been fighting in Syria in defence of Bashar al-Assad and in Iraq in defence of the Shia government there. And the majority of Arabs see Iran's interventions in both Syria and Iraq as defence of sectarianism, for Tehran's active support for the Iraqi and Syrian governments has come at the expense of the Sunni population of these countries, which in Syria make up most of that country's population and in Iraq its most substantial non-Shia Arab community.

Turmoil and violence in the Arab region following the Arab uprisings forced Iran to recalculate its embrace of what it initially called 'Islamic awakening' in the region. Iran had rushed to judge Arab revolts as Islamic awakening before, of course, notably the Palestinian intifada of December 1988, which Kamal Kharrazi, later to become Iran's foreign minister in Khatami's cabinet, had stressed was "100 percent Islamic".[223] This was no different, and mass uprisings in Tunisia, Egypt and Libya over twenty years later were all viewed in terms of Islamist stirrings inspired by Iran's example and its actions, variously seen as being modelled on the 1979 Islamic revolution, inspired by Iran's defiance, and even aiming to create the same in their own countries. The uprisings were viewed as positive and the beginning of a new era of cooperation with like-minded Arab regimes and overtures of friendship, and offers of assistance were made to the new Islamist-leaning leaderships of Egypt, Tunisia and Libya. Rise of neo-revolutionary Islamist regimes was seen as strengthening Iran's 'resistance front' and weakening of the Saudi-led Arab regional alliance structure. Then, the scale of change taking place in pro-US states was seen as weakening of American influence in the region, leading to its greater vulnerability and so potentially less able and threatening. Finally, the revolutions were regarded as game-changing events that would both make pro-US regimes more vulnerable and Israel more isolated.

While the turmoil unquestionably changed the region's strategic landscape and, with Egypt weakened and the Arab monarchies exposed, transformed the regional balance of power equation, Iran (and Turkey) saw in the changes a golden opportunity to enter the heart of the region and directly shape it. The uprisings, then, forced Iran to review its own role. But also at a practical level, the upheavals affected the republic's relations with Arab countries, which for a long time had followed a familiar pattern of cooperation and animosity.[224] The problem for Tehran was that it needed a new foreign policy approach towards the emerging Arab regimes, and it needed to understand how to interact with forces which for so long had been absent from the region's political arena. Iran was as far removed from the emerging Arab voices and forces as its Western counterparts, given that its influence in the Sunni world did not tend to go much beyond Hamas and Islamic Jihad in Palestine. In any case, Tehran continued to approach these organizations as national liberation movements and had little experience of dealing with popular Arab movements and the emerging Arab Islamist regimes; the experience it did have had been accumulated through cooperation with the Sudanese Islamist government of the 1990s and hardly identical to these new forces taking centre stage. Iran, in short, had no point of reference for dealing with its counterparts occupying the seats of power in Cairo, Tunis, and Tripoli (even though short-lived) after 2011.

At another level, the rise of Islamist-leaning regimes in the Arab region raised the temperature on identity politics, and as new regimes and social forces discovered their voices in Arab publics, they began to forge new ideas about themselves and the region. In this, they not only rejected Iran's claim to be an exemplar of revolutions but also questioned its role as a positive force for change in the region. The rise of what Iran portrayed as authentic regimes in the Arab region ironically raised questions about Iran's own self-perception as the first and most prominent revolutionary Islamist state. For a long time, Iran had been able to claim first place as the only real Islamic state in the entire Muslim world, but after 2010 several new Arab regimes, and after them Sunni organizations such as Daesh, were able to claim the same, thus offering alternatives to the Iranian model while eroding this essential component of the republic's own identity.

Furthermore, Iran's rulers failed to understand that, having got rid of one set of masters, the Arab world's emerging elites were not about to surrender their revolutionary narratives to Iran. Iran's role in stoking the fires of Bahrain's largely Shia protests in 2011 and 2012 also brought added pressure from the rest of the Arab monarchies (Jordan, Kuwait, UAE, and, to a lesser extent, Oman and Saudi Arabia) who saw in Iran's behaviour and statements evidence of meddling at a time when they themselves were feeling the tension rise in their own societies. Protests in Saudi Arabia's eastern province were quickly linked to Iranian agitation of the Kingdom's own Shia populations, particularly when Tehran sat on its hands as Sunni and Shia Iraqi protesters demanded the departure of their incompetent and corrupt Prime Minister Nouri al-Maliki. Iran's apparent double standards in dealing with the uprisings – supporting ruling regimes in Baghdad and Damascus while subverting them in Bahrain, Yemen, and Saudi Arabia – seriously weakened and undermined its claim as champion of revolutionary change in the rest of the region. Its intense political, security and economic support for the Syrian and Iraqi regimes reinforced the sense of regional polarization, and Tehran was seen as driving sectarianism. Regional dynamics following the uprisings then opened a new and dangerous chapter in the sectarian fires which had been burning in Afghanistan, Pakistan and Iraq (after 2003).

A mobilized Arab world was rediscovering and increasingly identifying with the Sunni voices of political Islam, whose message was significantly different and distinct from Iran's political Islam. And the differences in tone and practices between the two main sects of Islam became a fault line in Syria, where the Iran-backed Assad regime found itself under attack by protesters demanding political change in March 2011. In the ensuing months Iran's exposure to the political dynamics following the violent clampdown on Syrian protesters began to strike home the hidden dangers of sudden political change in a volatile region such as this one. Tehran soon adjusted its narrative of the Arab uprisings and, in a Kafkaesk tour de force, saw in Syria terrorists challenging the legitimate ruling regime and in Bahrain an illegitimate regime suppressing its freedom-loving citizens. In its realist pursuit of the national interest throughout this tense period, the incongruity in its position of assisting the Alawite minority-led regime of Assad in the pummelling of his own society (of largely Sunni and Kurdish Arabs), while claiming to support the Arab masses' struggle for freedom had been lost on Iran. As it massaged its message, the regime made itself more unpopular in the Arab world and even more vulnerable to accusations of sectarianism in the service of dictators. The effort to mobilize its political, economic and military assets in defence of deeply vulnerable allies in Iraq and Syria had deepened Arab anxieties of growing Iranian interference in the Arab world.

American inaction in the face of Iranian aggression fed the notion of American incompetence and indifference in the remaining moderate Arab states, which encouraged them to create their own security partnership. The Saudi Arabia–led coalition of Arab states (GCC+Egypt+Jordan+Morocco+Sudan) has since challenged Iran in Syria and Iraq as well as in Yemen. Iran's approach to the Arab uprisings contributed to the region's changing dynamics and in the process helped to create a new Saudi-led Arab alliance bent on weakening Iran's regional presence and its influence. Iran's forward strategy generated a strong Arab response, and it was difficult for Tehran to formulate an effective response. This is so because the backlash against the Islamic republic has opened two fronts against the country. On the one hand, the backlash has been led by Sunni jihadis intent on unpicking and destroying Shia communities across the region. Their ideology makes it impossible for Tehran to reason with them even if it wanted to. This has become all the more potent in the context of Syria, the Quranically important balad al-Sham, which for Sunnis is part of the heritage of the prophet and his legacy. Iran's buttressing of the Assad regime is seen by politicized Sunnis as depriving of their legacy and Islamic heritage being taken hostage by Shia Iran and Alawi Syria.

And, on the other hand, because the coalition of Arab states that has emerged has set itself the task of destroying Daesh and Gulf-affiliate al-Qaeda networks alongside rolling back Iran's influence by targeting its allies (in Syria, Yemen, Lebanon and Palestine), it is extremely difficult for Tehran to lodge itself as part of the solution to the first problem when it is seen as the core of the Arab states' second problem. So, while it is new for Saudi Arabia to refer to Iran as "occupier of Arab lands" (in Syria), it is not unexpected and certainly not surprising for the Saudi foreign minister to state robustly that "we are determined to confront any Iranian moves and we will do everything we can with what we have in political, economic and military means to protect our lands and people".[225] Other quarters were equally blunt. Rather unexpectedly, President Recep Tayyip Erdogan declared in March 2015: "Iran means to dominate the region. How can this be allowed? Iran has to abandon this ambition. It should withdraw its forces from Yemen, Syria, and Iraq".[226]

In the last analysis, the one thing that the Islamic republic has valued above all else is its credibility, and this has since 2011 been badly tarnished across the Muslim world as Tehran has doggedly pursued a geopolitically led power agenda at all cost. So despite the expressed desire to reduce regional tensions, Iran, under Rouhani, continued to build on the geopolitical gains made after the 2003 Iraq War and thus played a regional role arguably closer with the worldview of the Khamenei-dominated establishment. One result has been deepening tensions with Saudi Arabia and its growing camp of Arab and non-Arab allies (Pakistan and Turkey in particular) – thus, Saudi Arabia's angry severing of its diplomatic ties with Tehran on 2 January 2016 following its provocative execution of the charismatic Saudi Shia cleric, Sheikh Nimr Baqir al-Nimr, on charges of terrorism and disturbance of the peace on behalf of a foreign power (Iran), and then the torching of the Saudi embassy in Tehran by an angry mob. That Iran (and other Shia communities) would protest this act was never in question, but the manner in which events unfolded subsequently deepened the antagonism between Iran and its most powerful Arab counterpart in the shape of Saudi Arabia.

The gravity of the crisis can be gleaned by Riyadh's response, whose foreign minister saw in Iran's protest more than a hint of hypocrisy and the "continuation of the Iranian hostile policy in the region aiming at destabilizing the region's security and stability and spreading sedition and wars. In addition to these hostile attacks", the foreign minister continued, "the Iranian regime has managed to smuggle weapons and explosives, plant terrorist cells in the region, including the Kingdom, aiming to spread chaos and unrest. The history of Iran is full of negative and hostile interference in Arab countries affairs, always accompanied with subversion, demolition and killing of innocent souls".[227] To leave no ambiguity, the Saudi foreign minister underlined the deepening chasm with Tehran by suggesting that it was confronting Iran in the region for the sake of regional stability: "we are determined not to allow Iran to threaten our safety and security and will not allow it to implant terror cells in our countries or our allies. We have decided to sever our relations with a terror-sponsor country and we urge all countries to consider seriously whether they could tolerate sharing relations with a terror-sponsor country".[228]

Bahrain and Sudan were the first Arab countries to comply with the Saudi request and severed their diplomatic ties with Tehran soon after Riyadh's decision, followed by the UAE, Kuwait and Qatar just days later who downgraded their diplomatic representations in support of Saudi Arabia. Sudan, notably, had been a beneficiary of Iranian financial, political and military support in the 1990s and 2000s, so its decision was symptomatic of a wider rift between Iran and its Arab hinterland. The mounting geopolitical pressures and the extent of Arab forces uniting against the Islamic republic at this critical juncture were further evident in the Egyptian foreign minister's comments following the torching of the Saudi embassy in Tehran: "We reject Iranian interference in the internal affairs of the Kingdom. We have stressed many times that we stand firmly with our brothers in the Kingdom and other Gulf states".[229]

This sentiment was again repeated following the Arab League's 10th of January emergency ministerial meeting in Cairo on relations between Iran and the Arab world which not only roundly condemned the attacks on the Saudi missions (in Tehran and Mashhad) but went considerably further in criticizing the Islamic republic for its 'interference' in Arab countries.[230] Alongside a diplomatic 'blockade', Riyadh also has eagerly implemented an economic containment strategy designed to limit the financial gains of the nuclear settlement for Iran. Pressure on the UAE to limit Iranian business growth in Dubai has prevented Iran from re-growing its substantial large commercial presence in that business hub to act as a conduit for its global interactions. The Kingdom has continued to maintain its high oil output which has kept oil prices relatively low and Iran's treasury empty. And Riyadh has made effective moves to disrupt Iran's oil-shipping trade: "Shipping insurers and brokers have been advising clients since February [2016] that ships carrying Iranian crude will not be permitted to enter Saudi or Bahraini waters, according to an April report by Control Risks. It said ships that have been to Iran as one of their last three points of entry must also receive special approval".[231]

Irrespective of the flaws in Riyadh's overall strategy with regard to Iran, or indeed the problems associated with Saudi Arabia's own regional role in the post-Arab uprisings environment, the Iranian response has done little to instil confidence in Tehran's declared aim of reviving regional relations with its 'near abroad' neighbours. So, the position, in response to the Saudi accusations, that Riyadh's behaviour was worse than Iran's, did little to keep the door of diplomacy open. Thus, the foreign ministry spokesman, Hossein Jaber Ansari, stated on 4th January that Saudi Arabia was "continuing the policy of increasing tension and clashes in the region. Saudi Arabia sees not only its interests but also its existence in pursuing crises and confrontations and attempts to resolve its internal problems by exporting them to the outside".[232] Foreign Minister Zarif was even more direct, writing in the *New York Times* that he parked much of the region's ills on the Saudi doorstep, deliberately fanning Western fears of Wahhabi-instigated violence:

Let us not forget that the perpetrators of many acts of terror, from the horrors of Sept. 11 to the shooting in San Bernardino and other episodes of extremist carnage in between, as well as nearly all members of extremist groups like Al Qaeda and the Nusra Front, have been either Saudi nationals or brainwashed by petrodollar-financed demagogues who have promoted anti-Islamic messages of hatred and sectarianism for decades.[233]

The Saudi response, in the same pages, was equally direct:

In an outlandish lie, Iran maligns and offends all Saudis by saying that my nation, home of the two holy mosques, brainwashes people to spread extremism. We are not the country designated a state sponsor of terrorism; Iran is. We are not the nation under international sanctions for supporting terrorism; Iran is. We are not the nation whose officials are on terrorism lists; Iran is. We don't have an agent sentenced to jail for 25 years by a New York federal court for plotting to assassinate an ambassador in Washington in 2011; Iran does.[234]

The net result was even deeper tensions in Iran's relations with its immediate GCC neighbours, and a blow to Rouhani's efforts to rebuild regional relations and political bridges with its neighbours had foundered on the mantle of the brutal justice meted out in Saudi Arabia, but a system of justice with which Iran itself was not only familiar but also an advent advocate of. Beyond the GCC and also its struggles in Iraq and Syria, Tehran's new bid to draw closer to the Palestinian communities added to the sense of encirclement in Arab circles and also Israel. The announcement made in February 2016 by Mohammad Fathali (Iran's ambassador to Lebanon) that the Islamic republic would provide $7,000 to the family of Palestinians who had died in operations against Israel and $30,000 to those whose houses were demolished by Israeli forces, at a time when money was incredibly scarce in Palestine, was interpreted as Tehran's bid for a widening of its influence (and popularity) at a time when the Palestinian Authority (PA) was in distress, the Arab world divided, and Iran's own popularity in the Arab world at a low ebb.[235] Tehran would expect, with this opportunistic move, to extend its political influence, work more closely with Hamas and Islamic Jihad in the Occupied Territories, marginalize the Arab partners of the PA and thus also add more pressure on Israel.

So, context, regional context, continues to shape Iran's foreign policy. The more complex and dynamic regional relations become, the harder it is for Iran to adjust course and to shed its revolutionary cloak. Former Secretaries of State Kissinger and Shultz have been clear on this when they opined that 'nuclear peace' with Iran cannot in itself change the regional dynamics for the better. They wrote in April 2015, in the midst of intensive negotiations between Iran and world powers:

The final stages of the nuclear talks have coincided with Iran's intensified efforts to expand and entrench its power in neighboring states. Iranian or Iranian client forces are now the pre-eminent military or political element in multiple Arab countries, operating beyond the control of national authorities. With the recent addition of Yemen as a battlefield, Tehran occupies positions along all of the Middle East's strategic waterways and encircles archrival Saudi Arabia, an American ally. Unless political restraint is linked to nuclear restraint, an agreement freeing Iran from sanctions risks empowering Iran's hegemonic efforts. Some have argued that these concerns are secondary, since the nuclear deal is a way station toward the eventual domestic transformation of Iran. But what gives us the confidence that we will prove more astute at predicting Iran's domestic course than Vietnam's, Afghanistan's, Iraq's, Syria's, Egypt's or Libya's?[236]

Tehran itself has been clear that its core interests in the region have not changed with an openly moderate president. On such issues as Iran's role in Syria, for example, Ali Akbar Velayati, foreign policy adviser to the Leader, reported to a local newspaper in July 2015 that Ayatollah Khamenei had issued clear orders to all government branches that "all possible assistance should be provided to Syria's President Bashar Al Assad in order to preserve him.... During our recent meetings with the leaders of Syria and Iraq, we reminded all that two years ago we said Assad will not fall. We were not sure then that he will indeed remain in power. But today I can say with full confidence that he will remain in power so will his regime".[237] Iran, however, will inevitably have to adjust its Syria policy in the light of Russia's role, and Assad's drain on Iran's purse, reputation and manpower in search of a political solution to the Syria crisis. But its fortunes in both Iraq and Syria have become less clear since 2013 and the rise of al-Qaeda offshoot Daesh, as the most aggressive Sunni jihadi movement in the region. Daesh, whose good fortune has been tied to state failure in Iraq and Syria (both Iranian allies), has emerged as a great challenger of Iran's geostrategic presence. Daesh's ability to occupy important population centers (Raqqa in Syria and Mosul in Iraq in particular) and vast tracts of land in Iraq and Syria to create a new 'Caliphate' at the heart of the region forced Iran to intensify its support for its allies, mobilize Shia militias in Iraq, Afghanistan, Pakistan, and Lebanon to take up arms against jihadi groups in Iraq and Syria and also commit more of its own treasure and revolutionary guard personnel in defence of these regimes.

Iran, let us be clear, has been as guilty as other parties in militarizing these societies and using violence to get its own way. So, its actions, on display to the wider region on a daily basis, have in turn intensified the hostility of core Arab states against Iran while also encouraging neighbouring Turkey to adopt a more interventionist role in both Iraq and Syria in a challenge to Iran's strategy. Iran's efforts have produced mixed results in both Iraq and Syria, as when the chips have been down against the ruling regimes, it has been the involvement of major powers – the US and NATO allies in support of Maliki's successor in

Iraq (Prime Minister Haider al-Abadi) and Russia in support of Assad – which helped stabilize these regimes and not Iran's tireless efforts on their behalf. Furthermore, Iran's position in Syria had, until November 2015, firmly excluded it from any discussions about Syria's future, which of course ran counter to its efforts to reach a modus operandi with the Saudi-led Arab coalition. Indeed, rather ironically, Iran was included in the Vienna talks only because of Daesh's apparent strengthening and the intensification of its bloody violence which had been unleashed against other Arab (in Egypt, Tunisia, Saudi Arabia, Kuwait, Turkey and Lebanon), Western (in France and Belgium), and other European (Russians in Egypt) targets. Tehran's 'success' therefore in positioning itself at the high-stakes discussions regarding Syria (and to a lesser extent Iraq) is not a result of its own diplomatic robustness but rather due to the mixed fortunes of the other actors. As they try to manage their own affairs in highly volatile circumstances, the combination of the pressures and stresses of others left the political door ajar for Iran to try to pry open.

Looking forward, it is hard to see how Iran can maintain its current strategic profile in the Iraq-Levant theatre and its alliance structure intact in the face of regional and international efforts to stabilize the region, no matter how (relative) stability might be achieved or look like; Iran will not be the party driving this. First, it is unlikely that the disenfranchised populations of these countries will forgive Iran for its role in prolonging their agony and for making refugees of whole segments of their societies. Second, while the Arab peoples will always look skeptically upon Western and Russian interventions in their region, their sense of outrage about a self-declared Islamic regime bolstering Assad's dictatorial regime and maneuvering against them elsewhere in the region has left a deep scar. Indeed, while Iran may be credited with a larger role in the fight against Daesh and its affiliates (in both Syria and Iraq), this will probably come about – following the horrors of terrorism in Paris in November 2015 – thanks to a realignment of forces across the Atlantic, between Russia, the EU and the United States, rather than through Tehran's own successful diplomacy. Not for the first time, Russia will have secured a place for Iran in the rapidly changing dynamics, again to the dismay of the other regional powers.

Yet beyond the region itself, following the nuclear deal, Iran's relations took a perceptible turn for the better after 2013: EU countries reached out to Tehran virtually en masse in search of new economic opportunities (the restoration of diplomatic relations between Iran and the UK in autumn 2015 was part of the same process), Russia declared its intention to take its already bountiful strategic and economic ties with Tehran to a new level (which were put on display for the world during President Putin's visit to Tehran in November 2015), and China declared in September 2015 that its relations with Iran were entering 'a new stage' following the nuclear agreement and time was right for the two to pave the way for creating a 'strategic partnership' between the two Asian countries. Iran also pursued closer links with India, focusing primarily on energy and Indian investment in Iran's substantial natural gas deposits following the lifting of UN sanctions. Following Prime Minister Narendra Modi's high-level visit to Iran in May 2016, these links were consolidated further, with Iran agreeing to work more strategically with India, intensify economic cooperation, and give access to its Chabahar port facilities – and with this, easier access to Central Asia for India. Building a concrete strategic relationship will help New Delhi check the Sino-Pakistan partnership.

Conclusion

Revolutions not only change the foreign policy of the revolutionary state itself but also cause seismic disruptions across the wider regional (and international) landscape. Iran's revolution was no exception. The revolution fundamentally altered the country's foreign policy priorities and role perception, as well as its alliance structures. Iran's foreign relations since 1979 have consistently tested the inherent tension in the country's worldview, that between enhanced relations with the Global South and profitable relations with the rich oil-consuming countries.

As neighbours and adversaries alike regularly testify, Iran's relations with other countries and international institutions are not just complex but at times rather mystifying. Iran's foreign relations stand out in an already complex region as a unique case of pragmatism coloured by ideational imperatives. This is a classic case of revolutionary politics grappling with power politics. The tension between what Majid Rafizadeh has called "rational state actors and an ideological state" has remained.[238] As Henry Kissinger opined in 2012, the Islamic republic seems unable to be "a nation-state, rather than a revolutionary religious cause".[239] Indeed, the Faqih himself is of the same opinion:

> Is the fight against arrogance suspendable? Fighting against arrogance, fighting against the dominant order, cannot be suspended.... This is one of the principles of the revolution. Without fighting against arrogance, we would not be followers of the Quran.... America is the embodiment of this arrogance par excellence.... We have told the honorable officials who negotiated on the nuclear issue... that they are authorized to negotiate only on the nuclear issue – they have no authority to negotiate on other issues, and they don't.[240]

Isolationism and engagement vie for ascendency: "the constitution places far greater emphasis on sovereignty and independence than on economic and social development. To be precise, one can conclude that the concept of political isolation is constitutionally legalized irrespective of the dynamics of interconnectedness".[241]

Yet despite these real tensions in Iran's international role, conception and conduct, one can discern several enduring themes in Iran's foreign policy. Unquestionably, the key to understanding Iran's foreign policy is to be found in the country's domestic political context and the compromises reached and concessions made in the ongoing battle of factions. Although the Leader has carved for himself a particularly strong platform for establishing the general principles and boundaries of the republic's international relations, managing foreign policy is the domain of the executive and the other institutional and para-institutional forces vying for influence. Like other semiautonomous elites, the Iranian establishment is often caught fighting with itself rather than worrying about public opinion or intervention. Public perceptions, particularly around election cycles, do play a part but never in a path-changing way. Given the role of factional politics in the country, its complex institutional structures, and distribution of formal power, it is no surprise that its foreign policy emerges as a direct product of the interplay between domestic political forces as much as ideology.

More broadly, its international relations take shape through the interplay of elite interactions and factional interpretations of the republic's imperatives, on the one hand, and a constant assessment of the immediate external pressures facing Iran and the opportunities presented, on the other. The Islamic republic also has a deeper level to foreign policy and that is the "legacy of Iran's ancient past, as the center of several 'world empires' of its day", which have remained as permanent/fixed features of "Iran's view of itself and its surroundings".[242] Call this geopolitical memory, if you will, but a national consciousness of the country's rich history provides a sense of pride and international relevance to the deliberations of the republic's political masters.

So in this context, one can make several observations about the Islamic republic's international relations. The first is realignment towards Asia, which heavy sanctions by the West in the 2010s merely encouraged. This was inevitable in many ways as Asian countries had already substituted for the West in keeping the economic wheels turning. As a member of the elite, Asadollah Asgaroladi, said to be one of Iran's wealthiest businessmen and also the head of the Iran-China chamber of commerce, put it: "after the revolution we exchanged the Western frowns with the smiles from the East. They continue to smile at us".[243]

Second, Iran's relations with its northern neighbours have remained non-confrontational and non-ideological since President Rafsanjani put in place Iran's responses to the collapse of the Soviet Union in 1991. Relations with Russia were recalibrated following the collapse of the Soviet state and flourished in the 2000s. In Central Asia and the Caucasus also all subsequent presidents have followed the policy lines laid down by his administration. So, while relations with the MENA region have remained complicated and problematic, those with Asia have remained stable and positive. One can see this in President Xi's commitment during his January 2016 visit to Iran to support Iran's application to become a full member of the Shanghai Cooperation Organization. Iran's 'Look East' strategy emerged as the core of its anti-imperial stance but has in the new millennium acquired a more positive, strategic realm to it, namely that the Islamic republic is positioning itself to benefit from the strategic shift taking place at the global level. Iranian leaders, arguably, are therefore increasingly operating on the basis of a different, multipolar global order, dominated by Asian powers, which are historically, culturally and geographically closer to Iran. This global shift is seen as providing Iran protection from American pressure and also opportunity for Iran to play a greater role in this new multipolar world order. Thus the newly elected Rouhani said at the September 2013 meeting of the Shanghai Cooperation Organization that "following the end of bipolar power tensions, the trend of cooperation and competition has taken the place of absolute competition or absolute cooperation. Regional cooperation and regional gravitation, alongside the use of intra-regional capacities, bring the promise of a multipolar world order".[244] Since then, the prospects for Iran's full membership of the SCO have been raised considerably. A month later, Major General Yahya Rahim Safavi, former commander of the IRGC and now senior military advisor to the Leader, echoed President Rouhani's analysis and argued at a domestic gathering that: "in all likelihood, the world, including the powers of the Asian continent, is heading towards multipolarity. There will not be any superpower on a global scale by 2030, and [we] will move in a world of multipolar powers or networks and coalitions of power".[245]

Third, for all the – covert and overt – efforts of Iran's accommodationist presidents (Rafsanjani, Khatami and Rouhani) in clearing the logjam in relations with the United States, this has proved well-nigh impossible. Rouhani came closest to reaching an enduring accommodation with the US in 2015, but the engagement was so conditional and focused that neither side dared talk of the historic nuclear deal leading to a rapprochement on all fronts. Indeed, many months after the nuclear deal was being implemented, senior Obama administration officials were at pains to show a sceptical Congress that Iran and the US had not suddenly become best friends – in the statement to a joint session of the House Foreign Affairs Committee and the Senate Banking Committee in May 2016, Adam Szubin (Acting Undersecretary for Terrorism and Financial Intelligence) declared that "we will continue to prohibit U.S. persons from investing in Iran, importing or exporting to Iran most goods and services, or otherwise engaging in commercial or financial dealings with most Iranian persons or companies. Iran will also continue to be denied access to U.S. markets".[246]

It has been argued that Iran's worldview is driven by geography and identity as much as by ideology and utopia. So it expressly opted for a non-aligned foreign policy, 'neither East nor West' as the founder of the Islamic republic put it. Iran carved the world into the *mustakbarin* (hegemonic) Satanic (mischievous) powers and the downtrodden *mustazafin* (innocent) countries and peoples. As inheritor of a 'divine' revolution, this Islamic republic is responsible for the well-being of Muslims and for resisting the mustakbarin. An official publication of the IRI's diplomatic missions in London has put the matter in more stark terms: "The Islamic nature of this Revolution necessitates a constant struggle against world oppressors and hegemonists in whatever form they might take and the establishment of friendly relations with those governments which are neither aggressive nor hegemonic".[247] Are these the determinants of Iran's foreign policy? Only to an extent, I would argue, and in putting forward a more textured analysis, I shall defer to an argument made in 1991, which said that the "future Iranian policies are likely to remain highly nationalist, anti-Western in instinct, nonaligned by preference, and in support of Iranian regional hegemony".[248] Why? Because these are the traits of its character, its personality.

Iran's foreign policy does not take shape in isolation, and the wider drivers of change in the region can create serious challenges and pose major difficulties for the Islamic republic. The MENA region today seems to be in free fall and the old axis of power appears increasingly irrelevant to the region's emerging strategic landscape. Far from a handful of states, such countries as Algeria, Egypt, Iran, Iraq, Israel, Saudi Arabia, Syria, and Turkey, dominating their hinterland and influencing the regional system, the MENA regional system is now totally fragmented as well as polarized and unstructured. Strong, or indeed 'fierce', states of the recent past, such as Egypt, Iraq, Libya, and Syria, have disappeared from the scene and have left in their wake voids of power which have been filled by non-state actors who draw their power from communalist forces emerging across the region in place of the old strong states' national narratives, and their inspiration from violent and uncompromising jihadi groups such as Daesh, Jubat al-Nusra, al-Qaeda in the Arabian Peninsula, Boko Haram, and countless other such groups. The diffusion of power alongside the weakening of many of the region's strong and geopolitically important Arab states has created its own unique problems for the remaining MENA 'centralized states' to manage, but in the case of Iran – which is both non-Arab and proudly Shia – Sunni and Arab radicalism brings new dangers and national challenges. So, we have been shown that the conditions and the context for Iran's regional relations have changed dramatically since 2011.

While the Rouhani administration made it a national priority to address the nuclear crisis in order to strengthen the regime's economic base at home and to create space for its regional efforts, a nuclear deal did not help Iran to find new partners in dealing with the twin region-wide crises of state collapse and mass Sunni violence. If anything, the deal heightened the concerns of Iran's regional detractors (Israel, Saudi Arabia and its GCC partners, Egypt) that removal of sanctions and diplomatic restrictions would embolden Tehran in pursuit of its destructive and adventurist policies, to the detriment of the Jewish state on the one hand and the wider Arab world on the other.

The more Iran has tried to defend and protect its allies in Iraq and Syria and the Shia communities of Yemen, Afghanistan, Pakistan, and elsewhere, the more other states and Sunni jihadists have characterized its behaviour as hegemonic, sectarian, and meddling. Moreover, the forces railed against it pose a challenge not only to its regional interests but also to the very identity of the Islamic republic as a Shia-formed regime and a defender of Shiis first and foremost. Saddam Hussein, of course, used anti-Persian and anti-Shia narratives to mask Iraq's aggression against Iran, but in the 1980s, Tehran was able to deflect such attacks by falling on the narrative of an imposed war, the virtues of its 'holy defence', the revolutionary country's victimization by Satanic powers and their regional lackeys. After 2011, however, since when Tehran has been at the forefront of defending the repressive and violent Assad regime in Syria, the successive openly sectarian Shia government in Iraq, and the Yazidi Shia Houthi rebels in Yemen against the will of the international community, it can hardly claim victimization when its armed forces are stationed in the neighbouring countries and when it acts as the main supplier of lethal weapons to its own favoured non-state actors. Iran appears as the aggressor on the so-called Arab street instead of the Muslim world's just power and liberator. Uncomfortably for Tehran, the Islamic republic is so bound by such a strong 'Iran-Shia' identity prism, the very basis of the regime's strategy of socializing the revolution, that it is unable to project a different role externally. It is a prisoner of this prism, which inhibits its abilities to pursue alternative policy options. This, as much as the policy consequences of the Islamic republic acting as what Khan calls a 'protracted conflict state' acutely aware of its precarious condition regionally, now shape its international relations.[249]

As such, Iran is again detached from the emerging new core taking shape around a Saudi/GCC axis, which also includes the other Arab monarchies as well as Egypt, NATO-member Turkey, and Pakistan. This is the closest that the Arab region has ever come to forming a broad multinational coalition, and its strategic focus being on the same enemies as Iran – namely Daesh and al-Qaeda – yet Iran has been excluded from this Saudi-led coalition for its (perceived) policies in Iraq, Syria, Bahrain, Lebanon, and Yemen. The Islamic republic then is again in strategic isolation – bereft of powerful and reliable regional allies and dependent on less than reliable external partners (such as Russia and China). In my estimation, far from the region becoming more receptive to Iranian influence since the Arab uprisings, it has in fact become not only more challenging for Iran but also more dangerous. This is shown in the statements made about Iran by its closest neighbours. Thus, Bahrain's Foreign Minister, Sheikh Khalid al-Khalifa, deliberately glossed over the change of guard in Iran and its re-launch of détente to paint an uncompromisingly negative picture of Iran's regional role to a large audience of regional and international experts and policymakers (in November 2015 at the outset of the Manama Dialogue's annual meeting on regional security), stating:

> Iran is a bigger threat to us than ISIS. We must put an end to Iran's interference in the affairs of regional states. We must not underestimate the damage to regional stability caused by Iran's actions in the region. If we are not serious enough about this, I'm afraid we will remain in a state of conflict indefinitely. Iran is at a crossroads, and it's their choice where they can either choose to have a major shift in their foreign policy and move to phase two of fixing their relationships with the world after their nuclear deal and hopefully it will succeed.[250]

Add to regional challenges Iran's own national makeup, and it is not hard to understand Tehran's focus on internal challenges to the state from, for want of a better phrase, 'ethnic awakening' resulting from the spread of communalism in the region, and is also painfully conscious of the fact that it is increasingly having to bolster, with treasure, diplomacy and military, two failing former Arab powerhouses of Iraq and Syria.

In this sense, the strategic horizon for Iran has narrowed arguably since 2011, and its ability to make regional actors dance to its tune diminished. On reflection, the Islamic republic's 1969 moment proved to be a brief one, and looking forward, not only will the Islamic republic need a new mission statement but also a clearer sense of what it wants regionally and internationally and what its own role should be in such fast-changing conditions. As to how the intertwined pillars of independence, justice, and resistance, which thus far have shaped the ideational basis of the regime's foreign policy conduct, can help it adapt to the changing regional dynamics going forward remains an open question.

But from Tehran's own perspective, Iran's strategic situation looks less bad than the facts might suggest.

- First, despite the deteriorating regional situation, Tehran has managed to keep its alliance structure intact and the 'resistance front' now not only includes Syria and Iraq and Hezbollah (and to a lesser extent Hamas) but also a large community of Shia militias from around the region (including from Afghanistan and Pakistan) recruited to fight for Iran's cause.
- Second, despite the domestic distaste in Lebanon for Hezbollah's active role in keeping the Assad regime in power, one also detects a sense of empowerment as the long-suffering Lebanese now see the shoe on the other foot and the Syrian regime being dependent on their forces.
- Third, Tehran has been able to capitalize on communalization of regional states – in such countries as Afghanistan, Yemen, Iraq, Syria, Lebanon, Bahrain, and also Saudi Arabia – to keep a high level of influence in these fractured or polarized states. In this situation, and so long as its own national diversity is not tested, Tehran uses access to selected communities for influence. In Yemen, for example, Iran's patronage of the Houthi community is partly to securitize Saudi Arabia's southern borders and force it to devote its energies to the security of the Arabian peninsula and therefore away from the Levant and the northern Gulf.
- Fourth, from its own perspective, Tehran has been able demonstrate its growing power at home and abroad by dealing with the United States (its 'great satan') as an equal and thus bringing it to the negotiating table. Tehran averted war, Rouhani's negotiating team have argued, without compromising its principles and interests, while also countering the influence of America's regional allies who were pressing for military strikes on Iran's military and economic assets.
- Fifth, with the resolution of the nuclear crisis, Tehran has untied its hands to play a greater role internationally. Indeed, since October 2013, Tehran successfully cultivated partnerships with powerful economic actors, which

showed signs of bearing fruit when the nuclear deal was finally implemented in January 2016. So Tehran usefully renewed its politico-economic relationships with Russia and China while pursuing better relations with Asia's other economic giants in the shape of India, Republic of Korea and Japan (all three also partners of the United States). Relinking with Japan and South Korea occurred in spring 2016, which cleared the way for Prime Minister Modi to pitch for a close strategic partnership with the Islamic republic in May, during the first official visit of an Indian PM to Iran since 2003. Energy, Indian investment in Iran's gas fields, and Indian interest in the development of Chahbahar port on the edge of the Arabian Sea for the benefit of Iran, Afghanistan and India itself were of particular interest.

At the same time, Tehran also rekindled relations with the powerful European Union and its core states of Germany, France, Italy, Austria and the United Kingdom. Through economic diplomacy with the major economic powers, it attempted to re-enter the international economic system, perhaps as an untapped market in the first instance but more strategically as an important 'global swing state' with the ability to influence the Eurasian strategic landscape.[251] The Islamic republic in the twenty-first century has aimed to shed the role of a 'semi-periphery' state under the influence of dominant powers for the status of an aspirant swing state with a confident and independent foreign policy that can stand up to pressure and also exercise a combination of economic, security and political muscles across Asia and the Mediterranean to satisfy its own interests and ambitions. Shifting power at the global level and the commensurate 'Asianization' of the international economic system has helped facilitate Iran's aspirations for becoming a swing state.

Looking at Iran's foreign policy and international behaviour through a multitude of approaches, an attempt has been made to weigh the impact that exceptionalism – awareness of the uniqueness of the Iranian political system and its ideological underpinning by its post-revolution, often un-united, political elite – has played in the country's rule perception, alliance building, and foreign policy conduct. What strikes close observation of the period since Bani-sadr is the simple dichotomy of the republic vacillating between revolutionary idealism and political realism. Both have been present in abundance, across presidencies and even within a president's term. Ahmadinejad's administration, for example, finally sat with the Americans in Geneva in 2008 to talk nuclear compromise, yet his government had undone much of the work that Khatami's chief nuclear negotiator (Hassan Rouhani) had accomplished between 2002 and 2005.[252]

As Sarioghalam has perceptively observed, these oscillations between idealism and realism will inevitably "breed discontinuity, increase vulnerability and limit diplomacy to tactical interactions".[253] The strategic dimension, assumed by so many to be driving much of Iran's foreign policy calculations, has increasingly been sacrificed at the altar of the immediate – the tactical. The Islamic republic's international relations have tended to travel along the pendulum of revolutionary idealism and political realism and, in the absence of a balance or clearly defined and explained set of national interests, have left the country's leaders open to a plethora of often contradictory, and at times unfair, criticisms from within and without – for being too ideological, dogmatic, opportunistic, devious, untrustworthy, not radical enough, not ideological enough, too weak in the face of 'arrogance', transnationalist, unpredictable, hegemonic, meek. As a social construct, it can be all of these things – and none.

Notes

1 Graham E. Fuller, *The "Center of the Universe": The Geopolitics of Iran* (Boulder, CO: Westview Press, 1991).
2 Ibid., p. 2.
3 Ibid.
4 Hossein Salimi, 'Foreign Policy as Social Construction', in Anoushiravan Ehteshami and Reza Molavi (eds.) *Iran and the International System* (New York, NY: Routledge, 2012), p. 134.
5 Shahram Chubin and Sepehr Zabih, *The Foreign Relations of Iran: Developing State in a Zone of Great Power Conflict* (Berkeley, CA: University of California Press, 1974).
6 Abbas Milani, *The Shah* (New York, NY: Palgrave Macmillan, 2011).
7 Fred Halliday, *Iran: Dictatorship and Development* (New York, NY: Penguin Books, 1979).
8 Maaike Warnaar, *Iranian Foreign Policy during Ahmadinejad: Ideology and Actions* (New York, NY: Palgrave, 2013).
9 See, for example, Maaike Warnaar, ibid.
10 Eric Selbin, 'Revolution in the Real World: Bringing Agency Back In', in John Foran (ed.) *Theorizing Revolutions* (New York, NY: Routledge, 1997), pp. 123–36.
11 Fred Halliday, *Revolution and World Politics: The Rise and Fall of the Sixth Great Power* (London: Macmillan, 1999).
12 Peter Avery, *Modern Iran* (London: Ernest Benn, 1967).
13 Bernard Lewis, *The Middle East: 2000 Years of History from the Rise of Christianity to the Present Day* (London: Phoenix Giant, 1996).
14 Ibid.
15 Roxane Farmanfarmaian, 'Introduction', in Roxane Farmanfarmaian (ed.) *War and Peace in Qajar Persia: Implications Past and Present* (London: Routledge, 2008), p. 5.
16 Napoleon Bonaparte's letter of 14th March 1807 to the Persian king and crown prince from Osterode, in Iradj Amini, *Napoleon and Persia: Franco-Persian Relations under the First Empire* (Richmond, Surrey: Curzon Press, 1999), p. 96.
17 Ibid., p. 195.
18 Avery, op. cit., p. 102.
19 Farmanfarmaian, op. cit., p. 10.
20 See W. S. Haas, *Iran* (New York, NY: 1946), p. 35.
21 Gerd Nonneman, 'Analyzing the Foreign Policies of the Middle East and North Africa: A Conceptual Framework', *The Review of International Affairs*, vol. 3, no. 2, Winter 2003, p. 119.
22 Sepehr Zabih, 'Iran's International Posture: De Facto Nonalignment within a Pro-Western Alliance', *Middle East Journal*, vol. 24, no. 3, Summer 1970, pp. 302–18.
23 Amin Saikal, *The Rise and Fall of the Shah: Iran from Autocracy to Religious Rule* (Princeton, NJ: Princeton University Press, 2009).
24 Alan R. Taylor, *The Arab Balance of Power* (New York, NY: Syracuse University Press, 1982).

25 John C. Campbell, 'Oil Power in the Middle East', *Foreign Affairs*, October 1977, pp. 89–110.
26 Nicholas Cumming-Bruce, *A MEED Special Report – Iran* (London: MEED, February 1977), p. 28.
27 Rouhollah K. Ramazani, 'Iran's Changing Foreign Policy: A Preliminary Discussion', *Middle East Journal*, vol. 24, no. 4, Fall 1970, p. 421.
28 Alinaghi Alikhani's editorial note to Asadollah Alam, *The Shah and I: The Confidential Diary of Iran's Royal Court, 1969–1977* (London: I. B. Tauris, 1991), p. 29.
29 John Duke Anthony, 'The Union of Arab Amirates', *Middle East Journal*, vol. 26, no. 3, Summer 1972, pp. 271–87.
30 Gary Sick, *All Fall Down: America's Fateful Encounter with Iran* (London: I. B. Tauris, 1985), p. 14.
31 *New York Times*, 17 January 1972.
32 Amin Saikal, op. cit.
33 Asadollah Alam, *The Shah and I: The Confidential Diary of Iran's Royal Court, 1969–1977* (London: I. B. Tauris, 1991), p. 517.
34 Mohsen M. Milani, *The Making of Iran's Islamic Revolution* (Boulder, CO: Westview Press, 1994).
35 Fred Halliday, 'Introduction – Iran and the World: Reassertion and Its Costs', in Anoushiravan Ehteshami and Manshour Varasteh (eds.) *Iran and the International Community* (New York, NY: Routledge, 1991), p. 3.
36 Andrew Scott Cooper, 'Showdown at Doha: The Secret Oil Deal That Helped Sink the Shah of Iran', *Middle East Journal*, vol. 62, no. 4, Autumn 2008, pp. 567–91.
37 Ali Rahnemi and Farhad Nomani, *The Secular Miracle: Religion, Politics and Economic Policy in Iran* (London: Zed Books, 1990), p. 302.
38 Fred Halliday, *The Middle East in International Relations: Power, Politics and Ideology* (Cambridge: Cambridge University Press, 2005), p. 37.
39 Islamic Consultative Assembly, *The Constitution of the Islamic Republic of Iran* (Tehran: International Department, Islamic Consultative Assembly, n.d.), pp. 89–90.
40 Manouchehr Mohammadi, 'The Islamic Republic of Iran and the International System: Clash with the Domination Paradigm', in Anoushiravan Ehteshami and Reza Molavi (eds.) *Iran and the International System* (New York, NY: Routledge, 2012), pp. 71–89.
41 J. Matthew McInnis, *Iran's Strategic Thinking: Origins and Evolution* (Washington, DC: American Enterprise Institute, 2015), p. 5.
42 Mahboubeh Sadeghinia, 'The Impact of Iran's Tenth Presidential Elections on its Relations with the EU and Mediterranean States', in Anoushiravan Ehteshami and Reza Molavi (eds.) *Iran and the International System* (New York, NY: Routledge, 2012), p. 189.
43 Abbas Maleki, 'The Islamic Republic of Iran's Foreign Policy: The View from Iran', *Iranian Journal of International Affairs*, vol. vii, no. 4, Winter 1996, p. 747.
44 M. Reza Ghods, *Iran in the Twentieth Century: A Political History* (Boulder, CO: Lynne Rienner, 1989), p. 223.
45 Shaul Bakhash, 'Iran's Foreign Policy under the Islamic Republic, 1979–2000', in L. Carl Brown (ed.) *Diplomacy in the Middle East: The International Relations of Regional and Outside Powers* (London: I. B. Tauris, 2001), p. 247.
46 Bakhash, op. cit.
47 R. K. Ramazani, *Revolutionary Iran: Challenge and Response in the Middle East* (Baltimore, MD: Johns Hopkins University Press, 1986).
48 Maziar Behrooz, 'Trends in the Foreign Policy of the Islamic Republic, 1979–1988', in Nikki R. Keddie and Mark J. Gasiorowski (eds.) *Neither East Nor West: Iran, the Soviet Union, and the United States* (New Haven, CT: Yale University Press, 1990), p. 14.
49 The rise of a revolutionary regime in Iran was, on another level, an irritant for Iraq as it threatened to dent Saddam Hussein's carefully choreographed bid for both Arab leadership – subsequent to Egypt's unilateral peace with Israel – and that of the NAM.

50 Note, for example, Edmund Ghareeb's evidence of Iraqi leaders actually courting their Iranian counterparts in 1979 to form a common front: 'The Roots of Crisis: Iran and Iraq', in Christopher C. Joyner (ed.) *The Persian Gulf War: Lessons for Strategy, Law, and Diplomacy* (New York, NY: Greenwood Press, 1990), pp. 21–38.
51 Efraim Karsh, *The Iran-Iraq War: A Military Analysis* (London: International Institute for Strategic Studies Adelphi Paper no. 220, Spring 1987), p. 58.
52 Anthony Parsons, 'Iran and the United Nations, with Particular Reference to the Iran-Iraq War', in Anoushiravan Ehteshami and Manshour Varasteh (eds.) *Iran and the International Community* (New York, NY: Routledge, 1991), p. 15.
53 Parsons, ibid., p. 24.
54 Data for this section has relied on the International Institute for Strategic Studies' annual *Military Balance* and the Stockholm Peace Research Institute's arms transfers database.
55 Karsh, op. cit.
56 Declassified Foreign and Commonwealth Office documents, for example, show that while the British government was fully aware of Iraq's illegal use of chemical weapons (CW) in the war, it chose silence over the matter because a UK company had, unbeknown to itself, supplied equipment which was being used in Iraq's al-Qaim chemical weapons plant and also because London felt vulnerable to criticism over its own CW stockpiles. See Cahal Milmo, 'Why Britain Backed Down on Banning Saddam Hussein's Chemical Weapons during Iran War', *The Independent*, 3 July 2015.
57 Shahram Chubin and Charles Tripp, *Iran and Iraq at War* (London: I. B. Tauris, 1988), p. 246.
58 M. E. Ahrari, 'Iran, GCC and the Security Dimensions in the Persian Gulf', in Hooshang Amirahmadi and Nader Entessar (eds.) *Reconstruction and Regional Diplomacy in the Persian Gulf* (New York, NY: Routledge, 1992), pp. 193–212.
59 Fred Halliday, *Revolution and World Politics: The Rise and Fall of the Sixth Great Power* (London: Macmillan, 1999).
60 Hussein J. Agha and Ahmad S. Khalidi, *Syria and Iran: Rivalry and Cooperation* (London: Pinter, 1995).
61 The value of this partnership was revealed in 1988 at the height of the crisis in Iran-GCC relations following the Hajj incident in August 1987 and the death of 402 pilgrims and policemen, and Iran's storming and ransacking of Kuwaiti and Saudi embassies in Tehran and attacking their diplomats, and the escalating 'tanker war' in the Persian Gulf waters. In January 1988 Damascus played an instrumental role in deescalating Iran-GCC tensions and bringing the parties together for their first high-level face-to-face contact in the UAE. This proved to be a turning point as by the summer Iran had accepted SCR 598 ceasefire resolution which preceded constitutional reforms in Iran and the recognition that Tehran needed to make amends with its Arab neighbours.
62 See Anoushiravan Ehteshami and Raymond A. Hinnebusch, *Syria and Iran: Middle Powers in a Penetrated Regional System* (New York, NY: Routledge, 1997).
63 H. E. Chehabi, 'Iran and Lebanon in the Revolutionary Decade', in H. E. Chehabi (ed.) *Distant Relations: Iran and Lebanon in the Last 500 Years* (London: I. B. Tauris, 2006), pp. 201–30.
64 The Islamic republic's first defence minister, Mostafa Chamran, in fact flew to Tehran in February 1979 from his base in Lebanon.
65 For details see Anoushiravan Ehteshami and Raymond Hinnebusch, *Syria and Iran: Middle Powers in a Penetrated Regional System* (New York, NY: Routledge, 1997).
66 Magnus Ranstrop, *Hizb'Allah: The Politics of the Western Hostage Crisis* (London: Macmillan, 1997).
67 From Joseph Alagha, *The Shifts in Hizbullah's Ideology: Religious Ideology, Political Ideology, and Political Pragmatism* (Amsterdam: Amsterdam University Press, 2006), p. 224.

68 *APS Diplomat*, 2–9 April 1988.
69 *APS Diplomat*, 21–28 May 1988.
70 Nadia von Maltzahn, *The Syria-Iran Axis: Cultural Diplomacy and International Relations in the Middle East* (London: I. B. Tauris, 2013).
71 *Al-Ahram*, 15 January 1985.
72 Islamic Republic News Agency (IRNA), 18 April 1988.
73 Western diplomats had estimated that perhaps as much as half of Iran's heavy armour had been captured by Iraqi forces in the 1988 battles and reports soon emerged that Iraq had donated billions of dollars worth of captured Iranian military hardware to Jordan in August 1988, which included 90 Chieftain, 60 M-47 and 19 Scorpion tanks and a further 35 armoured personnel carriers. See *APS Diplomat*, 13–20 August 1988.
74 *APS Diplomat*, 7–14 May 1988.
75 *APS Diplomat*, 1–9 July 1988.
76 He made this sweeping speech on 22nd February 1989, a day after Iran opened an all-important Consulate-General in Shanghai and the announcement that China's Vice-Premier would lead a high-level delegation visit to Tehran in March. See *APS Diplomat*, 18–15 February 1989.
77 *APS Diplomat*, 18–25 February 1989.
78 Statement of the IRI Ministry of Foreign Affairs, 7 March 1989. *APS Diplomat*, 4–11 March 1989.
79 Speaking at a large gathering of DPRK officials which also included President Kim Il Sung. IRNA, 17 May 1989. This statement captures at once the radicalism and pragmatism of Iran's foreign policy, for here is the president of arguably the only revolutionary Islamic state on earth, which claims to put Islam as its guide, urging closer links with the most authoritarian, anti-religion, communist regime on earth for the sake of challenging the United States – their common foe.
80 Shireen T. Hunter, 'Iran from the August 1988 Cease-fire to the April 1992 Majlis Elections', in Robert O. Freedman (ed.) *The Middle East after Iraq's Invasion of Kuwait* (Gainesville, FL: University Press of Florida, 1993), p. 200.
81 John Calabrese, *Revolutionary Horizons: Regional Foreign Policy in Post-Khomeini Iran* (London: Macmillan Press, 1994).
82 Alex Edwards, *"Dual Containment" Policy in the Persian Gulf: The USA, Iran, and Iraq, 1991–2000* (New York, NY: Palgrave Macmillan, 2014).
83 Warren Christopher, 'Introduction', in Paul H. Kreisberg (ed.) *American Hostages in Iran: The Conduct of a Crisis* (New Haven, CT: Yale University Press, 1985), p. 1.
84 Quoted by Elaine Sciolino, 'Christopher Signals a Tougher U.S. Line Toward Iran', *Washington Post*, 31 March 1993.
85 IISS, *Strategic Survey 1991–1992* (London: International Institute for Strategic Studies, 1992).
86 *APS Diplomat*, 18–25 March 1989.
87 Ibid.
88 Mehran Kamrava (ed.) *International Politics of the Persian Gulf* (Syracuse, NY: Syracuse University Press, 2011).
89 Between 1992 and 1995 as many as five rounds of talks were held between the two sides, covering anything from the Middle East peace process to human right, terrorism, proliferation, and the situations in Bosnia and Afghanistan.
90 Shahriar Sabet-Saeidi, 'Iranian-European Relations: A Strategic Partnership?', in Anoushiravan Ehteshami and Mahjoob Zweiri (eds.) *Iran's Foreign Policy: From Khatami to Ahmadinejad* (Reading: Ithaca Press, 2011), pp. 55–72.
91 *APS Diplomat*, 17–14 June 1989.
92 IISS, op. cit, p. 109.
93 In 1996 Iran agreed its largest arms deal after the revolution (for $4.5 billion) with the country that had denied it nuclear power a year earlier, namely China.

International relations 261

94 Comment made by the IAEA Iran inspection team leader, cited in IISS, *Strategic Survey 1991–1992* (London: International Institute for Strategic Studies, 1992), p. 108.
95 Information that Iran had secretly imported from China 1.8 tonnes of nuclear material in 1991 only came to light subsequent to the IAEA's inspection of Iranian nuclear sites in 2003.
96 Hassan Rouhani, *National Security and Nuclear Diplomacy (Amniyat-e Meli va Diplomacey-e Hastehyee)* (Tehran: Center for Strategic Studies, 2011). Pakistan, Rouhani, says, was approached in 1987 for the transfer of a complete centrifuge machine for Iranian technicians to copy, but as this option proved problematic Tehran decided to tap into the black market and thus purchased 'several hundred' (Pakistan-origin) centrifuges through a Swiss-based middleman known as Taher. On arrival Iranians found these to be secondhand and thus contaminated, which has been the root cause of Iran's dispute with the IAEA ever since: Was Iran experimenting with nuclear products without notifying the Agency as required?
97 *APS Diplomat*, 24 September–1 October 1994.
98 Eva Rakel, 'Paradigms of Iranian Policy in Central Eurasia and Beyond', in Mehdi Parvizi Amineh and Henk Houwelling (eds.) *Central Eurasia in Global Politics: Conflict, Security and Development* (Leiden: Brill, 2005), pp. 235–57.
99 Eric Hooglund, 'Iran and Central Asia', in Anoushiravan Ehteshami (ed.) *From the Gulf to Central Asia: Players in the Great New Game* (Exeter: University of Exeter Press, 1994), pp. 114–28.
100 ECO has survived all the upheavals of the region and despite a low intra-ECO trade of some 9 per cent of the total for the group, with a population of 445 million people, a labour force of 164 million, and a total GDP of $1.9 trillion, it has emerged as a significant economic grouping in Asia. See *ECO Statistical Report 2015* (Tehran: Secretariat of the Economic Cooperation Organization, 2015.).
101 Mohammad Farhad Atai, 'Iran and the Newly-Independent States of Central Asia', in Ali Mohammadi and Anoushiravan Ehteshami (eds.) *Iran and Eurasia* (Reading: Ithaca Press, 2000), pp. 171–98; Edmund Herzig, 'Iran and Central Asia', in Roy Allison and Lena Jonson (eds.) *Central Asian Security: The New International Context* (London: Royal Institute of International Affairs, 2001), pp. 111–23.
102 Anoushiravan Ehteshami (ed.) *From the Gulf to Central Asia: Players in the Great New Game* (Exeter: University of Exeter Press, 1994).
103 Relations are discussed in some detail in Ali Mohammadi and Anoushiravan Ehteshami (eds.) *Iran and Eurasia* (Reading: Ithaca Press, 2000).
104 Abbas Maleki, 'Cooperation: A New Component of the Iranian Foreign Policy', *Iranian Journal of International Affairs*, vol. v, no. 1, Spring 1993, pp. 16–20.
105 Worth noting that at the height of the Rushdie crisis with the West, in February–March 1989, Tehran welcomed Soviet Foreign Minister Shaverdnadze and Vice-Premier Tian Jiyung in quick succession, building relations. Khamenei, in one of his last major acts as president, paid an official visit to China in May 1989, the first such visit by an Iranian head of state since 1979, to strengthen relations with the PRC. This was billed as a 'significant event' by the Chinese news agency, *Xinhua* (9 May 1989).
106 Pierre Pahlavi and Afshin Hojati, 'Iran and Central Asia: The Smart Politics of Prudent Pragmatism', in Emilian Kavalski (ed.) *The New Central Asia: The Regional Impact of International Actors* (Singapore: World Scientific Publishing, 2010), pp. 215–38.
107 Ziba Moshaver, 'Revolution, Theocratic Leadership and Iran's Foreign Policy: Implications for Iran-EU Relations', *The Review of International Affairs*, vol. 3, no. 2, Winter 2003, pp. 283–305.
108 He received 70 per cent of votes cast in an election with an 80 per cent voter turnout.
109 Speech at the Ninth OIC Summit in Doha, IRNA, 12 November 2000.
110 Full text translated ad distributed by salamiran.org.

111 Alireza Ansari, 'Iranian Foreign Policy under Khatami: Reform and Reintegration', in Ali Mohammadi and Anoushiravan Ehteshami (eds.) *Iran and Eurasia* (Reading: Ithaca Press, 2000), pp. 35–58.
112 President Khatami's speech at the UN-sponsored 'Conference of Dialogue Amongst Civilizations', IRNA, 5 September 2000.
113 Ibid., p. 55.
114 Edward Wastnidge, 'The Modalities of Iranian Soft Power: From Cultural Diplomacy to Soft Power', *Politics Journal* (online article), 24 December 2014, pp. 1–14.
115 Sabet-Saeidi, op cit., notes that the meeting on the margins of the September 1998 UN General Assembly between the two countries' foreign ministers helped bury the hatchet over the Rushdie affair and paved the way for the restoration of relations between Tehran and London.
116 Shireen Hunter, *Iran's Foreign Policy in the Post-Soviet Era: Resisting the New International Order* (Westport, CT: Praeger, 2010).
117 In the course of his May 1999 trip to Syria, Khatami met with the leaders of Hamas and Islamic Jihad as well as those of the Popular Front for the Liberation of Palestine and the PFLP-General Command – all designated as terrorist organizations by the West.
118 Khatami and Hariri had got on so well that Hariri returned to Tehran in June 2001 to congratulate Khatami on his second electoral success, and the two met again in May 2003 when Khatami visited Lebanon.
119 Al-Bawaba News, 15 January 2001.
120 Mona Ziade, 'Khatami backs Syria and Lebanon against US Threats', *Daily Star*, 15 May 2003.
121 Shireen Hunter, 'Iran, Turkey, and Central Asia: The Islamic Connection', in Elizabeth Van Wie Davis and Rouben Azazian (eds.) *Islam, Oil, and Geopolitics: Central Asia after September 11* (Lanham, MD: Rowman and Littlefield, 2007), pp. 187–202.
122 *Payvand Iran News*, 21 April 2002.
123 Alidad Mafinezam and Aria Mehrabi, *Iran and its Place Among Nations* (Westport, CT: Praeger, 2008), p. 50.
124 Bill Samii cited by Charles Recknagel, 'Iran: Khatami Tours Central Asia to Press for Iran Energy Routes, Lower U.S. Presence', RFE/RL, 25 April 2002.
125 Economic Cooperation Organization, *ECO Statistical Report 2014* (Tehran: Secretariat of ECO, 2014).
126 For a detailed discussion, see Anoushiravan Ehteshami, 'Iran's Assessment of the Iraq Crisis and the Post-9/11 International Oreder', in Ramesh Thakur and Waheguru Pal Singh Sidhu (eds.) *The Iraq Crisis and World Order* (Tokyo: United Nations Press, 2006), pp. 134–60.
127 Mary Buckley and Robert Singh (eds.) *The Bush Doctrine and the War on Terrorism: Global Responses, Global Consequences* (New York, NY: Routledge, 2006).
128 The White House, Office of the Press Secretary, 29 January 2002.
129 'Remarks by National Security Advisor Condoleezza Rice on Terrorism and Foreign Policy', The White House, Office of the Press Secretary, 29 April 2002.
130 Ray Takeyh, *Guardians of the Revolution: Iran and the World in the Age of the Ayatollahs* (Oxford: Oxford University Press, 2009).
131 Saira Khan, *Iran and Nuclear Weapons: Protracted Conflict and Proliferation* (New York, NY: Routledge, 2010).
132 Mel Gurtov, *Superpower on Crusade: The Bush Doctrine in US Foreign Policy* (Boulder, CO: Lynne Reinner, 2006).
133 This view had become so prevalent amongst the conservative elite that President Ahmadinejad dared repeat the myth of 9/11 as an American conspiracy – "the US government orchestrated the attack in order to save the Zionist regime in the Middle East" – from the tribune of the United Nations general assembly in September 2010, nine years after the acts of terror on US soil. IRNA, 23 September 2010.

International relations **263**

134 Donette Murray, *US Foreign Policy and Iran: American–Iranian Relations since the Islamic Revolution* (New York, NY: Routledge, 2010).
135 Ibid., p. 127.
136 Interview given to *Omid-e Atomi* (Nuclear Hope) magazine, IRNA, 27 October 2015.
137 Shahram Chubin, 'Arms Build-Up and Regional Military Balance', in Hooshang Amirahmadi and Eric Hooglund (eds.) *US-Iran Relations: Areas of Tension and Mutual Interest* (Washington, DC: Middle East Institute, 1994), p. 46.
138 Rouhani, op. cit., p. 37.
139 Rouhani, ibid. To give stronger direction to the nuclear programme, Khatami set up a uranium-enrichment council in1998, chaired by the president himself, to coordinate and oversee the multi-strand enrichment drive being undertaken. It was here that two critical decisions were taken: to install 54,000 centrifuges at Natanz and to begin work on the Arak 40-megawatt heavy water reactor.
140 Ibid.
141 Michael Eisenstadt, 'Living with a Nuclear Iran', *Survival*, vol. 44, no. 3, Autumn 1999, p. 131.
142 http://www.nci.org/06nci/01-31/Revelations.htm.
143 Robert J. Einhorn, 'A Transatlantic Strategy on Iran's Nuclear Program', *The Washington Quarterly*, vol. 27, no. 4, pp. 21–32.
144 IRNA, 10 February 2003.
145 Mohamed Elbaradei noted in his memoirs that the IAEA found "that nearly all of Iran's centrifuge technology had been imported from other countries". Mohamed Elbaradei, *The Age of Deception: Nuclear Diplomacy in Treacherous Times* (London: Bloomsbury, 2011), p. 117.
146 Mehran Kamrava, 'The United State and Iran: A Dangerous but Contained Rivalry' (Washington, DC: Middle East Institute *Policy Brief* no. 9, March 2008).
147 Interview in Jordan with a senior administration official on the margins of the World Economic Forum meeting held on the east bank of the Dead Sea, 21–23 June 2003.
148 Iran's safeguard agreement gave it 180 days to declare changes to its existing nuclear profile before it, for example, introduced any nuclear materials in Natanz.
149 David Albright and Corey Hinderstein, 'Iran, Player or Rogue?', *Bulletin of Atomic Scientists*, vol. 59, no. 5, September–October 2003, pp. 52–58.
150 Elbaradei, op. cit.
151 See full report at www.iaea.org.
152 State investigation of Pakistan's famous Khan Research Laboratory and subsequent arrest of several of its nuclear scientists in 2004 revealed that they had worked intimately with their Iranian counterparts, advising them on their nuclear programme: "We confided in them about the items needed to construct a nuclear bomb, as well as the makes of equipment, the names of companies, the countries from which they could be procured and how they could be procured". See Massoud Ansari, 'Nuclear Scientists from Pakistan Admit Helping Iran with Bomb-making', *Sunday Telegraph*, 25 January 2004.
153 Elbaradei, op. cit., p. 117.
154 Elbaradei, op. cit., p. 135.
155 This analysis is a condensed summary of the balance of opinion in Tehran in 2003–04 based on close interviews with members of both the political and intellectual elites during 2005–06.
156 Nima Gerami, *Leadership Divided? The Domestic Politics of Iran's Nuclear Debate* (Washington, DC: The Washington Institute for Near East Policy, February 2014).
157 Heidar Ali Balouji, 'The Process of National Security Decision Making in Iran: The Signing of the Additional Protocol', in Shannon N. Kile (ed.) *Europe and Iran: Perspectives on Non-proliferation* (Oxford: Oxford University Press for SIPRI, 2005), pp. 72–96.

158 Seyed Hossein Mousavian, *The Iranian Nuclear Crisis: A Memoir* (Washington, DC: Carnegie Endowment for International Peace, 2012).
159 AFP, 3 October, 2003.
160 Full text from Reuters, 21 October 2003.
161 Rouhani, op. cit., p. 57.
162 Jim Muir, 'Nuclear Deal Splits Iran Hardliners', BBC News, 22 October 2003.
163 Anne Penketh, 'Iran 'Will Resume Nuclear Programme' if Rebuked by Watchdog', *Independent*, 17 June 2004.
164 IISS, *Strategic Survey 2002/3* (Oxford: Oxford University Press for IISS, 2003), p. 172.
165 Daniel Dombey and Gareth Smyth, 'Iran Defiant in Face of IAEA Criticism over Nuclear Stance', *Financial Times*, 26 September 2005.
166 Elbaradei, op. cit., p. 144.
167 Statement of Foreign Minister Kamal Kharrazi, quoted in Elaine Sciolino, 'France Chastises Iran on Nuclear Inspections', *International Herald Tribune*, 22 April 2004.
168 Ibid., p. 194.
169 UN Security Council adopted resolution 1696 at the end of July demanding immediate suspension of all enrichment activities as a precondition of negotiations. This pushed into long grass the 'freeze-for-freeze' formula of negotiations being worked on by Larijani and the EU's high representative for common foreign and security policy, Javier Solana. Under the freeze-for-freeze arrangements, Iran would not raise its number of centrifuges and the West would not introduce UN sanctions on Iran.
170 Elbaradei, op. cit., p. 199.
171 Mousavian, op. cit.
172 Barbara Slavin, *Bitter Friends, Bosom Enemies: Iran, the U.S., and the Twisted Path to Confrontation* (New York, NY: St. Martin's Press, 2007), p. 225.
173 Elbaradei, op. cit., p. 203.
174 The sanctions included an international ban on all military trade with Iran, imposition of a travel ban on political and security figures deemed to be involved in the nuclear programme, limiting Iran's access to international finance, and the freezing of more Iranian assets overseas.
175 Seyed Hossein Mousavian, *The Iranian Nuclear Crisis: A Memoir* (Washington, DC: Carnegie Endowment for International Peace, 2012), p. 263.
176 Reuters, 15 March 2012. SWIFT handles more than $6 trillion payments daily, and managed 2 million Iranian cross-border transactions at the time.
177 More tensions followed this announcement in 2009, for the IAEA stated that information from other sources had traced Iran's site designs for this facility to 2006, "when Iran itself accepts that it was bound by the modified Code 3.1 to have informed the agency" then. Iran has reported that its design work had begun in 2007. Under Code 3.1 (introduced in 2003), Iran had agreed to provide the IAEA with design information for new facilities as soon as the decision to build had been made. Iran in December 2009 said that it was ending the application of Code 3.1, which technically it cannot do unilaterally under the terms of Article 39 of Iran Safeguards Agreement.
178 *Financial Times*, 29 May 2008.
179 IAEA Board of Governnors, *Implementation of the NPT Safeguards Agreement and Relevant Provisions of Security Council Resolutions 1737 (2006), 1747 (2007), 1803 (2008) and 1835 (2008) in the Islamic Republic of Iran* (Vienna: International Atomic Energy Agency), 18 February 2010.
180 Ibid., p. 3.
181 Quoted in Doyle McManus, 'Talking with Iran – and Sending a Message', *Los Angeles Times*, I November 2009.
182 Elbaradie, op. cit.

183 David Patrikarakos, *Nuclear Iran: The Birth of an Atomic State* (London: I. B. Tauris, 2012), p. 237.
184 Mousavian, op. cit., p. 287.
185 The White House, *The National Security Strategy of the United States of America* (Washington, DC: The White House, 2006), pp. 20–21.
186 Kamrava, op. cit.
187 Nicole Stracke, 'GCC and the Challenge of US-Iran Negotiations', *GRC Analysis*, 5 March 2009.
188 Ibid.
189 Jay Solomon, 'U.S. Doubts Iran will Respond to Overtures, Clinton says', *Wall Street Journal*, 3 March 2009.
190 *New York Times*, 18 June, 2009.
191 Though Hugo Chavez of Venezuela had been a regular visitor to Iran since 2001 (under Khatami) and was making his ninth visit in October 2010 in support of Iran's defiance of UN sanctions.
192 Jonathan Wheately and Najmeh Bozorgmehr, 'Ahmadi-Nejad tests Brazilian Diplomacy', *Financial Times*, 22 November 2009.
193 Hilal Khashan quoted in Robert Tate, 'Ahmadinejad gets Hero's Welcome in Lebanon, as Israel, West Watch with Suspicion', RFE/RL, 14 October 2010.
194 Oil prices remained above $100 per barrel right to the end of Ahmadinejad's presidency but, for reasons beyond Iran's control, started to decline within months of Rouhani's election victory in June 2013. OPEC data shows that the price of oil had fallen to just $60 per barrel in December 2014, around its 2008 figure, which was detrimental to Iran whose economy was straining under sanctions and structural deficiencies.
195 IISS, *The Military Balance 2007* (London: Routledge for IISS, 2007), pp. 209–13.
196 The United States provided millions of dollars in support of Israel's war effort, in terms of emergency aviation fuel, precision-guided weaponry, missiles, and cluster bombs. See Henrietta Wilkins, *The Making of Lebanon's Foreign Policy: Understanding the 2006 Hezbollah-Israel War* (New York, NY: Routledge, 2013).
197 Ironically, some years after the war, Hezbollah's leadership apologized for starting the war, by taking two Israeli soldiers hostage on July 12th, and the devastation it brought.
198 Saudi offer of over $1.5 billion in humanitarian aid to Lebanon was part of this strategy.
199 Joe Stirling, 'Obama Says he's not Bluffing on Iran Nukes', CNN, 3 March 2012.
200 Richard Spencer, 'UAE Moves on Illegal Nuclear and Weapons Trade', *The Telegraph*, 1 July 2010.
201 BBC News, 4 June 2013.
202 Peter Goodspeed, 'As Arab Spring Topples Dictators, Iran's Influence Grows', 26 November 2011.
203 *Financial Times*, 20 October 2013.
204 'Hamas 2010 Budget Mainly 'Foreign Aid' from Iran', *World Tribune*, 5 January 2011.
205 Hamid Fadhel (Iraq-based political commentator) quoted in 'Iraq's Shiites Grudgingly back Syria's Baath', *Kuwait Times*, 26 April 2011.
206 Ali M. Ansari, *Iran under Ahmadinejad: The Politics of Confrontation* (London: Routledge for IISS, Adelphi Paper 393, 2007), p. 45.
207 Saeed Kamali Dehgan, 'Iran Elections: Former Presidents Endorse Moderate Hassan Rouhani', *The Guardian*, 11 June 2013.
208 Rouhani, op. cit., p. 77.
209 *Asharq al-Awsat*, 7 December 2013.
210 Mohammad Javad Zarif, 'A Message from Iran', *New York Times*, 20 April 2015.

211 Adnan Tabatabai, 'Nuclear Talks: Paradigm Shift in Iran Foreign Policy', lobelog.com, 25 June 2015.
212 Interview given to the *Sharq al-Awsat*, 21 November 2013.
213 Jason Burke, 'Riyadh Will Build Nuclear Weapons if Iran Gets Them, Saudi Prince Warns', *The Guardian*, 29 June 2011.
214 Rouhani's publicized telephone conversation with President Obama on 27 September 2013 in New York as he was leaving the country was a message that he was not afraid of negotiating with Washington.
215 Siegfried S. Hecker, 'For Iran, a Nuclear Option More Trouble than it was Worth', *Bulletin of the Atomic Scientists*, 18 January 2016.
216 'Explanatory Note by the Permanent Mission of the Islamic Republic of Iran to the IAEA on the report of the Director General on the Implementation of Safeguards in the Islamic Republic of Iran (GOV/2013/40 dated 28 August 2013), 12 September 2013', IAEA Information Circular INFCIRC, 26 September 2013, 20pp.
217 Siegfried S. Hecker, op. cit.
218 RFE/RL, 16 October 2013.
219 Reuters, 17 October 2013.
220 International Crisis Group, *Iran After the Nuclear Deal* (Brussels: International Crisis Group, Middle East Report no. 166, 15 December 2015).
221 Kenneth Katzman and Paul K. Kerr, *Iran Nuclear Agreement* (Washington, DC: Congressional Research Service, 31 May 2016).
222 IRNA, 26 August 2015.
223 *APS Diplomat*, 6–13 February 1988.
224 See Peter Jones, 'Hope and Disappointment: Iran and the Arab Spring', *Survival*, vol. 55, no. 4, August 2013, pp. 73–84.
225 AFP, 19 October 2015.
226 http://www.gmfus.org/publications/iranian-moment-and-turkey.
227 Foreign Minister Adel bin Ahmed al-Jubeir's statement provided by the Saudi Ministry of Foreign Affairs, 3 January 2016: http://www.mofa.gov.sa/m/en/info/Pages/viewarticle.aspx?pageurl=/sites/mofaen/ServicesAndInformation/news/MinistryNews/Pages/ArticleID2016140473500.aspx.
228 Saudi Press Agency, 3 January 2016.
229 Foreign Minister Sameh Shoukry's comments were made on 5th January. *Arab News*, 6 January 2016.
230 See Saudi Press Agency, 10 January 2016.
231 Ladane Nasseri and Glen Carey, 'Saudi Arabia Has a Plan B to Try to Stop Iran's Economic Rise', Bloomberg, 26 May 2016.
232 BBC News, 4 January 2016.
233 Mohammad Javad Zarif, 'Saudi Arabia's Reckless Extremism', *New York Times*, 10 January 2016.
234 Adel bin Ahmed al-Jubeir, 'Can Iran Change?', *New York Times*, 19 January 2016.
235 Shlomi Eldar, 'Iran Stakes out Position Ahead of PA Collapse', *al-Monitor*, 1 March 2016.
236 Henry A. Kissinger and George P. Shultz, 'The Iran Deal and Its Consequences', *Wall Street Journal*, 7 April 2015.
237 Interview given to *Keyhan* and reported in Middle East Briefing, 13 July 2015.
238 Majid Rafizadeh, 'On Iran's Future Dealings with the 'Great Satan'', *al-Arabiya*, 7 November 2014.
239 Henry A Kissinger, 'Job One Abroad: Iran', *Washington Post*, 18 November 2012.
240 Ayatollah Khamenei speaking on 12 July 2015 in Tehran to a gathering of university students – just two days before the landmark nuclear deal was signed in Vienna. Cited by Mehdi Khalaji, 'The Nuclear Deal May Weaken Rouhani', *PolicyWatch* 2453, 14 July 2015.

241 Mahmood Sariolghalam, 'Iran's Emerging Regional Security Doctrine: Domestic Sources and the Role of International Constraints', in ECSSR, *The Gulf: Challenges of the Future* (Abu Dhabi: Emirates Center for Strategic Studies and Research, 2005), p. 174.
242 Fuller, op. cit., 241.
243 Quoted in Thomas Erdbrink, 'China Deepens Its Footprint in Iran After Lifting of Sanctions', *New York Times*, 24 January 2016.
244 See Amir Toumaj, *Iran's Economy of Resistance: Implications for Future Sanctions* (Washington, DC: American Enterprise Institute, November 2014), p. 8.
245 Ibid., p. 9.
246 This was after the US declared, for the benefit of non-US businesses, that its agencies would not prevent legitimate and permissible business activities taking place between Iran and third parties. See Kambiz Foroohar, 'Nuclear Deal Promised new Investment. Iran's still Waiting', Bloomberg, 25 May 2016.
247 Embassy of IRI, *After the Revolution: Islamic Republic of Iran* (London: Embassy of the Islamic Republic of Iran, n.d.), p. 24.
248 Fuller, op. cit., p. 268.
249 Khan, op. cit., pp. 27–44.
250 See Ismaeel Naar, 'Yemen's Present and Iran's Future Dominate Talks at Manama Dialogue', al-Arabiya, 1 November 2015.
251 The concept of a global swing states has been adapted from Daniel M. Kliman and Richard Fontaine, *Global Swing States: Brazil, India, Indonesia, Turkey and the Future of International Order* (Washington, DC: Center for a New American Security and the German Marshall Fund of the United States, 2012).
252 Foreign Minister Manouchehr Mottaki went so far as to say: "I think there can be a meeting both on the opening of a United States Interests Section in Iran and also on starting direct flights. We have proposed direct flights between the United States and Iran last year, given the intense demand from both American and Iranian people". Quoted in Sebnum Arso, 'Iran Open to U.S. Diplomatic Talks, Official Says', *New York Times*, 19 July 2008.
253 Mahmood Sariolghalam, 'Perceptions of Power and Multiplicity of Interests: Iran's Regional Security Policy', in ECSSR *Arabian Gulf Security: Internal and External Challenges* (Abu Dhabi: Emirates Center for Strategic Studies and Research, 2008), p. 95.

CONCLUSION

Iran's revolution was not a *fait accompli*, and the resultant regime emerged in the course of a fairly short but decisive revolutionary process. All revolutions are environment-specific waves, but this one was very different from all recognized previous revolutions. To begin with, it changed the old order with the weapon of religion and turned the Marxist slogan of 'religion is the opium of the masses' on its head. Its leadership was largely religious, with the liberal elements of the anti-Shah movement using religion and Islamic narratives and concepts in their campaigns. The core of the revolutionary leadership, moreover, was made up of the men of the cloth – clerics occupied the leadership role quickly once the movement had started. This was also the first of modern revolutions in which the 'vanguard party' was established after the successful overthrow of the old order and not before it. In fact, as we saw, the vanguard party itself was dissolved less than ten years after the revolution due to the absence of a coherent strategy for government and a well-structured political ideology with clearly-stated goals and objectives.

The vagueness that had created and kept together the revolutionary coalition came apart within a year of the republic's establishment and since then the (largely clerical) inner circle of the regime has found it impossible to create a cohesive blueprint, or acceptable vision, for this Islamic republic. The post-revolution political system is complex and, despite formal institutions of governance and a constitutionally mandated division of power, informal networks – which ebb and flow across factions – and the unelected organs of the state set parameters of continuity (and possible change) for the political system. The two major political blocs of today, loosely defined around a right-leaning group of conservatives/traditionalists and centre/left-leaning group of reformists, represent the culmination of decades of political interactions in search of a viable Islamic state. The competing camps represent starkly different visions of Iran and its place in the world, as much as of the international system itself, and this prohibits the emergence of a regime at peace with itself and the world.

In Iran, the revolutionary process itself continues to cast a long shadow on the nezam and, thanks to the contradictions in the system of governance established after the revolution, the regime finds it almost impossible to chart a new, or at least viable, path towards a post-revolutionary order. This is perhaps to be expected, as examples of China and France illustrate how long a revolutionary legacy can last and, because of this, how difficult it is for the political masters of the revolutionary regime to steer the state in a new direction without undermining their own authority or, worse, at the cost of the regime itself. Chinese and Iranian leaders are fully aware that when this was tried, as in the Soviet Union in the mid-1980s, very soon the regime in its entirety collapsed.[1] But whereas China seems to have found a way of adapting and indeed profiting from the globalization of capital, the Islamic republic, for all its pragmatism, has found it well-nigh impossible to break free from the unique ideological bend of the nezam and some of the elite's fear of change at the cost of religio-cultural annihilation. In this sense, the Leader's obsession with a cultural invasion of his beloved Iran is as much about preservation of the existing order as about how opening up to the world would force a redefinition of the Islamic republic and thus make it unrecognizable. Moreover, as the first generation masters of the nezam reach an advanced age, the battle of ideas and policies has also acquired a generational edge to it.

Data presented in this book also suggests that mass participation in the political process is indicative of a high degree of engagement with the political system, though often in anticipation of bringing about change through the ballot box. The process in itself bestows upon the regime a degree of legitimacy and a high level of ownership, but this in itself does not legitimize its policies, whether at home or abroad. It has been shown that voters use the ballot box time and again to intervene in the political process and force a change of course on the regime, as in the 1997, 2005 and 2013 presidential elections. But, as we have seen, institutional, legal and political limits exist on how much change the voters can actually bring about.

In the Khatami period, they engaged in the political process arguably with a view to changing governance, knowing full well that they could change only government. And when even this was apparently denied to them, in 2009, the masses revolted in large numbers – 'where is my vote' became an actual and symbolic cry for structural change. But this episode also showed how much change the regime can actually tolerate. June 2009 was perhaps Iran's Tiananmen Square moment and regime reaction here, much like in China, was to forcibly block off all avenues for dissent. Unlike China in 1989, however, which chose accelerated international economic integration as the means for deferring political protests, Iran is yet to decide whether it is prepared to integrate globally. The much-touted 'resistance economy' model arguably seems to suggest continuing separation as the country's grand economic strategy. Whether a decision on the country's long-term economic strategy, particularly in the context of Iran's desire to attract foreign direct investment, can be delayed for long in the post-sanctions environment remains to be seen, however.

The book has shown that 'narrating Iran' is a profound theoretical and methodological challenge, made harder by the fact that international comparisons are almost impossible to make. A subject of great importance, which indirectly also speaks to the residual national power of the Islamic republic, is Iran's regional and international role. Opinion remains deeply divided over whether Iran is a 'weakling or hegemon', to paraphrase Cordesman.[2] Will the nuclear deal, in this context, help further strengthen Iran and embolden it to pursue its not-so-secret regional hegemonic ambitions, or will the lifting of sanctions force open the closed doors of the Iranian state and, in the process of international integration, erode the nezam as it pressurizes its bloated and rusting institutions to adapt to change? Competing views of the Iranian leadership linger on, and those who see the elite as dominated by fanatical, messianic, unhinged even, elements can find plenty of examples of Iranian leaders' pronouncements or Iranian actions to corroborate this. Ahmadinejad exemplified this view of Iran.

But for those who see only rationality in Tehran's conduct, the danger of a resurgent Islamic republic is equally great, this being the point of Cordesman's words. The nuclear settlement, thus, has failed to address the problem because

> [It] recognizes Iran's right to enrich uranium and eventually industrialize that capacity. It concedes that Iran can construct an elaborate nuclear infrastructure for research and development. It establishes a verification system that gives Iran far too much advance notice of inspections and does not meaningfully limit the development of ballistic missiles, a pillar of any nuclear weapons program. It does not provide adequate access to the facilities and scientists involved in Iran's past work on nuclear weapons.... And after 15 years, once the agreement expires, Iran will be free to build as many nuclear installations as it wants, accumulate as much enriched uranium as it wishes, and enrich that uranium to whatever level it deems necessary.[3]

Far from removing the threat of an 'atomic Iran', in this view, the agreement has established the Islamic republic as a "threshold nuclear power... and paves the way for an eventual Iranian bomb".

A calculating Tehran can use the nuclear settlement to reach accommodation with the West and restore its ailing economy and military and thus return with a vengeance in search of opportunity and regional domination. This is at least how America's regional allies view the situation.[4]

Either way, a considerable number of regional states and many Western politicians see more trouble ahead in Iran's accommodationist policies. But the question is not whether Iran is weak or geopolitically ravenous but rather whether its revolutionary system is prosperous and sustainable. In the Leader's mind, of course, there is no question that Iran is today a strong, respected and authoritative country. In practice, however, it is less clear that Iran is actually 'winning' its regional battles:

- In Syria, it has to play second fiddle to Russia in defence of Bashar al-Assad but still has to pour into Syria personnel and treasure and suffer the label of 'occupier' from the rest of the Arab world.
- In Iraq, it has been shown that while it cannot fully defend Baghdad's Shia-dominated government and indeed the Iraqi state, it still has to provide military and economic support, which makes Tehran vulnerable to scathing criticism from Iraq's Arab neighbours and Sunni Muslims in Iraq.
- In Lebanon and Palestine, it has a limited voice, and the more that Hezbollah gets involved in Syria (or Bahrain, Kuwait or Yemen), the more suspicion is cast on its ties with Iran and its regional role.
- In Gaza, it has to sit back and watch Hamas reorient towards the Arab centre and away from Tehran's cherished 'resistance front'.
- In Afghanistan, it is now in direct competition with Pakistan, yet it is unable to push the Afghani government and Taliban opposition towards a compromise.
- In the Caucasus, Tehran's relations with Shia Azerbaijan have deteriorated, and the more that Baku appears to lean on the West (and Israel), the tighter Tehran's embrace of Yerevan appears, which means that Tehran has been unable to build an alliance with the only non-Arab Shia-majority country in the world.
- In Yemen, it has unwisely hitched up with a politicized community (Houthis) who enjoy legitimacy at home but are fighting their battles without regard to Tehran's interests and, worse still, are fighting the UN-recognized government (in exile) with support of the discredited and hated former president Ali Abdullah Saleh and his cronies.
- And with Turkey, Tehran's relations have become so tense that Ankara has pointedly joined forces with the Gulf Arab bloc on Syria and Iraq, also wider Muslim world issues.

And meanwhile, IS threatens Iran itself and has acquired a foothold around Iranian territory. In this context, it is hard to see how one can put a positive gloss on Iran's regional position.

But the revolution, in changing the country's ruling establishment and with it Iran's foreign policy priorities, has caused a serious rupture in the country's hitherto West-leaning alliance structure. In adopting a 'neither East nor West' doctrine, Tehran in fact moved away from the West just as smoothly as it drew closer to the East. In military, economic, cultural and political terms, the Islamic republic effectively shifted its gaze eastwards from the early days of the revolution. The West's alienation of Iran during its war with Iraq in the 1980s contributed considerably to the republic's 'Asia pivot'. But it was in the post-Cold War order that we see Iran's 'look East' policy blossom. It should be noted that Iran had already developed extensive links with virtually every major Asian power – China (and Taiwan), India, Japan and South Korea – well before the 1979 revolution. The imperial regime had cultivated links with all of those powers for strategic as well as economic reasons, and while Tehran was still sailing close to the American flag in its ventures eastwards (close support for the US forces in the Vietnam war, member of the anti-Communist League in Asia, for example), it was nevertheless increasingly conscious of the need to cultivate closer relations with a rising Asia. In this, Iran was well ahead of many of its neighbours, which for political, ideological or diplomatic reasons had been unable to establish relations with all the key Asian powers simultaneously. After the revolution, the process of 'Asianization' accelerated and over time many of Iran's neighbours also started to refocus eastwards.

As has been argued, national politics of the Islamic republic and the complexities of its structures and competitive system make development of a widely acceptable analytically robust framework for explaining it rather difficult. But a combination of insights from political economy and political theory can give us a focus. From Mohammadi's analysis of Iran's political system – as being 'path-dependent' – we learn that the factional disorder that has followed the dissolution of the regime's ruling party (the Islamic Republic Party) within ten years of the republic's establishment has become so ingrained that it is hard to see how a 'rules-based' party political system can replace the current factionalism of the system.[5] As Mohammadi argues, it will require strong agency (members of the elite) that can robustly "interact with the powerful actors in the system".[6] Evidence of this taking place in a systematic fashion is sketchy at best. Path dependency in this context has institutionalized an anti-party system. Such an analysis shows how factionalism has come to dominate the politics of the country and also how factions have changed and evolved over the lifetime of the republic.

Iran's electoral politics has shown how election cycles act as triggers for infighting and intensive efforts to rebalance power between factions. These cycles highlight the rise and decline of social forces in the struggle for power – from the reform movements, the surge of the Green Movement, to the securitization of the state under the neoconservative factions. Detailed examination has illustrated the delicate balancing act between legitimized political participation and management of the process and outcome of elections. The analysis drew particular attention to the political 'tipping points' in the nezam and their impact on the management of the political order. The tension between tolerance and flexibility on the one hand and rigidity and intolerance on the other has become a core problem for the regime to address since 2009.

Iran's political system offers a paradox: How can it possess and operate virtually all the key institutions of republicanism yet behave so repressively? Despite having clear institutions of governance, distinct and separate executive, legislative and judiciary branches of government, clear constitutionally defined remits for all its officials and official organs, checks and balances, competitive municipal, parliamentary, presidential elections (amongst others), according to Freedom

House, Iran is one of the least 'free' countries in the world. In the 2000s period, Iran's rating of 'six' for freedom, civil liberties, and political rights, with seven being the worst rating, placed it near the very bottom of the international table. Answer to the question why pluralist components of the republic have, thus far, not been able to triumph over its (dominant) authoritarian elements is to be found in the resilience of the dominant groups and the ability of the conservative and traditionalist forces in the regime to 'upgrade' their authoritarian responses and be remarkably adaptive.[7] Resilience of authoritarianism in the Islamic republic is partly disguised by the durability of its republican institutions and the regularity of electoral cycles which legitimize the nezam on a regular basis and, at the same time, act as a conveyor belt for regime insiders to get onto the ladders of power.

Elections also can provide the context for inhibiting attempts at pluralization of the political system, notes Tezcür.[8] Voters gravitated towards Ahmadinejad in 2005 precisely because his campaign prioritized the demands of the marginalized social groups, the often-neglected rural communities and of course the religious conservatives, and by also targeting the corrupt elements of the establishment for their excesses the neoconservatives further widened their electoral appeal. The state's distributive and redistributive powers, moreover, particularly when the private sector has been weak and ineffectual in providing job and income security, and the government's monopoly of welfare have also enhanced its ability to control competing social forces.[9] A state-linked bourgeoisie beholden to the nezam and the rentier system putting the political elite in control of the country's economic wealth converge to give the regime a degree of continuity, particularly in crises. But this does not offer Iran a way out of the economic gridlock its elite has created.[10]

For all the factional divisions and institutional rivalries, the regime has shown real deftness for accommodating contestation at the intra-elite level while contracting the scope for political inclusion from below, which of course gives it elasticity. Brittleness is further avoided by the fact that the state can effectively manage and control society through non-repressive measures and such forms as legal regulation.

Analysis of political interactions and policy outcomes suggests a strong correlation between policy fluctuations in the international arena and political power at home. Foreign relations act as an externality for the regime's domestic political competition.[11] International relations can be seen as an auxiliary of internal relations. But in the dialectical relationship between external and domestic, society and economy bear the brunt of the factional struggle to secure the policy upper hand. So success in the nuclear negotiations by the reformist-centrist camp, for example, can lead to the imposition of tighter social controls at home, on women (over hejab and use of makeup), the youth (for hairstyle to clothing and use of social media), and the intelligentsia and socially popular figures (spurious arrest and prosecution for media comments, advertising of motion pictures on externally based satellite channels, posing in photographs with the wrong people, wearing of the wrong gear by sportsmen in the public eye), as much as political pressures for propagating the wrong image of Islamic Iran, insulting the leader, or deemed to be spreading malicious rumours about the republic.

Taking the long view, the point is well made that "ideological foreign policy has utilized much of Iran's national resources, further consolidating state control of the economy. The continuing paradox of the Islamic Republic is that, politically, it is anti-Western but if it wants to develop economically, it needs the West.... A strategy of growth for Iran requires cooperation with the West and the abandoning of anti-American policies".[12] Iran is an emerging Asian power on the crossroads of Eurasia, which can – in the medium term – help it walk away from the mess of the MENA regional system in ways that Turkey was able to do in the 1990s by hooking up with Europe and join the Asian economic slipstream. But the key to its regional success and domestic prosperity lies in the country's ability to implement radical structural reforms. The need for such a step change has been recognized by the leadership for decades and has been evident since President Rafsanjani's efforts to liberalize the economy in the 1990s. The conservative backlash against him, which left him vulnerable in the absence of the progressive and centrist forces in the Majlis that Rafsanjani himself had wilfully marginalized as potential enemies of his reforms, not only diminished the impact of his administration's policies but also actually tilted the balance of power in favour of the right wing of the conservative forces. The tension between economics and politics remains unresolved.

So while President Rouhani celebrated 'implementation day' of the nuclear agreement with a promise of a 'flood of investment' following the deal, his conservative opponents complained that he was exposing society to Western social corruption by opening the gates of the country to Western investment. The regime has shown its satisfaction with the status quo and a lack of interest in instigating wholesale change. Not surprising then that the Rouhani administration's measures to open the economy to trade and foreign investment should result in rising pressure of the security establishment on society. There is then arguably an inverse relationship between détente and economic openness, and social freedoms. Examples from elsewhere – Republic of Korea, Brazil, Argentina, Mexico, and Indonesia – suggest that for political leaders to single-handedly dismantle state capitalist institutions is almost impossible and can happen either through domestic trauma or in the context of engagement with international capital and institutions.[13] Changing Iran's political economy, in which the state's overwhelming socioeconomic influence is checked, will prove difficult, even if the leadership believed in such a strategy. Changing clientelist relationships will also be hard without disrupting the power structure of the Islamic republic – the latter not being in any group's interest in the political system.

Factionalism, as we have seen, drives political rivalries and manifests itself in ideological competition. The same encourages theological reinterpretation of the revolutionary order's founding father, so the struggle for the soul of this 'Islamic government' continues. But other factors also contribute to the crisis of leadership in the Islamic republic, and of these perhaps the most significant is what Brumberg has called the "system of contending authorities".[14] The best example of this is to be found in the country's constitutional arrangements. In an effort to iron out the institutional tensions in the roles assigned to the president, prime minister and the Majlis in the original constitution, the amended constitution created even more structural and political problems for the nezam. By introducing a popularly elected executive president who was also responsible for 'implementing the constitution', the post-1989 structure has clearly intensified tensions at the head of the regime, for in the last analysis,

> All of Iran's presidents... have to live with a political system that left them with two uncomfortable options: exercise authority as the democratically elected guardian of the Constitution, thus risk alienating the *faqih*; or subordinate themselves to the Supreme Leader, and in so doing defer to traditional authority at the expense of the modern office of president and the constitutional authority of the *Majles*.[15]

A further problem is to be found in institutionalized arbitrary rule and arbitrary decisions – that is, in the unspecified (and at times arbitrary and therefore political) ways in which the Council of Guards, for example, passes judgement on the suitability of candidates for elected office and the mass disqualifications that tend to follow. How can candidates prove their suitability if they are being judged behind closed doors and have very limited right of appeal against the CG's decisions?

For these reasons, some argue that the "Iranian ship of state thus continues to drift from course to course, in its search for a proper equilibrium between dedication to its revolutionary convictions and the pressuring demands of governance, between religion and state, and between Islam and the West".[16] Drift is a direct product of the republic's confused constitutional order, the unlimited powers that it has given the Faqih, and the factional rivalries that the regime has provoked. It is arguably a product of the still contested visions of Khomeini's Islamic republic.

Notes

1 Though it should be noted that the USSR was already on its knees due to the system's inefficiencies, economic stagnation, the competition with the West, which required it to invest heavily in its global alliances, and of course the costly Afghan war, which, for the Soviet Union at least, lasted until 1989.
2 Anthony H. Cordesman, *Iran: "Weakling" or "Hegemon"?*, (Washington, DC: Center for Strategic and International Studies, February 2007).
3 Eliot Cohen, Eric Edelman and Ray Takeyh, 'Time to Get Tough on Tehran: Iran Policy After the Deal', *Foreign Affairs*, vol. 95, no. 1, January/February 2016, p. 65.
4 Ibid, pp. 64–75.
5 Ariabarzan Mohammadi, *The Path Dependent Nature of Factionalism in Post-Khomeini Iran* (UK: Al-Sabah Paper no. 13, December 2014).
6 Ibid, p. 35.

7 Steven Heydemann and Reinoud Leenders, 'Authoritarian Governance in Syria and Iran: Challenged, Reconfiguring, and Resilient', in Steven Heydemann and Reinoud Leenders (eds.) *Middle East Authoritarianisms: Governance, Contestation, and Regime Resilience in Syria and Iran* (Stanford, CA: Stanford University Press, 2013), pp. 1–31.
8 Güneş Murat Tezcür, 'Democratic Struggles and Authoritarian Responses in Iran in Comparative Perspective', in Steven Heydemann and Reinoud Leenders (eds.) *Middle East Authoritarianisms: Governance, Contestation, and Regime Resilience in Syria and Iran* (Stanford, CA: Stanford University Press, 2013), pp. 200–21.
9 Kevan Harris, 'A Martyrs' Welfare State and its Contradictions: Regime Resilience and Limits through the Lens of Social Policy in Iran', in Steven Heydemann and Reinoud Leenders (eds.) *Middle East Authoritarianisms: Governance, Contestation, and Regime Resilience in Syria and Iran* (Stanford, CA: Stanford University Press, 2013), pp. 61–80.
10 Amin Saikal, *Iran at the Crossroads* (Cambridge: Polity Press, 2016).
11 Anoushiravan Ehteshami, Raymond Hinnebusch, Heidi Huuhtanen, Paolo Raunio, Maaike Awarnaar, and Tina Zintl, 'Authoritarian Resilience and International Linkages in Iran and Syria', in Steven Heydemann and Reinoud Leenders (eds.) *Middle East Authoritarianisms: Governance, Contestation, and Regime Resilience in Syria and Iran* (Stanford, CA: Stanford University Press, 2013), pp. 222–42.
12 Mahmood Sariolghalam, 'Iran's Emerging Regional Security Doctrine: Domestic Sources and the Role of International Constraints', in ECSSR, *The Gulf: Challenges of the Future* (Abu Dhabi: Emirates Center for Strategic Studies and Research, 2005), p. 173.
13 Alex E, Fernández Jilberto and André Mommen (eds.) *Liberalization in the Developing World: Institutional and Economic Changes in Latin America, Africa and Asia* (Mew York, NY: Routledge, 1996).
14 Daniel Brumberg, *Reinventing Khomeini: The Struggle for Reform in Iran* (Chicago, IL: University of Chicago Press, 2001), p. 149.
15 Ibid, p. 246.
16 David Menashri, 'Whither Iranian Politics? The Khatami Factor', in Patrick Clawson, Michael Eisenstadt, Eliyahou Kanovsky and David Menashri, *Iran under Khatami: A Political, Economic and Military Assessment* (Washington, DC: Washington Institute for Near East Policy, 1998), p. 43.

BIBLIOGRAPHY

Ervand Abrahamian, 'Ali Shari'ati: Ideologue of the Iranian Revolution', *MERIP Reports 104*, March–April 1982, pp. 25–28.
Ervand Abrahamian, *Khomeinism: Essays on the Islamic Republic* (Berkeley, CA: University of California Press, 1993).
Hussein J. Agha and Ahmad S. Khalidi, *Syria and Iran: Rivalry and Cooperation* (London: Pinter, 1995).
M. E. Ahrari, 'Iran, GCC and the Security Dimensions in the Persian Gulf', in Hooshang Amirahmadi and Nader Entessar (eds.) *Reconstruction and Regional Diplomacy in the Persian Gulf* (New York, NY: Routledge, 1992), pp. 193–212.
Joseph Alagha, *The Shifts in Hizbullah's Ideology: Religious Ideology, Political Ideology, and Political Pragmatism* (Amsterdam: Amsterdam University Press, 2006).
Asadollah Alam, *The Shah and I: The Confidential Diary of Iran's Royal Court, 1969–1977* (London: I. B. Tauris, 1991).
Kazem Alamdari, 'The Power Structure of the Islamic Republic of Iran: Transition from Populism to Clientelism, and Militarization of Government', *Third World Quarterly*, vol. 26, no. 8, 2005, pp. 1285–1301.
David Albright and Corey Hinderstein, 'Iran, Player or Rogue?', *Bulletin of Atomic Scientists*, vol. 59, no. 5, September–October 2003, pp. 52–58.
Hamid Algar (trans) *Islam and Revolution: Writings and Declarations of Imam Khomeini* (Berkeley, CA: Mizan Press, 1981).
Parvin Alizadeh (ed.) *The Economy of Iran: The Dilemmas of an Islamic State* (London: I.B. Tauris, 2000).
Roy Allison and Lena Jonson (eds.) *Central Asian Security: The New International Context* (London: Royal Institute of International Affairs, 2001).
Tawfiq Alsaif, *Islamic Democracy and its Limits: The Iranian Experience Since 1979* (London: Saqi, 2007).
Iradj Amini, *Napoleon and Persia: Franco-Persian Relations under the First Empire* (Richmond, Surrey: Curzon Press, 1999).
Hooshang Amirahmadi, *Revolution and Economic Transition: The Iranian Experience* (New York, NY: State University of New York press, 1990).

Hooshang Amirahmadi, 'Economic Destruction and Imbalances in Post-revolutionary Iran', in Hooshang Amirahmadi and Nader Entessar (eds.) *Reconstruction and Regional Diplomacy in the Persian Gulf* (London: Routledge, 1992), pp. 65–108.

Hooshang Amirahmadi and Nader Entessar (eds.) *Reconstruction and Regional Diplomacy in the Persian Gulf* (New York, NY: Routledge, 1992).

Hooshang Amirahmadi and Eric Hooglund (eds.) *US-Iran Relations: Areas of Tension and Mutual Interest* (Washington, DC: Middle East Institute, 1994).

Amnesty International, *Iran: Violations of Human Rights 1987–1990* (London: Amnesty International, 1990).

Jahangir Amuzegar, 'The Role of Oil in the Economic Development of Iran 1949–1973', in Baqer Mostofi and Keith McLachlan (eds.) *The Development of the Iranian Oil Industry 1954–1973* (London: School of Oriental and African Studies, 1991), pp. 23–45.

Jahangir Amuzegar, 'The Iranian Economy before and after the Revolution', *Middle East Journal*, vol. 46, no. 3, Summer 1992, pp. 413–25.

Jahangir Amuzegar, *Iran's Economy under the Islamic Republic* (London: I.B. Tauris, 1993).

Alireza Ansari, 'Iranian Foreign Policy under Khatami: Reform and Reintegration', in Ali Mohammadi and Anoushiravan Ehteshami (eds.) *Iran and Eurasia* (Reading: Ithaca Press, 2000), pp. 35–58.

Ali M. Ansari, *Modern Iran Since 1921: The Pahlavis and After* (London: Longman, 2003).

Ali M. Ansari, *Iran under Ahmadinejad: The Politics of Confrontation* (London: Routledge for IISS, Adelphi Paper 393, 2007).

John Duke Anthony, 'The Union of Arab Amirates', *Middle East Journal*, vol. 26, no. 3, Summer 1972, pp. 271–87.

M. Javad Ardalan, 'Comments on the Iranian Economy', *The Iranian British Chamber of Commerce*, Autumn 2014.

Said Amir Arjomand, 'The Reform Movement and the Debate on Modernity and Tradition in Contemporary Iran', *International Journal of Middle East Studies*, vol. 34, no. 4, November 2002, pp. 719–33.

Said Amir Arjomand, 'Constitutional Implications of Current Political Debates in Iran', in Ali Gheissari (ed.) *Contemporary Iran: Economy, Society, Politics* (Oxford: Oxford University Press, 2009), pp. 247–74.

Said Amir Arjomand, *After Khomeini: Iran Under His Successor* (Oxford: Oxford University Press, 2009).

Ahmad Ashraf, 'From the White Revolution to the Islamic Revolution', in Saeed Rahnema and Sohrab Behdad (eds.) *Iran after the Revolution: Crisis of an Islamic State* (London: I.B. Tauris, 1995), pp. 21–44.

Mohammad Farhad Atai, 'Iran and the Newly-Independent States of Central Asia', in Ali Mohammadi and Anoushiravan Ehteshami (eds.) *Iran and Eurasia* (Reading: Ithaca Press, 2000), pp. 171–98.

Peter Avery, *Modern Iran* (London: Ernest Benn, 1965).

Michael Axworthy, *Revolutionary Iran: A History of the Islamic Republic* (London: Penguin, 2014).

Shirzad Azad, 'The Politics of Privatization in Iran', *Middle East Review of International Affairs*, vol. 14, no. 4, December 2010, pp. 60–71.

Shaul Bakhash, 'Iran since the Gulf War', in Robert O. Freedman (ed.) *The Middle East and the Peace Process: The Impact of the Oslo Accords* (Gainesville, FL: University Press of Florida, 1998), pp. 241–64.

Shaul Bakhash, 'Iran's Foreign Policy under the Islamic Republic, 1979–2000', in L. Carl Brown (ed.) *Diplomacy in the Middle East: The International Relations of Regional and Outside Powers* (London: I. B. Tauris, 2001), pp. 247–58.

Bahman Baktiari, *Parliamentary Politics in Revolutionary Iran: The Institutionalization of Factional Politics* (Gainseville, FL: University Press of Florida, 1996).

Heidar Ali Balouji, 'The Process of National Security Decision Making in Iran: The Signing of the Additional Protocol', in Shannon N. Kile (ed.) *Europe and Iran: Perspectives on Non-proliferation* (Oxford: Oxford University Press for SIPRI, 2005), pp. 72–96.

Ali Banuazizi, 'The Crisis of Legitimacy, Resistance, and Civil Society', *Iran Nameh*, vol. xiv, no. 1, Winter 1996, pp. 61–78.

Richard E. Barrett and Martin K. Whyte, 'Dependency Theory and Taiwan: Analysis of a Deviant Vase', *American Journal of Sociology*, vol. 87, 1982, pp. 1064–1089.

G. Barthel (ed.) *Iran: From Monarchy to Republic* (Berlin: Akademie-Verlag, 1983).

Hassan Bastani, *How Powerful Is Rouhani in the Islamic Republic?* (London: Royal Institute of International Affairs, November 2014).

Sara Bazoobandi, *Iran's Domestic Political and Economic Challenges* (Jeddah: Gulf Research Center, November 2012).

Hazem Beblawi and Giacomo Luciani (eds.) *The Rentier State* (London: Croom Helm, 1987).

Maziar Behrooz, 'Trends in the Foreign Policy of the Islamic Republic, 1979–1988', in Nikki R. Keddie and Mark J. Gasiorowski (eds.) *Neither East Nor West: Iran, the Soviet Union, and the United States* (New Haven, CT: Yale University Press, 1990), pp. 13–35.

Julian Bharier, *Economic Development in Iran: 1900–1970* (London: Oxford University Press, 1971).

James Bill, *The Eagle and the Lion: The Tragedy of American-Iranian Relations* (New Haven, CT: Yale University Press, 1988).

Haim Bresheeth and Nira Yuval-Davis (eds.) *The Gulf War and the New World Order* (London: Zed Books, 1991).

L. Carl Brown (ed.) *Diplomacy in the Middle East: The International Relations of Regional and Outside Powers* (London: I. B. Tauris, 2001).

Daniel Brumberg, *Reinventing Khomeini: The Struggle for Reform in Iran* (Chicago, IL: University of Chicago Press, 2001).

Mary Buckley and Robert Singh (eds.) *The Bush Doctrine and the War on Terrorism: Global Responses, Global Consequences* (New York, NY: Routledge, 2006).

Hars J. Budig and Mehmet Süer, *Middle East and North Africa Markets Review 1973–74* (London: Gower Economic Publishing, 1973).

Business International Limited, *Iran: A Manual for Foreign Business. Opportunities and Operating Conditions to 1994* (London: The Economist Group, 1991).

John Calabrese, *Revolutionary Horizons: Regional Foreign Policy in Post-Khomeini Iran* (London: Macmillan Press, 1994).

John C. Campbell, 'Oil Power in the Middle East', *Foreign Affairs*, October 1977, pp. 89–110.

Houchang E. Chehabi, 'Iran and Lebanon in the Revolutionary Decade', in H. E. Chehabi (ed.) *Distant Relations: Iran and Lebanon in the Last 500 Years* (London: I. B. Tauris, 2006), pp. 201–30.

Houchang E. Chehabi (ed.) *Distant Relations: Iran and Lebanon in the Last 500 Years* (London: I. B. Tauris, 2006).

Shahram Chubin, 'Arms Build-Up and Regional Military Balance', in Hooshang Amirahmadi and Eric Hooglund (eds.) *US-Iran Relations: Areas of Tension and Mutual Interest* (Washington, DC: Middle East Institute, 1994), pp. 44–55.

Shahram Chubin and Charles Tripp, *Iran and Iraq at War* (London: I. B. Tauris, 1988).

Shahram Chubin and Sepehr Zabih, *The Foreign Relations of Iran: Developing State in a Zone of Great Power Conflict* (Berkeley, CA: University of California Press, 1974).

Patrick Clawson, 'Islamic Iran's Economic Politics and Prospects', *Middle East Journal*, vol. 42. no. 3, Summer 1988, pp. 371–88.

Patrick Clawson, Michael Eisenstadt, Eliyahou Kanovsky and David Menashri, *Iran under Khatami: A Political, Economic and Military Assessment* (Washington, DC: Washington Institute for Near East Policy, 1998).

Eliot Cohen, Eric Edelman and Ray Takeyh, 'Time to Get Tough on Tehran: Iran Policy After the Deal', *Foreign Affairs*, vol. 95, no. 1, January/February 2016, pp. 64–75.

Andrew Scott Cooper, 'Showdown at Doha: The Secret Oil Deal That Helped Sink the Shah of Iran', *Middle East Journal*, vol. 62, no. 4, Autumn 2008, pp. 567–91.

Anthony H. Cordesman, *Iran: "Weakling" or "Hegemon"?*, (Washington, DC: Center for Strategic and International Studies, February 2007).

Stephanie Cronin, *The Army and the Creation of the Pahlavi State in Iran, 1910–1926* (London: Tauris Academic Studies, 1997).

Farhad Daftary and Maryam Borghey, *Multinational Enterprises and Employment in Iran* (Geneva: International Labour Office, 1976).

Niheer Dasandi, *The Politics-Bureaucracy Interface in Developing Countries: Characteristics, Determinants, and Impact on Reform* (Singapore: UNDP Global Centre for Public Service Excellence, 2014).

Elizabeth Van Wie Davis and Rouben Azazian (eds.) *Islam, Oil, and Geopolitics: Central Asia after September 11* (Lanham, MD: Rowman and Littlefield, 2007).

James Defronzo, *Revolutions and Revolutionary Movements* (Boulder, CO: Westview Press, 1996).

Mohsen Dehgani (ed.) *Religion and Politics from Imam Khomeini's Viewpoint: A Collection of Articles* (Tehran: The Institute for Compilation and Publications of Imam Khomeini's Works, 2007).

Alex Edwards, *"Dual Containment" Policy in the Persian Gulf: The USA, Iran, and Iraq, 1991–2000* (New York, NY: Palgrave Macmillan, 2014).

Kaveh Ehsani, '"Tilt but Don't Spill": Iran's Development and Reconstruction Dilemma', *Middle East Report*, November–December 1994, pp. 16–21.

Kaveh Ehsani, Arang Keshavarzian and Noram Claire Moruzzi, 'Tehran, June 2009', *Middle East Report Online*, 28 June 2009.

Anoushiravan Ehteshami, 'Iran', in Tim Niblock and Emma Murphy (eds.) *Economic and Political Liberalization in the Middle East* (London: British Academic Press, 1993), pp. 214–36.

Anoushiravan Ehteshami (ed.) *From the Gulf to Central Asia: Players in the Great New Game* (Exeter: University of Exeter Press, 1994).

Anoushiravan Ehteshami, *After Khomeini: The Iranian Second Republic* (London: Routledge, 1995).

Anoushiravan Ehteshami, 'The Foreign Policy of Iran', in Raymond Hinnebusch and Anoushiravan Ehteshami (eds.) *The Foreign Policies of Middle East States* (Boulder, CO: Lynne Rienner, 2002), pp. 283–309.

Anoushiravan Ehteshami, 'Iran's Assessment of the Iraq Crisis and the Post-9/11 International Order', in Ramesh Thakur and Waheguru Pal Singh Sidhu (eds.) *The Iraq Crisis and World Order* (Tokyo: United Nations Press, 2006), pp. 134–60.

Anoushiravan Ehteshami and Mahjoob Zweiri, *Iran and the Rise of Its Neoconservatives* (London: I. B. Tauris, 2007).

Anoushiravan Ehteshami and Mahjoob Zweiri (eds.) *Iran's Foreign Policy: From Khatami to Ahmadinejad* (Reading: Ithaca Press, 2011).
Anoushiravan Ehteshami and Manshour Varasteh (eds.) *Iran and the International Community* (New York, NY: Routledge, 1991).
Anoushiravan Ehteshami and Raymond Hinnebusch, *Syria and Iran: Middle Powers in a Penetrated Regional System* (New York, NY: Routledge, 1997).
Anoushiravan Ehteshami, Raymond Hinnebusch, Heidi Huuhtanen, Paolo Raunio, Maaike Awarnaar, and Tina Zintl, 'Authoritarian Resilience and International Linkages in Iran and Syria', in Steven Heydemann and Reinoud Leenders (eds.) *Middle East Authoritarianisms: Governance, Contestation, and Regime Resilience in Syria and Iran* (Stanford, CA: Stanford University Press, 2013), pp. 222–42.
Anoushiravan Ehteshami and Reza Molavi (eds.) *Iran and the International System* (New York, NY: Routledge, 2012).
Michael Eisenstadt, 'Living with a Nuclear Iran', *Survival*, vol. 44, no. 3, Autumn 1999, pp. 124–148.
Mohamed Elbaradei, *The Age of Deception: Nuclear Diplomacy in Treacherous Times* (London: Bloomsbury, 2011).
Melvyn J. Else, *Iran: Business Opportunities for the 1980s* (London: Metra Consulting Group, 1978).
Embassy of IRI, *After the Revolution: Islamic Republic of Iran* (London: Embassy of the Islamic Republic of Iran, n.d.).
Peter Evans, *Dependent Development: The Alliance of Multinational, State, and Local Capital in Brazil* (Princeton, NJ: Princeton University Press, 1979).
Roxane Farmanfarmaian (ed.) *War and Peace in Qajar Persia: Implications Past and Present* (London: Routledge, 2008).
Louise Fawcett, *Iran and the Cold War: The Azerbaijan Crisis of 1946* (Cambridge: Cambridge University Press, 1992).
John Foran (ed.) *Theorizing Revolutions* (New York, NY: Routledge, 1997).
Hesam Forozan, The *Military in Post-Revolutionary Iran: The Evolution and Roles of the Revolutionary Guards* (New York, NY: Routledge, 2016).
Robert O. Freedman (ed.) *The Middle East after Iraq's Invasion of Kuwait* (Gainesville, FL: University Press of Florida, 1993).
Robert O. Freedman (ed.) *The Middle East and the Peace Process: The Impact of the Oslo Accords* (Gainesville, FL: University Press of Florida, 1998).
Freedom House, *Iran: Freedom on the Net 2015*, http://www.freedomhouse.org.
Graham E. Fuller, *The "Center of the Universe": The Geopolitics of Iran* (Boulder, CO: Westview Press, 1991).
Nima Gerami, *Leadership Divided? The Domestic Politics of Iran's Nuclear Debate* (Washington, DC: The Washington Institute for Near East Policy, February 2014).
Masoud Ghaffari, *Political Economy of Oil in Iran* (London: Institute of Islamic Studies, 2000).
Edmund Ghareeb, 'The Roots of Crisis: Iran and Iraq', in Christopher C. Joyner (ed.) *The Persian Gulf War: Lessons for Strategy, Law, and Diplomacy* (New York, NY: Greenwood Press, 1990), pp. 21–38.
Ali Gheissari (ed.) *Contemporary Iran: Economy, Society, Politics* (Oxford: Oxford University Press, 2009).
Ali Gheissari and Kaveh-Cyrus Sanandaji, 'New Conservative Politics and Electoral Behavior in Iran', in Ali Gheissari (ed.) *Contemporary Iran: Economy, Society, Politics* (Oxford: Oxford University Press, 2009), pp. 275–98.

Ali Gheissari and Vali Nasr, *Democracy in Iran: History and the Quest for Liberty* (Oxford: Oxford University Press, 2006).
Pankaj Ghemawat and Steven A. Altman, *DHL Global Connectedness Index 2014: Analyzing Global Flows and their Power to Increase Prosperity* (Bonn: Deutsche Post DHL, 2014).
M. Reza Ghods, *Iran in the Twentieth Century: A Political History* (Boulder, CO: Lynne Rienner, 1989).
Robert Graham, *Iran: The Illusion of Power* (London: Croom Helm, 1979).
Mel Gurtov, *Superpower on Crusade: The Bush Doctrine in US Foreign Policy* (Boulder, CO: Lynne Reinner, 2006).
William S. Haas, *Iran* (New York, NY: Columbia University Press, 1946).
Nader Habibi, 'The Economic Legacy of Mahmoud Ahmadinejad', *Middle East Brief*, no. 74, June 2013, 9pp. Published by Brandeis University's Crown Center for Middle East Studies.
Fred Halliday, *Iran: Dictatorship and Development* (New York, NY: Penguin Books, 1979).
Fred Halliday, *Revolution and World Politics: The Rise and Fall of the Sixth Great Power* (London: Macmillan, 1999).
Fred Halliday, *The Middle East in International Relations: Power, Politics and Ideology* (Cambridge: Cambridge University Press, 2005).
Kevan Harris, 'The Rise of the Subcontractor State: Politics of Pseudo-privatization in the Islamic Republic of Iran', *International Journal of Middle East Studies*, vol. 45, no. 1, February 2013, pp. 45–70.
Kevan Harris, 'A Martyrs' Welfare State and Its Contradictions: Regime Resilience and Limits through the Lens of Social Policy in Iran', in Steven Heydemann and Reinoud Leenders (eds.) *Middle East Authoritarianisms: Governance, Contestation, and Regime Resilience in Syria and Iran* (Stanford, CA: Stanford University Press, 2013), pp. 61–80.
Edmund Herzig, 'Iran and Central Asia', in Roy Allison and Lena Jonson (eds.) *Central Asian Security: The New International Context* (London: Royal Institute of International Affairs, 2001), pp. 111–23.
Z. Heyat, *Iran: A Comprehensive Study of Socio-economic Condition* (CA: Eastern Publishing Society, 1983).
Steven Heydemann and Reinoud Leenders, 'Authoritarian Governance in Syria and Iran: Challenged, Reconfiguring, and Resilient', in Steven Heydemann and Reinoud Leenders (eds.) *Middle East Authoritarianisms: Governance, Contestation, and Regime Resilience in Syria and Iran* (Stanford, CA: Stanford University Press, 2013), pp. 1–31.
Steven Heydemann and Reinoud Leenders (eds.) *Middle East Authoritarianisms: Governance, Contestation, and Regime Resilience in Syria and Iran* (Stanford, CA: Stanford University Press, 2013).
Raymond Hinnebusch, 'Globalization, Democratization, and the Arab Uprising: The International Factor in MENA's Failed Democratization', *Democratization*, vol. 22, no. 2, March 2015, pp. 335–57.
Raymond Hinnebusch and Anoushiravan Ehteshami (eds.) *The Foreign Policies of Middle East States* (Boulder, CO: Lynne Rienner, 2002).
Dilip Hiro, *Iran Today* (New York, NY: Nation Books, 2005).
Samanvya Hooda, 'Iran's Economic Renaissance: Will the IRGC Profit? – Analysis', *Institute for Peace and Conflict Studies*, 5 June 2016.
Eric Hooglund, 'Iran and Central Asia', in Anoushiravan Ehteshami (ed.) *From the Gulf to Central Asia: Players in the Great New Game* (Exeter: University of Exeter Press, 1994), pp. 114–28.

Shireen Hunter, 'Iran from the August 1988 Cease-fire to the April 1992 Majlis Elections', in Robert O. Freedman (ed.) *The Middle East after Iraq's Invasion of Kuwait* (Gainesville, FL: University Press of Florida, 1993), pp. 183–206.
Shireen Hunter, 'Iran, Turkey, and Central Asia: The Islamic Connection', in Elizabeth Van Wie Davis and Rouben Azazian (eds.) *Islam, Oil, and Geopolitics: Central Asia after September 11* (Lanham, MD: Rowman and Littlefield, 2007), pp. 187–202.
Shireen Hunter, *Iran's Foreign Policy in the Post-Soviet Era: Resisting the New International Order* (Westport, CT: Praeger, 2010).
Shireen Hunter, *Iran Divided: The Historical Roots of Iranian Debates on Identity, Culture and Governance in the Twenty-First Century* (London: Rowman and Littlefield, 2014).
General Robert E. Huyser, *Mission to Tehran* (London: Andre Deutsch, 1986).
International Crisis Group, *Iran: Struggle for the Revolution's Soul* (Brussels: ICG Middle East Report no. 5, August 2002).
IHRDC, *Deadly Fatwa: Iran's 1988 Prison Massacre* (New Haven, CT: IHRDC, 2009).
Charles Issawi (ed.) *The Economic History of Iran, 1800–1914* (Chicago, Il: University of Chicago Press, 1971).
Ramin Jahanbegloo, 'A Harsh Crackdown is Coming in Iran', *New Perspectives Quarterly*, vol. 27, no. 2, Spring 2010, pp. 29–30.
Ramin Jahanbegloo and Abdolkarim Soroush, 'Iran on the Edge', *New Perspectives Quarterly*, vol. 27, no. 2, Spring 2010, pp. 32–33.
David Ramin Jalilvand, 'Recent Developments and Challenges in Iranian Oil and Gas Sector', *Orient*, vol. 54, no. iv, 2013, pp. 67–73.
Alex E, Fernández Jilberto and André Mommen (eds.) *Liberalization in the Developing World: Institutional and Economic Changes in Latin America, Africa and Asia* (New York, NY: Routledge, 1996).
Christopher C. Joyner (ed.) *The Persian Gulf War: Lessons for Strategy, Law, and Diplomacy* (New York, NY: Greenwood Press, 1990).
Mehran Kamrava, *Iran's Intellectual Revolution* (Cambridge: Cambridge University Press, 2008).
Mehran Kamrava, 'The United States and Iran: A Dangerous but Contained Rivalry' (Washington, DC: Middle East Institute *Policy Brief* no. 9, March 2008).
Mehran Kamrava (ed.) *International Politics of the Persian Gulf* (Syracuse, NY: Syracuse University Press, 2011).
Mehran Kamrava and Houchang Hassan-Yari, 'Suspended Equilibrium in Iran's Political System', *The Muslim World*, vol. 94, October 2004, pp. 495–524.
Eliyahu Kanovsky, *Iran's Economic Morass: Mismanagement and Decline under the Islamic Republic* (Washington, DC: Washington Institute for Near East Policy, Policy Paper no. 44, 1997).
Majid Karimi and Manssor Limba (eds.) *Sahifeh-ye Imam* (Tehran: The Institute for Compilation and Publication of Imam Khomeini's Works, vol. 21, 2008).
Efraim Karsh, *The Iran-Iraq War: A Military Analysis* (London: International Institute for Strategic Studies Adelphi Paper no. 220, Spring 1987).
Massoud Karshenas, *Structural Adjustment and the Prospects of the Iranian Economy* (London: SOAS Department of Economics Working Paper no. 57, September 1995).
Massoud Karshenas, 'Structural Adjustment and the Iranian Economy', in Nemat Shafik (ed.) *Economic Challenges Facing Middle Eastern and North African Countries: Alternative Futures* (London: Macmillan, 1998), pp. 202–24.
Kenneth Katzman and Paul K. Kerr, *Iran Nuclear Agreement* (Washington, DC: Congressional Research Service, 31 May 2016).

Emilian Kavalski (ed.) *The New Central Asia: The Regional Impact of International Actors* (Singapore: World Scientific Publishing, 2010).

Nikki R. Keddie, *Modern Iran: Roots and Results of Revolution* (New Haven, CT: Yale University Press, 2006).

Nikki R. Keddie and Mark J. Gasiorowski (eds.) *Neither East Nor West: Iran, the Soviet Union, and the United States* (New Haven, CT: Yale University Press, 1990).

Arang Keshavarzian, 'Contestation without Democracy: Elite Fragmentation in Iran', in Marsha Pripstein Posusney and Michele Penner Angrist (eds.) *Authoritarianism in the Middle East: Regimes and Resistance* (Boulder, CO: Lynne Rienner, 2005), pp. 63–87.

Saeed Madeh Khaksar (translator), *Sahifeh-ye Imam* (Tehran: The Institute for Compilation and Publication of Imam Khomeini's Works, vol. 4, 2008).

Saira Khan, *Iran and Nuclear Weapons: Protracted Conflict and Proliferation* (New York, NY: Routledge, 2010).

Majid KhosraviNik, *Discourse, Identity and Legitimacy: Self and Other in Representations of Iran's Nuclear Programme* (Amsterdam: John Benjamins Pubs, 2015).

Shannon N. Kile (ed.) *Europe and Iran: Perspectives on Non-proliferation* (Oxford: Oxford University Press for SIPRI, 2005).

George Kirk, *Survey of International Affairs 1939–1946: The Middle East in the War* (Oxford: Oxford University Press, 1947).

Daniel M. Kliman and Richard Fontaine, *Global Swing States: Brazil, India, Indonesia, Turkey and the Future of International Order* (Washington, DC: Center for a New American Security and the German Marshall Fund of the United States, 2012).

Paul H. Kreisberg (ed.) *American Hostages in Iran: The Conduct of a Crisis* (New Haven, CT: Yale University Press, 1985).

Bernard Lewis, *The Middle East: 2000 Years of History from the Rise of Christianity to the Present Day* (London: Phoenix Giant, 1996).

John W. Limbert, *Iran: At War with History* (Boulder, CO: Westview Press, 1987).

Robert Looney, *The Economic Development of Iran – A Recent Survey with Projections to 1981* (New York, NY: Praeger, 1973).

Alidad Mafinezam and Aria Mehrabi, *Iran and Its Place Among Nations* (Westport, CT: Praeger, 2008).

Ali Akbar Mahdi, 'The Student Movement in the Islamic Republic of Iran', *Journal of Iranian Research and Analysis*, vol. 15, no. 2, November 1999, pp. 5–32.

Abbas Maleki, 'Cooperation: A New Component of the Iranian Foreign Policy', *Iranian Journal of International Affairs*, vol. v, no. 1, Spring 1993, pp. 16–20.

Suzanne Maloney, 'Agents or Obstacles? Parastatal Foundations and Challenges for Iranian Development', in Parvin Alizadeh (ed.) *The Economy of Iran: The Dilemmas of an Islamic State* (London: I.B. Tauris, 2000), pp. 145–76.

Nadia von Maltzahn, *The Syria-Iran Axis: Cultural Diplomacy and International Relations in the Middle East* (London: I. B. Tauris, 2013).

Vanessa Martin, *Creating an Islamic State: Khomeini and the Making of a New Iran* (London: I. B. Tauris, 2000).

Edward S. Mason, Mahn Je Kim, Dwight H. Perkins, Kwang Suk Kim, and David C. Cole, *The Economic and Social Modernization of the Republic of Korea* (Cambridge, MA: Harvard University Press, 1980).

J. Matthew McInnis, *Iran's Strategic Thinking: Origins and Evolution* (Washington, DC: American Enterprise Institute, 2015).

E. Melikaf, *Development of Manufacturing in Iran, 1962–74* (Keele: PhD thesis, Keele University, 1979).

David Menashri, 'Whither Iranian Politics? The Khatami Factor', in Patrick Clawson, Michael Eisenstadt, Eliyahou Kanovsky and David Menashri, *Iran under Khatami: A Political, Economic and Military Assessment* (Washington, DC: Washington Institute for Near East Policy, 1998), pp. 13–51.

Abbas Milani, *The Shah* (New York, NY: Palgrave Macmillan, 2011).

Mohsen M. Milani, *The Making of Iran's Islamic Revolution: From Monarchy to Islamic Republic* (Boulder, CO: Westview Press, 1994).

Ziba Mir-Hosseini and Richard Taper, *Islam and Democracy in Iran: Eshkevari and the Quest for Reform* (London: I.B. Tauris, 2006).

Kamran Mofid, *Development Planning in Iran: From Monarchy to Islamic Republic* (Wisbech: MENAS Press, 1987).

Kamran Mofid, *The Economic Consequences of the Gulf War* (London: Routledge, 1990).

Mohammad Reza Abedini Moghanaki and Mohsen Shariatinia, 'Global Power Transition, Sanctions and Iran's Export Orientation', *Iran Review of Foreign Affairs*, vol. 5, no. 1, Spring 2014, pp. 5–28.

Ali Mohammadi and Anoushiravan Ehteshami (eds.) *Iran and Eurasia* (Reading: Ithaca Press, 2000).

Ariabarzan Mohammadi, *The Path Dependent Nature of Factionalism in Post-Khomeini Iran* (UK: Al-Sabah Paper no. 13, December 2014).

Manouchehr Mohammadi, 'The Islamic Republic of Iran and the International System: Clash with the Domination Paradigm', in Anoushiravan Ehteshami and Reza Molavi (eds.) *Iran and the International System* (New York, NY: Routledge, 2012), pp. 71–89.

Ayatollah Hossein-Ali Montazeri, *Khatirat-i Ayatollah Montazeri, Majmu'iyyih Payvastha va Dastnivisha* [Memoir of Ayatollah Montazeri, the Collection of Appendices and Handwritten Notes] (2001).

Ziba Moshaver, 'Revolution, Theocratic Leadership and Iran's Foreign Policy: Implications for Iran-EU Relations', *The Review of International Affairs*, vol. 3, no. 2, Winter 2003, pp. 283–305.

Mehdi Moslem, *Factional Politics in Post-Khomeini Iran* (New York, NY: Syracuse University Press, 2002).

Baqer Mostofi and Keith McLachlan (eds.) *The Development of the Iranian Oil Industry 1954–1973* (London: School of Oriental and African Studies, 1991).

Negar Mottahedeh, *#iranelection: Hashtag Solidarity and the Transformation of Online Life* (Stanford, CA: Stanford University Press, 2015).

Seyed Hossein Mousavian, *The Iranian Nuclear Crisis: A Memoir* (Washington, DC: Carnegie Endowment for International Peace, 2012).

Mehdi Mozaffari, 'Islamism in Algeria and Iran', in Abdel Salam Sidahmed and Anoushiravan Ehteshami (eds.) *Islamic Fundamentalism* (Boulder, CO: Westview Press, 1996), pp. 229–47.

H-G Muller, 'Remarks on the Role of the State Capital Sector and National Private Capital in the Revolutionary Process of Capitalism in Iran up to the End of the 1970s', in G. Barthel (ed.) *Iran: From Monarchy to Republic* (Berlin: Akademie-Verlag, 1983).

Donette Murray, *US Foreign Policy and Iran: American–Iranian Relations since the Islamic Revolution* (New York, NY: Routledge, 2010).

Kasra Naji, *Ahmadinejad: The Secret History of Iran's Radical Leader* (London: I. B. Tauris, 2008).

Afsaneh Najmabadi, 'Depoliticisation of a Rentier State: The Case of Pahlavi Iran', in Hazem Beblawi and Giacomo Luciani (eds.) *The Rentier State* (London: Croom Helm, 1987), pp. 211–27.

Siamak Namazi, 'The 6th Majlis Elections in Iran: What Happened and What Can We Expect', *Journal of Iranian Research and Analysis*, vol. 16. No. 1, April 2000, pp. 14–21.

Tim Niblock and Emma Murphy (eds.) *Economic and Political Liberalization in the Middle East* (London: British Academic Press, 1993).

Ramy Nima, *The Wrath of Allah: Islamic Revolution and Reaction in Iran* (London: Pluto Press, 1983).

Farhad Nomani and Sohrab Behdad, *Class and Labor in Iran: Did the Revolution Matter?* (Syracuse, NY: Syracuse University Press, 2006).

Gerd Nonneman, 'Analyzing the Foreign Policies of the Middle East and North Africa: A Conceptual Framework', *The Review of International Affairs*, vol. 3, no. 2, Winter 2003, pp. 118–30.

Homa Omid, *Islam and the Post-Revolutionary State in Iran* (London: Macmillan Press, 1994).

Arzoo Osanloo, 'Contesting Governance: Authority, Protest, and Rights Talk in Postrepublican Iran', in Steven Heydemann and Reinoud Leenders (eds.) *Middle East Authoritarianisms: Governance, Contestation, and Regime Resilience in Syria and Iran* (Stanford, CA: Stanford University Press, 2013), pp. 127–42.

Pierre Pahlavi and Afshin Hojati, 'Iran and Central Asia: The Smart Politics of Prudent Pragmatism', in Emilian Kavalski (ed.) *The New Central Asia: The Regional Impact of International Actors* (Singapore: World Scientific Publishing, 2010), pp. 215–38.

Maryam H. Panah, 'State and Society in the Islamic Republic: The Impact of Post-revolutionary War', *Journal of Iranian Research and Analysis*, vol. 16, no. 1, April 2000, pp. 73–95.

Rouzbeh Parsi, 'The Usual Surprise? Iran's Presidential Elections', *European Union Institute for Security Studies*, June 2013.

Sir Anthony Parsons, 'Iran and the United Nations, with Particular Reference to the Iran-Iraq War', in Anoushiravan Ehteshami and Manshour Varasteh (eds.) *Iran and the International Community* (New York, NY: Routledge, 1991), pp. 7–30.

Mehdi Parvizi Amineh and Henk Houwelling (eds.) *Central Eurasia in Global Politics: Conflict, Security and Development* (Leiden: Brill, 2005).

David Patrikarakos, *Nuclear Iran: The Birth of an Atomic State* (London: I. B. Tauris, 2012).

Nicola Pedde, 'The Nuclear Agreement: Tehran's Take', *Aspenia*, no. 68–69–70, 2015, pp. 141–48.

Nicola Pedde, 'Challenges for the New Persia', *Aspenia International*, no. 71–72, 2016, pp. 81–92.

Evaleila Pesaran, *Iran's Struggle for Economic Independence: Reform and Counter-reform in the Post-revolutionary Era* (London: Routledge, 2011).

M. Hashem Pesaran, *Iranian Economy during the Pahlavi Era* (Cambridge: University of Cambridge Department of Applied Economics Working Paper no. 9418, October 1994).

James F. Petras and Morris H. Morley, 'Development and Revolution: Contradictions in the Advanced Third World Countries – Brazil, South Africa, and Iran', *Studies in Comparative International Development*, vol. XVI, no.1, Spring 1981, pp. 5–43.

Stephen C. Poulson, 'Nested Institutions, Political Opportunity, and the Decline of the Iranian Reform Movement Post-9/11', *American Behavioral Scientist*, vol. 53, no. 1, September 2009, pp. 27–43.

Marsha Pripstein Posusney and Michele Penner Angrist (eds.) *Authoritarianism in the Middle East: Regimes and Resistance* (Boulder, CO: Lynne Rienner, 2005).

Ali Rahnema and Farhad Nomani, *The Secular Miracle: Religion, Politics and Economic Policy in Iran* (London: Zed Books, 1990).

Saeed Rahnema and Sohrab Behdad (eds.) *Iran after the Revolution: Crisis of an Islamic State* (London: I. B. Tauris, 1995).
Eva Rakel, 'Paradigms of Iranian Policy in Central Eurasia and Beyond', in Mehdi Parvizi Amineh and Henk Houwelling (eds.) *Central Eurasia in Global Politics: Conflict, Security and Development* (Leiden: Brill, 2005), pp. 235–57.
Rouhollah K. Ramazani, 'Iran's Changing Foreign Policy: A Preliminary Discussion', *Middle East Journal*, vol. 24, no. 4, Fall 1970, pp. 421–37.
Rouhollah K. Ramazani, *Revolutionary Iran: Challenge and Response in the Middle East* (Baltimore, MD: Johns Hopkins University Press, 1986).
Magnus Ranstrop, *Hizb'Allah: The Politics of the Western Hostage Crisis* (London: Macmillan, 1997).
Report of the Economic and Social Council (prepared by Reynaldo Galindo Pol) to the UN General Assembly, *Situation of Human Rights in the Islamic Republic of Iran* (New York, NY: United Nations, 2 November, 1989).
Alan Richards and John Waterbury, *A Political Economy of the Middle East* (Boulder, CO: Westview Press, 1996).
Hassan Rouhani, *National Security and Nuclear Diplomacy (Amniyat-e Meli va Diplomacey-e Hastehyee)* (Tehran: Center for Strategic Studies, 2011).
Ian Roxborough, *Theories of Underdevelopment* (London: Macmillan, 1979).
Shahriar Sabet-Saeidi, 'Iranian-European Relations: A Strategic Partnership?', in Anoushiravan Ehteshami and Mahjoob Zweiri (eds.) *Iran's Foreign Policy: From Khatami to Ahmadinejad* (Reading: Ithaca Press, 2011), pp. 55–72.
Mahboubeh Sadeghinia, 'The Impact of Iran's Tenth Presidential Elections on Its Relations with the EU and Mediterranean States', in Anoushiravan Ehteshami and Reza Molavi (eds.) *Iran and the International System* (New York, NY: Routledge, 2012), pp. 175–91.
Karim Sadjadpour, *Reading Khamenei: The World View of Iran's Most Powerful Leader* (Washington, DC: Carnegie Endowment for International Peace, 2008).
Amin Saikal, *The Rise and Fall of the Shah: Iran from Autocracy to Religious Rule* (Princeton, NJ: Princeton University Press, 2009).
Amin Saikal, *Iran at the Crossroads* (Cambridge: Polity Press, 2016).
Hossein Salimi, 'Foreign Policy as Social Construction', in Anoushiravan Ehteshami and Reza Molavi (eds.) *Iran and the International System* (New York, NY: Routledge, 2012), pp. 130–49.
Mahmood Sariolghalam, 'Iran's Emerging Regional Security Doctrine: Domestic Sources and the Role of International Constraints', in ECSSR, *The Gulf: Challenges of the Future* (Abu Dhabi: Emirates Center for Strategic Studies and Research, 2005), pp. 163–83.
Mahmood Sariolghalam, 'Perceptions of Power and Multiplicity of Interests: Iran's Regional Security Policy', in ECSSR *Arabian Gulf Security: Internal and External Challenges* (Abu Dhabi: Emirates Center for Strategic Studies and Research, 2008), pp. 81–100.
Giovanni Sartori, *Parties and Party Systems: A Framework for Analysis* (Cambridge: Cambridge University Press, 1976).
Asghar Schirazi, *The Constitution of Iran: Politics and the State in the Islamic Republic* (London: I. B. Tauris, 1997).
Peter Seeberg, 'The Iranian Revolution, 1977–79: Interaction and Transformation', *British Journal of Middle Eastern Studies*, vol. 41, no. 4, pp. 483–97.
Eric Selbin, 'Revolution in the Real World: Bringing Agency Back In', in John Foran (ed.) *Theorizing Revolutions* (New York, NY: Routledge, 1997), pp. 123–36.
William Shawcross, *The Shah's Last Ride: The Story of the Exile, Misadventures and Death of the Emperor* (London: Chatto and Windus, 1989).

Gary Sick, *All Fall Down: America's Fateful Encounter with Iran* (London: I. B. Tauris, 1985).
Abdel Salam Sidahmed and Anoushiravan Ehteshami (eds.) *Islamic Fundamentalism* (Boulder, CO: Westview Press, 1996).
Theda Skocpol, *State and Social Revolutions* (Cambridge: Cambridge University Press, 1979).
Theda Skocpol, *Social Revolutions in the Modern World* (Cambridge: Cambridge University Press, 1994).
Barbara Slavin, *Bitter Friends, Bosom Enemies: Iran, the U.S., and the Twisted Path to Confrontation* (New York, NY: St. Martin's Press, 2007).
Nicole Stracke, 'GCC and the Challenge of US-Iran Negotiations', *GRC Analysis*, 5 March 2009.
Sir Percy Sykes, *History of Persia* (London: Macmillan, 1921).
Ray Takeyh, *Guardians of the Revolution: Iran and the World in the Age of the Ayatollahs* (Oxford: Oxford University Press, 2009).
Alan R. Taylor, *The Arab Balance of Power* (New York, NY: Syracuse University Press, 1982).
Ghoncheh Tazmini, *Khatami's Iran: The Islamic Republic and the Turbulent Path to Reform* (London: I. B. Tauris, 2009).
Güneş Murat Tezcür, 'Democratic Struggles and Authoritarian Responses in Iran in Comparative Perspective', in Steven Heydemann and Reinoud Leenders (eds.) *Middle East Authoritarianisms: Governance, Contestation, and Regime Resilience in Syria and Iran* (Stanford, CA: Stanford University Press, 2013), pp. 200–21.
Ramesh Thakur and Waheguru Pal Singh Sidhu (eds.) *The Iraq Crisis and World Order* (Tokyo: United Nations Press, 2006).
Parisa Najafi Tonekaboni, 'Iranian Bloggers and Internet Censorship', International Society for Human Rights, http://www.ishr.org.
Amir Toumaj, *Iran's Economy of Resistance: Implications for Future Sanctions* (Washington, DC: American Enterprise Institute, November 2014).
Sanam Vakil, 'Despite Election Triumph, Rouhani Still Faces Formidable Foes', RIIA Expert Comment, 1 March 2016.
Mehrdad Valibeigi, 'The Private Sector in Iran's Post-Revolutionary Economy', *Journal of South Asian and Middle Eastern Studies*, vol. XVII, no. 3, Spring 1994, pp. 1–18.
Immanuel Wallerstein, *The Capitalist World-Economy* (Cambridge: Cambridge University Press, 1979).
Maaike Warnaar, *Iranian Foreign Policy during Ahmadinejad: Ideology and Actions* (New York, NY: Palgrave, 2013).
Edward Wastnidge, 'The Modalities of Iranian Soft Power: From Cultural Diplomacy to Soft Power', *Politics Journal* (online article), 24 December 2014, pp. 1–14.
Henrietta Wilkins, *The Making of Lebanon's Foreign Policy: Understanding the 2006 Hezbollah-Israel War* (New York, NY: Routledge, 2013).
Yael Yishai, *Civilian Society in Israel towards the Year 2000 – Between State and Society* (Jerusalem: Paul Baerward School of Social Work, 1998).
Sepehr Zabih, 'Iran's International Posture: De Facto Nonalignment within a Pro-Western Alliance', *Middle East Journal*, vol. 24, no. 3, Summer 1970, pp. 302–18.
Marvin Zonis, *The Political Elite of Iran* (Princeton, NJ: Princeton University Press, 1971).
Mahjoob Zweiri (ed.) *The Eighth Majlis (Parliamentary) Election – Where Is Iran Headed?* (Amman: Center for Strategic Studies, University of Jordan, March 2008).

INDEX

Abadi, Haider al- 249
Abdullah, Crown Prince 202
Abedini Moghanaki, Mohammad Reza 130
Abramian, Ervand 33
Absolute Guardianship 43–4
accountability 146
Achaemenid dynasty 17
addiction 11, 206
AE *see* Assembly of Experts (AE)
Afghanistan 205, 253, 271; economic relationship with 175, 197, 205
Afkham, Marzieh 241
aghazadeh 151
Agreement between Iran and the Consortium of Western oil companies (1954) 118
Ahmadinejad, Mahmoud 1; criticisms of 64–6, 70; economy under 64–5, 73, 91, 142–6; international relations under 182, 219–35, 256; 'justice shares' programme 143; president (2005–2013) 61–3, 87–91, 112n141; presidential candidate (2005) 5, 59, 60–1; presidential candidate (2009) 68, 69–70
Ahvaz Rolling Mill 137
Airbus 148
Alamolhoda, Ayatollah Ahmad 98
Alexander the Great 17
Algeria 193–4, 253
Algiers Agreement (1975) 185
Alikhani, Alinaghi 175
Almaty-Tehran railway service 204
Amal 188, 189

Amirahmadi, Hooshang 134, 151–2
Amnesty International 46
Amuzegar, Jamshid 23, 119, 135
Anglo-Persian Treaty (1919) 172
Anglo-Russian Convention (1907) 172
Ansari, Ali M. 235
Ansari, Hossein Jaber 246
Anti Money Laundering and Countering Financing of Terrorism (AML/CFT) 149
Arab Cold War (1958–71) 174
Arab League 246
Arab Spring 5, 233–5
Arabs in Iran 16, 17
Arak Aluminum Rolling Mill 137
Arak heavy water reactor 212, 214, 222, 239, 240
Arak Steel Company 137
Araki, Grand Ayatollah Mohammad Ali 44
Ardebili, Ayatollah Abdolkarim 78
Ardeshir I 17
Aref, Mohammad Reza 93, 94, 100
Argentina 196
Arjomand, Said Amir 54
Aryan, Hossein 75
Asgaroladi, Asadollah 251
Askari, Ali 153
Assad, Bashar al- 242, 248, 271
Assad, Hafez al- 189
Assembly of Experts (AE) 28, 37, 101–2; election of 97–8, 100; role of 4
Association of Combatant Clerics/ Preachers 101

Association of Militant Clerics 41, 48, 59
Association of Researchers and Teachers 78
Association of the Self Sacrifices of the Islamic Revolution 81
Atomic Energy Agency 224
Avery, Peter 22, 172–3
Axworthy, Michael 49, 53
Azad, Shirzad 132, 141
Azerbaijan 198, 204–5, 271
Azeris 15, 16, 17

Baghdad Pact 21, 174
Bahais 16, 30n1
Bahar 99
Bahonar, Mohammadreza 97
Bahrain 233, 235, 246; Khatami visit to 202; relationship with 246, 254; support for Shia majority in 187, 202, 233, 243, 244; US forces in 8, 182
Bakhash, Shaul 6–7, 181–2
Bakhtiar, Shapour 25
Bakhtiaris 16
Baluch 16, 17
Bani-Sadr, Abolhassan 40, 41, 256
Bastani, Hossein 93
Bazargan, Abdolali 86
Bazargan, Mehdi 37, 40, 41
Behdad, Sohrab 123, 150
Beheshi, Ali Reza 77–8
Beit Rahbari 5, 27, 37
Benin 229
bin Laden, Osama 205
blogging 12, 106
Boko Haram 253
Bolivia 228
Bolton, John R. 68, 73
Bonaparte, Napoleon 172
bonyads 10, 140, 154
Bosnia 193
Brazil 129, 186, 229
Brumberg, Daniel 25, 275
Burkino Faso 229
Bush, George W. 207, 208, 209
Bushehr nuclear power plant 196, 224

Campbell, John C. 121, 175
Cardoso, Fernando Henrique 126
Carter, Jimmy 24
Caspian Sea Cooperation Organization 197
censorship 6, 10, 53, 99, 116, 146
Center for Strategic Research 51, 52
CENTO 174
CG *see* Council of Guardians (CG)
Chile 186

China 269; economic relationship with 130, 148, 150, 196; relationship with 8, 182, 198, 199, 204, 249
China Railway Construction Corporation 148
Christianity 16
Christopher, Warren 193
Chubin, Shahram 210, 212
Clawson, Patrick 157
Clinton, Bill 193
Clinton, Hillary 84, 228
Coalition of Reformists 101
Coalition of the Imam's Line 48
competitiveness 10
Conservative Majority Coalition 97
Constitution of the Islamic Republic of Iran 4, 13, 27, 34–9; Article 2 179; Article 4 4; Article 5 4–5; Article 44 132, 141; Article 152 179; Article 153 179; Article 154 179; checks and balances in 4; contradictions in 35–6
Constitutional Revolution (1905–11) 128, 173
Control Risks 246
Coordinating Council of the Reformist Front 58, 59
Cordesman, Anthony H. 270
corruption 10, 146
Council for a Conservative Alliance 98
Council of Guardians (CG) 4, 53, 55, 63, 73, 81, 97, 99, 141, 275; appointment of 27; role of 36, 37, 69
Cuba 228

Daesh 234, 243, 244, 248, 249, 253, 254
Daimler 148
Danesh-Jafari, Davud 64
Democracy Party of Iran 59
Denmark 121
Devotees and Path-Seekers of the Islamic Revolution 101
DHL Global Connectedness Index 2014 115
dissent, elimination of 43–4, 46, 51, 52, 89
divorce 11
Dovoum-e Khordad Movement 50, 51

EC *see* Expediency Council (EC)
Economic Commission for Asia and the Far East Region (ECAFE) 123
Economic Cooperation Organization (ECO) 197, 205
Economist 73, 102, 138, 145
Economist Intelligence Unit 10

economy 9–11, 12, 115–61; Ahmadinejad, under 64–7, 73, 91, 142–6; deregulation 139; exports 115, 120, 123; Iraq war impact on 133–5; Khatami, under 140–2; land reform 121–2, 132; Pahlavi dynasty, during 23, 117, 118–29; post-sanctions 158–61; potential of 115–17; privatization of state-controlled assets 137, 138, 141, 142, 143–4; Rafsanjani, under 137–40, 141; revolution impact on 129–35; Rouhani, under 145, 146–50, 158; sanctions and 146, 154–8, 231–2; self-sufficiency 132, 144; state, role of in 125–8, 132, 138; state-society relations 150–4; *see also* oil economy
education 9, 11
Egypt 174, 234, 242, 253; assistance to 175; economy of 116; Morsi administration 233; Mubarak departure 233; relationship with 7, 181, 186, 241, 246
Eisenstadt, Michael 211
Ejei, Gholamhossein Mohseni 99
Elbaradei, Mohamed 215, 222
elections 5, 104, 273; candidates, approval of 6, 91; 2016 97–102; *see also* presidential elections
Erdogan, Recep Tayyip 245
Etala'at 24
ethnicities 16–17
European Community 191
European Investment Bank (EIB) 149
European Union (EU): economic relationship with 149–50; 1992 summit 194; nuclear crisis involvement 155, 156, 214, 231; relationship with 155, 199, 231; sanctions 155, 156, 231
Evans, Peter 126
exceptionalism 256
Executives of Construction 48
Expediency Council (EC) 4, 27, 55, 141, 147
export-substitution industrialization (ESI) 126, 158

factionalism 6, 38–9, 40–1, 79, 180, 272, 274
Fadayeen 41
Fahd, King 189–90
Faisal, Turki al- 238
Fallahian, Ali 92
Faqih: absolute guardian 44; Beit Rahbari 5, 27, 37; importance of 4–5, 27–8, 37, 46; qualifications of 4; responsibilities of 5, 27, 36; Vali-e Faqih 35, 105; Velayat-e Faqih 27, 37, 38, 53; Velayat-e Faqih-e Motalaq 43

Farmanfarmaian, Roxane 172
Fars 98–9
Fathali, Mohammad 247
Firooz-Abadi, Dehghani 12–13
Followers of the Velayat 97
Fordow enrichment facility 223, 224
foreign policy *see* international relations
Foreign Reserve Fund 145
Forozan, Hesam 155
Foundation of the Oppressed 154
France: economic relationship with 121, 148, 149; relationship with 172, 176, 201
Franco-Persian Treaty of Finkenstein (1807) 172
Free Syrian Army 234
free-trade zones (FTZs) 146
freedom: financial 116; labour, of 116; press, of 6, 10, 53, 99, 116, 146
Freedom House 272–3
Friedman, George 233
Front of Islamic Revolution Stability 101
Fuller, Graham E. 168, 253

Ganji, Akbar 86
Gaza 271
gender issues 11
geography 16, 171
Gerdab 98
Germany: economic relationship with 20, 121, 130, 148; relationship with 18, 174, 176, 201
Ghafari, Hadi 45
Ghaffari, Masoud 134
Ghana 229
Gharazi, Mohammd 95
Gheissari, Ali 56
Ghods, M. Reza 181
globalization 10, 115–16, 146
Goethe Institute 24
Goldman Sachs 9, 115
Golpaygani, Grand Ayatollah Mohammad Reza 44
government of Iran: creditability of 84; as nonliberal democracy 105; as revolutionary Islamic model 5; structure of 4–5, 27–9, 272
Graham, Robert 122
Great War 18, 117
Greece 201
Green Movement 2, 52, 75, 76, 85–6, 89, 102, 103, 272
Guard *see* Revolutionary Guard
Guardians Council *see* Council of Guardians (CG)

Habermas, Jürgen 52
Habibi, Hassan 42
Haddad-Adel, Gholam-Ali 93, 100
Hajjarian, Saeed 52, 53, 56
Halliday, Fred 29–30, 169, 178, 179, 187
Hamas 199, 222, 227, 233, 255, 271
Hanke, Steve 139
Hariri, Rafiq 202
Hasanzadeh, Mohammad Tagi 11
Hazrati, Elias 92
Heritage Foundation 146
Heyat, Z. 122
Hezbollah 188–9, 199, 202–3, 209, 222, 227, 229, 230, 234–5, 242, 255, 271
Hill, Chris 222
Hinnebusch, Raymond 159
Hong Kong 129
Houthi 254, 255
Hoveyda, Abbas 23, 25
Hussein, Saddam 192, 253

ideationalism 170
identity, Iranian 2, 7, 17, 171, 173
IIPF see Islamic Iran Participation Front (IIPF)
India 8, 123, 175, 182, 198, 199, 249–50, 256
Indonesia 123
International Energy Agency 231
International Monetary Fund (IMF) 65, 123, 137
international relations 12, 168–257; Ahmadinejad, under 182, 219–35; Arab Spring and 5, 233–5; domestic context for 170; historical features of 171–3; Iraq war, during 183–92; Islamic republic, under 178–250; Khatemi, under 199–218; 'Looking East' 8, 182, 198, 251, 271–2; 9/11 impact on 207–10; Pahlavi dynasty, under 173–8; Rafsanjani, under 192–9; Rouhani, under 235–50; see also nuclear crisis
Internet use 11–12, 106
Iran Khodro Diesel 148, 149
Iran Marine Industries 137
Iranian Central Bank 156
Iranian-Islamic Freedom Party 101
Iranian Revolution 23–7, 33–4, 250, 268; causes of 23–4, 33
Iraq 174, 242, 244, 253, 254, 255, 271; assistance to 177; relationship with 7, 176, 181, 220, 227; Shia in 32, 184; see also Iraq War
Iraq War 39, 133–5, 183–92

IRGC see Revolutionary Guard
Isfahan plant 196, 212
ISIS 254, 271
Islamic Coalition Party 101
Islamic Cooperation Organization 197
Islamic Iran Participation Front (IIPF) 54, 55, 58, 59, 64, 89
Islamic Jihad 227
Islamic Labour Party 101
Islamic Republic Party (IRP) 41, 42
Islamist Islamic National Front 193
Israel 7, 68, 227, 253; Defence Force 209; Hezbollah attack against (2006) 230; relationship with 176, 181, 202, 220
Italy 130, 186; economic relationship with 148, 149; relationship with 201

Jafari, Peyman 133, 136
Jahangiri, Eshaq 145, 159
Jahromi, Mohammad 65
Jalili, Kazem 100
Jalili, Saeed 92–3, 95
Jame'ay-e Rouhaniyat-e Mubarez 41
Jannati, Ayatollah Ahmad 101, 102, 215
Japan: economic relationship with 121; relationship with 256
Joint Comprehensive Plan of Action 157
Jordan 7, 175, 181, 193
Jubat al-Nusra 253
Judaism 16
judicial independence 10, 146

Kaabi, Hamad al- 231
Kadivar, Hojjatoleslam 83
Kadivar, Mohsen 52, 53, 86
Karroubi, Mehdi 40, 41, 45; incarceration of 87; presidential candidate (2005) 58, 59, 60; presidential candidate (2009) 68, 70, 72, 77, 78
Karsh, Efraim 186
Karshenas, Massoud 128–9
Kashani, Ayatollah Imami 13
Kavakevian Mohammad 92
Kazakhstan 203
Keshavarzian, Arang 39
Khalifa, Sheikh Khalid al- 254
Khalkhali, Sadegh 45
Khamenei, Ayatollah Ali 8, 40, 41, 67, 75, 76, 81, 90, 94, 103, 191, 248, 250; Beit Rahbari 5, 27, 37; Leader 43, 44, 45, 47; president 47, 7444
Khan, Reza see Pahlavi, Reza Shah
Kharrazi, Kamal 242
Khatam al-Anbiya 155

Khatami, Ayatollah Ahmad 86
Khatami, Hojjatoleslam Mohammad 1, 41, 45, 47, 81–2, 92; economy under 140–2; international policies under 199–218; president (1997–2005) 43, 51–7, 75; presidential candidate (1997) 49–51; presidential candidate (2001) 54, 55; restrictions on 89
Khoei, Grand Ayatollah Adolqasem 44
Khoeinia, Mohammad 45
Khomeini, Ayatollah Ruhollah 36, 56, 136, 184; death of 43; executions ordered by 43, 46; Islamic government, thoughts on 5, 26, 29, 34–5, 39, 44, 75; role in revolution 22, 24, 25, 26, 27; Rushdie affair 190–1
Khuzestan 16
Kim Il Sung 260n79
Kissinger, Henry 247–8, 250
Kurdish Regional Government 68
Kurdistan 183
Kurds 15, 16, 17
Kuwait 68, 234; Iraq invasion of 192; relationship with 48, 187, 246
Kyrgyzstan 203

land reform 121–2, 132
languages 16
Larijani, Ali 66, 100, 221; presidential candidate (2005) 58, 59; speaker of Majlis 62, 97, 102, 147
Leader *see* Faqih
Lebanon 68, 187–8, 227, 229, 234, 255, 271; Amal in 188, 189; relationship with 202; Shia in 32, 188, 189; war in (2006) 230; *see also* Hezbollah
Liberation Front (Movement) 40, 41
Libya 186, 214, 233, 234, 242
Limbert, John W. 117
List of Hope 100, 101, 102
local councils 28
'Looking East' 8, 182, 198, 251, 271–2
Lurs 16, 17

McInnis, J. Matthew 180
Madani, Ahmad 41
Majlis 19, 28; First (1980–84) 40, 42; Second (1984–88) 40, 42; Third (1988–92) 40, 42; Fourth (1992–96) 45, 48; Fifth (1996–2000) 47–9, 53; Sixth (2000–04) 54–5, 56; Seventh (2004–08) 55–6, 57; Eighth (2008–12) 62, 63; Ninth (2012–16) 63; Tenth (2016) 97–102; dissolution of 22; responsibilities of 28

Majma-e Rouhaniyoun-e Mubarez 41
Maleki, Abbas 180, 181
Maloney, Suzanne 154
Mamluk dynasty 171
Mammut Group 148
Manama Dialogue 254
Mansour, Sherif 99
Marash, Hossein 82
Marashi, Seyyed Hossein 97
Mashad-Sarakhs-Tedzhen railroad 198
Mashaei, Esfandiar Rahim 89, 90, 92
Mauritius 175
Mazaheri, Tahmasb 64
Mazandarani & Gilaki 17
Mehralizadeh, Mohsen 58, 59
Menashri, David 275
Mesbah-Yazdi, Ayatollah Mohammad-Taqi 98, 101
Michel, David 161
Milani, Mohsen M. 178
Mir-Hosseini, Ziba 45
Mirdamadi, Mohsen 64, 89
Mobile Communication Company (MCI) 155
Mobin Trust Consortium (MTC) 155
Moderation and Development Party 101
Modi, Narendra 250, 256
Mofid, Kamran 134
Mogherini, Federica 149
Mohajerani, Ataollah 86
Mohammadi, Ariabarzan 272
Mohtashemi, Ali Akbar 41, 45
Moin, Mostafa 58, 59
Mojahedin-e Khalq Organization (MKO) 40, 41, 46
Mongols 17
Monotheism and Justice Front 63
Montazeri, Ayatollah Hossein Ali 40, 44, 46, 56, 77, 83, 86–7
Morocco 7, 181, 193
Moslehi, Hojjatoleslam Heydar 90
Mossadegh, Mohammad 118, 174
Mossadeq, Mohammad 19, 21
Mostofi, B. 118
Motahari, Ali 100
Mottahedeh, Negar 111n107
Mottaki, Monouchehr 92, 229
Mousavi, Mir Hossein 40, 43, 49, 73, 137–8, 191; incarceration of 87; presidential candidate (2009) 68, 69, 70, 72, 73, 74, 78–9, 81, 82, 85; prime minister 44, 47, 135, 136
Mousavi-Khoeinia, Mohammad 41, 108n27
Mousavi-Tabrizi, Hossein 45

Mousavian, Seyed Hossein 225
Moutaki, Manouchehr 89
Mozaffari, Mehdi 37–8, 66, 88
Muslim Brotherhood 233

Nabavi, Behzad 45
Nahavandian, Mohammad 147
Nasser ed-Din Shah 173
Natanz uranium enrichment facility 212, 214, 221, 223, 240
Nateq-Nouri, Ayatollah Ali Akbar 41, 48, 49, 50, 58, 59, 93–4
National Council of Resistance of Iran 212
National Front 24, 39, 40, 41
National Iranian Industries Organization 137
National Iranian Oil Company 143
National Liberation Army of Iran 46
National Tax Administration 152–3
Nedaye Iranian 101
neoconservatism 57–63, 219
New York Times 236, 246–7
nezam 34, 37
Nicaragua 228
Nima, Ramy 36
Nimr, Sheikh Nimr Baqir al- 245
9/11 206, 207–10
Nomani, Farhad 123, 150, 179, 180
Non-Proliferation Treaty (NPT) 7, 214, 215, 222; Additional Protocol 215, 216
North Korea 186, 222
Northern Alliance 205
Nouri, Abdullah 52
nuclear crisis 1, 7, 84–5, 103, 210–18, 221–6, 270; development of nuclear programme 195–6, 210–11, 222; end of 237–41; national pride in nuclear programmes 211, 212, 215, 216, 225; Paris Agreement (2004) 217–18; politics in 96–103; purchases of uranium 195–6; uranium enrichment facilities 212, 214, 221, 222, 223, 224, 239, 240; *see also* sanctions
Nusra Front, al- 234

Obama, Barak 8, 66–7, 224, 231
oil economy 117, 119–21, 124, 177, 231–2; importance of 10, 21, 119, 122, 131; Iraq war impact on 133–4; prices 65, 123, 124, 134, 142–3, 178
Oman 177, 187
Omid, Homa 36
Operation Iraqi Freedom 213
Organization of Islamic Conference (OIC) 200
Oriental Oil Kish 155
Ottoman Empire 18, 171–2

Pahlavi, Mohammad Reza Shah 8, 20–3; downfall of 24–6, 26; economy under 21, 23, 118–29; international relations under 174–8; modernization programme 22–3, 121, 128; White Revolution 22, 118, 119, 121
Pahlavi, Reza Shah 18–20, 117–18, 173–4; modernization programme 19, 20, 117–19; politics under 32–3
Pahlavi dynasty 15, 19; economy under 21, 23, 117, 118–29; end of 24–6; international relations under 173–8; *see also* Pahlavi, Mohammad Reza Shah; Pahlavi, Reza Shah
Pakistan 175, 197, 210, 253, 263n152, 271
Palestine 227, 271
Palestinian Authority (PA) 247
Paris Agreement (2004) 217–18, 220
Park Chung Hee, President 125
Parsons, Sir Anthony 185
Paydar Front 98
Pedde, Nicola 17–18
People's Experts 101
People's Voice Coalition 100, 102
Persia 17–18
Pesaran, M. Hashem 122, 128
Peugeot-Citroen 149
Peykar 41
Philippines, The 8, 123, 182
Plan and Budget Organization 134
PLO 7, 181
politics 12, 32–107; presidential elections; 2009 election 63–74; 2013 election 92–6; constitution impact on 34–9; flexibility of system 105; Iraq war, during 39–42; neoconservatism 57–63; nuclear crisis 96–103; political parties 38; second republic 43–9; Tehran Spring 49–57; velvet revolution 75–84; *see also* Majlis
populism 61, 66, 141, 226
Pourazizi, Saeed 56
president 28, 183
presidential elections: 1989 election 43; 1997 election 49–57; 2001 election 54, 55; 2005 election 57–61; 2009 election 63–74, 269; 2013 election 6, 92–6, 235–6; qualifications of candidates 6, 91
press, freedom of 6, 10, 53, 99, 115, 146
Principlists Grand Coalition 100, 101, 102
Purmohammadi, Mostafa 64
Putin, Vladimir 249

Qaeda, al- 84, 205, 207, 209, 244, 253, 254
Qajar, Ahmad Shah 19
Qajar dynasty 15, 18, 19, 172; economy under 116, 117; fall of 173
Qalibaf, Mohammad B 66; presidential candidate (2005) 58, 59; presidential candidate (2013) 93, 95
Qatar 230, 234, 246
quality of life 10, 146
Qu'ran 35

Rafizadeh, Majid 250
Rafsanjani, Ayatollah Ali Akbar Hashemi 25, 40, 41, 66, 79–81, 83, 98, 104, 134, 190, 216; economy under 136–40, 141; international relations under 192–9, 251; president (1989–1997) 43, 45–6, 49; presidential candidate (2005) 59, 60–1; presidential candidate (2013) 6, 92
Rahnema, Ali 179, 180
Ramazani, Rouhollah K. 175
Rastakhiz 23, 32, 33
Reformist Policymaking Council 97
regional power 7, 182, 244–50
Reporters without Borders 6, 99
resistance economy 144, 147–8, 269
Revolutionary Guard 51–2, 62, 90–1; economic interests of 155; Intelligence Organization 98, 99; website 98
Reyshahri, Mohammad 50
Rezaei, Mohsen 70, 72, 93, 95
Rice, Condoleezza 207–8
Richards, Alan 152
Rouhani, Hojjatoleslam Hassan 2, 39, 41, 65, 101, 104, 196, 210, 274; economy under 145, 146–50, 158, 159; international relations under 235–50, 252; *National Security and Nuclear Diplomacy* 217; president (2013–2017) 92, 103; presidential candidate (2013) 92–5
Roxborough, Ian 133, 151
Rushdie, Salman 190–1
Russia 18, 242; economic relationship with 148, 196, 249; relationship with 21, 172, 198, 199, 251; *see also* Soviet Union

Sadeghinia, Mahboubeh 180
Sadjadpour, Karim 87–8
Safavi, Yahya Rahim 252
Safavids 171
Safi, Ayatollah 77
Saleh, Ali Abdullah 271
Salehi-Isfahani, Djavad 10–11, 91

Salimi, Hossein 169
Sanandaji, Kaveh-Cyrus 56
sanctions: economy and 146, 154–8, 231–2; EU 155, 156, 231; lifting of 146, 148, 240; UN 155, 156, 185, 223, 231; US 155, 156, 231
Sanei, Ayatollah Yousef 78
Sarioghalam, Mahmood 256
Sassanian Dynasty 17
Saudi Arabia 4, 178, 243, 244, 253; assistance to 177; Khatami visit to 202; relationship with 7, 181, 187, 189–90, 202, 233, 235, 238, 241, 242, 245–7
Schirazi, Asghar 25, 35, 36
sectarianism 234
security concerns 7–8, 182, 216
Security Council (UN) 155, 206, 214, 216, 221–2, 225; resolution 479 185; resolution 514 185; resolution 598 185, 190; resolution 1696 223, 264n169; resolution 1747 223; resolution 1803 223; resolution 1835 223; resolution 1929 223
Seifzadeh, Mohammad 69
Selbin, Eric 170
Selim, Sultan 171
setadema.com 71
Shabestari, Mohammad Mojtahed 52–3
Shah-Daei, Marzieh 150
Shamsolvaezin, Mashaollah 71
Shanghai Cooperation Organization (SCO) 69, 227, 251, 252
Shariati, Ali 34
Shariatinia, Mohsen 130
Shawcross, William 33
Shia Islam 82, 254; in Bahrain 187, 202, 233, 243, 244; clerics role in government 4; in Iran 16, 171; in Iraq 32, 184; in Lebanon 32, 188–9; in Syria 189
Shirazi, Ayatollah Makarem 77
Shultz, George 247–8
Sick, Gary 176
Silk Road 17
Singapore 8, 182
Skocpol, Theda 33
Sobh-e Emrouz 53
social media 71, 89, 106
Society for the Defence of Islamic Values 48
Society of Seminary Teachers, The 101
Society of the Combatant Clergy 41, 48
Soleimani, Davood 89
Soroush, Abdolkarim 45, 86
South Korea 123, 125, 129; relationship with 8, 182, 256

Soviet Union: relationship with 174, 195; weapons purchases from 186; *see also* Russia
Spain 186, 201
Standard Oil Company of America 19
Sudan 193, 246
Sunni Islam 84, 234, 244, 253; in Iraq 16; radicalized 234
Supreme Leader *see* Faqih
Supreme National Security Council 28
SWIFT (Society for Worldwide Interbank Financial Telecommunication) 156, 223
Switzerland 121, 130
Syria 233, 234, 242, 244, 253, 255, 271; assistance to 175, 241, 248; relationship with 7, 181, 186, 187, 189, 234–5; Shia in 189
Szubin, Adam 252

Tabatabae, Shahebedin 85
Tabatabai, Adnan 237
Taheri, Ayatollah Jalaledin 57, 77
Taiwan 8, 129, 182
Tajik, Dr. Mohammad Reza 51, 52
Tajikistan 203
Tajzadeh, Mostafa 89
Takeyh, Ray 224
Taliban 50, 205, 206, 209
Tapper, Richard 45
TAV 141
Tayyebnia, Ali 152
Tazmini, Ghoncheh 51
Tehran agreement (2003) 220
Tehran Bureau 52
Tehran Spring 49–57
Telecommunications Company of Iran (TCI) 142, 155
Tezcür, Güneş Murat 273
Tobacco Concession (1890) 173
Togo 229
Torkan, Akbar 159
Transparency International 145
Tudeh 21, 41
Tunisia 233, 234, 242
Turkcell 141
Turkemens 16, 17
Turkey 175, 194, 234, 253, 271; assistance to 177; economic relationship with 197, 205
Turkmenistan 203
Turkomanchai Treaty (1828) 172

UAE 199, 202, 231, 246
Union of Islamic Iran People Party 101
United Front of Principlists 63
United Kingdom (UK) 172; economic relationship with 121, 148; withdrawal of 175, 176
United Nations 200, 201; Charter 221; sanctions 155, 156, 185, 223, 231; *see also* Security Council (UN)
United States (US): economic relationship with 121, 148, 158, 193; National Security Strategy 226; relationship with 21, 127, 130, 174, 176, 209, 227–8, 252; sanctions 155, 156, 231
Universal Coalition of Reformists 101
US National Intelligence Estimate 73
Uzbekistan 203

Vakil, Sanam 100
Vali-e Faqih 35, 105
Valibeigi, Mehrdad 135
Vatican 201
Velayat-e Faqih 27, 37, 38, 53
Velayat-e Faqih-e Motalaq 43
Velayati, Ali Akbar 92, 93, 95, 248
velvet revolution 75–84
Venezuela 182, 228, 229
Vietnam 177
Voice of the Nation 101

Wahhabi 84
Wallerstein, Immanuel 126
Waterbury, John 152
White Revolution 22, 118, 119, 121
Woolsey, James 196
World Bank 137, 147, 153; Doing Business 146
World Trade Organization 150
Wright, Robin 77

Xi, President 148, 149, 251

Yas-e Nou 56
Yazdi, Ayatollah Mohammad 81, 83–4, 98, 101
Yekta Front 97
Yemen 253, 255, 271; relationship with 244; support for rebels in 241, 243, 245, 254
Yishai, Yael 105

Zanjani, Ayatollah Babak 77, 166n110
Zarif, Javad 157, 236, 237, 238, 239, 246
Zavarei, Reza 50
Zemin, Jiang 204
Zoroastrianism 16